CCEA
GCSE
HISTORY
THIRD EDITION

Finbar Madden
John D. Clare

HODDER
EDUCATION
AN HACHETTE UK COMPANY

Every effort has been made to trace all copyright holders, but if any have been inadvertently overlooked, the Publishers will be pleased to make the necessary arrangements at the first opportunity.

Although every effort has been made to ensure that website addresses are correct at time of going to press, Hodder Education cannot be held responsible for the content of any website mentioned in this book. It is sometimes possible to find a relocated web page by typing in the address of the home page for a website in the URL window of your browser.

Hachette UK's policy is to use papers that are natural, renewable and recyclable products and made from wood grown in well-managed forests and other controlled sources. The logging and manufacturing processes are expected to conform to the environmental regulations of the country of origin.

Orders: please contact Hachette UK Distribution, Hely Hutchinson Centre, Milton Road, Didcot, Oxfordshire, OX11 7HH. Telephone: +44 (0)1235 827827. Email education@hachette.co.uk Lines are open from 9 a.m. to 5 p.m., Monday to Friday. You can also order through our website: www.hoddereducation.co.uk

ISBN: 9781471889721

© Finbar Madden, John D Clare 2017

First published in 2017 by

Hodder Education,
An Hachette UK Company
Carmelite House
50 Victoria Embankment
London EC4Y 0DZ
www.hoddereducation.co.uk

Impression number 10 9 8

Year   2023

Cover photo ©Markus Matzel/ullstein bild/Getty Images

Illustrations by DC Graphic Design Limited

Typeset in Caecilia 45 Light 10/12pt by DC Graphic Design Limited, Hextable, Kent

Printed by CPI Group (UK) Ltd, Croydon CR0 4YY

A catalogue record for this title is available from the British Library.

Acknowledgments

The publishers would like to thank the following individuals, institutions and companies for permission to reproduce copyright illustrations in this book:

p. 1, © Bettmann/Getty Images; **p. 2**, © World History Archive / Alamy Stock Photo; **p. 3**, AKG-images/Ullstein Bild; **p. 5**, AKG-images; **p. 6**, David Low, Evening Standard, 3 July 1934/British Cartoon Archive, University of Kent; **p. 9**, © PRISMA ARCHIVO / Alamy Stock Photo; **p. 10**, © Bettmann/Getty Images; **p. 12**, © Archivart / Alamy Stock Photo; **p. 15**, © FALKENSTEINFOTO / Alamy Stock Photo; **p. 16**, © INTERFOTO / Alamy Stock Photo; **p. 17**, © INTERFOTO / Alamy Stock Photo; **p. 18**, © Peter Horree / Alamy Stock Photo; **p. 19**, © Peter Horree / Alamy Stock Photo; **p. 20**, © Mary Evans Picture Library / Alamy Stock Photo; **p. 22**, © Heritage Image Partnership Ltd / Alamy Stock Photo; **p. 24**, © INTERFOTO / Alamy Stock Photo; **p. 25**, © Mary Evans Picture Library / Alamy Stock Photo; **p. 26**, © Mary Evans Picture Library / Alamy Stock Photo; **p. 27**, © Hulton-Deutsch Collection/CORBIS/Corbis via Getty Images; **p. 28**, © World History Archive / Alamy Stock Photo; **p. 32** t, © Keystone-France/Gamma-Keystone via Getty Images; **p. 32** b © World History Archive / Alamy Stock Photo; **p. 35**, © INTERFOTO / Alamy Stock Photo; **p. 36**, © dpa picture alliance / Alamy Stock Photo; **p. 38**, © Mary Evans Picture Library / Alamy Stock Photo; **p. 39**, © Kumar Sriskandan / Alamy Stock Photo; **p. 40**, © John D Clare; **p. 44**, © Bundesarchiv, Bild 146-1972-025-10 / CC-BY-SA 3.0; **p. 46**, © Pictorial Press Ltd / Alamy Stock Photo; **p. 47**, © IanDagnall Computing / Alamy Stock Photo; **p. 50** (background), © Science History Images / Alamy Stock Photo; **p. 52**, © Granger Historical Picture Archive / Alamy Stock Photo; **p. 54**, © Granger Historical Picture Archive / Alamy Stock Photo; p. 55, © ClassicStock / Alamy Stock Photo; **p. 56**, © Everett Collection, Inc. / Alamy Stock Photo; **p. 57**, l: SPC Plains Dakota NAA 4988 00606600, National Anthropological Archives, Smithsonian Institution, **p. 57** r: SPC Plains Dakota NAA 4988 00606700, National Anthropological Archives, Smithsonian Institution; **p. 58**, © GL Archive / Alamy Stock Photo; **p. 62**, © Hartsook/Library of Congress/Corbis/VCG via Getty Images; **p. 63**, © Everett Collection Historical / Alamy Stock Photo; **p. 64** l, © ScreenProd / © Photononstop / Alamy Stock Photo; **p. 64** r, © Everett Collection Inc / Alamy Stock Photo; **p. 66**, © Pictorial Press Ltd / Alamy Stock Photo; **p. 67**, © Lordprice Collection / Alamy Stock Photo; **p. 68**, © ClassicStock / Alamy Stock Photo; **p. 72**, © Chronicle / Alamy Stock Photo; **p. 73**, © World History Archive / Alamy Stock Photo; **p. 74**, © Pictorial Press Ltd / Alamy Stock Photo; **p. 76**, © Joy Global; **p. 80**, © Chronicle / Alamy Stock Photo; **p. 82**, © Everett Collection Historical / Alamy Stock Photo; **p. 85**, © Granger Historical Picture Archive / Alamy Stock Photo; **p. 86**, © Photo Researchers, Inc / Alamy Stock Photo; **p. 87**, © Granger Historical Picture Archive / Alamy Stock Photo; **p. 88** t, © Everett Historical – Shutterstock; **p. 88** b, © Marmaduke St. John / Alamy Stock Photo; **p. 89**, © IanDagnall Computing / Alamy Stock Photo; **p. 90**, © Granger Historical Picture Archive / Alamy Stock Photo; **p. 93**, © Bettmann / Getty Images; **p. 94**, © The Print Collector / Alamy Stock Photo; **p. 95**, © Crawford Art Gallery, Cork / DACS 2017; **p. 98**, Courtesy of the National Library of Ireland; **p. 99**, © Hulton Archive / Stringer / Getty Images; **p. 100**, © Punch Limited; **p. 105**, © Windows To Ireland; **p. 109**, © Central Press/Getty Images; **p. 113** b, © Haywood Magee/Getty Images; **p. 119**, © Leslie Gilbert Illingworth / National Library of Wales / Solo Syndication; **p. 122**, © British Library/Colindale; **p. 123**, © Ulster Museum; **p. 124**, © Irish Examiner; **p. 126**, © Punch Limited; **p. 128**, © People's History Museum (ref. NMLH.2014.26.1.54); **p. 134**, © Linenhall Library; **p. 137**, © Bettmann / Getty Images; **p. 140**, © Anonymous/AP/REX/Shutterstock; **p. 144**, © PA Archive PA Archive/PA Images; **p. 145**, © PA Archive PA Archive/PA Images; **p. 146**, © John Downing/Express/Hulton Archive/Getty Images; **p. 149**, © Bentley Archive/Popperfoto/Getty Images; **p. 150**, © Anonymous/AP/REX/Shutterstock; **p. 152**, © Belfast Telegraph; **p. 153**, © Keystone/Getty Images; **p. 155**, © A. Jones/Evening Standard/Getty Images; **p. 156**, © Popperfoto/Getty Images; **p. 158**, © Topham / AP via Topfoto; **p. 159**, © Keystone Pictures USA / Alamy Stock Photo; **p. 161**, © Belfast Telegraph; **p. 164**, © Popperfoto/Getty Images; **p. 167**, © Hulton-Deutsch/Hulton-Deutsch Collection/ Corbis via Getty Images; **p. 168**, © Belfast Telegraph; **p. 170**, © Belfast Telegraph; **p. 171**, ©2003 Topham / PA; **p. 172**, © Bettmann /Getty Images; **p. 173**, © amer ghazzal / Alamy Stock Photo; **p. 176**, Peter Kemp/AP/REX/Shutterstock; **p. 178**, © Topham / PA; **p. 180**, © REUTERS / Alamy Stock Photo; **p. 181** t, © REUTERS / Alamy Stock Photo; **p. 181** b, © Allstar Picture Library / Alamy Stock Photo; **p. 183**, © REUTERS / Alamy Stock Photo; **p. 184**, © Chris Jackson - WPA Pool/ Getty Images; **p. 185**, © Steve Eason/Hulton Archive/Getty Images; **p. 186**, © Allstar Picture Library / Alamy Stock Photo; **p. 189**, © REUTERS / Alamy Stock Photo; **p. 190**, © Jose Gil – Shutterstock; **p. 191**, © Crown Copyright; **p. 194**, © Everett Collection Historical / Alamy StockPhoto; **p. 197**, © Bettmann/ Getty Images; **p. 199**, © Prisma Bildagentur AG / Alamy Stock Photo; **p. 204**, © Leslie Gilbert Illingworth / National Library of Wales / Solo Syndication; **p. 206**, © Punch Limited; **p. 207**, © The Print Collector / Alamy Stock Photo; **p. 210**, © Punch Limited; **p. 215**, © Everett Collection Historical / Alamy Stock Photo; **p. 216**, © Imagno/Getty Images; **p. 218**, © CTK / Alamy Stock Photo; **p. 219**, © 2000 Topham / AP; **p. 222**, © Everett Collection Historical / Alamy Stock Photo; **p. 230**, © Rolls Press/Popperfoto/Getty Images; **p. 231**, © Leslie Gilbert Illingworth / National Library of Wales / Solo Syndication; **p. 236**, © Sovfoto/UIG via Getty Images; **p. 237**, © Ulrich Baumgarten via Getty Images; **p. 242**, © dpa picture alliance / Alamy Stock Photo; **p. 243**, © World History Archive / Alamy Stock Photo; **p. 245**, © Spencer Platt/Getty Images; **p. 246**, © Gado Images / Alamy Stock Photo; **p. 248** l, © DOD Photo / Alamy Stock Photo; **p. 248**, r, © REUTERS / Alamy Stock Photo; **p. 249**, © Steve Greenberg.

The publishers would also like to thank the following for permission to reproduce material in this book: DUP Deputy Leader Peter Robinson, MP, reflecting on the Framework Documents in an article published *The Independent*, 24 February 1995.

CONTENTS

UNIT 1 SECTION B: LOCAL STUDY

Option 1 Changing Relations: Northern Ireland and its Neighbours, 1920–49

Option 2 Changing Relations: Northern Ireland and its Neighbours, 1965–98

UNIT 2 OUTLINE STUDY

International Relations, 1945–2003

INTRODUCTION

About the course

The course you are studying is split into two units: Unit 1, Modern world studies in depth and the Local study, and Unit 2, the Outline study. There are four options in Unit 1.

Unit 1: Modern world studies in depth and the Local study

Unit 1 Section A: Modern world studies in depth

Unit 1	You will study this ...	... or this
Section A: Modern world studies in depth	Option 1: Life in Nazi Germany, 1933–45	Option 2: Life in the United States of America, 1920–33

Unit 1 Section B: Local study

Unit 1	You will study this ...	... or this
Section B: Local study	Option 1: Changing Relations: Northern Ireland and its Neighbours, 1920–49	Option 2: Changing Relations: Northern Ireland and its Neighbours, 1965–98

You only need to study two of the options, one from Section A and one from Section B.

Unit 2: Outline study

All of Unit 2 is compulsory: the topic you will study is International Relations, 1945–2003.

About the book

This book covers all of the options and units of your course.

Features

Each chapter in this book contains:
- activities to help you understand and consolidate your knowledge
- practice questions to help you refine the skills needed for your exam
- revision tips to advise you on preparing for your exam
- glossary terms, in bold and colour the first time they appear.

There is also a map on the opening page of each topic to help you get a sense of where places are.

Sources and interpretations

There are both sources (contemporary) and interpretations (non-contemporary) throughout the book to help you gain knowledge of key events and different viewpoints of them.

- In the chapters covering Unit 1, there are both sources and interpretations: interpretations are in blue and they are called 'Interpretations' to show that they are not contemporary. Interpretations will not appear in your Unit 1 exam and you will only answer questions on sources in Unit 1, Section B.
- In the chapters covering Unit 2, there are both sources and interpretations, but as you will answer questions on both in your Unit 2 exam, they are all called 'sources'. However, the interpretations are still a different colour so you can identify them.

The examination

There are two papers in the examination. Paper 1 covers the Modern world studies in depth and the Local study, while Paper 2 focuses on the Outline study.

The layout of the papers is fairly straightforward. To begin, make sure that you are doing the right sections on the day of the exam.

Revision techniques

Everyone revises differently. For some people it is a matter of sitting at a desk; for others pacing up and down. While some people can work with music in the background, others require total silence. The bottom line is – there's no single best way.

Whatever your revision style, there are a number of practical suggestions as to how you should approach revision and use your time:

▶ Start your revision in plenty of time.

▶ Organise a revision timetable for each section of the course.

▶ Draw up a revision checklist that allows you to focus on the parts of the course that you are most concerned about.

▶ Set yourself a target of material to cover in each session – for example, Nazi attempts to reduce unemployment – and stick to it.

▶ Revise for short periods – 15–20 minutes, for example – and take breaks in between.

▶ Review what you have covered at the end of the day and again the next day to make sure you have internalised the information.

▶ Be open to using a range of ways of remembering material. For example, rhymes, mnemonics, coding and diagrams.

▶ Look at the specimen papers on the CCEA website and use those questions to practise your exam skills.

▶ Consult all relevant CCEA Mark Schemes and Chief Examiner's Reports to see what you need to aim for and – more importantly – the mistakes to avoid.

▶ Leave yourself enough time to revisit material that you have already revised closer to the time of the examination.

Sitting the examination

General points

▶ Make sure you're **looking at the right questions**. This is particularly relevant to the two Northern Ireland sections in Paper 1.

▶ Look for **all of the questions** – some may be over the page. Don't forget to check.

▶ Follow the **instructions** on the front of the exam paper - and within each section.

▶ **Read** each question carefully – ideally more than once.

▶ Use a highlighter pen to emphasise **key points/ words** in a question.

▶ Answer the question that has been set – not the one you wish had been set.

▶ Remember the connection between the amount of marks for each question, how many lines are given in the paper for you to write your answer, and how much you are expected to write (see tables below).

▶ Stick rigidly to whatever dates are given in a question. You will get no marks for going beyond the dates given.

▶ If you want to score strongly in each part of the examination, you must spend the appropriate amount of time on each question. Too much time spent on one section will mean too little left for others and will cost you significant amounts of marks.

▶ Stay in the room for the **full amount** of time. You can't get marks if you're not there.

Timing

Here are suggested timings for each question part.

Paper 1: Section A

Question	Mark	Suggested timing
Question 1	4 marks	4 minutes
Question 2	6 marks	5 minutes
Question 3	6 marks	5–7 minutes
Question 4	8 marks	10 minutes
Question 5	16 marks	15–20 minutes

Paper 1: Section B

Question	Mark	Suggested timing
Question 1	2 marks	2–3 minutes
Question 2	4 marks	5–6 minutes
Question 3	5 marks	5–7 minutes
Question 4	6 marks	6–8 minutes
Question 5	5 marks	4 minutes
Question 6	18 marks	20 minutes

Paper 2

Question	Mark	Suggested timing
Question 1	4 marks	5 minutes
Question 2a	4 marks	5 minutes
Question 2b	2 marks	3 minutes
Question 3	8 marks	10 minutes
Question 4	16 marks	20 minutes
Question 5	4 marks	5 minutes
Question 6	22 marks	25 minutes

Remember!

▶ Your answers must demonstrate a detailed knowledge. This book provides you with the key facts on each topic. Learn these thoroughly!

▶ Structure your answer. Most frequently a chronological framework will be the best way to achieve this.

▶ Select appropriate facts to answer the question asked.

▶ Many pupils lose marks by failing to identify all relevant information. Instead of writing a lot about one point, try to write less about a number of points.

UNIT 1

Option 1 Life in Nazi Germany, 1933–45

This option focuses on the impact of the Nazi dictatorship on people's lives in Germany, and on the effect of political, economic, social and racial forces in Germany at this time.

The opening years of the 1930s saw the rapid rise of Hitler to totalitarian power and the beginning of a police state. German workers, women and youth found their lives hugely changed as the Nazis imposed their ideas of *Gleichschaltung* and *Volksgemeinschaft*. Jewish people, Roma and other minorities were persecuted.

During World War II, the Nazi state came under pressure and began to fail. Life became much harder for German people and opposition

and resistance increased. The Nazis tried to implement their 'final solution' (genocide) for Jewish people.

This option examines the following key areas:

▶ Hitler takes political control, 1933–34
▶ Control and opposition
▶ Life for workers in Nazi Germany
▶ Life for women and the family in Nazi Germany
▶ Life for young people in Nazi Germany
▶ Life for the Jewish community and minorities in Nazi Germany
▶ Germany at war

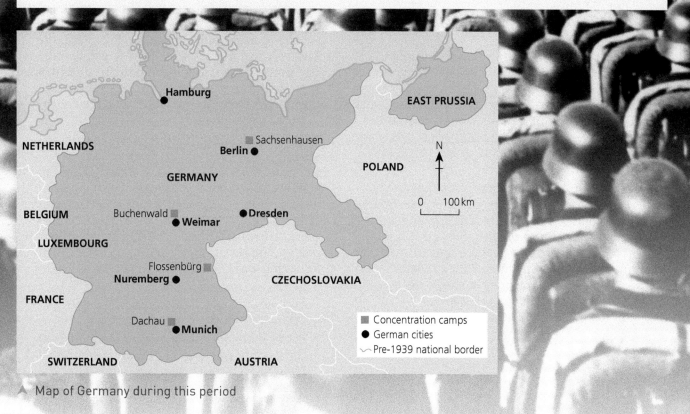

▲ Map of Germany during this period

Hitler's appointment as Chancellor

Weimar Germany, 1919–33

The government of Germany in the 1920s was known as the 'Weimar Republic', after the town where the government was declared in 1919. It had a President, but real power was in the hands of an elected parliament, the *Reichstag*, which made the laws and guaranteed the German people's political and religious rights and freedoms.

It was a weak government, constantly attacked by both the communists and by right-wing nationalist groups such as the Nazi Party (NSDAP) – a fascist organisation led by Adolf Hitler.

Hitler's message was one of violence – he hated Jewish and communist people (whom he blamed for Germany's defeat in the First World War), and vowed to make Germany into a great military power again. Hitler was backed by two paramilitary organisations – the 60,000-strong SA (*Sturmabteilung*) and the smaller SS (*Schutzstaffel*) – who intimidated and murdered his opponents.

The rise of the Nazis

The Nazi Party remained small and unpopular until 1929, when the Great Depression wrecked the German economy. The Nazi message of hate found a ready audience, particularly amongst the middle classes and farmers, whose businesses were going bankrupt. The number of Nazi seats in the *Reichstag* rose from 12 in 1928 to 230 in July 1932.

By January 1933, the *Reichstag* was hopelessly divided and, unable to run a stable government, the President, Paul von Hindenburg, and former Chancellor, Franz von Papen, offered Hitler the post of Chancellor in a coalition government. Von Hindenburg and von Papen hoped to use the Nazi deputies to gain a majority in the *Reichstag*, but believed they could control Hitler.

On 30 January 1933, Hitler accepted the post and von Hindenburg appointed him Chancellor.

> The SA celebrates on 30 January 1933 with a huge torch-lit procession, watched by large crowds of Nazi supporters giving the Nazi salute. Was Hitler certain of becoming a dictator at this point?

The removal of opposition

In order to gain total control over Germany, Hitler would have to overcome a number of obstacles. He would have to deal with the President, the *Reichstag* and the army, each of which could still prevent his rise to total power. In addition, there might be opposition from other parties, Germany's state governments and the country's trade union movement.

Hitler moved almost immediately to gain an overall majority in the *Reichstag*, calling new elections for 5 March 1933. If Hitler wanted to achieve a Nazi Party majority of seats, he would need to stop people voting for two of Germany's main parties, the SPD (the moderate Social Democratic Party) and KPD (the communist party). The Nazis attempted to achieve this in the following ways:

▶ In early February a new law forbade newspapers and public meetings from criticising the Chancellor and his administration.

▶ In the state of Prussia, which made up two thirds of the whole of Germany, leading Nazi Hermann Göring was made Minister of the Interior. He ensured that the SA was enrolled into the police and was used to disrupt opposition parties' election campaigns.

The *Reichstag* Fire

It was the burning of the *Reichstag* building on 27 February that gave Hitler his best chance of destroying the KPD's election campaign. Because a Dutch communist, Marinus van der Lubbe, was captured at the scene, the Nazis blamed the communists for the blaze and suggested that it could be the start of a communist rebellion.

The blaze was so convenient for Hitler that many people suspected that the Nazis were involved in setting the fire. Hitler used the fire to exploit President von Hindenburg's fear of a communist takeover. He also persuaded the President to approve the Decree for the Protection of People and State. This new law, which remained in place for the duration of Nazi rule, gave the government the power to suspend many of the civil rights that had been guaranteed in the Weimar constitution. Essentially, the Decree restricted:

▶ the right to speak freely
▶ the right to meet or form groups for meetings
▶ the right to print opinions in newspapers
▶ and the right to send private post and have private phone conversations.

The new government lost no time in using its emergency powers and went on to imprison opponents, disrupt the election campaigns of opposition parties and intimidate left-wing voters.

Source A Sefton Delmer, a British journalist, provides an account of Hitler's reaction to the *Reichstag* Fire.

Twenty to thirty minutes after the fire was discovered, Hitler said to von Papen: 'This is a God-given signal. If this fire, as I believe, turns out to be the handiwork of the Communists, then there is nothing that will stop us from crushing out the murderous pest with an iron fist.' … That evening Hitler said to me, 'God grant that this be the work of the Communists. You are witnessing the beginning of a new age in German history.'

▲ Berliners watch the *Reichstag* Fire in February 1933. Why was the burning of the *Reichstag* so frightening for German people?

Revision tip

Questions 1 and 2 in the exam will be based on factual knowledge. What is a fact? How does it differ from an inference, an opinion and a judgement?

Activities

1 Explain what the following organisations were:
  ● the SPD
  ● the KPD
  ● the Reichstag
  ● the SA
  ● the SS.
2 What was the Decree for the Protection of People and State?
3 How did the *Reichstag* Fire help the Nazis?
4 Does Source A support, or not support, the claim that the Nazis started the *Reichstag* Fire?

The election of 5 March 1933

Held just six days after the *Reichstag* Fire, the 1933 election took place amidst an outpouring of Nazi propaganda and intimidation. In Prussia, Göring issued a 'shooting decree' which gave the police the right to shoot political protesters. Thousands of the KPD's members and trade unionists were imprisoned and the SPD leaders fled the country.

Even so, when the results were declared, the Nazis had won only 288 seats (see Table 1). While this was far more than any other party, it was still not enough for an overall majority. The KPD managed to win 81 seats despite the government's underhand tactics, while the SPD won a very respectable 120 seats.

However, with the support of nationalist deputies from other parties, the Nazis now had just over 50 per cent of the votes in the *Reichstag*. This left the Nazis in a stronger position within both the cabinet and the government.

Party	Seats	Percentage
Nazis (NSDAP)	288	45
Social Democrats (SPD)	120	19
Communists (KPD)	81	13
Centre Party (Z)	74	11
Others	84	12

Table 1 Election results, March 1933.

The Enabling Act, 23 March 1933

Hitler, however, wanted even more power and moved to amend the constitution to allow the government to introduce laws without the *Reichstag's* or President's approval for a period of four years. Such a change to the constitution required the support of two-thirds of the *Reichstag* members present. However, at this point Hitler could count on the support of only 50 per cent of deputies.

To ensure his two-thirds majority, Hitler simply ensured that most of his opponents were not there to vote against the measure. He used the powers of the Decree for the Protection of People and State to ban the KPD, thus preventing the communists from voting against the new law. With the communist deputies now in jail, Hitler just needed the support of the Catholic Centre Party (ZP) to achieve the 66 per cent of votes needed. Its support was achieved by a promise to cancel the Decree for the Protection of People and State and an agreement to protect the rights of the Catholic Church within Germany.

The final vote was passed by 441 votes to 94 in March 1933. Only the Social Democrats bravely opposed the measure, despite the presence of SA and SS men chanting 'We want the Enabling Act' (Source B).

> **Source B** Extract from an account by a member of the SPD of the *Reichstag* meeting where the Enabling Act was passed, March 1933.
>
> We tried to dam the flood of Hitler's unjust accusations with interruptions of 'No!', 'An error!', 'False!' but that did us no good. The SA and SS people, who surrounded us in a semicircle along the walls of the hall, hissed loudly and murmured: 'Shut up!', 'Traitors!', 'You'll be strung up today'.

Gleichschaltung

Hitler's government might have been given sweeping powers for four years, yet within months it had eliminated most of the remaining political opposition in Germany. This was achieved by a process known as *Gleichschaltung* (a German word meaning 'bringing into alignment' – coordinating all aspects of life to fit in with Nazi ideals).

Gleichschaltung took the following forms:

▶ In late March 1933 all of Germany's state parliaments were closed down, then re-established with Nazi majorities.

▶ In April 1933, Jewish people and other individuals that the Nazis regarded as their political enemies were removed from jobs in the legal profession and civil service. At the same time, key positions within Germany's state governments were taken over by Nazis.

▶ In May 1933, all trade unions were outlawed and replaced by a Nazi union, the DAF (German Labour Front).

▶ Youth Clubs and initiatives such as Strength through Joy (or *Kraft durch Freude*, KdF) and Beauty of Labour (or *Schönheit der Arbeit*, SdA) tried to make the German people think like Nazis. (These organisations are discussed in more detail on page 18.)

▶ In July 1933, the 'Law against the Establishment of Political Parties' made the Nazis the only legal political party.

In July 1933, therefore, Germany became a one-party state. However, by this stage there were few other parties to get rid of. The Social Democrats had already been outlawed, while the Centre Party had ceased to exist.

In November 1933, yet more *Reichstag* elections were held. This time the Nazis won 92 per cent of the vote.

In January 1934, Hitler introduced the Law for the Reconstruction of the State. This law abolished all of Germany's state governments, apart from Prussia's, which continued to be run by Hermann Göring, a key Nazi leader.

Activities

1 What was the Enabling Act?
2 How did Hitler manage to get the Enabling Act passed by the *Reichstag*?
3 Explain *Gleichschaltung*.
4 Why did Hitler want to control Germany's state governments?

▲ The SA moves to occupy trade union buildings in Berlin on 2 May 1933. How would closing down the trade unions increase Hitler's power?

The threat from Röhm and the SA

Hitler's position was still under threat; however, now the danger came from the SA, commanded for the last two years by Ernst Röhm, one of Hitler's longest-serving co-workers. Under Röhm's leadership the SA had expanded to over two million members (some historians say 4.5 million).

Röhm was one of the more left-wing members of the Nazi Party. He believed that Hitler's takeover would be followed by a 'second revolution', in which the authority of Germany's economic old guard and the army would be crushed and the SA would become Germany's new army. Röhm now wanted this second revolution to start. His plans worried the German Army, which looked down on the SA as a group of thugs and made clear its displeasure to Hitler.

This concerned Hitler because:

▶ He feared the Army. It was the only group that could stop his achievement of dictatorship.

▶ He needed the Army to implement his foreign policy aims. Many in the army high command supported these aims.

Röhm was also opposed by other leading Nazis such as Heinrich Himmler (head of the SS) and Hermann Göring (Source A). They believed that the SA leader had become too big for his boots and they tried to convince Hitler that Röhm was disloyal and that aspects of his private life, such as his open homosexuality, were inappropriate for a leading Nazi.

The Night of the Long Knives

Hitler finally moved against the SA on the night of 30 June 1934, an event that became known as the 'Night of the Long Knives'. Anyone he suspected of preventing his achievement of dictatorship was executed. Key SA leaders, including Röhm, were arrested and executed.

Estimates vary widely, but it is believed that around 100–200 people were killed on this night. Hitler's achievement of dictatorship took another step forward. The Nazis justified the actions that they had taken by claiming that they had prevented an SA *putsch* (revolution) from taking place. On 3 July, the government approved a law stating that: 'the measures taken on 30 June and 1 and 2 July to suppress the acts of high treason are legal, being necessary for the self-defense of the state.' Both the Army leadership and President von Hindenburg spoke of their appreciation for the actions that Hitler had taken.

Source A Extract from a speech by Hermann Göring, 18 June 1934.

It does not lie with us to say if a second revolution is necessary. The first revolution was ordered by the Leader and finished by him. If the Leader wishes a second revolution, we stand tomorrow, if he wants us, in the streets. If he wishes no further action we will suppress everyone who wants to make a second revolution against the wishes of the Leader.

▶ A British cartoon from 1934 commenting on the Night of the Long Knives; the caption states 'They salute with both hands now'. How did the Night of the Long Knives increase Hitler's power?

The death of von Hindenburg: Hitler becomes *Führer*

With the SA threat gone, von Hindenburg was the only person standing in Hitler's way as he moved towards dictatorship. Yet any threat that the elderly President might have posed proved very short-lived, as von Hindenburg died on 2 August 1934. A day earlier, a new law had been passed, which merged together the jobs of President and Chancellor and replaced both with the all-powerful position of *Führer* and Reich Chancellor.

The army now showed its thanks to Hitler for the removal of the SA threat by swearing an oath of personal loyalty to the *Führer*. Previously, soldiers had promised their loyalty to the constitution. In this new oath, each soldier promised to completely obey Adolf Hitler, the *Führer* of the German nation. From this point on the army's fate was totally linked to Hitler's.

Shortly after Hitler became *Führer*, the German people were asked to vote in a plebiscite to indicate their approval for Hitler's new position. Forty-three million Germans – almost 90 per cent of those who voted – agreed with the actions that the *Führer* had taken.

Little more than 18 months after his appointment as a relatively weak Chancellor, Hitler had turned Germany into a totalitarian state. What was most remarkable was that most of the revolutionary changes introduced had been implemented legally, using the powers granted by the 1933 Enabling Act.

Activity

1 Who were:
   - Paul von Hindenburg
   - Franz von Papen
   - Ernst Röhm?
2 Explain the German word *Führer*.
3 Why did the Night of the Long Knives take place?
4 Create a timeline to describe the sequence of events that led to Hitler declaring himself Germany's *Führer*.

Revision tip

The following were all factors helping Hitler take control of Germany in 1933: *Reichstag* Fire; 1933 election; Enabling Act; *Gleichschaltung*; Abolition of Trade Unions; Law against the Establishment of Political Parties; Night of the Long Knives.

You need to be prepared for a question which suggests that ANY of the factors was the most important, and then asks whether you agree.

Practice questions

1 How did Hitler use the Enabling Act to help him consolidate his power?
2 'Hitler achieved power in Germany by one means only: the use of terror.' Do you agree? Explain your answer.

The creation of the police state

Just in case anyone was still resisting Nazism and its ideas, Germany's security and justice systems also came under increasing Nazi control.

Himmler, the SS and the Gestapo

Following the destruction of the SA (see page 6) Heinrich Himmler's SS took over responsibility for police, security and intelligence in Germany, and the enforcing of Nazi race rules.

The SS had three main branches:

▶ The *Kripo* (*Kriminalpolizei*) who carried out general policing duties.

▶ The *Gestapo* (*GEheime STAatsPOlizei* – the secret state police) which had responsibility for hunting down the Nazis' opponents, who became known as 'enemies of the state'. The *Gestapo* Law of 1936 put the *Gestapo* above the law; they could do whatever they wanted in the line of duty. The *Gestapo* also had the right of imprisonment without trial (custody), which affected thousands of people during Hitler's rule, who simply disappeared.

▶ The SD (*Sicherheitsdienst*) was the intelligence arm of the SS; headed by Himmler's 'trainee' Reinhard Heydrich, it monitored the security of the Reich.

Potential SS members were trained in '*Junker* Schools' to be ruthless and cruel, and were told that they were the 'master race' and the forces of light. They were taught total unquestioning loyalty, which is why they formed Hitler's personal bodyguard, and why SS officers were always used to carry out massacres and illegal actions.

In 1935, Himmler conducted a purge to get rid of unfit officers, members with a problem with alcohol and gay people, and members who could not prove that they did not have Jewish ancestors. Even so, there were almost a quarter of a million members of the SS in 1939.

As a result of his total control of Germany's police and security forces, Himmler had immense power within Nazi Germany; his power continued to grow until the final months of World War II. Some historians have argued that the SS became so powerful that it became a 'state within a state'.

The law courts

The judicial system also came under state control. The aim was to ensure that the legal system did not protect those the state wanted to punish. After Germany's law courts found a number of communists not guilty of setting the *Reichstag* Fire in 1933, a furious Hitler set up a special People's Court in 1934 which would give the 'right' verdict on those accused of crimes against the state. Trials had Nazi judges, no juries, and defendants were often simply accused and not allowed to defend themselves.

It is estimated that in the period up to 1939, the judicial system sentenced nearly a quarter of a million Germans found guilty of political crimes to more than 600,000 years in prison.

Concentration camps

The Decree for the Protection of People and State allowed for opponents to be arrested and placed in 'protective custody' in newly constructed concentration camps, the first of which was established at Dachau in the state of Bavaria in March 1933. By mid-1934, these camps were being run by a part of the SS known as the Death's Head Units. Those imprisoned had to endure extremely harsh conditions.

While most early inmates of concentration camps were political prisoners, before long other groups (minority groups such as Jewish people, communists, Roma and Sinti, gay people, people with a problem with alcohol, and sex workers) suffered internment.

The impact of the Police State

The Nazis controlled everything at every level – from area leaders to the local group leaders and wardens of a street or block of flats. Everybody was watched.

The Nazis sought to create a people's community (*Volksgemeinschaft*). Here – alongside charity and neighbourliness – people were taught that their primary duty was loyalty to the German state and to its *Führer*.

One result of this was that informers reported troublemakers to the *Gestapo*. Germans could find themselves signing papers giving the *Gestapo* permission to take them into prison for 'crimes' as minor as anti-Nazi graffiti, owning a

Option 1 Life in Nazi Germany, 1933–45

banned book, or saying business was bad. This – given the brutal torture which accompanied being questioned by the *Gestapo* – made people terrified to speak out. Germans learned to 'speak through a flower' (say only nice things about the government), even with their closest friends. Who knew who might be the informer in their midst?

Even more terrifyingly, the Nazis believed in 'clan responsibility': if one member of the family broke the law, all the family was guilty and could be punished. This made it all but impossible to organise any opposition to the Nazis.

The impact on people's lives was huge. Many non-Nazi officials were arrested; those who did not 'disappear' lost their jobs and ended up in poverty.

All opposition was crushed. In the tiny rural village of Oberschopfheim, when the local Young Men's Club clashed with the Hitler Youth in 1935, its leaders were arrested and the SS conducted a house-to-house search of the village for non-Nazi flags and emblems.

Did German people live in fear? They did not trust their neighbours and worried when they forgot to say '*Heil Hitler*'. But many Germans approved of the elimination of the 'enemies of the state' – it actually made them feel safer. Most people joined the Nazi Party, left 'political matters' to the government, followed the new rules, and got on with their lives.

▲ Cover of the 3 December 1936 edition of *Illustrierter Beobachter* (Illustrated Observer), the Nazi Party's illustrated weekly magazine, which carried that week a report on the concentration camp at Dachau. Why do you think the Nazis were so open about the existence of the concentration camps?

Source A Hans Leidler's story was told by the American historian WS Allen (1965). Leidler was a member of the SPD and of the *Reichsbanner* (the paramilitary wing of the SPD). He lost his job as a railway worker and was refused unemployment pay. Local employers were too frightened to give him work. His house was searched by the *Gestapo* more than 20 times.

An unknown man knocked at Leidler's door and asked for him by name. Leidler took him in. It was raining and the man was wet. The man showed Leidler a *Reichsbanner* membership book and told him that he was a fugitive [runaway] from the *Gestapo*. He told Leidler that the *Reichsbanner* had risen in the Ruhr and was fighting the Nazis. Did Leidler have any weapons? Could he supply the names of any loyal *Reichsbanner* men in the area?

Leidler answered 'no' to each question and added, 'I'm through, I've had the sh*t kicked out of me. All I can do is put you up overnight and feed you, which I'd do for any human being on a night like this'.

In the morning, after breakfast, the man went to the door and, just before he left, turned his lapel back and showed Leidler an SS button. Then he left wordlessly.

Activities

1 What was *Volksgemeinschaft*, and what was its purpose?
2 What was the *Gestapo*?
3 What is a police state?
4 Explain the different ways that Source A is evidence of the Nazi Police State.
5 Was the police state successful in eliminating opposition to the Nazi government?

Propaganda and censorship

Goebbels and Nazi ideas

One of the easiest ways of ensuring obedience was by getting people to support the new government. This was the job of Dr Josef Goebbels, Minister for Popular Enlightenment and Propaganda. To help him in this task, Goebbels established the *Reich Chamber of Culture*. Goebbels' work was as much about stopping harmful culture (Source B) as about promoting Nazi values and ideas.

The Ministry of Propaganda

One of the most impressive propaganda methods the Nazis used was the annual Nuremberg rallies. Light, sound and costume were used to create an awe-inspiring atmosphere among crowds of up to half a million people. Other small-scale rallies and festivals were held throughout the year in order to glorify Germany, Hitler (for example, on his birthday), or other Nazi anniversaries. Nazi propaganda efforts probably reached their height with the spectacle of the 1936 Olympic Games, which were held in Berlin.

Source B Nazi Minister Albert Speer comments on the importance of radio for Nazi propaganda.

Through technical devices like the radio and the loudspeaker, 80 million people were deprived of independent thought. It was thereby possible to subject them to the will of one man.

The Propaganda Ministry also undertook a wave of censorship in the cinema, theatre, music and literature as it tried to ensure that all culture reflected Nazi thinking. A 1934 law against malicious gossip outlawed anti-Nazi stories and jokes. Exhibitions of 'degenerate' art were organised, showing people the 'bad' work of modern artists such as George Grosz and Otto Dix. Unacceptable music such as jazz was condemned. The writings of over 2500 authors were banned (in May 1933, 20,000 books by banned authors were burned in Berlin). Propaganda films such as *The Eternal Jew* were produced to portray the Jewish race in a negative way. And listening to radio broadcasts from countries outside Germany was also made illegal.

▼ The Nuremberg rally of 1936. What might be the effect of rallies like this on the participants?

Hitler in his book, *Mein Kampf* (1925), had praised the power of propaganda to control the masses (whose perception he held to be 'extremely limited and weak'). Control of the media was therefore a key Nazi aim. This was achieved in a variety of ways:

▶ Most newspapers were bought up by *Eher Verlag*, the Nazi publishers. By 1939, the Nazis owned 69 per cent of the newspaper titles in circulation. Newspapers that printed stories the regime disapproved of were shut down.

▶ The Editors' Law held editors responsible for the content of their newspapers – editors went to a daily Propaganda Ministry briefing to be told what to print. Only journalists that were approved by the government could work in the media.

▶ Posters used powerful images and slogans to convey Nazi messages.

▶ The Nazis took control of all radio stations while radio stations from countries outside Germany could not be picked up. Efforts were made to persuade Germans to buy cheap 'people's receivers' radios made by the Reich Radio Company. These could only pick up Nazi broadcasts. By 1939, 70 per cent of households owned one, the highest percentage of radio ownership for any country in the world.

▶ Loudspeakers were erected in public places and in workplaces.

▶ Propaganda films were produced. Some (like *Triumph of the Will*, about the 1934 Nuremberg rally) tried to inspire people with the Nazi message, but others – such as *The Eternal Jew*, 1940 – just promoted hatred.

The impact of propaganda and censorship on the German people

It is difficult to decide the extent to which ordinary Germans believed Nazi ideas.

Some historians suggest that the Nazi government failed to establish a new Nazi *Volksgemeinschaft* and that some propaganda – for example, Nazi attacks on the Church – backfired.

Other historians have suggested that Nazi propaganda was successful when it appealed to values many Germans already possessed: nationalism, antisemitism and admiration for Hitler's leadership (the so-called 'Hitler Myth').

The Nazis realised that young people were more impressionable than older people (Source C). They were able to create a generation of people so fanatically loyal that they fought to the bitter end in World War II.

Also, recent studies have suggested that many Germans simply closed their ears to anything which presented the government in a bad light (to political opponents, to Jewish people) – they knew what was going on but chose to ignore it. If this is true, Nazi propaganda can be said have been highly effective, because it persuaded the German people to allow the Nazis to implement their policies.

Source C Hitler, speaking in 1933.

When an opponent says, 'I will not come over to your side', I calmly say, 'Your child belongs to us already ... you will pass on. Your descendants, however, now stand in the new camp. In a short time they will know nothing else but this new community.

Activities

1 Who was in charge of propaganda in the Nazi government?

2 What was *Eher Verlag*?

3 What were the Nuremberg Rallies?

4 Why was propaganda so important to the Nazi state?

5 Construct a spider diagram to show the different ways that the Nazis tried to control the German people. Add notes to your spider diagram to show how these different ways worked together to keep the German people under Nazi control.

Revision tip

Make sure you are able to identify all the different methods of propaganda and censorship, and to explain for each how and why they were so successful.

Opposition to Hitler and the Nazis

The extent of support for the Nazis

Although the Nazi police state greatly affected opposition to the Nazi regime, this did not mean that every German person supported them. One historian has argued that if your measure of extent of support is whether the German people were totally absorbed into a Nazi *Volksgemeinschaft*, then the Nazis failed. Working class Germans, in particular, never totally accepted Nazi ideals, and neither did the Churches. Overall, however, he says, if you are just looking at what the Nazis achieved, then the Nazi *Volksgemeinschaft* was very successful. Although individuals might have grumbled about aspects of the Nazi state, in general there was no organised opposition to the regime until the start of World War II.

It is debatable how much the Nazi government affected people's lives. Elections were controlled. People were forced to be obedient and patriotic. There was no freedom of speech. If you opposed the Nazi regime or belonged to one of the minority groups it persecuted, your life would be very difficult, to say the least.

On the other hand, most Germans at every level willingly went along with the regime: some actively believed in their policies and supported them, while others put on a show of supporting them because they were scared to oppose them.

Studies have shown that:

▶ The Nazis were hugely popular in rural Protestant areas.

▶ Many lower middle class people – small businessmen and shopkeepers – were pro-Nazi.

▶ The Nazis were less likely to be supported by the urban working classes and unemployed people.

▶ Young people, recruited into the fun, adventure and comradeship of the Hitler Youth, were most likely to be keen Nazis.

Undoubtedly the fact that several hundred thousand Germans ended up being imprisoned for political crimes would have had a significant impact on the willingness of Germans to speak out against the regime. Nevertheless, it is clear that, in the years 1933–39, the vast majority of Germans were happy at least to accept their new government and *Führer*.

Source D Report from an exiled SPD member, writing in 1936.

Hitler succeeds in simply everything, it is said, and hopes which had not quite been buried for a fall of the regime are again deeply disappointed.

Activities

Find evidence from pages 2-12 to explain the comments in source D.

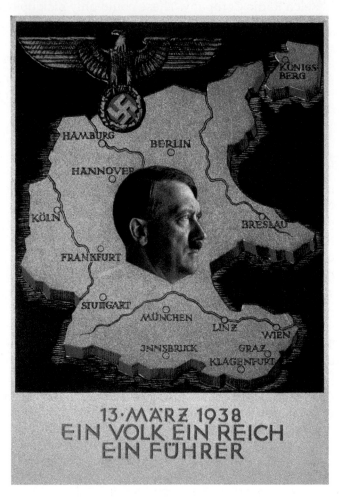

▲ 'One People, One Empire, One *Führer*': a propaganda poster from 1938. Does this poster prove Hitler was all-powerful?

Opposition from the churches

Given the country's long tradition of Christianity, Hitler knew that it would be almost impossible to destroy Germany's different Churches; however, he was determined to limit their influence as much as possible.

Overall, the Nazis were relatively successful in their aim of undermining the influence of Germany's Churches. Although a number of individual clerics spoke out against aspects of the regime, by and large the Churches as organisations remained more concerned about ensuring their survival.

The Catholic Church

In July 1933, a special agreement (The Concordat) was signed with the Catholic Church. The Church agreed not to involve itself in German politics; in return it was permitted to continue to run its own services, schools and youth groups for young people.

Initially, this arrangement worked well, but by 1936 some of its terms – particularly those guaranteeing the rights of Catholic organisations such as youth groups – were being ignored. In 1937, therefore, Pope Pius XI responded by condemning the Nazi regime, whilst later some German Church leaders such as Bishop von Galen of Münster spoke out strongly and successfully against Nazi policies (see page 42).

The Lutheran Church

The Protestant (Lutheran) Church was split over its attitude to Nazism. Pro-Nazi Lutherans were known as 'the German Christians' and their aim was to control all Germany's Protestants. Their symbol was a cross with the swastika at its centre and their version of the Bible was altered to omit many references to Jewish people. The German Christians were led by Ludwig Müller, who became the first *Reich Bishop* in July 1933.

In 1934, those Lutherans who disagreed with Nazism set up the rival 'Confessional Church'. One of their leaders was Pastor Martin Niemöller who was arrested by the Nazis in 1937 and sent to Dachau concentration camp (see page 42).

Nazi religion

The Nazis also tried to create their own Church, the 'German Faith Movement'. Its beliefs owed much more to medieval and even occult values (such as worship of the sun and the old Viking religions) and the Hitler Myth than to the ideas of Christianity. Hitler hoped that it would draw people away from their loyalty to Christianity, but it had only around 200,000 followers and Hitler was forced to deal with the established churches.

Opposition from young people

Many young Germans loved the Nazi Youth organisation, the Hitler Youth. However, not all young people supported the Nazi regime.

Before 1933, the Social Democrat and Communist Parties had youth wings, and these continued (as 'Friends of Nature' hiking clubs) until 1936, when the government made it compulsory to join the Hitler Youth movement – although many young German people (maybe as many as a million) avoided this by simply not attending.

Some young people rebelled against the Hitler Youth by forming their own groups. One group, Swing Youth, grew their hair long and danced to jazz. Another group, the Edelweiss Pirates, wore checked shirts, shorts, white socks and a lapel pin of the edelweiss flower – they hung around in parks and committed acts of vandalism.

However, until World War II, few young Germans actively opposed the government politically. Most were just being rebellious teenagers who did not want to be told how to behave. One exception was the Leipzig Hounds (1937), a communist group who listened to Moscow radio.

Activity

1 What steps did the Nazis take to control the Catholic and Lutheran Churches?
2 Which youth groups opposed Hitler Youth and why?
3 Use evidence from pages 8–13 to fill out the following table identifying the extent of support for the Nazi regime:

German people supported the Nazi regime by choice	German people were forced to support the Nazi regime

Practice questions

1 Describe two ways that the Nazis tried to control the German churches between 1933 and 1937.
2 How did propaganda affect the German people between 1933 and 1937?

Examination practice for Life in Nazi Germany, 1933–45

This page provides guidance on how to answer questions 1 and 2 in the exam.

Question 1

Below is a list of people linked with control and opposition in Nazi Germany.

Heinrich Himmler	Clemens von Galen	Marinus van der Lubbe	Baldur von Schirach	Claus von Stauffenberg

Match each person to the correct description and write your answer in the space provided. The first one has been done for you.

Leader of the SS and *Gestapo*	Heinrich Himmler	[1]
Army officer involved in a plot to kill Hitler	_____	[1]
Catholic Bishop who opposed Nazi policies	_____	[1]
Leader of the Hitler Youth	_____	[1]
Dutch communist accused of setting the *Reichstag* on fire	_____	[1]

Guidance

First, enter the answers you know. After that, you should be able to figure out the remaining answers. While being accurate, do this question as quickly as you can.

Question 2

Guidance

Describe two methods used by the Nazi Police State to hunt down opponents. **[3+3]**

You should be looking to spend about five minutes on this question. Remember that it does not need a long answer. You need to identify two ways and describe them both: your description needs to be as detailed as possible within the time allowance you have.

Follow the steps below for each part of the answer.

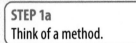

STEP 1a
Think of a method.

Example
One method the Nazis hunted down opponents was the Gestapo.

STEP 1b
Fully describe the method with a detailed sentence.

Example
Gestapo agents hunted down and arrested 'enemies of the state' — though informers identified troublemakers for them.

STEP 2a
Think of another method.

Example
A second method the Nazis hunted down opponents was the SD.

STEP 2b
Fully describe the method with a detailed sentence.

Example
The SD was the intelligence arm of the SS who were trained in 'Junker Schools' to be ruthless and cruel.

Nazi attempts to reduce unemployment

Hitler realised that the German economy had to be a focus of his attention for two reasons:

1 The Depression had created great hardship and political instability, so he would have to sort it out if he wanted to stay in power.

2 He wanted to go to war and make Germany great again, and that meant constructing a strong war economy.

In March 1933, the respected economist Dr Hjalmar Schacht became President of the *Reichsbank*. Within a year he had been appointed Minister of Economics. Schacht's 1934 New Plan, which was introduced to deal with a trade deficit, oversaw the revival of the German economy by traditional methods:

▶ Introducing massive cuts to welfare spending.

▶ Imposing limits on imports.

▶ Trade agreements with other countries.

▶ Government spending on key industries.

Under Schacht's guidance, the German economy recovered. However, by 1936 Hitler was pressurising him to increase spending on military resources and, unwilling to do this, Schacht resigned in 1937.

The Four-Year Plan

Despite his total lack of economic expertise, Hermann Göring was the man Hitler appointed to create an economy that was 'ready for war'. In 1936, he introduced the Four-Year Plan. One of its key aims was to ensure in advance of any future conflict that Germany had become an Autarky: that it would be able to survive by itself economically.

The Four-Year Plan introduced a range of strategies to ensure autarky:

▶ New factories were constructed and industries placed under strict government control.

▶ The amount of goods imported by Germany was cut.

▶ Higher targets were set for the production of essential materials such as oil, rubber and steel.

▶ Industries were encouraged to develop artificial substitutes for raw materials, particularly rubber and oil.

▶ A programme of inventions was started to try to reduce imports, notably the development of synthetic fibres and genetic research on plants.

▶ Targets were imposed for the production of foodstuffs. The *Reich Food Estate*, which all farmers had to join, provided very strict guidelines on what and how much should be produced.

◁ This 1937 school textbook describes the key infrastructure of *Das Dritte Reich* ('The Third Empire'). Use the pictures to make a list of the issues which the Nazis claimed were their economic priorities.

Reducing unemployment

Reducing Germany's massive levels of unemployment was one of Hitler's biggest challenges. 'Within four years,' he promised, 'unemployment must be decisively overcome'. The Nazis introduced a number of policies to tackle unemployment. The Nazis' vote had increased partly as a result of their promises to get Germans back to work. At first glance it would seem that he was largely successful, with only 300,000 people listed as being without work by 1939.

Targeted groups

Many people, especially professional women and Jewish people, were forced from the workplace and their jobs were then given to those who were unemployed. Neither of these groups was then counted as 'unemployed'.

Conscription and rearmament

The introduction of conscription (forced recruitment into the army) in 1935 had a significant impact on unemployment levels through the creation of new jobs. In 1933, there were 100,000 jobs in the German Army. By 1939, there were 1.4 million.

As Germany prepared for war, through the New and Four-Year plans (see page 15), thousands more jobs were created in the armament military weapons and equipment and associated industries (such as steel and coal).

Public works

The Reinhard Programme of June 1933 – named after the Nazi Secretary of State for Finance – was a massive one billion-marks programme of public works, to build *autobahns* (the German motorways), waterways and railways. A second Programme was announced in September 1933, which gave tax incentives for construction projects in rural areas and for house-building in towns.

A fifth of government spending on public works was on the *autobahns* and work began on 15 *autobahns* with 15,000 workers.

> **Revision tip** ↻
>
> It is important that you are able to explain the differences between the New Plan and the Four-Year Plan, and the different steps the Nazis took to reduce unemployment. You also need to be able to explain whether or not Hitler was successful in making Germany into an Autarky.

The National Labour Service (RAD)

The scale of existing public work schemes was increased with the establishment in 1934 of the National Labour Service (*Reichsarbeitsdienst* – RAD).

The RAD, which brought together similar schemes begun by earlier governments, was a compulsory national civic service scheme. Conscripts were clothed in military-style uniforms and were housed in army-style barracks. They drilled with spades, trained like soldiers and worked a 76-hour week. While no wages were paid, workers did receive their food and a small amount of spending money in return for providing cheap labour for state infrastructure programmes. They built schools, hospitals and motorways. Six-month membership of the RAD for all men aged 18–25 became compulsory in 1935. Members were removed from the unemployment register.

The Government also introduced the *Reich* Nature Protection Act (1935) to plant trees and prevent cruelty to animals.

▲ A RAD work contingent march to work. Why are they carrying their spades like rifles?

> **Activities** ✎
>
> 1 What was the New Plan? How successful was it?
> 2 Create a spider diagram showing the key elements of the Four-Year Plan.
> 3 How did conscription and rearmament help create jobs?
> 4 What did the National Labour Service (RAD) do to reduce unemployment?
> 5 Why was it so important for the Nazis to reduce unemployment in Germany?

The impact and effectiveness of Nazi actions to reduce unemployment

Nazi economic successes

At first glance, it would seem that the Nazis were largely successful in their attempts to reduce unemployment. In 1933, the unemployment rate had been 26 per cent; in 1939 it was below 1 per cent.

The Reinhard Programme built 1.8 million new apartments in the years 1933–39, and employment in construction rose from only 666,000 to more than 2 million in 1933–36.

By 1941, at a cost of 6.6 billion marks, the system of *autobahns* had reached 4,000 kilometres, including 9,000 bridges. Knowing the propaganda value of this, Hitler called himself 'Father of the *autobahn*'.

The failure of Autarky

The Nazis were less successful, however, in their efforts to achieve Autarky, or become economically self-sufficient. By 1939, Germany was still importing over one-third of the natural resources essential to its economy. It had become clear that the only way to make its economy self-sufficient would be to conquer other countries and so gain complete access to their natural resources.

Ultimately, the Nazis wrecked, not rescued, the German economy.

▶ The switch of production to munitions and rearmament weakened the economy.

▶ To pay for the rearmament and public works programmes, the Nazis printed 12 billion marks of 'Mefo bills' (a way of paying without borrowing). This created inflation and by 1939 the economy was in crisis. Some historians have suggested that Hitler had to go to war in 1939 to head off an economic collapse.

▶ Food prices rose, there was a 'nutritional crisis' in northern Germany in the 1930s and the death rate actually rose in 1933–38.

At the same time, Nazi propaganda promises failed to materialise, although Nazi Party members got good jobs, houses and special privileges, and businessmen who joined the Nazi Party got government orders.

Alle Frauen geht das an! Was fordert der Vierjahresplan?

Kartoffel
Ich schmecke doch wirklich gut,
wenn man mich richtig zubereiten tut.
Drum, liebe Hausfrau, laß dir sagen,
ich bin billig und fülle den Magen.
Ich enthalte Eiweiß und sehr viel Stärke.
Und geb' dir Kraft zu deinem Werke.

Fisch
Ich bin der Fisch!
Und gehöre auf jeden deutschen Tisch!
Mindestens einmal alle Wochen,
sollst du mich braten oder kochen.
Bin gut bekömmlich und nährstoffreich –
drum rasch zum Händler, und hole mich gleich!

Quark
Ich bin der Quark!
Ich mach' dich groß, gesund und stark!
Werd' dir nicht über auf die Dauer
und schmecke gut, ob süß, ob sauer.
Bin preiswert und deshalb allen bekannt:
bei uns werd' Topfen ich genannt.

Marmelade
Ich bin billig und doch vorzüglich,
drum schlecken mich alle so vergnüglich.
Man genießt mich verdünnt zu Brei,
und sonst noch zu verschiedenerlei.
Statt Butter man aufs Brot mich streicht
das Haushaltgeld dann länger reicht.

Kohl
Wenn Bohnen, Erbsen rarer werden,
kommt der Kohl erst aus der Erden.
Da er so nahrhaft und bescheiden,
drum kann ihn auch ein jeder leiden.
Die Kinder greifen zu so frisch,
dampft die Schüssel auf dem Tisch.

Hedwig Aichinger.

▲ One side effect of Autarky was a barrage of propaganda on German housewives from the Domestic Economy department. This is a poem for housewives about approved foods – potatoes, fish, cheese, preserves, cabbage – in the *Kraft durch Freude* magazine, 1938.

Activities

1 What were Mefo bills?
2 Why was Autarky so important to the Nazi government?
3 How did the Nazis try to achieve Autarky and how successful were they?

Nazi attempts to change the lives of workers

Changing the mind set of Germany's urban workers was a key aspect of Nazi *Volksgemeinschaft*, and the Nazis introduced three organisations to try to accomplish this.

The German Labour Front (DAF)

Hitler was afraid that trade unions – which had proved challenging during the years of the Weimar Republic – could interfere with his plans, so in May 1933 they were outlawed. At the same time, taking industrial action (striking) to obtain better pay and conditions was declared illegal.

Instead, the Unions were replaced by the German Labour Front (*Deutsche Arbeitsfront* – DAF), a Nazi workers' organisation. It was led by Dr Robert Ley, who promised the workers that it would look after them as well as the unions had done (Source A). Within two years all workers – more than 20 million people – were members.

In Germany in 1928, 20 million days' work was lost to strikes; in 1939 there were none.

> **Source A** Robert Ley speaking about the DAF, May 1933.
>
> For we know that without the German worker there is no German nation ... Workers, I swear to you we shall not only preserve everything that exists, we shall build up even further the protection of the worker's rights.

The Beauty of Labour (SdA)

A branch of the DAF, the 'Beauty of Labour' (*Schönheit der Arbeit* – SdA) was set up to encourage workers to be proud of their work. Essentially a propaganda department, it ran campaigns to improve working conditions through, for example, better lighting, washing facilities or noise reduction.

The Government discouraged heavy drinking and people with a problem with alcohol were sent to concentration camps. It was also the first government in the world to realise that smoking caused cancer and to introduce regular screening of women for breast cancer.

> ➤ A 1933 poster encouraging workers to join the DAF. The German slogans mean: 'At that time as today ... we remain comrades'. All Nazi posters carry **subliminal messages** – what is this poster trying to brainwash the people to believe?

Strength through Joy (KdF)

The Nazis were also keen to ensure that their workers were happy outside the workplace. Therefore 'Strength through Joy' (*Kraft durch Freude* – KdF) was established in November 1933 to improve workers' free time and offer incentives.

The KdF provided workers' picnics, cheap cinema and theatre tickets and organised a broad range of sporting activities. Cheap holidays were arranged, including trips abroad and Mediterranean cruises, as a reward for hard work. These brought fun into workers' lives and made them feel valued. A huge holiday camp with 10,000 family rooms was built at Prora on the Baltic Sea for German workers to get some 'true relaxation' – by which the Nazis meant sun, sport and propaganda.

The flagship KdF scheme was a savings scheme to own a car, the Volkswagen (people's car), by contributing five Marks each week (until 750 Marks had been paid).

> **Activity** 🖉
>
> Match up the following organisations and definitions:
> 1 The DAF   A Set up to offer incentives during workers' free time
> 2 The KdF
> 3 The SdA   B Set up to replace trades unions
>   C Set up to encourage workers to take pride in their work

The impact and effectiveness of Nazi actions on the lives of workers

While the DAF was meant to represent the workers in discussions with their employers, it tended to side with employers and workers found their freedoms restricted (for example, their ability to move to better-paid jobs or leave their jobs) and their working hours increased (Source B).

Wages and prices

In 1939, after six years of Nazi government, it was employers who came out the clear winners with their real incomes (i.e. the 'spending' power of people's incomes, taking account of rises in prices) increased by 130 per cent. Ordinary workers, whose wages had been slashed during the 1929–33 Depression, did not see real wages recover to pre-Depression levels until 1938.

Nevertheless, for most Germans in work, incomes improved steadily, whilst prices grew only slowly (and actually fell for goods such as electrical appliances, clocks and watches), so real wages rose by 20 per cent under the Nazis.

Working conditions also improved in some ways. For instance, many workplaces introduced showers, canteens and crèches. But no German citizen ever received a Volkswagen car and the war broke out before the Prora holiday camp had seen a single visitor.

There were also some improvements in welfare, notably for mothers and children, and the government provided universal health care, job protection, rent controls and low taxes. The Nazis doubled the amount of paid holiday, from three days to six days a year. However, as money was poured into rearmament, a number of public facilities declined. There were reductions, for instance, in the number both of hospital beds and of doctors per head of population.

> **Source B** Government statement on the role of the DAF, November 1933.
>
> The high aim of the Labour Front is to educate all Germans who are at work to support the National Socialist State and to indoctrinate them in the National Socialist mentality.

Revision tip

There is a danger, if you are asked how Nazi labour policies affected German workers, only to list the organisations – DAF, SdA, KdF – and say what they did.

You must also explain how the workers' lives were affected by these organisations.

Practice questions (?)

1 Describe two ways in which the lives of German workers changed between 1933 and 1939.
2 'The Nazis' attempts to improve life for Germany's workers were successful.' Do you agree? Explain your answer.

▲ This poster advertises the DAF and KdF. What is its message? Compare this poster to the DAF poster on page 18.

Nazi views of women and the family

Aryan ideals

The Nazi treatment of women grew out of the Nazi idea that the German people were descended from a perfect 'Aryan' race – a 'Master Race' which was strong, blond, white-skinned and noble – but which had been 'contaminated' by 'impure blood'. In the 1930s, many scientists believed in eugenics (the idea of applying selective breeding methods to people). The Nazis therefore sought to re-establish the purity of the German people by making Aryan-type women (and stopping 'degenerates') have more babies.

Therefore, the main role of Germany's women was to produce as many racially pure children as possible in pursuit of the Master Race.

▲ *The Aryan Family*, a painting by Wolfgang Willrich. Identify ten ways this family represents the Nazi ideal.

Employment

In Weimar Germany there had been 100,000 female teachers and 3,000 female doctors. Within a year most had been sacked or 'encouraged' to leave. After 1933, they could not be appointed to civil service positions. In 1936, women were forbidden to become a judge. Most women's associations closed down voluntarily and some women's leaders were arrested or assassinated. Instead, the Nazis set up the Nazi Women's League. It took no part in politics and, through its twice-weekly magazine *Frauen Warte* which had a circulation of almost two million, encouraged its members to be good housekeepers.

Family life: *Kinder, Küche, Kirche*

As well as meeting Aryan race ideals, to fit into the Nazi *Volksgemeinschaft*, German women had to also meet Nazi social requirements. These, essentially, can be summed up in the phrase: Children, Kitchen, Church (*Kinder, Küche, Kirche*): the 'three Ks'.

The Nazis believed that the family was the foundation unit of the German nation. They taught that Weimar society had devalued the family, but that they aimed to support and enhance it.

The Nazi family was based on the traditional medieval notion of society rooted in love of homeland and ties of kinship, where the father was strong and the worker/provider, while the mother was gentle and the nurturer.

The Nazis turned Mother's Day into a national festival day celebrating family life.

Appearance

Nazi women were expected not to wear makeup, trousers or high heels. Their hair should be arranged in plaits or a bun. Slimming was discouraged because it might harm the woman's ability to bear children. Smoking was discouraged because it was 'un-German'. The women's section of the DAF ruled that 'painted and powdered' women and those who smoked 'in hotels, cafés, in the street and so on' would be excluded from their meetings.

Nazi actions and policies to change the lives of women and the family

Marriage and babies

The ideal Nazi mothers had lots of children and German women were given incentives to do so:

▶ The Law to Reduce Unemployment (1933) offered a 600 mark marriage loan to employed women who married and left work. The debt was reduced by a quarter for every child, so couples had children specifically to 'baby-off' the loan.

▶ After 1935, families were given welfare allowances. At first, this was a single grant for families with six children; in 1936 it was replaced by regular payments for the 5th child onwards, and in 1938 from the 3rd child … all paid for by increased taxes on the childless.

▶ Mothers of many children were celebrated and given the right to go to the front of queues. After 1938, on significant days such as Mothering Sunday or the day of Hitler's mother's birthday, 12 August, women with four or more children were given an 'Honour Cross' (bronze for four children, silver for six and gold for eight). These women were also able to benefit from lower taxation levels and increased state benefits.

▶ Contraception and abortion became much harder to get.

▶ SS members were expected to have four children. After 1935, unmarried women were encouraged to live in 'Life-Source' (Lebensborn) homes where SS men could impregnate them.

▶ Childless couples were encouraged to divorce so that the woman could have the chance of becoming pregnant with someone else. In 1938, divorces to end childless marriages were made easier to obtain.

Sterilisation and imprisonment

Having babies was not without its risks. The Nazis only wanted 'valuable' mothers, who would have Aryan babies. Consequently, if you wanted a marriage loan, you had to have a Certificate of Suitability for Marriage, signed by a doctor. What the doctor was looking for was defined in the *Law for the Prevention of Hereditarily Diseased Offspring* (1933) – mental illness, such as schizophrenia or depression, epilepsy, blindness, deafness, physical disability and alcoholism. Women who were physically unable to bear children, or who had extra- or pre-marital sex were also rejected. About one in 25 women failed to get a Certificate.

The 1933 *Diseased Offspring* law also enacted that: 'anyone who is hereditarily ill within the meaning of this law … can be sterilised'. Thus, the woman, who had gone joyfully to ask her doctor for a wedding Certificate, instead found herself, not only refused permission to marry, but being sterilised. By 1939, an estimated 350,000 women had been sterilised by 'Genetic Health Courts'.

And since refusal was linked to some kind of mental, physical or social unsuitability for the *Volksgemeinschaft*, women who had failed the Certificate could then find themselves being put in a workhouse or a concentration camp.

Similarly, after 1938, mothers proposed for an Honour Cross were vetted by the League of Large Families. If it was found that they neglected their children or their housework, they would be 're-educated' and if they proved unreformable, they were sent to a concentration camp.

Source A Joseph Goebbels commenting on the role of women under National Socialism, 1929.

The mission of women is to be beautiful and bring children into the world. This is not at all as rude and unmodern as it sounds. The female bird pretties herself for her mate and hatches eggs for him. In exchange, the male takes care of gathering the feed, and stands guard and wards off the enemy.

Source B *'To Be German is to Be Strong'* – a speech by the Nazi Women's League leader Gertrud Scholtz-Klink, printed in a 1936 issue of *Frauen Warte*.

The deepest calling we women have is: motherhood … We know and believe that all German women will accept this calling. More and more faithful helpers will join our ranks, working cheerfully and strongly as we have done in the past. Not only those women with children will become mothers of the nation, but rather each German woman and each girl will become one of the *Führer's* little helpers.

The impact and effectiveness of Nazi policies

The Nazi regime was a huge set-back for women's rights in Germany. The Nazis replaced the equality women had gained under the Weimar Republic, with 'equivalence' – the idea that men and women should have different roles which were equally valuable to society. In reality, women were simply excluded from public life and leadership – as Göring put it: 'Take a pot, a dustpan and a broom, and marry a man'.

Few women protested at their being pushed back into domesticity and some of them adopted Nazi values enthusiastically. In 1938, the *NS-Frauenschaft* had two million members.

However, Nazi attitudes regarding women and the family hugely affected private life – as one *NS-Frauenschaft* member said: 'Marriage is not merely a private matter, but one which directly affects the fate of a nation.'

Moreover, all the evidence suggests that the Nazi attempts to get women to have more babies failed. Though the number of marriages, and the number of babies born, rose slowly through the 1930s, neither ever reached the rates achieved in the early 1920s. The Nazis were giving benefits to parents who had large families, but it seems that they were merely giving money to people who would have had large families anyway, rather than encouraging people to have large families.

And it appears that the dangers surrounding the Certificate of Marriage actually discouraged marriage – when the rules were relaxed in 1938, the marriage rate rose.

Finally, the Nazi attempt to exclude women from the workplace failed. Although the numbers of professional women did go down, a large number of women in less-skilled employment kept their jobs because of a lack of replacement workers. The numbers of women in jobs actually went up in the later 1930s as the drive for rearmament and Autarky took off.

Indeed, the Nazis came to regret excluding women. Faced with a growing skills shortage, the Nazis after 1937 required women to do a 'Duty Year' in a factory. And, when the war broke out, women were needed to help the war effort.

Activities

1 What were 'the three Ks'?
2 Explain why the Nazis tried to change the role of women in German society.
3 How successful were the Nazis' policies towards women?

Practice question

Below are two methods used by the Nazis to change the lives of German women between 1933 and 1939:

Law for the Prevention of Hereditarily Diseased Offspring (1933)
Nazi Women's League (1937)

Choose **one** method and explain how it affected the lives of German women.

▲ This Nazi poster was produced in 1936. The words mean: 'The Nazi Party ensures *Volksgemeinschaft*. The German people need its advice and help so get yourselves to the local group.' Discuss as a whole class the messages of the poster.

This page provides guidance on how to answer question 3 in the exam.

Question 3

Below are two groups of German people affected by Nazi rule in the 1930s.

Choose one group and explain how Nazi rule affected their lives. [6]

Workers	Women

Guidance

You should be looking to spend about seven minutes on this question. To access all the available marks, your answer needs not only to give facts about your chosen topic, but to 'provide an accurate, well-developed explanation and analysis' which answers the question (in this example, of **how their lives were affected**).

Follow the steps below for each part of the answer.

STEP 1
Chose a topic, *stating the whole question.*

Example

One group whose lives were affected by Nazi rule was the workers.

STEP 2a
Take a fact, and explain how it affected workers' lives.

Example

One way was because their Unions were banned in May 1933. The German Labour Front (DAF) which replaced it promised to support them, but usually sided with the employers. They were affected by this because their wages remained low and they were not allowed to go on strike.

STEP 2b
Repeat for another fact.

Example

A second way was through the Kraft durch Freude (KdF), which provided workers' picnics and sporting activities, cheap cinema and theatre tickets and cheap holidays, although the promise of a holiday camp at Prora and a Volkswagen 'people's car' never materialised.

STEP 2c
Repeat for a third fact.

Example

A third way was through the Schönheit der Arbeit (SdA) which the Nazis set up to encourage workers to be proud of their work. Although primarily a propaganda department, it did achieve some improvements to their working conditions.

Nazi actions and policies to change the lives of young people

The Nazis saw indoctrination of youth with National Socialist ideas as the key to their future control of the country. Young people would be easier to control and indoctrinate. The Nazis saw young boys as Germany's future military and political leaders and young girls as the country's future mothers. So they set about influencing children inside and outside school.

Youth movements

Age	Boys	Girls
6–10	Cubs (*Pimpfe*)	
10–14	Young German Folk (*Deutsches Jungvolk*)	Young Maidens (*Jung Mädel*)
14–18	Hitler Youth (*Hitlerjugend*)	League of German Maidens (*Bund Deutscher Mädel*)
18–21		Faith and Beauty (*Glaube und Schönheit*)

Table 1 The main Nazi youth movements.

The Hitler Youth (*Hitlerjugend*)

Set up in 1922, the Hitler Youth had two main aims – to indoctrinate racism and develop physical fitness in Germany's youths. After the Nazis came to power, a Youth Law (1936) decreed that children must be educated according to Nazi principles, which all but made the Hitler Youth compulsory. The old Boy Scouts movement was banned and pressure was put on Catholic Youth Clubs to disband. Teachers set punishment essays for children who did not go to the Hitler Youth.

Upon joining the Hitler Youth, a boy would be put on probation, during which time he was taught about the Hitler Youth and Hitler and had to learn the words of the *Horst Wessel Song* (written by a Hitler Youth hero who died for the Nazi cause). He would then run 60 metres, go on a hike and complete a 'courage test', to win his membership, and be given the uniform, a badge and a dagger inscribed 'Blood and Honour'.

The leader of the Hitler Youth, Baldur von Schirach, organised the Hitler Youth into a hierarchy of organisations for different ages (see Table 1) and gave their activities a yearly focus – the Year of Training, Year of PE, Year of Young People.

Hitler Youth members took part in exciting, military-style activities (such as marches, camps and war games) and sang rousing songs based on stories from German folklore. In 1937, rifle practice was introduced (which trained 1.5 million boys to shoot). For lucky members, there was the *Flieger-Hitler Youth* (flying gliders, plus visits to the *Luftwaffe*, the German air force), the *Motor-Hitler Youth* (to learn to ride motorcycles) and the *Marine-Hitler Youth* (sailing and visits to German training ships). Members received a monthly magazine called 'Will and Power'.

By 1938, the Hitler Youth had more than 7 million members and in September 1938, 80,000 Hitler Youth members held a huge 'Rally of Greater Germany' at Nuremberg.

After war broke out in 1939, all German boys were automatically conscripted into the Hitler Youth, which was reformed into the 'home guard' force which manned searchlights and anti-aircraft guns. In 1945, with Germany's army destroyed and the USSR advancing, Goebbels organised a German Home Defence Force made up of Hitler Youth members and older men, for a last-ditch defence of Berlin.

▼ A recruitment poster for the Hitler Youth. The German words mean: 'Join Us! Into the Hitler Youth'. What about this poster would have attracted German boys into joining?

HER ZU UNS!

Hinein in die Hitler-Jugend

The League of German Maidens (*Bund Deutscher Mädel* or BDM)

Source A Trude Mohr, leader of the BDM, explains her vision for its members.

Germany needs a generation of girls which is healthy in body and mind, sure and decisive, proud and confident … free of sentimental and excessive emotions, in sharply defined femininity, to be the comrade of a man, whom she regards not as a superior but as a companion.

The BDM was the mirror girls' youth organisation to the Hitler Youth. It had a female leader – Trude Mohr, a former postal worker – and, like the Hitler Youth, it was organised into age groups.

Its activities were designed to teach German girls how to be good mothers and to keep themselves fit for childbirth. 'Home Evenings' during the week included lessons in cooking and cleaning, but also story-telling, learning about Hitler and German folklore and singing patriotic songs round a fire. It was purposely made to be romantic and comradely.

Saturdays involved exercise – sports, gymnastics, marching, and swimming. A good BDM member could run 60 metres in 14 seconds, complete a long march, swim 100 metres … and make a bed. The girls had their own magazine, called 'Maiden's Works'.

Senior BDM members were sent on outward bound courses designed to build good character, and the organisation also offered skiing and camping holidays, (girls from poor families went free). 'Aryan' girls might be sent to a *Lebensborn* home (see page 21).

Through everything the BDM did ran the idea of self-sacrifice – that a good Nazi woman put others and the nation first. BDM girls took part in community service, and during the war collected money, knitted socks, visited wounded soldiers and helped refugees. After 1943, as the tide of the war turned against Germany, many BDM girls went into 'home guard' service, though rarely to fight.

Source B Ilse McKee remembered in 1960 what it was like to be a member of the BDM.

It was all fun in a way and we certainly got plenty of exercise, but it had a bad effect on our school reports … We were of course lectured a lot on National Socialist ideology, and most of this went right over our heads … We were told from a very early age to prepare for motherhood.

▲ A poster for the BDM. The German words mean: 'Build Youth Hostels and Homes'. Compare this poster with the Hitler Youth poster on page 24. What can you learn from the comparison about Nazi actions to change the lives of young people?

Activities

1 Who were Baldur von Schirach and Trude Mohr?
2 Explain the purpose of the 1936 Youth Law.
3 Fill in the table below.
4 After filling out the table, what do you notice about the two organisations? What does this say about the Nazis' ideas of boys and girls?

	Aims of organisation	Activities of organisation
The Hitler Youth		
The League of German Maidens (BDM)		

Education

The American historian Louis Snyder suggested that Nazi education was based around 'a sense of race', and 'getting German youth ready for war'. In addition, the Nazis sought to train students to accept that 'individuals must be willing and ready to sacrifice themselves for nation and *Führer*'.

Therefore the government:

▶ Dismissed Jewish teachers and those regarded as unreliable. One teacher who told a joke about Hitler lost her job and spent three weeks in prison.

▶ Encouraged teachers to join the National Socialist Teachers' League (NSLB) and to promote Nazism at all times. Within six years all but three per cent of teachers had joined the NSLB.

▶ Sent primary school teachers to special camps for a month-long training course.

▶ Asked Hitler Youth and BDM members to report teachers who were not 'Nazi' enough.

Source A The Nazi Minister of Education explains the role of education under National Socialism.

The whole purpose of education is to create Nazis.

▲ This schoolbook – *The Poisonous Mushroom* (1936) – shows Jewish teachers and pupils being driven out of school. Discuss the meaning of the image.

The Nazi curriculum

The curriculum was also Nazified – for example:

▶ In Biology, pupils studied 'blood purity' and eugenics, and learned how to recognise Jewish people. Jewish pupils were humiliated and, after 1935, banned from attending school altogether.

▶ Maths involved 'social arithmetic', where pupils calculated the flight of a missile, or the cost of caring for a mentally ill patient.

▶ Geography explained Hitler's claim in his book *Mein Kampf* that Germany needed to conquer *lebensraum* ('living space') from the countries of Eastern Europe.

▶ History taught national pride; Hitler thought it ridiculous that historians should try to be objective.

Girls followed a different curriculum, which taught them to be good wives and mothers – cookery, needlework, housekeeping and PE.

Fifteen per cent of the timetable was spent on PE and pupils who failed a fitness test were expelled.

Nazi special schools

For young men whom the Nazis hoped would form the Nazi elite of the future, special schools were established:

▶ Boys aged 11–18 could be sent to the National Political Institutes of Education. These were boarding schools where they were trained to be young soldiers; many went into the SS.

▶ In Adolf Hitler Schools, boys were taught by a 'Commander' and 'Leaders' (not 'Principal' and 'teachers'); four-fifths of the curriculum was given to PE and they were also taught German 'folklore'.

▶ The Order Castles were the elite schools. There, students were brutally prepared to be SS officers, and the curriculum included war games with live ammunition. One student writing about one of these exercises commented casually: 'of course, some of our chaps are killed'.

Revision tip ⟳

It is essential that you can explain the Nazis' policies both inside and outside of school. Make sure you are able to explain whether these policies were successful.

The impact and effectiveness of Nazi actions and policies by 1939

The Nazis' youth policies had mixed results. Most young people accepted them unquestioningly and would have been influenced by the Nazi policies both inside and outside the classroom.

Arguments 'for' the impact of Nazi actions and policies

German people who were members of the Hitler Youth often remember the time very fondly. As young people, they loved the Hitler Youth and BDM, the exciting activities and most of all marching through town, with adults standing respectfully giving the Nazi salute, forcing off the road adults who were in their way.

It is also obvious that the Nazis achieved their aim of brainwashing young people. In 1936, on Hitler's birthday, thousands of Hitler Youth members paraded and promised: 'I swear to devote all my energies and my strength to the saviour of our country, Adolf Hitler. I am willing and ready to give up my life for him, so help me God.' In 1945, true to their word, with Germany's armies destroyed, they fought and died for him.

A darker, but just as successful side of the Hitler Youth, was the Patrol Force, whose job was to inform on opponents. Its model member was a boy named Walter Hess, who turned his father in for imprisonment for calling Hitler a 'crazed maniac'. Adults were scared of what young people might tell the authorities and this gave young people a power they enjoyed.

Arguments 'against' the impact of Nazi actions and policies

On the other hand, evidence suggests that the quality and breadth of education suffered badly, with traditional subjects losing out to PE, ideology and folklore under the regime. Students' education was harmed by their continual absences to attend the Hitler Youth and BDM.

Also, as we saw on page 12, as many as one million youths avoided joining the Nazi youth movements, and even established rival youth groups of their own (see below, page 41).

▲ Every class had a compulsory 'Press Period'. In 1939, an American reporter from *Ken* magazine photographed these pupils reading the Nazi propaganda newspaper *Völkischer Beobachter*.

Activities

1 Why did the Nazis see Germany's young people as so important for the future of the Third Reich?
2 What were the main features of Nazi education policy, 1933–39?
3 Were Nazi education policies successful?
4 Hitler boasted to his opponents: 'Your child belongs to us already' (page 11). Was he correct?

Practice questions

1 Describe two ways in which the Nazis tried to control young people's free time between 1933 and 1939.
2 How did Nazi education policies affect young people between 1933 and 1939?

The persecution of minorities

In the early twentieth century, many scientists and doctors taught that some races were superior to others, in a way which we would find racist today. Most Germans believed that they were descended from a 'Master Race' which they called the Aryan Race.

This belief trickled down from academics into the German folklore movement, which looked back romantically to Germany's mythical past. (Look back through pages 24–27 to see how many times folklore was part of the Nazi indoctrination of youth.) Thus Nazi policy became a generally-accepted German belief.

Nazi racial ideas and policies

Some races, it was said, were not so bad; the English and Danes – even the French – had some Germanic blood in them. Other races, however, were held to be inferior. An Austrian monk called Jörg Lanz-Liebenfels – whose books Hitler read – suggested that the 'lower races' (such as the African and Asian races) had been born of a union between Eve and a demon. The Slav races of Europe, said the Nazis, were fit only to be their slaves. Many black Germans were sterilised or killed.

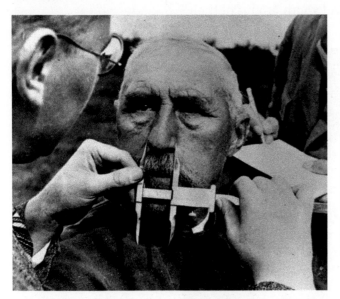

▲ Race Determination Test (1940). The Nazis claimed that their racial policies were based on 'scientific' research and data. What does this photograph tell us about Nazi race policies?

The Nazis also believed that marriage or relationships between people of different races was wrong and would 'pollute' German blood. The Nazis concluded that many people were simply *Untermenschen* (sub-human).

Many scientists of the time also believed that the answer to this was 'eugenics'. As you have seen, this was why the Nazis encouraged Aryan-type mothers to have as many children as possible (pages 20–21). However, they also recommended sterilisation of the 'unfit'. One of the leading champions of keeping the German race 'pure' was the psychiatrist Ernst Rüdin – a man who after the war would be described as 'one of the most evil men in Germany.' In 1930, however, he was one of the speakers at the International Congress for Mental Hygiene, held in Washington, America. After the Nazis seized power, Rüdin wrote the *Law for the Prevention of Hereditarily Diseased Offspring* (July 1933) – which set up the 'Genetic Health Courts' (see page 21).

Thus the Nazis considered a whole range of races and groups *Untermenschen*, whom they believed had to be eliminated in one way or another from the gene-pool, including Jewish people, Roma people, Jehovah's Witnesses, gay people, political opponents and the 'asocial'.

All of these groups were targeted by the Nazis and many individuals ended up in concentration camps where they lived under extremely harsh conditions. The Nazis enacted policies designed to prevent them from reproducing, to remove them from society or to eliminate them altogether.

Activities

1 What did the Nazis believe about the Aryan race?
2 Which social groups did the Nazis regard as *Untermenschen*?
3 After reading page 29, create a spider diagram with 'Nazi treatment of minorities' in the centre. Summarise the information by adding notes to your diagram. Can you see any similarities in the ways Nazis treated different minority groups?

The treatment of minorities

Prisoners in Nazi concentration camps were forced to wear a coloured triangle representing their 'crime'.

'Asocial' Germans – people who did not 'fit' into the *Volksgemeinschaft* – were regarded as 'useless mouths' by the Nazis. They included the 'work shy', vagrants, people with a problem with alcohol, and sex workers. A 'Beggars Week' in 1933 rounded up many 'asocials' and there was another 'Campaign against the Workshy' in 1938.

Pacifists were 'asocial' too, because they refused to defend the Fatherland.

Although not guilty of any crime, thousands of 'asocial' Germans were sent to concentration camps, where they were brutally treated and died from starvation, disease, gassing, hanging, torture, or execution.

People with mental and physical disabilities and illnesses, or who were deaf or blind. The *Diseased Offspring Law* of 1933 allowed sterilisation of disabled people, and after 1935 doctors were allowed to terminate pregnancies by force. In 1939–41, the Nazis conducted a programme of euthanasia. Mentally disabled people in concentration camps were made to wear a black triangle with the word *Blöd* ('stupid').

It has been estimated that the Nazis killed 72,000 mentally ill people during the Second World War and that 300,000 men and women were sterilised from 1934–45.

The Roma people. The Nazis thought 'Gypsies' (the Roma people) as great a danger to Aryan blood purity as Jewish people. Persecution began in 1936, when many Roma were rounded up and sent to concentration camps in 'crime prevention' campaigns. By 1938, Himmler was calling for a 'Solution' to the 'Gypsy Question'. The Roma holocaust is called the *Porajmos* ('cutting up'); perhaps a third of the estimated 700,000 Roma people in Europe were killed.

Gay men. In 1933, the Hitler Youth attacked the *Institute for Sex Research*, which studied homosexuality. 100,000 gay men were arrested; 15,000 were sent to concentration camps. Some were castrated; others were experimented on to try to find a 'cure'. The Nazis forbade lesbianism, but classified it as an asocial rather than criminal act.

There were about 25,000 active **Jehovah's Witnesses** in Germany, where they were known as 'Bible Students'. Although in 1933 they declared in public that they did not oppose the regime and were 'in agreement with its goals', they refused to swear allegiance to Hitler or join the army. Their religion was banned and they were placed in prison or put into mental institutions. Some 2,000 were sent to concentration camps and 250 were executed. Since all they had to do to be left alone was renounce their religion, they showed great courage.

Political opponents of the Nazis were sent to concentration camps from the very start of the Nazi regime. Brutal treatment included floggings, 'standing cells' (that forced the prisoner to stay permanently in an uncomfortable position) and 'pole-hanging' prisoners by their hands tied behind their backs. Many political prisoners were students and intellectuals, and many died.

'Career criminals' (gangsters) were sent to labour camps; there, some were used by the SS as 'prisoner-policemen' and were given special privileges to beat and bully the inmates. Ordinary criminals were sent to prison, where conditions were brutal. During the war, prisoners were required to defuse unexploded bombs and, when one Berlin jail became overcrowded, some prisoners were simply executed.

Nazi persecution of the Jewish community

The Nazis reserved their greatest hatred for Germany's Jewish people. Jewish people had experienced antisemitism in many European countries for several centuries. In Germany, there was a perception that Jewish people were more influential than their numbers merited. There was a belief that Jewish people were greedy and held too many of the most important jobs in the country. Hitler and the Nazis had long used propaganda to tell the Germans that Jewish people were to blame for many of the problems that they had faced, including the end of the First World War, the Treaty of Versailles and all that had gone wrong since.

Once in power, Hitler wasted no time in putting his antisemitism into operation. His policies were particularly intended to intimidate Germany's Jewish population by showing it as being different from other German citizens. He also hoped to isolate Jewish people and prevent them from having any influence on German society.

> **Source A** Hitler outlining his aims for Jewish people, 1922.
>
> As soon as I have power, I shall have gallows after gallows erected … Then the Jews will be hanged one after another, and they will stay hanging until they stink.

Revision tip

You can use the information on pages 32–33 to help you understand what day-to-day life was like for Jewish people in Germany at the time.

Activities

1 Why was there so much antisemitism in Germany in the 1930s?
2 Sort the persecutions on the timeline into the following categories: economic, civic rights, exclusion, violence.
3 What are the six most important dates from the timeline? Justify your choices.
4 Explain whether there was any progression in the persecution of Jewish people in the timeline from 1933–39. Did their persecution get worse?

To achieve these aims, the Nazis took the following steps:

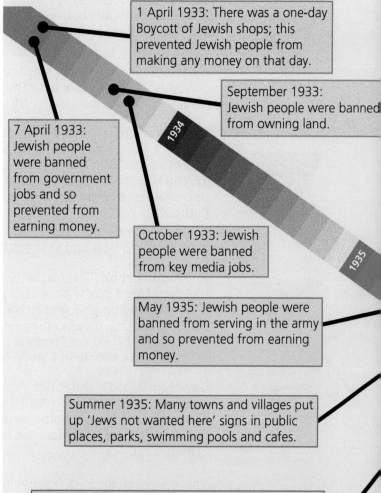

1 April 1933: There was a one-day Boycott of Jewish shops; this prevented Jewish people from making any money on that day.

7 April 1933: Jewish people were banned from government jobs and so prevented from earning money.

September 1933: Jewish people were banned from owning land.

October 1933: Jewish people were banned from key media jobs.

May 1935: Jewish people were banned from serving in the army and so prevented from earning money.

Summer 1935: Many towns and villages put up 'Jews not wanted here' signs in public places, parks, swimming pools and cafes.

September 1935: **Nuremberg Laws**. There were two main elements:
- The *Reich Citizenship Law*: Jewish people were were deprived of many political and economic rights and were made wards of the state.
- The *Law for the Protection of German Blood and German Honour*: It became illegal for Jewish people and Aryans to marry or engage in sexual relations outside marriage.

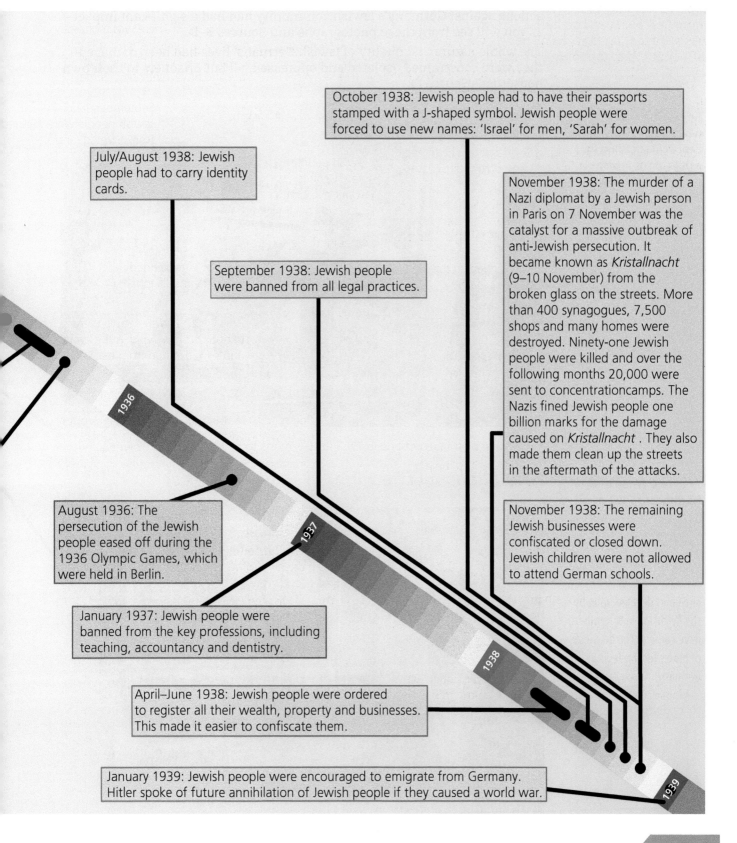

October 1938: Jewish people had to have their passports stamped with a J-shaped symbol. Jewish people were forced to use new names: 'Israel' for men, 'Sarah' for women.

July/August 1938: Jewish people had to carry identity cards.

November 1938: The murder of a Nazi diplomat by a Jewish person in Paris on 7 November was the catalyst for a massive outbreak of anti-Jewish persecution. It became known as *Kristallnacht* (9–10 November) from the broken glass on the streets. More than 400 synagogues, 7,500 shops and many homes were destroyed. Ninety-one Jewish people were killed and over the following months 20,000 were sent to concentrationcamps. The Nazis fined Jewish people one billion marks for the damage caused on *Kristallnacht* . They also made them clean up the streets in the aftermath of the attacks.

September 1938: Jewish people were banned from all legal practices.

1936

1937

August 1936: The persecution of the Jewish people eased off during the 1936 Olympic Games, which were held in Berlin.

November 1938: The remaining Jewish businesses were confiscated or closed down. Jewish children were not allowed to attend German schools.

January 1937: Jewish people were banned from the key professions, including teaching, accountancy and dentistry.

1938

April–June 1938: Jewish people were ordered to register all their wealth, property and businesses. This made it easier to confiscate them.

January 1939: Jewish people were encouraged to emigrate from Germany. Hitler spoke of future annihilation of Jewish people if they caused a world war.

1939

The impact and effectiveness of Nazi actions and policies by 1939

By the time the Second World War started in September 1939, the Nazis' actions against Germany's Jewish community had had a significant impact – as you will see from these photographs and Sources B–D.

The whole nature and quality of Jewish Germans' lives had been damaged – they were constrained, isolated and oppressed, all but prisoners in their own houses (see Source E).

The boycott of Jewish businesses

Source B The Nazi newspaper, *Völkischer Beobachter*, calling for a boycott of Jewish-owned businesses, 30 March 1933.

On 1 April 1933, at the stroke of 10, the boycott of all Jewish businesses, doctors, lawyers begins – 10,000 mass gatherings. The Jews have declared war on 65 million, now they are to be hit where it hurts them most.

▲ SA men post instructions in 1933 for Germans to boycott a Jewish-owned shop.

Kristallnacht (The Night of Broken Glass)

Source C When the Nuremberg Laws of 1935 were passed, a Jewish body called the 'Representation of the German People' announced:

The Laws decided upon by the *Reichstag* in Nuremberg have come as the heaviest of blows for the Jews in Germany.

▲ The aftermath of *Kristallnacht* in 1938.

Source D Instructions issued by the Reich Security Bureau about the events of *Kristallnacht*, 9–10 November 1938.

Only such measures may be employed as will not endanger German lives or property, for example, synagogues may only be burnt when there is no risk that fire will spread to neighbouring structures. Jewish stores and dwellings may be destroyed ... The police must not interfere with the demonstrations that will occur.

Source E An extract from the *Diary of Anne Frank*, a Dutch Jewish girl.

Our freedom was severely restricted by a series of anti-Jewish decrees: Jews were required to wear a yellow star; Jews were required to turn in their bicycles; Jews were forbidden to use trams; Jews were forbidden to ride in cars, even their own; Jews were required to do their shopping between 3.00 and 5.00 p.m.; Jews were required to frequent only Jewish-owned barbershops and beauty salons; Jews were forbidden to be out on the streets between 8.00 p.m. and 6.00 a.m.; Jews were forbidden to go to theatres, cinemas or any other forms of entertainment; Jews were forbidden to use swimming pools, tennis courts, hockey fields or any other athletic fields ...; Jews were forbidden to sit in their gardens or those of their friends after 8.00 p.m.; Jews were forbidden to visit Christians in their homes; Jews were required to attend Jewish schools, etc.

You couldn't do this and you couldn't do that, but life went on. Jacque always said to me, 'I don't dare do anything anymore, 'cause I'm afraid it's not allowed.'

Faced with these attacks on their quality of life and self-esteem, many Jewish people (including the scientist Albert Einstein, the psychoanalyst Sigmund Freud and the author Victor Hugo) fled Germany.

Thus the Jewish community's role in German life was successfully strangled by the economic, political and social policies introduced by the Nazis.

Nor were these actions opposed by many ordinary Germans. A combination of support (especially resulting from propaganda), education, ignorance or fear ensured that persecution of Jewish people was able to go ahead.

Revision tip

This is a very important topic. Make sure you are aware of the different ways in which the Nazis discriminated against Jewish Germans and other minority groups.

Activities

1 Split the class into groups of three or four. Each group takes one of the following topics:
   - the Boycott of 1933
   - the Nuremberg Laws of 1935
   - *Kristallnacht*, 1938
   - Nazi persecution of minorities
2 Using pages 30–33, discuss and note for your topic:
   - why it happened
   - what happened
   - how it would have affected Jewish Germans.
3 Share your ideas with the rest of the class, presenting them in an appropriate way – for example:
   - as a wall chart – for example a spider diagram or Venn diagram
   - as a cartoon

Practice questions

1 Below are two methods used by the Nazis to persecute minority groups:

Concentration camps
'Crime prevention' campaigns

Choose **one** method and explain how it affected the lives of minority groups.

2 'Nazi persecution of the Jewish people was planned.' Do you agree? Explain your answer.

This page provides guidance on how to answer question 4 in the exam.

Question 4

How did Nazi persecution impact on the lives of Jewish Germans in the years 1933–39? [8]

Guidance

You have 10 minutes to complete this answer, so that means quite a lot of writing! You must be able to outline the aims of Nazi persecution of Jewish people, describe the types of persecution, and analyse clearly the impact on Jewish people. Your answer needs to be well informed, and provide an accurate, well-developed explanation and analysis of the impact.

Follow the steps below for each part of the answer.

STEP 1

Start with an introductory sentence stating the whole question.

Example

The lives of Jewish Germans were impacted by Nazi persecution in many ways.

STEP 2a

Take a point, and explain the impact on people's lives.

Example

One form of persecution was economic. The Nazis boycotted Jewish shops in 1933. Jewish people were forbidden to hold jobs in the government or the army, as teachers or doctors. This took away their ability to earn money, reducing many to poverty.

STEP 2b

Repeat for another point.

Example

A second form was removing their civic rights. In the 1935 Nuremberg Laws, the Reich Citizenship Law removed their political and economic rights. The Law for the Protection of German Blood and German Honour made it illegal for Jewish people and Aryans to marry. This led to Jewish people having to live their lives with their freedom severely restricted.

STEP 2c

Repeat for a third point.

Example

A third form of persecution was to exclude Jewish people. Towns put up 'Jews not wanted here' signs. Jewish people had to have their passports stamped with a J-shaped symbol. Jewish children were excluded from school. The impact of this was to isolate Jewish people and make them targets.

STEP 2c

Repeat for a fourth point.

Example

Finally, another form of persecution was violence. On Kristallnacht in 1938, 400 synagogues, 7,500 shops and many homes were destroyed. Ninety-one Jewish people were killed and over the following months 20,000 were sent to concentration camps.

7 Germany at war

Life in Germany during World War II

The impact of the war on the German people

At first, the outbreak of war seemed to have a relatively limited impact on ordinary Germans.

One exception would have been the general celebrations that resulted from news of early military successes. As a result of such victories, not only did Hitler's popularity increase, ordinary Germans experienced few shortages, since, as their Armies conquered new territory, the spoils of war were sent home. In such circumstances there was little need for propaganda to remind the population of the importance of supporting the nation's military endeavours.

Playing a part

That said, rationing was introduced at the start of the war as a means of avoiding shortages (see page 37); as a consequence many Germans were able to enjoy a healthier diet.

Nor was the impact of war limited to rationing; in September 1940 the evacuation of children from Berlin was ordered. This was because of the belief that Germany would soon be subjected to bombing by the RAF. In the end, this bombing did not begin until 1942. In any case, many children did not leave the city at that time and it was only following the Allied bombing of Hamburg in 1943 that such evacuation became compulsory.

Ordinary Germans were encouraged to play their part in supporting the war effort. One such example was the part members of the Hitler Youth played in collecting materials that could be used for recycling.

The role of propaganda

As the war went on and successes became more limited, the role of propaganda increased. In the aftermath of defeats at Stalingrad (February 1943) and the impact of the Allied bombing of German cities, the population was urged by Goebbels to work harder and to make even greater sacrifice to achieve ultimate victory.

▲ Germany 1940: a crowd listens to the latest war report outside a radio shop. Germans had limited access to the news. What propaganda advantages did this give the government?

Air raids and bombing

Although expected much earlier, it was really 1942 before ordinary Germans began to experience the devastation of bombing raids by the Allies (Britain, the USA and the USSR) upon their major cities. In the early years of the war, Allied bombing was directed against industrial targets, but this had limited success. The Allies decided to shift from strategic bombing to the night-time targeting of towns and cities. The intention was to force an early end to the war by the destruction of Germans' spirits.

Allied bombing raids

A number of key German cities came under attack as a consequence of these raids.

▶ On 30 May 1942 Cologne was the target of the RAF's first ever 'thousand bomber raid', codenamed Operation Millennium.

▶ Hamburg was bombed on two main occasions. During the first raid – July 1943 – an estimated 50,000 died (including civilians) and an estimated one million were left without homes. As a result of the second raid (August 1943), nearly two-thirds of the city's buildings were destroyed. In addition, tens of thousands died (historians' estimates vary from 60,000 to 100,000).

▶ One of the war's most infamous bombing raids was that which was targeted against Dresden which was attacked over two nights in February 1945 by 1,300 heavy bombers; nearly three-quarters of the city's buildings were destroyed while 150,000 civilians were killed.

Results

By the time that the war in Europe ended in May 1945 it is estimated that at least 3.5 million civilians had lost their lives as a consequence of the Allies' bombing campaign. Some historians argue that the Allied raids helped unite the country, but there is also evidence that while active resistance was limited (see pages 41–44), disaffection was growing amongst the population in the latter stages of the war, particularly after the German Army's defeat in the Battle of Stalingrad.

> **Activities**
>
> 1 Why did the Allies target Germany's cities in air raids?
> 2 What were the key Allied bombing raids, and what happened?
> 3 What impact did the raids have on Germany?

> **Revision tip**
>
> It is important that you are able to show that you understand how Germany was changed at home by World War II. Make sure that you know the key impacts economically and socially and can show how life altered for many people.

▲ Dresden, 1945. 'What is amazing is, not that Germany surrendered, but that the German people fought on for so long.' Do you agree?

Total War and rationing

Total War was first declared by Joseph Goebbels in a speech made in February 1943. By then it was becoming more obvious that Germany was not winning the war, not least due to the German Army's defeat at Stalingrad. It was also clear that Germany's previous economic structures were not able to provide an economy suited to the kind of war that Germany was now fighting. The idea of Total War was that all economic activity would be focused on the task of winning the war; everything else would cease.

Total War

The first individual tasked with rationalising the economy and its structures was Fritz Todt. Following his death in a plane crash in February 1942, Hitler's architect, Albert Speer, replaced him as Minister for Armaments and Production. Speer's job was to increase war production within the economy. Speer took over the running of the economy and reinforced the drive for Total War by ensuring that the production of civilian goods ceased and all factories were solely focused on production to support the war effort. As a result, working hours increased, while more women were employed as factory workers. Even though non-German workers were also used, and German industry suffered from the effects of Allied bombing, Speer's mass production techniques ensured that industrial productivity increased. Munitions output grew by 60 per cent per worker between 1939 and 1944.

Rationing

Whilst some degree of rationing (for meat, bread, fats and sugar) had been introduced when the war started in September 1939, the German Army's early victories had meant that food shortages were not at first a major problem.

However, Germany's economy had not been ready for a major war and so this situation began to change in 1942. The German Army's failure to secure victory over the USSR meant that the amount of rationing – including that of cigarettes – had to be increased, while artificial substitutes had to be found for those goods now deemed scarce.

In 1939, each person was entitled to 700g of meat each week; by 1945 this had been reduced to 250g per week and as a consequence many Germans experienced real hunger. In addition, public parks and private gardens were given over to the production of vegetables whilst the population was encouraged to embrace new recipes such as the 'daisy salad', to make use of unusual ingredients such as aubergines and artichokes and to eat a one-dish meal on Sundays. Additional rations were made available to those working in heavy industries such as mining, whilst pregnant women and blood donors also benefited from extra supplies.

'Fake' food

With foodstuffs in short supply, many shop window displays showed make-believe produce. For example, milk bottles were filled with salt to make it appear as if they contained milk. Nor was food the only kind of rationing. From November 1939, clothes and footwear were subject to rationing and any household suspected of having more than its fair share of the latter was open to inspection by Nazi officials. Soap was also subject to rationing, although this was less of a problem because people were only allowed to use hot water on two days each week (in order to save fuel). The rationing of toilet paper proved more difficult. In 1943 the production of non-military clothing stopped altogether. Following this, Exchange Centres were established to enable Germans to swap both clothing and household items such as furniture.

Not surprisingly, such shortages resulted in the emergence of a black market with items such as foodstuffs, luxury clothing and perfume being easily obtainable.

As the war entered its final year, there were genuine shortages of both clothing and food. That said, the introduction of rationing was not all bad. The rationing of foodstuffs meant that for a time more people were eating a more balanced diet – even if it was less than varied.

Activity

Create a spider diagram showing the key aspects of rationing in wartime Germany.

Labour shortages and the role of women in the workplace

Throughout the 1930s, the Nazis' 'three Ks' doctrine (see page 20) promoted the ideal of a woman's place being at home looking after her family. Even before the war began, the reality proved to be rather different. With increasing numbers of men being conscripted into the military, there were in excess of six million women at work, particularly in industry.

The Nazi government discovered, however, that many women were less than willing to join the workforce to replace the men who had gone off to fight. In January 1943, the lack of men meant that Hitler's government was left with no option but to conscript women into the workforce. Women between the ages of 17 and 45 were required to engage in work outside the home. By 1944, more than 40 per cent of women were working, making up more than half of the workforce.

That more women did not take up work outside the home was due to a range of factors. Despite Nazi ideology, many women were already involved in the workplace when the war started in 1939.

Thus, Hitler's reluctance to mobilise Germany's women – seeking rather to maintain their traditional role as homemakers – meant that many women were either not employed at all or were only employed on a part-time basis.

However, even these measures proved insufficient to make up the shortfall and so the regime was also forced to make use of non-German workers and prisoners of war. By the end of 1944, it is estimated that in excess of eight million foreign workers were employed in Germany. Many more were employed as compulsory labourers in the countries occupied by the Nazis.

▲ German women train as firefighters, 1940.

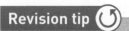

Revision tip

The war affected the lives of Germans in many ways – rationing, bombing, evacuation of children, 'Total War', youth activities, women's work, labour shortages, escalation of racial persecution and so on.

For each of these effects, make sure you have considered not only how they affected life in Germany, but how much, so you are ready for a question which suggests that ANY of the effects was most important, and then asks whether you agree.

Activities

1 How did Germany engage in 'Total War'?
2 Who were Fritz Todt and Albert Speer?
3 How did the Nazis deal with labour shortages during the war years? How successful were they?

Escalation of racial persecution

The Nazis' racial policies changed with the onset of war. Those Jewish people who were German citizens, had the option of emigration until 1941. This option was voluntarily taken by those German Jewish people who had the means to escape. From 1938, such emigration was encouraged and was overseen by the Reich Central Office for Jewish Emigration. It is estimated that as many as half of Germany's Jewish population left in this manner before the start of the war. However, the regime's decision to ban such emigration in 1941 meant that this route of escape was closed off.

However, as Germany invaded Poland (and other territories) in 1939 and the years that followed, it is estimated that in excess of three million additional Jewish people came under Germany's control. This number increased significantly following Germany's invasion of the USSR in June 1941. Such numbers led the Nazis to decide that previously used methods of control would no longer be sufficient to deal with the 'Jewish issue'.

As a consequence, the Nazis considered a number of approaches to deal with their inherited Jewish population. In Summer 1940, the Nazi government's 'Jewish Department' suggested the 'Madagascar Plan' – exiling all Europe's Jewish people to Madagascar, but this proved impossible because the British Navy was blockading German ports. There would have to be a different solution.

▲ In the Pinkas Synagogue in Prague is a memorial which simply covers every wall with the names of all the 78,000 Czech Jewish people who died in the Holocaust. In what other ways might we commemorate the Holocaust?

The *Einsatzgruppen* and Ghettos

Between 1939 and 1942, SS *Einsatzgruppen* squads (special units of soldiers which followed behind the advancing German armies) rounded up Jewish people in the newly-occupied territories – particularly Poland and the USSR – and executed them in their thousands. They also burned towns and villages where Jewish people were living. Their initial focus was on Jewish men, but after August 1941 this was broadened to include all Jewish people. Often the victims were identified by local informants. Before they were executed, these Jewish people were taken to execution sites where trenches had already been prepared. In many cases those about to be executed were forced to dig their own graves. Historians estimate that by 1943, two million people, mainly Jewish people, had been murdered in this way.

Many of the Jewish people living in Polish cities such as Warsaw and Lodz found themselves living in Ghettos after the start of the war. These were segregated areas where Jewish communities were forced to live. At first they were 'open', but later they were 'sealed' – the Nazis surrounded them with walls and guards. Anybody trying to leave was shot.

The Nazis created at least 1,000 ghettos in Eastern Europe, each with a Jewish Council nominally in control. The Nazis used these Jewish people as forced labour in their factories.

The largest Ghetto was in Warsaw, where 400,000 Jewish people were forced into an area of 3.4 square km. They struggled to survive, running workshops which traded illegally with the local Polish people and even the German army. They organised social events and set up a Self-Help Organisation which provided welfare.

However, in such overcrowded areas, living conditions were harsh and dirty and many people died of disease (such as typhus). The Nazis imposed a deliberate policy of starvation rations, so thousands of people starved or froze to death, and small children risked execution, squeezing through cracks in the wall to smuggle food.

The Final Solution

The increasing number of Jewish people under Nazi control meant that new methods of control and elimination – other than the use of the *Einsatzgruppen* and the use of Ghettos – would have to be found. In late 1941, the decision was taken that another more efficient method of eliminating the Jewish population would be needed. Hermann Göring ordered Reinhard Heydrich to work out a plan and as a result on 20 January 1942 a group of 15 senior Nazis met at a house in Wannsee (a suburb of Berlin) with the intention of deciding upon how best to deal with the 'Jewish Problem'. Following much discussion, it was decided to establish special 'Death Camps' to execute Europe's Jewish population. Their decision became known as the 'Final Solution'.

The Death Camps

A number of these camps were built in locations in Eastern European countries that had been occupied by the Nazis. The most infamous was the double labour–extermination camp of Auschwitz-Birkenau, located in southern Poland. We have detailed information about what happened to those sent there.

Upon arrival – often by train from the Ghettos – the Nazis confiscated people's possessions. Then, any people whom the Nazi medics deemed unfit for work (the old, the ill, the children) were immediately sent, up to 2,000 at a time, to the gas chambers. Jewish *Sonderkommando* prisoners encouraged them to enter the gas chambers by telling them they were going for a shower, or to be deloused. Once inside they were executed using a gas known as Zyklon B (hydrogen cyanide). The *Sonderkommando* units then extracted any gold teeth from the dead and burned their bodies in vast ovens.

Those deemed fit for work were used for forced labour. The Administrative and Business Office of the SS ran farms, clothing and armaments factories, and sold slave labour to other companies for three *Reichsmarks* a day; it was a huge business enterprise. When too tired to work any longer, the Jewish prisoners were sent in their turn to the gas chambers.

Operations at Treblinka, Sobibor, Belzec and Chelmno were slightly different. There, prisoners were killed in the gas chambers by exhaust fumes.

Towards the end of the war, the Nazis began establishing the so-called 'destruction Ghettos' across Eastern Europe. Unlike the open and sealed Ghettos of earlier in the war, these were simply marshalling yards for the collection of Jewish people. Most only lasted a couple of months, until all the Jewish people in the area had been sent them to the death camps. The last Ghetto to be 'liquidated' was Lodz in August 1944.

By the time the war in Europe ended in May 1945, an estimated six million Jewish people had been murdered by the Nazis through the use of the gas chambers and other forms of execution (including medical experimentation, or simply being worked to death). Such strategies were also used against the Roma under Nazi control.

> **Interpretation A** From the 'Holocaust Encyclopaedia' of the United States Holocaust Memorial Museum.
>
> The genocide of the Jews was the culmination of a decade of German policy under Nazi rule and the realization of a core goal of the Nazi dictator, Adolf Hitler.

Activities

1 Explain the roles of Hermann Göring and Reinhard Heydrich in the persecution of Jewish people.
2 What were the following?
    - Einsatzgruppen
    - Ghettos
    - Death camps
    - The Final Solution
3 How and why did the Nazis racial policies change after 1939?

Revision tip

This is a difficult topic but one that you need to know fully. Remember to refer back to the Nazis' actions against Germany's Jewish population before 1939 to provide a context for the horrors that then took place in the Second World War.

▲ The entrance to the Auschwitz Death Camp has become a symbol of the Holocaust. Can we ever understand what went on behind those gates?

Growing opposition and resistance in Germany, 1939–45

It is fair to say that the majority of Germans remained loyal to the regime – or at least to Hitler – during the war years. There was limited civilian opposition as the continued existence of the Police State made such resistance almost impossible.

However, opposition to the regime did emerge. There was some opposition from German conservatives in the form of the Kreisau Circle (a group of aristocrats, socialists, clergymen and foreign office officials led by Helmuth von Molkte and Peter von Wartenberg) and the Beck-Goerdeler Group (see page 43). The main difference between the two groups was that the Kreisau Circle was against the use of force – unlike the the Beck-Goerdeler Group. While there was also opposition from the Red Orchestra, a resistance group set up by the communist movement which had been driven underground by the regime, the most effective opposition to the Nazi regime largely came from some youth groups, the Churches and from within the military.

Youth groups

As already outlined, the Nazis had placed a great deal of emphasis on the indoctrination of Germany's youth. Whilst many young people did conform, others did not and their opposition came to the fore during the war years. Three main groups of young people showed their opposition to the Nazis during these years, the Swing Youth, the Edelweiss Pirates and the White Rose movement.

Swing Youth

The Swing Youth membership was drawn mostly from the upper and middle classes and was largely urban-based. These young people were not particularly political but enjoyed listening to jazz music (which the Nazis regarded as degenerate – having been produced by an inferior race) and attending bars and clubs. In response the Nazis closed down those locations that the Swing Youth frequented.

Edelweiss Pirates

Those who joined the Edelweiss Pirates (named after the flower, which was their emblem) were generally from a working class background and wore checked shirts and dark-coloured trousers. The name was a collective name given to the members of groups, some of whom had their own individual names such as Roving Dudes and Navajos. These young people had refused to join the Hitler Youth movement; instead they spent their time mocking and beating up that group's members. During the war years, members of the Pirates made it their business to distribute propaganda leaflets that had been dropped by Allied aircraft.

The White Rose

The non-violent White Rose movement was set up in 1942 by Munich University undergraduates Hans and Sophie Scholl. The distribution of anti-Nazi leaflets (which outlined the atrocities being carried out by the Nazis in Eastern Europe and the USSR, and which strongly criticised the regime) was one of the activities undertaken by the group, which also appealed to Germans not to support the war effort. The main members were executed by the *Gestapo* following their betrayal by a university caretaker, who saw them placing anti-Nazi leaflets in university lecture theatres.

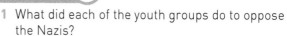

Activities

1 What did each of the youth groups do to oppose the Nazis?
2 Which groups of people (apart from youth groups) showed some resistance to the Nazis?
3 How did the Edelweiss Pirates demonstrate their opposition to the Nazis?

The Churches

The Confessional Church

Whilst none of Germany's main churches spoke out as organisations against the Nazis, there were examples of individual religious leaders who did publicly oppose the regime. Lutheran pastors such as Dietrich Bonhoeffer and Martin Niemöller were opposed to the regime's setting up of the National Reich Church and established the Confessional Church. Bonhoeffer also became more politically involved and participated in anti-Nazi activities; he passed secrets to the Allies, and was part of the assassination attempts of 1943 and 1944. In 1943 he was arrested and sent to Buchenwald concentration camp, then sent to Flossenbürg concentration camp where he was executed in April 1945. Niemöller also ended up imprisoned in concentration camps between 1938 and 1945, first in Sachsenhausen and then in Dachau. Unlike Bonhoeffer, however, Niemöller survived the experience.

The Catholic Church

Some Catholic priests opposed Hitler; many hid Jewish people during the Holocaust and thousands were sent to concentration camps. The Catholic Bishop of Münster, Clemens von Galen, later spoke out against the Nazi regime, preaching a number of strongly-worded sermons in 1941, particularly against the Nazis' use of euthanasia which had started in 1939 and which resulted in the deaths of 100,000 mentally-ill people (Source A). As a result of the outcry that followed, the Nazis were forced to abandon the policy. Von Galen also spoke out against forced sterilisation, concentration camps and the activities of the Gestapo. As a consequence he lived under virtual house arrest from that time until the end of the war. Von Galen was arrested in 1944 following the July bomb plot but was released in 1945. He was created a Cardinal by Pope Pius XII in February 1946, but died the following month.

> **Source A** Bishop von Galen condemning Nazi policies, August 1941.
>
> If you establish the principle that you can kill unproductive fellow human beings then woe betide us all when we become old and frail …

Jewish reactions to the Nazis

By constantly listing only the atrocities of the Holocaust, historians run the danger of giving the Nazis the victory all over again. One negative result is the myth that the Jewish people simply went 'as sheep to the slaughter'. This is not true.

Armed resistance

In April–May 1943, Jewish people in the Warsaw Ghetto revolted. They fought for a month, killing 300 Germans; 13,000 Jewish people died. There were dozens of other Ghetto rebellions.

Many Jewish people fought in 'partisan' resistance groups. In the forests of eastern Poland, 1941–44, the Bielski brothers led a Jewish resistance group which attacked Nazis and helped more than 1,200 Jewish people to escape.

Even in the death camps there was resistance. At Treblinka in August 1943 and Sobibor in October 1943, Jewish people attacked their guards and organised mass-escapes. In Auschwitz, in October 1944, the *Sonderkommando* prisoners (see page 40) stole some explosives and blew up a crematorium. As she died on the gallows, one of the conspirators, Rosa Robota, shouted: 'Be strong and courageous'.

You have to remember that all these rebellions were undertaken by people who knew it was hopeless and that death was inevitable.

Emigration and hiding

Another form of resistance was to try to avoid the Nazi holocaust. More than half the Jewish people in Germany and Austria (including 83 per cent of Jewish people under the age of 24) managed to emigrate or flee. Some 15,000 Jewish children were sent out of Germany unaccompanied, many of them on the *Kindertransport* trains organised by British stockbroker Nicholas Winton.

Many Jewish emigrants went to Palestine, where they worked to establish the state of Israel.

Many Jewish people hid – some in secret rooms like Anne Frank in Holland – others in plain sight, pretending to be Christians. Survival was a miracle, but thousands did so – the Jewish Austrian Edith Hahn fled to Munich, where she met and married a Nazi officer.

Non-violent resistance

Many more Jewish people worked to subvert the Nazi oppression. In the Ghettos they smuggled food, produced underground newspapers, forged papers and destroyed files. The Minsk Ghetto organised a hospital, a welfare centre and a school. In Warsaw, they assembled a record of the Holocaust as it happened (the 'Oneg Shabbat').

Cooperation

Sometimes, even Jewish people who seemed to be cooperating with the Nazis were working against them. In Hungary, the lawyer Rezső Kasztner was known as a friend of the Nazis, but he organised the Kasztner train, which diverted 1,684 Jewish people from Auschwitz to Switzerland.

Everywhere they conquered, the Nazis set up 'Jewish Councils', which helped them run the ghettos. Often denounced as collaborators, many were trying to reduce the suffering by cooperating. In Holland, the Jewish Council organised deportations to the death camps – but arranged 15,000 exemptions and tried to make sure there were endless delays and no brutality.

Personal heroism and survival

In Krakow, imprisoned Jewish underground fighter Gusta Draenger wrote her story on toilet paper and smuggled it out to the world. The day before he was sent to Auschwitz, Warsaw headteacher Janusz Korczak was given a chance to escape; he refused, preferring to stay with his 200 pupils for their final, terrifying journey.

Finally, in a world of death and despair, sometimes just holding onto your humanity – keeping clean, holding onto your faith – was a triumph of resistance. As the family took their train ride to Auschwitz, teenager Helen Stine's father bought her mother a belt from another woman … so she would look nice on the journey.

The Army

Whilst the above-mentioned groups were active in their opposition to Hitler's regime, the most serious attempt to remove him during the war years came from some members of the German military.

The Army had sworn its loyalty to Hitler following Hindenburg's death in August 1934. Although some senior officers could not have been described as fans of the Führer, it was difficult to oppose him whilst the war was going Germany's way.

By 1943, the war was going badly for Germany, particularly in the East against the USSR; as a result opposition to Hitler grew within the ranks of the Army. In that same year, seven attempts to kill Hitler were planned; all failed as did three further efforts in early 1944.

Operation Valkyrie

In 1944, a group of military opponents agreed a plan to assassinate Hitler. The group was led by General Ludwig Beck and Dr Carl Goerdeler, a politician. The assassination attempt was to be carried out in July 1944 by Claus von Stauffenberg, an army officer and member of the German aristocracy. Initially supportive of Hitler, von Stauffenberg's personal experience of the dreadful conditions being endured by the German Army in its war against the USSR and the brutality of the SS, led him to conclude that Hitler had to be removed.

In a plan known as Operation Valkyrie, von Stauffenberg was to attend a meeting with Hitler in his Wolf's Lair field headquarters in Rastenburg (East Prussia) and leave a bomb in a suitcase. As Chief of Staff to General Fromm, the Commander-in-Chief of the Home Army, von Stauffenberg had regular access to Hitler, thus making a bomb easier to plant. After the bomb had exploded, the plot leaders would use the Army to seize control of Berlin.

Initial attempts to plant the bomb came to nothing; on 17 July, Hitler ordered the arrest of Dr Goerdeler. He managed to evade capture, but this meant that time for the plot to work was running out. On 20 July, therefore, von Stauffenberg placed and primed the bomb in Hitler's staff meeting as planned, and left to return to Berlin.

After von Stauffenberg left, however, someone else present moved the case further away from Hitler. When it exploded, four of those attending the meeting were killed; Hitler, however, survived, suffering only minor injuries. It would then seem that the failure of those involved in the plot to act quickly enough to gain control of Berlin meant that when von Stauffenberg arrived back in the capital from Rastenburg, little had happened. By that evening the plot had failed.

Following the failure of the plot, Beck attempted suicide and was then shot. Von Stauffenberg was arrested and executed. In total, 5,746 individuals were executed following the failure of the July bomb plot. A variety of methods were used to kill those involved including firing squads, garrotting, hanging or torture. Some of those hanged were executed using piano wire. Many others committed suicide, including Field Marshall Erwin Rommel, one of Germany's most successful military commanders. In the aftermath of the failed plot, all members of the German Army had again to swear an Oath of Loyalty to Hitler as *Führer*.

▲ The Wolf's Lair after the bomb. Why did the von Stauffenberg bomb plot fail?

The effectiveness of opposition and resistance up to 1945

Judging the success of opposition is relatively straightforward in that no German-based group or citizen was able to stop or defeat Hitler and the Nazis. The population's fear of the regime and its security forces played a significant part in ensuring wholescale conformity. At the same time, the destruction of the party system and the weakening of trade unions robbed Germans of a means of demonstrating any opposition to the regime. Despite some domestic opposition, the Nazi regime was largely able to continue with its programme of racial purification and its desire to exercise military control over other nations until its ultimate defeat at the hands of its opponents in the shape of Britain, France, the USA and the USSR.

At the same time, the determination of some groups and individuals to express their opposition to the regime and its policies was proof of Hitler's failure to gain control over every German citizen and not every Nazi policy was able to be implemented successfully.

Revision tip

It is important that you can explain – for each of the different groups who opposed the Nazi regime – what they did and how successful they were.

Practice questions ❓

1 Describe two ways in which rationing affected German people between 1939 and 1945.
2 'Opposition and resistance to the Nazi regime was stronger during 1939–1945 than from 1933–1939.' Do you agree? Explain your answer.

Activities

1 How successfully did the Army resist Hitler during World War II?
2 Use the information on pages 41–44 to fill in the table:

	Reasons for opposing the Nazi regime	Actions for opposing the Nazi regime	Outcomes of opposing the Nazi regime
Youth groups			
The churches			
The Army			

This page provides guidance on how to answer question 5 in the exam.

Question 5

'The main opposition to the Nazis in the years 1939-45 came from the Church.' Do you agree?

Explain your answer. [16]

Guidance

You should be looking to spend about 20 minutes on this question. This is the longest answer that you have to provide in this section of the examination. It needs to be twice the length of your answer for Question 4. The question type is different too; you are being presented with a statement and are asked to consider whether or not you agree with it. To be able to get the highest marks for your answer you will need to show that you have considered the arguments for and against the statement – before coming to a judgement which is supported by appropriate historical evidence. You can either agree or disagree with the statement – just make sure that the evidence is there to support what you say!

Follow the steps below for each part of the answer.

STEP 1

Introduce the first idea, stating the whole question.

Example

There is a strong case to be made for the idea that the main opposition to the Nazis came from the Church, 1939-45.

STEP 2a

Explain how this is so, supporting your ideas with facts and reasoning. For this question, introduce each way the Church's organisations and people opposed the Nazis then explain how they did this.

Example

The Church opposed the Nazis in several ways. For example, Pastor Niemöller was a key figure in opposing the Nazis ... Additionally, the Catholic Bishop von Galen ...

STEP 2b

Measure how significant this is and explain why you think this. Remember to support your explanation with facts. For example, you could say that von Galen spoke out against the Nazi policy of euthanasia which helped force the Nazis to abandon the policy.

Example

The Church's opposition was <very/mildly/not very> powerful because ...
This is shown by ...

STEPs 3a and 3b

Introduce the opposing idea, again stating the whole question, and measure how significant this is (as in Steps 2a and 2b).

Example

However, there is a strong case to be made for the idea that the main opposition to the Nazis came from other groups, such as the Army and youth groups.

STEP 4

Make a justified judgement and relate it back to the question.

Example

Therefore, we can see that the Church <was/was not> the main opposition to the Nazis.

This option focuses on how the lives of American people were affected by the political, economic and social changes that took place in the United States of America between 1920 and 1933.

These were the years when minority groups in American society – black Americans, Native Americans and immigrants – faced racial and economic barriers. They were the years of jazz, cinema, the radio and the automobile, and of significant change in the lives of women. This was the era of Prohibition, gangsters and Al Capone.

The 1920s were also a time of economic change – an apparent economic boom in the

1920s, followed by the Wall Street Crash and the Great Depression.

This option requires students to know about the causes of these events and also about the impact they had on different people's lives.

This option examines the following key areas of content:

▶ Life for minority groups

▶ Prohibition

▶ Social change and popular entertainment

▶ The 'Roaring Twenties'

▶ Economic problems in the 1920s

▶ The Wall Street Crash, 1929

▶ The Great Depression, 1929–33

▲ Map of the USA during this period

1 Life for minority groups

Problems faced by black Americans in the southern states

In 1865, the 13th Amendment to the United States Constitution abolished slavery.

However, in the United States, each state can make its own laws, in addition to federal laws.

So, although slavery was abolished, the southern states which had supported slavery quickly began making laws to restrict the rights and freedoms of black Americans. These regulations came to be called the 'Jim Crow' laws.

Jim Crow laws and civil rights

Examples of Jim Crow Laws include:

▶ black children were not allowed to attend white schools

▶ black people had to sit in 'their' train carriage and not in the 'white' section

▶ black people were forbidden from drinking from the same water fountain as white people

▶ black people were excluded from white libraries, restaurants, cinemas, churches and swimming pools.

Southern states in particular enforced this kind of segregation because they resented black Americans' newfound freedom. In 1896, the US Supreme Court – in the case of Plessy v. Ferguson – upheld this by ruling that 'separate but equal' racial segregation was legal.

Thereafter, until 1954, black Americans were reduced to second-class citizens. Literacy tests were used to exclude them from the vote and from sitting on juries. This meant that they had no power to influence the laws being made against them and, when on trial, they were often convicted even when the evidence showed them to be innocent. The Scottsboro trials of 1931 were a particularly famous example of this – although the Supreme Court overruled the verdicts of the local courts, five of eight young black men accused of raping two white women were eventually given sentences ranging from 75 years to death.

▲ This photo from the 1930s shows a black American going up a stairway to the 'colored' entrance of a cinema, with a 'White Men Only' restroom below. Explain all the ways this photo illustrates discrimination against black Americans.

Although they could no longer treat their black workers as enslaved people, white landowners in the southern states found a new way to force black people to work for them. Instead of paying wages, they gave black workers a share of the profit when the crop was sold. Until then, they lent money to the workers, who had to keep working for them to pay off the debt. This system was called 'sharecropping' and it was just another kind of slavery.

Finally, anti-miscegenation laws forbade inter-racial marriage. These laws had been declared constitutional by the US Supreme Court in 1883 and were not totally repealed until 2000 – yet one more example of the racism, exclusion and oppression which black Americans faced on a daily basis in the southern states.

The rise of the Ku Klux Klan

Any black American suspected of challenging white supremacy lived in fear of the mob, and of lynching – 1,360 black Americans were lynched in the period 1900–19, with 281 more in the 1920s and a further 119 in the 1930s. When some black Americans tried to prevent a lynching in Tulsa, Oklahoma, in 1921, a white mob raided the black neighbourhoods, burning 1,256 homes and killing 26 black Americans.

Not all southern Americans approved. In the 1930s, the *Association of Southern Women for the Prevention of Lynching* declared lynching 'an indefensible crime'. But American Presidents feared losing votes and no law was ever passed against it. Two anti-lynching bills (in 1922 and 1934) were defeated by the senators from the southern states.

Against this background of race hatred, a former church-minister called William J Simmons set a fiery cross on top of Stone Mountain in Georgia and re-established an organisation called the Ku Klux Klan – a right-wing extremist group which wanted to 'purify' American society.

The actions of the KKK

The Klan adopted clothing of long white robes and hoods, appointed paid recruiting officers called 'Kleages', held secret meetings and spoke in secret codes called 'Klonversations'. They denied being racist or violent and insisted that they were merely a brotherhood of like-minded people who wanted to protect 'American principles'.

However, they flogged and lynched anyone who stepped outside their white, Anglo-Saxon, Protestant (WASP) definition of American-ness. They attacked Catholics, Jewish people, communists, gay people and divorcees, set fire to saloons, and tried to drive out immigrants who were moving into the neighbourhood. Most of all, the KKK attacked black Americans for any excuse, but especially those under suspicion of crimes.

Membership rose to almost five million and, in August 1925, 50,000 Klansmen marched through Washington to show their strength and popularity. Many Klan members were middle class and it had a strong women's section.

When caught and brought to trial, Klansmen found themselves in front of police, judges and juries who were Klansmen too, and were let off.

Many white Americans, especially in the north, opposed the Klan and its violence. Others joined, but then left when they realised what the Klan was really doing. And after the Grand Dragon (leader) of the Indiana Klan was found guilty of the rape and murder of a teacher in 1925, membership fell dramatically.

Source A From a Klan publication, c.1922.

The Klan does not cultivate nor deal in hatred or division between the races and religion ... [But] a man born and reared on American soil, under the American flag, is more likely to be true to American principles.

Activities

1 Explain the significance of the Plessy v Ferguson case of 1896.
2 What were the Jim Crow laws?
3 After you have read the information on this page, choose five adjectives to describe the Ku Klux Klan and find facts to support your choices.

Black Americans in the northern states

During the First World War, when the factories in the northern states experienced a shortage of labour, wages rose until they were three times as much as a black worker's wages in the south. Half a million black Americans in the southern states moved north, partly for the better wages and job opportunities, and partly to escape the poverty and racial oppression they faced in the south. A further 800,000 black Americans left the South in the 1920s and 400,000 more in the 1930s.

This movement is called 'the Great Migration'. Black men took jobs in dangerous industries such as steel, automotive and meatpacking, while women often became maids. The Pennsylvania Railroad was so keen to recruit black people that it paid their travel expenses north. Another employer of black labour was the automobile manufacturer Henry Ford. The number of black people living in New York increased by 66 per cent and in Detroit by 600 per cent.

Racism and riots

They were not welcome. Alongside open racism, the larger workforce caused wages to fall, whilst pressure on housing caused rents to rise, which angered local poor white workers. There were race riots in a number of northern towns in 1919 – most notably in Chicago, where 38 people were killed. Some white neighbourhoods made rules forbidding residents to sell their houses to non-whites; in other places, when new black families moved in, all the white families moved out. These reactions created a racial divide in many northern towns.

The result was that these new migrants crowded into areas of poor housing called 'ghettos'. Residents became victims of 'redlining' (denial of loans or insurance), so called after the red lines with which businesses identified black American areas on maps.

Many trade unions had a 'whites-only' policy and black Americans were usually the last to be hired and the first to be fired. The new migrants were not even welcomed by the existing black American population in the north, who looked down on the new poorly-educated people from the south and blamed them for the tension and violence.

Activities

1 Why did many black Americans move from the southern states to the northern states in the 1920s and 1930s?
2 What were ghettos?
3 What was 'redlining'?
4 How were the lives of black Americans different in the northern states from in the southern states?

Revision tip

Questions 1 and 2 in Option 2 of the exam will be simply factual knowledge.

Political and cultural responses of black Americans

Faced by legal, political and economic discrimination, black Americans began to take action to achieve equality. The 1920s were the time when they first began to break through.

1 The **HARLEM RENAISSANCE** was a cultural explosion centred on the black neighbourhood of Harlem in New York. It was centred on black racial pride – 'the expression of our individual dark-skinned selves' as poet Langston Hughes put it. Famous people of the Harlem Renaissance include the artist Aaron Douglas, the singer and actor Paul Robeson, the author Alain Locke and the novelist and folklore expert Zora Neale Hurston.

2 **FASHION.** Black performers such as the singer Bessie Smith and the dancer Josephine Baker (see page 67) were major fashion trendsetters (Baker bought her gowns from a French fashion designer, and owned a pet cheetah).

3 **MUSIC.** Black Jazz musicians including Fats Waller and Duke Ellington played at clubs such as the (whites-only) Cotton Club in New York and (during Prohibition – see pages 58–61) at the speakeasies. Black musicians also developed a new way of playing the piano called the Harlem Stride style – with a rocking ('striding') left hand and a swing rhythm.

4 **DANCES** like the Charleston, the Black Bottom and the Lindy Hop were adopted by the fashionable 'flappers' (see page 64), who wanted to break free from the restrained 'proper' dances of their parents.

5 The **NEW NEGRO** (the title of a book by the Harlem author Alain Locke) popularised the idea that Black Africans could, through intelligence and culture, break the white racist stereotype of what black Africans were like.

6 The **NATIONAL ASSOCIATION FOR THE ADVANCEMENT OF COLORED PEOPLE (NAACP)** – founded in 1909 by W.E.B. du Bois – campaigned for 'political, educational, social and economic equality of rights'. In the 1920s, it led a campaign against lynchings and in 1923 won a legal victory (Moore v. Dempsey) which stopped mobs intimidating trials.

7 The **UNIVERSAL NEGRO IMPROVEMENT ASSOCIATION.** Founded by Marcus Garvey in 1914, UNIA claimed four million members in 1921. Garvey encouraged black Americans to celebrate their blackness and even tried to persuade them to emigrate back to Africa.

8 **HOWARD UNIVERSITY** was formed in the 1860s to educate black students in medicine, engineering, law and the arts, with the aim of overcoming inequalities of race, colour or wealth. Among its graduates were Alain Locke, Zora Neale Hurston and Carter G. Woodson (the historian who in 1926 invented 'Negro History Week' – the forerunner of our Black History Month).

9 Black Americans went into business, and formed a growing middle class – in Chicago, for instance, the neighbourhood of Bronzeville was known as the '**BLACK METROPOLIS**'. In a show of economic strength, black Africans boycotted Chicago's chain stores until they promised to employ black staff.

10 **POLITICS.** After the abolition of slavery, black Americans voted Republican, but towards the end of the 1920s many began to vote Democrat – they began to realise that they could use their vote to secure improvements to their civil rights.

11 **LABOR UNIONS.** During the Great Depression, black Americans who had gained jobs in factories began to organise to resist redundancies and wage cuts (for example, in Ford's factories – see page 49). In 1935, the Congress of Industrial Organisations (CIO) was formed which was open to black Americans.

12 **FILM.** In 1920, film director Oscar Micheaux produced *Within our Gates* – the harrowing story of the children of a black American couple lynched by a white mob.

Activities

Working with a partner:
1 Prepare 24 cards – 12 with the titles and 12 with the facts, from the points on this page. Mix them up, turn them face down, then take turns to pick them up two at a time to try to match the titles with their associated facts, in order to help you learn the topic.
2 For each point on this page, explain how it helped to increase the status and self-esteem of black Americans.
3 Discuss with your partner either the statement 'Life for black Americans improved in the 1920s' or 'The experience of black Americans in the 1920s was, overall, negative', each taking a different side of the argument.

Problems faced by immigrants

For many people, America was the 'land of opportunity', and represented freedom (from religious and political persecution, and poverty). More than 30 million Europeans flocked there in the nineteenth century.

At first, the immigrants were from western and northern Europe, but towards the end of the century there were large influxes of very poor and poorly-educated people from Eastern Europe, Asia and Mexico. In 1907 (the highest year for immigration until 1990), almost 1.3 million persons entered the country.

Attitudes towards immigration

Although almost all Americans were originally from immigrant families, there were several reasons for a generally hostile attitude to immigration in the 1920s.

30,000,000 IMMIGRANTS

▲ This picture, *30,000,000 Immigrants* by Bernarda Bryson, shows Jewish immigrants outside the main inspection building on Ellis Island in New York Bay, where they were quizzed (name, occupation and how much money they had), and given a medical inspection. Many immigrants were sent back home if they were too poor, or were physically or mentally ill, or could not work. Ellis Island was nicknamed 'Heartbreak Island' because of this. How do you think the artist feels about these immigrants?

Racism: You have seen how intolerant white Americans could be (pages 47-49). It was claimed that while northern Europeans were skilled and hard-working, more recent immigrants from Asia and Europe were 'inferior stock', and could not easily become American, especially as many could not speak English.

Religion: White Anglo-Saxon Protestants or WASPs, the dominant group in the USA (see page 48), hated the poor Catholics and Jewish people from Eastern Europe, and feared the 'mysterious' religions of East Asia.

HOSTILITY

Trade unionists were worried that immigrants would be 'cheap labour' (work for less money) and take their jobs; people also complained about immigrants moving into their neighbourhoods and taking their houses.

Isolationism: After the horrors of the First World War and the Russian Revolution, many Americans in the 1920s wanted to 'keep to themselves' and 'shut out the world'. They did not want to welcome any political, radical extremists such as **communists** and anarchists to America, as they might try to overturn their freedom and democracy.

Restrictions on immigration in the 1920s

Consequently, the US government in the 1910s and 1920s passed a series of measures to restrict immigration – not just to limit numbers, but to only let in 'desirable' people.

The effect of the 1921 and 1924 Immigration Acts (see the 'anti-immigration legislation' diagram to the right) was not only to reduce immigration, but to restrict it to the white, northern European countries. Thus, the number of Italians emigrating to America was reduced from 200,000 to 4,000 a year, but the number of Germans actually rose (to 57,000 a year).

Meanwhile, the Federal Bureau of Naturalization organised patriotic 'Americanization Day' rallies and courses on democracy. These were aimed to prepare immigrants for a 'citizenship exam' and assimilate them into the American way of life – to try to force them to abandon their original culture and attitudes and become 'true Americans'.

Impact on the lives of immigrants

In the 1920s, poor immigrants who had come to America seeking wealth and freedom usually found themselves living in overcrowded slums alongside other immigrants from their own country. In New York, for example, they ended up in the Lower East Side (the Jewish community), 'Little Italy', and 'Chinatown'. These immigrants often worked long hours in poorly-paid manual jobs.

Seeing the government create laws that essentially discriminated against them would have scared immigrants into keeping to themselves. The immigrants were overwhelmingly honest and decent, but living in poverty meant that some inevitably became ill, or took to alcohol and gambling. Some Americans mistakenly linked these behaviours with the people, rather than thinking about the conditions (for example, people living close together in slums meant disease spread more easily).

Revision tip 🔄

Make sure you can explain at least one reason why immigrants faced hostility and at least one restriction placed on immigrants in the 1920s.

Decade	Millions of immigrants
1900-1909	8.2
1910-1919	6.3
1920-1929	4.3
1930-1939	0.7

Table 1 Immigration to the United States, 1900–1939.

Anti-immigration legislation in the USA

The **1917 *Immigration Law*** insisted that immigrants must be able to read English, increased the tax paid by arriving immigrants, and banned all immigration from Asia, except Japan.

⬇

The **1918 *Dillingham-Hardwick Act*** forbade anarchists to enter the country.

⬇

The **1921 *Emergency Quota Act*** set a maximum of 357,000 immigrants a year using the 'National Origins Formula' (which capped nations to three per cent of the number of emigrants to the US in 1910).

⬇

The **1924 *Reed-Johnson Act*** tightened up the 'National Origins Formula' from three per cent to two per cent of the 1890 emigration, and proposed an absolute cap of 150,000, to come into force from 1929.

Activities

1. What were the reasons for the generally hostile attitude towards immigration in the 1920s?
2. Look back at 'attitudes towards immigration' on page 52, then look at the laws passed to restrict immigration 1917–24. For each law, discuss how much you feel was affected by:
   - racism
   - religion
   - isolationism
   - trade unionism.
3. Explain to a partner what the statistics in Table 1 show about the effect of US anti-immigration legislation.

Hostility towards immigrants

In the 1920s, therefore, immigrants lived under a shadow of suspicion and hostility.

The Red Scare

The success of the Russian Revolution of 1917 frightened Americans:

▶ a US Senate investigation warned that Bolshevism (Communism) would bring atheism.

▶ Newspapers labelled communists as 'assassins and madmen'

▶ Films such as *Bolshevism on Trial* (1919) portrayed communists as dangerous and ridiculous at the same time.

The US government saw how the American public were panicking about communism and passed the *Sedition Act* in 1918. This made it illegal to criticise or abuse the US government, flag, or army. There was a general fear that immigrants were plotting a revolution in America.

The Palmer Raids

In April–May 1919, 36 mail bombs were sent to US politicians; in June eight bombs exploded in US cities. The bombs were set by radicals who were effectively declaring war on capitalists. 1919 was also a year of violent strikes, which people believed were also due to communists. The US Attorney-General, Mitchell Palmer, had his house damaged by a bomb. He told Congress that radicals were planning to destroy the government.

Palmer began arresting suspects. The Union of Russian Workers was raided in November 1919. Then, in January 1920, thousands of people (estimates vary from 3,000 to 10,000) were rounded up from 30 towns across 23 states, and arrested and held in prison. Most were members of the Communist Party, although others were trade unionists, Jewish, Catholic, or black Americans.

Palmer's actions created a great deal of opposition. When the revolution he had predicted for May 1920 did not happen, the raids were stopped and most of those imprisoned were released, although some were deported.

Activity 🖉

Construct a spider diagram about these three events, and use it to explain the impact of these events on the lives of immigrants.

The Sacco and Vanzetti case

In 1920, two Italian anarchists, Nicola Sacco and Bartolomeo Vanzetti, were accused of killing two guards during a robbery at a Massachusetts shoe factory.

The two were brought to trial in 1921. Although both had alibis at the time (Sacco had met an official at the Italian consulate, and 107 people testified they had bought fish from Vanzetti), they were found guilty – the jury did not believe the Italian witnesses who spoke on their behalf. Even when a criminal confessed to the murders in 1925, the courts refused to believe him.

Over the next six years, Sacco and Vanzetti appealed to the courts to let them go. All their appeals failed. Eventually, despite a mass protest of 20,000 people at Boston Common, Sacco and Vanzetti were executed in the electric chair in August 1927. Both faced their death with bravery, saying that the clear injustice of their case would help end hostility towards other immigrants.

▲ This cartoon of 1919 shows a 'Red', a Bolshevik and an 'alien slacker' (lazy worker) running away from the American Legion (a patriotic war veterans organisation, formed in 1919). The animal is saying 'They're going away for their health!' How does this cartoon depict immigrants?

Problems faced by Native Americans

Background

The westwards expansion of the United States across the Great Plains of North America was at the expense of the Native Americans (or 'Indians', as they were known at the time). There were many Native American tribes living on the Great Plains at the time the white settlers wanted to expand. Each tribe had its own language and set of cultures and traditions. White settlers saw them as primitive and a threat; battles and wars fought during the nineteenth century left hundreds of thousands of Native Americans dead. White settlers wanted to use the Native American land to develop railroads, mining, and building dams: they believed in the idea of manifest destiny:

▶ that Americans were the bringers of 'civilisation'

▶ that Americans had a mission to spread civilisation across the land

▶ that Americans were given this destiny by God to carry out.

The Native American way of life

By the 1920s, therefore, all the ideas about the Native American way of life which you might have taken from books or films – of nomadic warriors travelling across the country hunting the buffalo and living in tipis – are utterly wrong. After 1867, all Native Americans were expected to live on reservations. The last large-scale Native American War ended in defeat in 1877. The buffalo were slaughtered – by 1885, only 200 buffalo remained alive in the US.

Life on the reservations was specifically designed to destroy the independence, traditions and way of life of the Native Americans. They were not allowed the same rights as other US citizens, and the reservations were run for them by the government's Bureau of Indian Affairs (BIA). They were expected to settle down and live like white famers. In return, they were promised supplies and medicines – promises which the US government failed to keep.

The policy of 'allotment'

Not even the agreed Native American reservations were safe. Under the BIA, white Americans were regularly given the right to use tribal lands for development.

Since the *Dawes Act* of 1887, the government had followed a policy of dividing the Native American reservations into 'allotments'. These allotments were given to individual Native Americans, who would then become US citizens. The US government wanted Native Americans to come around to the American way of living: owning property or land and making a living from it, by farming. Many Native Americans were persuaded and bullied into this, only to find that they could not make a living on their land and had to sell it. In this way, by the end of the 1920s, two thirds of the tribal lands had been sold to white settlers.

▲ Native American farmer ploughing a field in New Mexico, USA, in 1930. Why would white Americans have regarded this man as a 'good Indian'?

The impact on Native Americans

The Meriam Report in 1928 was the first study into Native Americans' living conditions since 1850. It reported the full horror of the situation of Native Americans. On average, Native Americans earned only one sixth as much as white Americans, and experienced poor health, malnutrition, and an infant mortality rate almost three times that of white Americans.

The Report especially criticised the health care provided by the government, and declared the land that had been given to the Native Americans 'unsuitable for family farming ... land which a trained and experienced white man could hardly wrest [make] a living'.

The experience of Native Americans

In 1883, the government had declared a 'Code of Indian Offenses' (abolished in 1933) banning the "evil practices" of the tribes. Since then, the Native American religion, Peyotism, and their traditional 'Sun Dance', were forbidden in many states. In 1923 in New Mexico a 'Dance Order' banned traditional Puebloan dances because dancers gave away their possessions during the dance – a very un-American thing to do.

In 1903 a Kiowa warrior named Lone Wolf challenged the right of the government to allot tribal lands. The US Supreme Court not only denied his claim (*Lone Wolf v. Hitchcock*), but went on to declare that the Native Americans were "an ignorant and dependent race" who should be treated as "wards of the nation".

This gave the government rights, not only over the Native American lands, but over their culture, language, religion, art, and education. The belief amongst white Americans at the time was that Native Americans should be encouraged to abandon their native culture and become 'true Americans'. This policy is termed 'assimilation'.

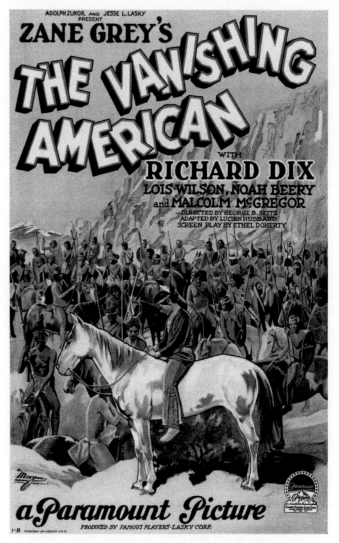

▲ The 1925 movie *The Vanishing American* told the story of a noble Native American man, Nophaie, who joined the US Army and fought bravely in World War One. Returning home, Nophaie realised that the Native American way of life was coming to an end, and died happy protecting Marion, the white teacher at the Native American school who taught him to read. All the main Native American roles were played by white Americans. How does this story show the racism against Native Americans?

Activities

1 Explain the allotment policy.
2 Why did white settlers want Native Americans to change their way of life?
3 Using the information on pages 55–56, create a spider diagram about all the problems Native Americans faced in the 1920s and early 1930s.

The education of Native Americans

Education was seen as the main way to assimilate Native Americans, and to do this the Bureau of Indian Affairs (BIA) set up boarding schools for Native American children.

Here, children were given European-style haircuts and uniforms, and even new English-sounding names. Pupils were forbidden to speak their own languages, even to each other, and made to go to Christian church services. The lessons taught European-American values, and much of the time was spent doing cleaning jobs with strict rules and harsh physical punishments. The aim, as one historian called it, was 'education for extinction'.

Although the schools were voluntary, Native American parents were bullied by the government into sending their children to the schools. In 1920, nearly 11,000 Native American children were educated in off-reservation boarding schools.

The Meriam Report in 1928 (see page 56) declared the boarding schools 'grossly inadequate', and recommended:

▶ that there should be no attempt to interfere with the children's religion or ceremonies

▶ that Native American children be taught about their own culture, history, art and language, by teachers who valued tribal ways

▶ vocational training for a rural lifestyle

▶ more day schools on the reservations.

Changing attitudes

As the public became more aware of the plight of the Native Americans, their situation slowly improved.

Changing attitudes towards Native Americans in the USA

1911	A group of leading Native Americans formed the Society of American Indians. It published the American Indian Magazine and campaigned for an 'American Indian Day'.
1923	The Indian Defense Association was formed by Collier who, after a visit to the Puebloans of New Mexico, decided that Native American culture was superior to American society.
1924	The Snyder Act gave Native Americans full US citizenship rights.
1928	The Meriam Report highlighted the poor way the US government had treated the Native Americans.
1933	US President Roosevelt appointed Collier as Commissioner of Indian Affairs. Collier's 'Indian New Deal' included an Indian Civilian Conservation Corps, an Indian Emergency Conservation Work program and an Indian Arts and Crafts Board.

⌃ These photos show three Sioux boys (left to right Wounded Yellow Robe, Henry Standing Bear and Chauncy Yellow Robe) as they entered a boarding school in 1883 (left photo), and three years later (right photo). How do these photographs illustrate the policy of 'assimilation'?

Practice questions

1 Describe two ways in which US government policies affected the lives of immigrants in the 1920s.

2 Why did Native Americans face problems in the USA in the 1920s?

3 'The most serious social problem America faced in the 1920s was the poor treatment of black Americans.' Do you agree? Explain your answer.

2 Prohibition

The introduction of Prohibition

In January 1919, Congress passed the 18th Amendment, prohibiting the 'manufacture, sale, or transportation of intoxicating liquors'. In October, the *Volstead Act* defined an 'intoxicating liquor' as anything over 5 per cent proof (i.e. anything stronger than a weak beer). Alcohol was banned in America and Prohibition Agents (such as The Untouchables, a group of ten agents led by Eliot Ness) were employed to stop any trade in alcohol and to destroy any stores of liquor they found.

Reasons for and aims of Prohibition

Temperance organisations such as the Anti-Saloon League and the Women's Christian Temperance Union had been campaigning against 'the demon drink' since the 1830s and had developed hard-hitting and effective propaganda. Posters, and songs and poems, such as The *Drunkard's Fall*, stressed the damage it did to the family. Pamphlets stressed the cost of beer and linked drink to accidents. The aim was not just to reduce alcohol consumption, but to stop it altogether.

The temperance message was supported by many sections of society. Ministers asked their congregations, 'Do you want Christ to come at the Judgment Day and find you drunk?' Women's leaders blamed alcohol for domestic violence and family poverty. The American Medical Association knew that alcohol caused liver disease and mental illness and declared its support for Prohibition in 1917. The Ku Klux Klan (see page 48) also opposed drunkenness.

The turning point in the campaign was the First World War, when the government decided that it needed to reduce alcohol consumption to improve workers' productivity and prevent absenteeism. At the time, Prohibition seemed to be a popular proposal and, by the time it was agreed, 31 states had already enacted their own Prohibition laws.

▼ Government agents destroying captured liquor during Prohibition. Only a fraction of illegal liquor was destroyed in this way. So what was the purpose of government photographs like this?

Source A John Strange, former lieutenant governor of Wisconsin, speaking during the First World War, named some popular German beers:

The worst of all our German enemies – the most treacherous, the most menacing, are Pabst, Schlitz, Blatz, and Miller.

The growth and impact of organised crime

Many people simply defied the law. Some built stills and made their own 'moonshine' (illegal liquor). Prohibition Agents found and destroyed 280,000 such stills. Others bought their booze from illicit sellers or visited one of the 250,000 'speakeasies' (illegal bars), which were so numerous that they have come to symbolise the 'Roaring Twenties'. The 2,300 Prohibition Agents could not cope at a local level, never mind patrol the 4,000-mile border with Canada, over which 'bootleggers' transported the alcohol. Others smuggled it in by sea – the phrase 'the real McCoy' derives from an American sea-smuggler who specialised in fine Scotch. One Agent visited a number of cities, recording how long it took him to get an illegal drink – the record was 35 seconds!

Even worse were the 'Big-Time' criminals and Mafia bosses who took advantage of Prohibition. They organised the bootlegging, ran protection rackets and murdered rivals. Before 1919, organised crime gangs had controlled prostitution and the black market, but were relatively small-scale. Prohibition provided an opportunity to make so much money that suddenly organised crime became big business.

Perhaps the most famous gangland boss, 'Scarface' Al Capone, was fabulously wealthy, was accepted in high society, and in 1928 was even considered for *Time Magazine*'s 'Man of the Year'. Meanwhile, on the streets, gangsters with names like 'The Scourge' Lombardo (killed 1928) and 'Tight Lips' Gusenberg (killed 1929) fought gangland wars for control of the liquor trade. At the same time, bribery and corruption spread through law enforcement and politics at every level, from the local cop to the judges and Senators.

The son of an Italian immigrant, Al Capone worked his way up from bouncer and gangland bodyguard to become the head of a Chicago gang called 'The Outfit'. He had an army of 700 'torpedoes' (assassins) and used bribery and threats to control police, councillors and judges. On Valentine's Day, 1929, his men, dressed as police officers, gunned down seven members of a rival gang.

By 1933, the criminal underworld was more organised and powerful than ever before. Ending Prohibition became essential, not so that people could have a drink, but to break the power of organised crime.

Revision tip

Make sure that you understand all the ways in which Prohibition helped the growth of organised crime.

Differing attitudes towards Prohibition

It was not just the gangsters who opposed Prohibition; the gangsters thrived because many Americans hated Prohibition:

▶ Millions of ordinary people simply ignored the law.

▶ Wealthy people such as Pierre DuPont – an industrialist who saw Prohibition as an attack on his personal freedom – poured money into the Association Against Prohibition Amendment (AAPA).

▶ The wealthy celebrity Pauline Sabin feared that a law which everybody disobeyed (even politicians) meant that 'children are growing up with a total lack of respect for the law'. In 1929 she founded the Women's Organization for National Prohibition Reform (WONPR). It was the biggest anti-Prohibition organisation in the country, much bigger than the pro-Prohibition Women's Christian Temperance Union (WCTU).

However, while it is true that the law was poorly obeyed in the cities, it tended to be supported by rural, Protestant, and middle-class communities:

▶ rural workers saw drinking and drunkenness as morally corrupt behaviours linked to immigrants and cities

▶ religious Protestant groups such as Quakers and Methodists saw drinking as a sin and drinking saloons as places where people could be corrupted by alcohol

▶ middle class communities linked drunkenness with the poor

Consequently, Prohibition created fierce debate, as these sources show:

Source B John Haynes Holmes in a Debate on Prohibition with the lawyer Clarence Darrow in 1924.

I have never believed that democracy involved the liberty to guzzle when that liberty to guzzle was a menace to me and to all other men and to the society which constitutes the America we love.

Source C Clarence Darrow, in a Debate on Prohibition with the Rev John Haynes Holmes in 1924.

This Prohibition Law has filled our jails with people who are not criminals. It has made criminals of men who otherwise would be honest. It is hateful, it is an abomination; and we ought to get rid of it.

Source D Anonymous letter to the *New York Times*.

It is a wonder to me that the Prohibitionists can sleep, they have thrown thousands of honest men out of work and caused great hardships. Many of the men in breweries had families to support. Now they are hunting jobs.

Source E The comedian Will Rogers.

Instead of giving money to found colleges to promote learning, why don't they pass an Amendment prohibiting anybody from learning anything? If it works as good as Prohibition, why, in five years we would have the smartest race of people on earth.

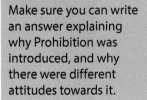

Revision tip

Make sure you can write an answer explaining why Prohibition was introduced, and why there were different attitudes towards it.

Activities

1 Describe two aims of Prohibition.

2 Using Sources B–E above, decide whether they are for or against Prohibition and why.

3 Using the ideas you have discovered, frame a debate about Prohibition, in which one of you argues for Prohibition, and the other against Prohibition.

Reasons for the failure of Prohibition

Historians have identified four reasons that Prohibition was repealed:

▲ Opposition: It was opposed by many wealthy and powerful interests (see page 60).

▲ Taxation: Prohibition caused problems for the government because before 1913 a third of all taxes came from taxes on alcohol.

▲ Problems in the alcohol industry: Saloons were closed and breweries went bankrupt – the beer-making town of St Louis went into recession.

▲ Disrespect for the law: While most Prohibition crime was minor, taken overall it created a culture of lawlessness which damaged society; it had become fashionable to go to a speakeasy for liquor.

In 1929, the Wickersham Commission (set up to report on the progress of Prohibition) reported that Prohibition was unenforceable, that people disrespected the law, and that they were angry with the extent of organised crime that had happened because of it. In 1933, shortly after he had become President, Franklin D. Roosevelt passed the Cullen-Harrison or Beer Permit Act, allowing the sale of alcohol. 'I think this would be a good time for a beer,' he said. Soon after, in December 1933, the 21st Amendment was passed which repealed (cancelled) Prohibition.

However, social historians have pointed out that Prohibition did not 'fail' in its key objectives of reducing the drinking of alcohol and improving health. In the early 1920s, drinking alcohol fell by up to 70 per cent, especially amongst the urban working-class communities (where people could not afford black market prices). Even after Prohibition was repealed, the drinking of alcohol and the number of deaths from liver disease were lower than in the 1910s.

Activities

1 Explain one reason for the failure of Prohibition.
2 Why did many wealthy and powerful people oppose Prohibition?
3 What were the economic reasons for the failure of Prohibition?

Practice questions ❓

1 Describe two ways in which Prohibition helped the growth of organised crime in the 1920s.
2 'It could be said that during the 1920s, crime killed Prohibition.' Do you agree? Explain your answer.

The changing role of women in American society

There were major changes in attitudes towards women, and in women's behaviour, in the 1920s.

Voting rights for women

In 1920, Congress ratified the 19th Amendment, giving women the vote. At the time, it was expected that women's votes (female suffrage) would change America by making women more powerful and have more of a say in running the country.

The significance of voting rights

Carrie Chapman Catt, the leader of the National American Women's Suffrage Association (NAWSA), immediately reformed the NAWSA into the League of Women Voters (LWV), to help motivate women to influence public affairs. Its Vice-President in the 1920s was Eleanor Roosevelt (who went on to oversee the United Nations' Declaration of Human Rights in 1948, and led the US Commission on the Status of Women in the 1960s).

In 1920, the LWV joined with other women's groups to form the Women's Joint Congressional Committee (WJCC). It represented ten million women. It lobbied for laws to protect women and children – on issues such as child labour, education, Prohibition and sexual diseases.

Its greatest success was the Sheppard-Towner Act of 1921, which provided federal funding for maternity and child care.

Other female activists scored successes elsewhere. In 1923 the Women's Bureau, created by Congress to help wage-earning women, established the principle of equal pay for female civil servants.

The Equal Rights Amendment 1923

However, after 1924, the women's movement ran out of steam. Right-wing politicians accused the WJCC of being communist, and Christian groups claimed it was trying to destroy the family. In 1924, a Child Labour Amendment (to protect young workers under 18) failed to become law, because of this opposition to the movement.

At the same time, the women's movement split. During the campaign for the vote, a group called the National Women's Party (NWP), led by Alice Paul, had tried more active tactics. After 1920, the NWP lobbied for women's equality and proposed the Equal Rights Amendment in 1923. The Equal Rights Amendment argued for completely equal rights between men and women – that is, there should be no protection or flexibility for women: they would be expected to do 'men's job's' even if that included heavy lifting and longer or night-time hours. The WJCC opposed the ERA, saying that it would harm their work, which was to protect women. In the end, Congress did not pass the Equal Rights Amendment until 1972.

Were women more powerful?

In terms of how much things changed for women and how much power they gained, a few women were named as judges in the 1920s, and Nellie Tayloe Ross was elected state governor of Wyoming in 1924. But even by 1930 only 13 women had been elected to Congress. It was not until the election of Franklin D Roosevelt in 1932 that large numbers of women turned out to vote in an election.

▲ League of Women Voters' delegates in 1920. What kind of world did they want?

Activities

1 What was the LWV?
2 What was the ERA?
3 How successful was the ERA?
4 Construct a timeline to show the main events to do with women's voting rights from 1920 to 1933.

Women in the workplace

You will read in some books that women before World War I were expected to stay at home and be housewives, and that work in some way 'liberated' them. This is not true. Poor women lived lives of harsh drudgery – in rural areas they worked as (if married, unpaid) farm labourers, and in the towns they doubled up factory work during the day with the work of a wife and mother at night.

It is true that women began to make some inroads into the jobs market in the 1920s.

▶ During World War I, some women worked in armaments (weapons) factories.

▶ The number of women working rose by two million in the 1920s.

▶ Some businesswomen did achieve success (for instance Dorothy Arzner, film director, and Estee Lauder, cosmetics).

▶ Women were employed as secretaries, typists and book-keepers. By 1930, the clerical profession was almost wholly female.

▶ In 1920, Congress created the Women's Bureau to 'promote the welfare of wage-earning women, improve their working conditions, increase their efficiency, and advance their opportunities'.

▶ The Women's Trade Union League helped women organise trade unions.

Significance of women's work

However, it is debatable whether these changes marked a significant improvement in women's lives:

▶ The lives and work of poor women did not change at all.

▶ Wage discrimination continued – women did not get equal pay for the same job, and part of the reason they came to dominate the clerical profession was because they were cheaper to hire.

▶ Only about 15 per cent of white and 30 per cent of black married women with wage-earning husbands held paying jobs. Female schoolteachers were fired when they married and workplaces like banks refused to hire them at all.

▶ There were actually fewer female doctors and lawyers in 1930 than in 1910.

Activities

1 How did women's prospects in the workplace change during the 1920s?

2 Make a list of qualities which a woman today might expect from a 'good job'. Using page 63, identify all the ways in which female employment in the 1920s fell short of this ideal.

3 Debate the statement: 'Nothing changed in the 1920s – women remained the slaves of society.'

◀ A photograph of women working in a government financial department in 1924. They are, of course, not using 'computers', but they are using the latest mechanical calculators.

Looking at the photograph, suggest what it tells us about the nature of some women's work in the 1920s.

The influence of the flappers

You may read in some books that, before the 1920s, women's lives were very restricted, that they could not wear make-up or play sport, and that they had to wear modest clothes and could only go out with a chaperone. While there were women in that situation, it applied only to wealthy middle-class households and even then the 'new woman' had been evident since the 1890s, going to college, going bicycling and on walks and wanting more control over her own life.

The First World War, however, had seen women take a more prominent role in the workplace and the 1920s saw a number of further developments which affected women's lives:

▶ Women got the vote in 1920 (see page 62).

▶ Growing wealth and the increased availability of domestic appliances such as vacuum cleaners and washing machines (see page 72 for how this affected women).

▶ A new urban social culture based on night-life (see pages 66–67).

▶ Improved communication (radio, records, automobiles and plane flights) made women aware of an exciting world beyond the home.

▶ Films such as Clara Bow's 'It' Girl portrayed adventurous and promiscuous women; millions of film-goers idolised the movie stars and copied their looks and behaviour.

Source A An article – written by a woman – in 1921.

Do they ever think … these lovely, brainless, unbalanced, cigarette-smoking morsels of undisciplined sex? Has the American girl no modesty, no self-respect, no reserve, no dignity?

Out of this, therefore, it is suggested, some women developed new self-confidence which was exemplified in the 'flappers' of the 1920s who:

▶ demanded independence, worked and got involved in politics

▶ wore looser, shorter clothes to allow greater freedom of movement (for example, a loose underwear garment called a 'step-in' replaced the old corset); many flappers favoured the flat-chested 'garconne' (boyish) look of the French fashion designer Coco Chanel – and some wore men's clothes

▶ enjoyed a scandalous social life which broke traditional rules – smoking, drinking, attending speakeasies and dancing to jazz music

▶ were sexually liberated (for example, kissing in public, flirting with men and accepting lifts from men in cars); some were openly lesbian.

➤ (Left) Edna Purviance and Charlie Chaplin in the silent movie *Easy Street* (a morality tale of 1917).

(Right) Clara Bow in *Call Her Savage* (a racy talkie of 1932 which was the first film to portray gay people on screen). What are the differences between how women are shown in these photos?

Continuity in the role of women

Did the flappers exist at all as they were portrayed on the films and in novels?

▶ To be a flapper, you needed money and leisure time. Working-class women could not afford the new appliances and remained tied to the hard work of home and/or a menial job. Women who worked in factories or sweatshops worked too hard and too long to be able to have a wild social life.

▶ In rural America, 'the modern world' of cars, nightclubs and movies had not yet begun. In the 1930s, 90 per cent of American farms still lacked electricity and the proportion of farms with a telephone actually fell during the 1920s. Farming suffered a recession and most farmers' wives did not have the money to buy the new appliances – they cooked on a woodstove and drew water from a well.

▶ In the 'Bible Belt' states of the south-eastern United States, people believed that God had created women as a helpmate for man, that they should be obedient and submissive, and that their God-given role was that of a mother and homemaker.

Most of these women actively disapproved of the new relaxed morality. The Anti-Flirt League was formed in 1923 to encourage proper behaviour in young women (its first rule was: 'those who flirt in haste oft repent in leisure').

Nevertheless, the mere fact that women watched the movies in such huge numbers (see page 67) suggests that many yearned for a more romantic and exciting life. It has been suggested that the rise in the number of divorces was a sign of growing feminism.

How far did women's lives change in the 1920s?

	Before World War One	In the 1920s
Politics	'Women had no vote and no power.'	'Women were politically engaged voters.'
Work	'Women stayed at home.'	'Women took over the clerical professions.'
Fashion	'Women wore corsets and restrictive clothes.'	'Women wore bobbed hair and short skirts.'
Behaviour	'Women were modest, prim and proper.'	'Women were wild, drunk and sexual.'

Table 1 Simplistic, traditional view of how women's lives changed in the 1920s.

Revision tip

For each of the ways women's lives changed (the right to vote, work, flappers) make sure you can answer **why** this aspect of their lives changed.

Revision tip

Make sure you understand both the arguments for change and the arguments for continuity.

Activities

1 What factors limited women's freedom in the 1920s?
2 Working in a group, and using pages 62–65 identify evidence which supports and which contradicts all eight statements.
3 Add and complete a fourth column to Table 1: 'Women's lives today', and discuss as a group how far along the road to feminism women had travelled by the end of the 1920s.

Changes in popular entertainment

Entertainment, as well as being 'the fun side' of life, was also important in forming the social attitudes and behaviour of the 1920s.

It is important to realise that America had a lively entertainment scene before the 1920s:

▶ Most public entertainment centred around Vaudeville, a kind of variety show featuring entertainment acts from juggling to tap dancing to singing. A popular form of show was the 'Minstrel Show', where white actors 'blacked up' and mocked and mimicked black people. Florenz Ziegfeld's shows (including daringly-dressed chorus dancers) also became famous at this time.

▶ Many people went to dance halls. New dances with names such as the Bunny-Hug and the Turkey Trot displaced traditional European dances. The popular music of the time was 'Ragtime' – you will almost certainly have heard '*The Entertainer*' by the ragtime composer Scott Joplin.

▶ The first movies were appearing. They were played in 'Nickelodeons' (so called after the small 5-cent 'nickel' coin people paid to go in to see them).

▶ In sport, watching baseball and college football was already hugely popular.

However, there were many exciting developments in entertainment in the 1920s, which became known as 'the roaring twenties'.

Jazz music

Jazz was first played in New Orleans by black musicians such as Fats Waller and Duke Ellington. After 1917, as racial tension grew, many of them went north to play in the night clubs of New York.

Impact and attitudes

The invention of radio and the phonograph (record-player) took jazz music into people's homes. They were called 'race records', because they were recorded by black musicians. Jazz music was part of the Harlem Renaissance and the growth of black pride (see page 50). It was also part of the rebellious attitude of the times – baggy trousers and short skirts, and new dances.

Jazz was seen as dangerous and exciting (because it was played in speakeasies and clubs, by black musicians) and this made it popular with the flappers, but it led other people to label it 'the devil's music'.

▶ The St Louis Cotton Club band, about 1925. What does the photo suggest about the band and their music?

New dances

In the 1920s, new and exciting dances replaced the European dances of the nineteenth century.

The Charleston was a fast dance developed in Black communities which was adopted by flappers (two of the famous movie actresses of the time, Joan Crawford and Ginger Rodgers, both began their careers by winning Charleston competitions).

The 'Black Bottom Stomp' was first recorded by Jelly Roll Morton and named after Black Bottom – a black neighbourhood in Detroit; after 1926 it became the most popular dance in America.

Impact and attitudes

Again, because they were associated with speakeasies, clubs and liquor, the new dances attracted the rebellious and the young, but their wild, unrestrained movements scandalised many Americans, who thought the dances were immoral.

Cinema

In the 1920s, movie-going replaced Vaudeville as the main form of popular entertainment. There were 8,000 cinemas in 1910 – this had increased to 300,000 by the end of the 1920s, when 100 million people were going to the cinema every week. Actors such as Charlie Chaplin, Rudolf Valentino and Mary Pickford became 'stars', idolised and copied by their fans.

Technology improved quickly. In 1927, *The Jazz Singer* starring Al Jolson, was the first 'talkie'. Walt Disney developed credible animation in his Mickey Mouse cartoons from 1928. Two-colour films were common by the end of the 1920s; from 1932 Walt Disney produced his animations in colour and colour movies became common from 1934.

Impact and attitudes

Films allowed people to escape into a fantasy world, far different from the poor, harsh reality of their lives. They taught people new fashions (such as smoking) and new ways to behave – many girls wanted to be like the 'It' girl, Clara Bow (see page 64). They also shocked more conservative people; after 1934 – in response to popular complaints – Hollywood enforced the 'Hays Code', which regulated how sex was portrayed on screen.

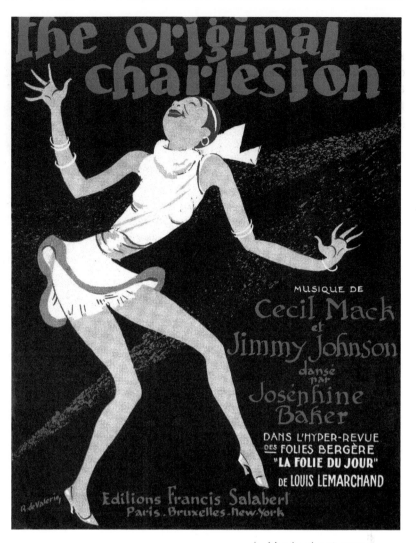

▲ Music sheet cover for a Charleston dance tune showing Josephine Baker, 1923. What does it suggest about entertainment in 'the roaring twenties'?

67

Radio

As mass-production reduced its price, radio replaced the newspapers as the main form of news and entertainment. By the end of the 1920s, ten million homes had a radio and there were 600 radio stations in 1930, from huge organisations such as the National Broadcasting Company to small local stations operating from isolated studios.

Impact and attitudes

The radio allowed people to keep up to date with news – and to listen to the latest jazz music. Families gathered round the radio and listened to their favourite programmes together. Radio revolutionised politics – President Franklin D. Roosevelt (1933–45) used the radio to give 'fireside chats' to the nation. The power of radio was revealed in 1938 with Orson Welles' production of *The War of the Worlds*. Presented as a news bulletin for dramatic effect, it caused widespread panic because people thought it was true.

The growing role of spectator sport

Radio helped sport to become a national obsession, because it made it possible for people to follow sports and teams they could never hope to go to see.

Baseball continued to be the biggest sport of the time, with the New York Yankees player Babe Ruth (nicknamed the 'Sultan of Swat') its biggest star. Boxing was also hugely popular – Jack Dempsey (the 'Manassa Mauler') was the first boxer to earn $1million for a fight.

Other sports became popular. The first Professional Tennis Tour was established in 1926. The PGA golf championship had been established in 1916, but it grew during the 1920s – its greatest star was a golfer called Bobbie Jones. American Football also flourished – the National Football League (NFL) was established in 1920 and the present-day system of leagues and play-offs developed from 1932.

Impact and attitudes

A government survey in 1933 reported that sport on the radio encouraged people to play sports, made huge stars of the top players and increased attendance at matches – although it tended to benefit the more successful clubs at the expense of the smaller ones. The report also noted that: 'broadcasting of sports has led to the developing of a special skill in announcing the movements of athletes not at times easy to see, a skill rather highly appreciated'.

▲ Listening to the radio in the 1930s.

Activities

1 Who were the following people:
   - Fats Waller and Duke Ellington
   - Charlie Chaplin
   - Clara Bow?
2 What effect did the mass production of the radio have on popular entertainment in the 1920s?
3 Using information from pages 66–68, create a table like the following and fill it in:

Change in popular entertainment	Attitude towards it	Impact on people's lives
Jazz music and dance		
The rise of Hollywood and actors		
Cinema and radio		
Spectator sport (boxing and baseball)		

Practice questions

1 Describe two ways in which the lives of women changed in America in the period 1920–33.
2 'The 19th Amendment was a major step forward for women.' Do you agree? Explain your answer.
3 How did cinema affect American people during the 1920s?

Revision tip

For each of the topics on pages 66–68 (jazz, dances, movies, radio and sport) make sure you could write an answer to a question asking you how it affected the lives of American people.

This page provides guidance on how to answer questions 1 and 2 in the exam.

Question 1

Below is a list of words linked with problems faced by black Americans in the 1920s.

Jim Crow	Segregation	Ku Klux Klan	Lynching	Ghettos

Match each word to the correct description and write your answer in the space provided. The first one has been done for you.

a Southern laws that restricted the rights of black Americans   Jim Crow   [1]
b Killing someone, especially by hanging, without a trial   _____   [1]
c A 'separate but equal' racial policy   _____   [1]
d Areas of poor, crowded housing   _____   [1]
e White supremacist organisation   _____   [1]

Guidance

First, enter the answers you know. After that, you should be able to figure out the remaining answers. While being accurate, do this question as quickly as you can.

Question 2

Describe two ways in which the lives of women changed in America in the period 1920–33. [3+3]

Guidance

You should be looking to spend about five minutes on this question. Remember that it does not need a long answer. You need to identify two ways and describe them both: your description needs to be as detailed as possible within the time allowance you have.

Follow the steps below for each part of the answer.

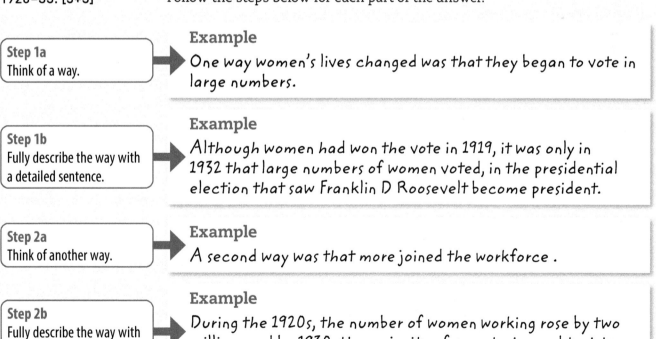

Step 1a
Think of a way.

Example
One way women's lives changed was that they began to vote in large numbers.

Step 1b
Fully describe the way with a detailed sentence.

Example
Although women had won the vote in 1919, it was only in 1932 that large numbers of women voted, in the presidential election that saw Franklin D Roosevelt become president.

Step 2a
Think of another way.

Example
A second way was that more joined the workforce.

Step 2b
Fully describe the way with a detailed sentence.

Example
During the 1920s, the number of women working rose by two million, and by 1930, the majority of secretaries and typists were working women.

The boom years

Reasons for the rapid economic growth of the 1920s

There were six main causes of the economic boom of the 1920s in the United States:

1 The First World War

The United States had stayed out of the war until 1917, with the result that whilst the main European countries had fought each other to destruction, America was relatively unharmed by the fighting. Also, European industry had been turned over to producing war goods, allowing American firms to take over their markets. Meanwhile, the western European governments had borrowed billions of dollars from American banks to buy munitions and armaments from American firms; not only did this stimulate the American firms, it meant that after the war European economies struggled to recover because they were having to pay back the loans.

All this meant **opportunity** for American firms, and the American economy grew.

2 Mass production

Two major advances in technology helped American firms increase their productivity. The first was the moving assembly line (by 1927 Ford was producing a new Model T automobile every ten seconds), and the second was 'time and motion' studies, which improved efficiency and reduced waste. At the same time, the sheer size of American industry allowed firms to achieve 'economies of scale' – buying raw materials in vast quantities allowed firms to force down the price they paid.

All this meant that, not only were American firms producing goods in huge quantities, they were producing them at a very **cheap price** – for instance, the price of a Model T automobile fell from $850 in 1911 to $295 in 1920.

3 Mass marketing and credit

Production only benefits firms if it is sold, but the US population rose from 106 million in 1920 to 123 million in 1930 – a huge and increasing market, and developments in marketing in the 1920s made sure those people spent their money! Adverts (including radio broadcasts after 1921) encouraged people to want and buy material goods, whilst half a million travelling salesmen went door-to-door selling everything from bibles to brushes. If the local shops didn't have what you wanted, you could buy it by mail order. And, if your bank account ran dry – no matter! The Americans developed 'Hire Purchase' (buying on credit) and weekly instalments ('easy payments') to encourage people to borrow-to-buy – six out of ten cars were bought this way in the 1920s.

As firms prospered, they employed more workers – who then had the wages to spend on buying more things. Average wages increased by 27 per cent during the 1920s, which further **increased demand**.

4 The Stock Market

Mass production requires investment, but the booming Stock Market supplied the capital which allowed firms to grow. The idea is that investors buy 'shares' in a firm, and the firm uses the money to expand; it then pays investors a 'dividend' in return. Later in the decade, the Stock Market 'overheated' and 'crashed ' (see pages 80–81), but at the start of the 1920s, sales of shares rose steadily (from 200 million a year in 1921 to 600 million a year in 1927) which poured millions of dollars into American industry, and gave it the investment to grow.

5 Government policies

The Party in power in the United States in the 1920s was the Republican Party. The Republican Presidents (Warren Harding, 1921–23 and Calvin Coolidge, 1923–29) believed that the best way to encourage economic growth was *laissez-faire* – by which they meant giving businesses the freedom to do as they wanted. The 'American Dream' was all about achieving success for yourself and Americans in the 1920s believed in 'rugged individualism' – the idea that anyone could become rich simply by hard work and determination.

The government therefore:

a) Reduced income tax (which favoured the rich) and instead increased tariffs (which hurt the poor by raising the prices of imported goods).

b) Allowed Trusts (super-corporations) and Cartels (alliances of companies) which were so huge that they could control the market and 'fix' prices.

c) Weakened the Trade Unions – the courts allowed American businessmen to forbid workers to join trade unions ('yellow dog' contracts) and to break strikes by force.

d) Set high tariffs on imported goods – the *Fordney-McCumber Act* (1922) set tariffs of up to 400 per cent (the highest in history). Tariffs protected American industry from international competition and helped it grow.

6 The cycle of prosperity

Wealth creates wealth. As the profits of industry went into workers' salaries and wages, this allowed more spending and demand, which led to more sales and increased production, which needed more workers. The American economy had become large enough to be self-generating.

The car industry especially, stimulated the entire economy. Its demand for raw materials led to expansion in the steel, glass and tyre industries (ancillary industries). Then the needs of motorists required expansion of the oil industry (for petrol), road-building and house-building in the 'suburbs' which people with cars were able to live in. And, of course, the automobile then allowed consumers to drive to new markets and go on holiday and spend their money, thus increasing demand.

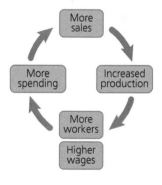

Activities

Work in a group of 3 or 4; each group takes a different cause of the boom.
1 Construct a spider diagram to map out the ways your cause helped to create the economic boom – find as many ways as you can, and explain in depth.
2 Share your ideas with other groups, who have been analysing other causes.
3 Explore the different ways the causes are inter-linked.

Revision tip ↺

For each of these causes of the boom, make sure you can explain HOW they caused the economic boom, taking the argument right through to the economic growth it caused.

Features of the boom and the impact on people's lives

There was an economic boom; the US economy grew by 40 per cent in the 1920s. Times were so good that in 1928 Herbert Hoover, the new American president proclaimed a 'triumph over poverty' and promised Americans 'a chicken in every pot and a car in every backyard'.

1 Consumer goods

There was a craze for 'household gadgets' in the 1920s (not just things like fridges, washing machines, vacuum cleaners, sewing machines and telephones, but popcorn makers, toasters, phonographs, irons, coffee percolators, electric fans, eyelash curlers and many more). The number of telephones doubled from 10 million to 20 million (100 per cent increase) and the number of radios rose from 60,000 to 10 million (a 1,667 per cent increase).

The typical American housewife had to spend 60 hours a week on meals, laundry and cleaning in 1900. In 1925, this became just 45 hours a week.

2 The automobile

The automobile industry boomed in the 1920s. In 1927, the 15 millionth Model T Ford rolled off the production line. Automobile production in 1928 was 4.4 million. In the 1920s, the number of automobiles on US roads rose from 8 to 23 million.

Middle class Americans could now live in the suburbs and travel into town to work. Town dwellers could take a trip to the country or to the seaside – country people had the opportunity of a trip to the city to shop. Motels, roadside 'fast-food' restaurants and drive-in movies were built, and motor racing became a popular sport – neither would have happened at all without the automobile. Traffic jams and road accidents became part of life.

◁ Advertisement for labour-saving devices from an electrical department catalogue in 1929.

▲ A construction worker on the Empire state building, New York, 1930.

3 The construction industry

There was a property boom in the 1920s. Most obvious were the new skyscrapers such as New York's Empire State Building, completed in 1931. A quarter of the financial district of New York was rebuilt in the 1920s and the image of New York as a skyline of skyscrapers was defined. Many gorgeous mansions were built for the fabulously wealthy; and many ordinary people managed to buy a family house in the suburbs.

The 1920s were also a time of great sophistication – buildings were designed in the Art Deco style. The great architect Frank Lloyd Wright developed the concept of small, 'organic' (natural-looking) suburban houses and experimented building with precast concrete blocks.

4 The chemicals industry

The 1920s were a time when the scientists of the chemicals industry developed a large number of commercial products:

▶ Rayon was a cheap, synthetic material, but it felt and looked like silk.

▶ In 1927, the huge chemicals firm DuPont patented cellophane film.

▶ Bakelite, an early brittle form of plastic (it was used for electrical goods like plugs and radios, and children's toys).

▶ Cosmetics and beauty products such as new hair dyes, Cutex nail polish (1917) and new lipsticks.

▲ Charlie Chaplin (on the right) in *Modern Times*.

Activities

1 Create a spider diagram summarising the features of the boom. Annotate it to show how each feature changed the nature and the quality of Americans' lives in the 1920s.
2 How did the economic developments of the 1920s affect the lives of Americans?

Practice questions

1 Below are two features of the 1920s in America.

| The development of the chemical industry |
| The development of consumer goods |

Choose one feature and explain its impact on 1920s America.
2 Why did American industry face problems in the 1920s?

5 The film industry

The film industry was centred on the Hollywood neighbourhood of Los Angeles. From 1910, it grew rapidly, until it became the most important film-making place in the world. 90 per cent of its films were made by the 'Big Five' studios – MGM, Paramount, Warner Bros, RKO and Fox – which between them produced some 500 films a year. The studios employed thousands of employees – from actors, directors and scriptwriters to stuntmen and carpenters. In 1929, the first Academy Awards (Oscars) were held.

You have already seen (page 67) how films affected people's lives, influencing fashion, attitudes, and how people behaved.

6 Mass production methods

Assembly-line working and time-and-motion studies came at a price. Their aim was to fit the worker into the production process almost as a piece of the machinery. Assembly workers were well paid, but their work was repetitive and boring, and they worked under great pressure, having to keep up with the pace of the assembly line.

In *Modern Times* (1936), Charlie Chaplin made fun of modern industrial work in his role as an accident-prone worker trapped on an assembly line which just went faster and faster.

7 Mass marketing and credit

In the nineteenth century, traditionally, Americans had tried to avoid getting into debt, which was seen as a bad thing. By the mid-1920s, most Americans' attitude to debt had completely changed, and debt had become an accepted part of the American way of life. Consumer debt in the United States doubled, until it stood at $3 billion by 1930.

By the end of the 1920s, the average American spent more than seven per cent of their income on repayments.

Examination practice for Life in the United States of America, 1920–33

This page provides guidance on how to answer question 3 in the exam.

Question 3

Below are two industries which changed American society in the period 1920–29.

Choose one industry and explain how it changed American society.

The automobile industry	The film industry

(6)

Guidance

You should be looking to spend about seven minutes on this question. Here you have a little choice. Spend a little time working out which of the two areas you understand and can write about best. Your answer needs to provide an accurate, well-developed explanation and analysis of how your choice changed American society.

Follow the steps below for each part of the answer.

STEP 1 Choose one industry and relate it to the question.	**Example** One industry which changed America in the period 1920–29 was the automobile industry.
STEP 2a Explain and analyse one way it affected American society.	**Example** One way it changed America was the way it pioneered mass-production methods. Workers had to fit into the production process and worked under great pressure, having to keep up with the pace of the assembly line.
STEP 2b Explain and analyse another way.	**Example** A second way was how it changed where Americans lived. Middle-class Americans went to live in the suburbs and travelled into town to work.
STEP 2c Explain and analyse another way.	**Example** A third way was how it changed social life. Town dwellers could take a trip to the country or to the seaside — country people had the opportunity of a trip to the city to shop. Motels, roadside 'fast-food' restaurants and drive-in movies were built, and motor racing became a popular sport.

▲ The Joy loading machine (1917) replaced hand-loading of coal into the wagons (which at that time employed more than half the workforce). The arms at the front gathered up the coal onto the conveyor belt.

Problems behind the prosperity

Whilst it is very easy to look at the huge increases in things like car production and get the impression of an economy which was booming in the 1920s, in fact there were a number of ways in which the US economy was in serious trouble.

Decline in the 'old industries'

Spectacular advances in the Electrical and oil-based Chemicals industries (see pages 72 and 73) were not good news for the 'old industries' – coal, textiles and railways – which had prospered up to the First World War.

Coal

The war years had been a time of great prosperity for the coal industry, and in 1919 the miners won a 14 per cent pay rise. After the war, however, oil began to replace coal as a source of power, and demand from the railroads also fell. The result was overproduction of coal, and the price of coal fell. This in turn hit profits and led to decline. Coal production – which had reached 657 million tonnes in 1920 – stood at just 536 million tonnes in 1929.

Jobs in mining were hit by this fall in demand, but also by mechanisation – particularly the Joy loading machine, electrically-powered mechanical cutters and underground locomotives.

The number of coal miners – nearly 700,000 in 1919, had fallen to 600,000 by 1929, and 450,000 by 1939. By 1929, a miner's wage was barely a third of the average national wage.

The industry also suffered from poor industrial relations. In 1921, an armed band of 10,000 West Virginia coal workers fought the so-called 'Battle of Blair Mountain' with 250 police and a private army of some 2,000 armed coal company guards.

Textiles

The traditional cotton mills found themselves facing competition from rayon, and falling demand because the new skimpy flapper's fashions used less cloth. In response, to reduce costs, and because most workers in the South did not belong to trade unions, the Southern manufacturers were able to make their workers tend more machines (this was known as 'the stretchout').

This led to overproduction, and – unable to compete – the textiles mills of the north failed. Instead of modernising, firms simply closed down. This then in turn caused a general recession. The number of textiles workers fell from 450,000 in 1920 to 372,000 in 1930, and there was widespread industrial unrest in 1929, although the strikes were uncoordinated and easily defeated.

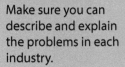

Revision tip ↻

Make sure you can describe and explain the problems in each industry.

Problems in agriculture

In the 1920s, the US government encouraged farmers to modernise their methods, and to introduce machines such as the tractor and the combine harvester, and better breeds and seeds.

The result was overproduction, which lowered prices and profits. The price of wheat, $80 a tonne during the First World War, fell to $35–40 a tonne during the 1920s.

> **Source A** US Secretary of Agriculture Henry C Wallace, writing in 1924:
>
> In times such as these the problems of farm management are reduced to the simplest terms: Produce as much as you can and as cheaply as you can of what you can produce best; spend as little as you can; do without everything you can; work as hard as you can; make your wife and your children work as hard as they can.

Government policies made the situation worse. Prohibition (see page 58) destroyed the brewing industry, a major market for wheat and barley. High tariffs (see page 71) on goods coming from Europe had provoked European countries to retaliate by imposing high tariffs on American wheat, which hit exports.

Farming was also hit by disease. Cotton-growing was plagued by the boll-weevil, and the curly-top virus destroyed the sugar-beet industry.

Congress tried a number of times in the 1920s to pass a Farm Relief Bill, which would have helped farmers by giving them a better price for their produce. However, President Coolidge (who believed in *laissez faire*) vetoed it.

As a result, between 1920 and 1932, agriculture suffered greatly. One in four farms was sold (half a million farmers lost their farms in 1929 alone). Many farmers migrated to urban areas – the number of agricultural workers fell from 27 per cent to 21 per cent of the working population.

Most rural workers did not prosper in the 1920s: farm wages were only a third of industrial workers' wages, and sharecroppers (see page 47) suffered especially.

Revision tip

You could be asked about any problem (such as overproduction, poor industrial relations or government policies) – not just mechanisation. So make sure you can answer questions based on any 'problem behind the prosperity'.

Activities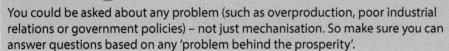

1 What is mechanisation?
2 How did mechanisation lead to overproduction?
3 Explain how overproduction harmed the older industries such as coal and textiles in America in the 1920s.

The unequal distribution of wealth

There were many groups in society that did not prosper in the 1920s.

▶ Since so much of the economic growth was due to mechanisation, the boom did not bring full employment and there were two million people unemployed throughout the 1920s. Welfare benefits were limited, so these people and their families lived in poverty.

▶ As the old industries struggled (pages 76–77), wages fell in agriculture, coal and textiles. There was particular poverty in rural areas, where less than a tenth of houses had electricity or running water.

▶ Most Black Americans worked as agricultural labourers and sharecroppers in the south, so they experienced this deprivation; one million lost their jobs in the 1920s. Black Americans in the north fared little better. They suffered discrimination (in low-paying, menial jobs). New York's Black Harlem district was severely overcrowded and residents struggled to make ends meet.

▶ Native Americans lived in poverty and repression (see pages 56–57).

In 1929, therefore, 60 per cent of Americans lived below the poverty line (earning $5 a day or less).

By contrast, meanwhile, government tax and industrial policies (see page 71) meant that the super-rich flourished. The number of millionaires quintupled from 7,000 to 35,000. By the end of the decade, the top five per cent of the population owned one-third of the wealth.

This unequal distribution of wealth was hugely damaging to the economy, because it meant that the people who had this excess money had little to do but save it, whilst those who would have spent it did not have any. Towards the end of the decade, therefore, demand began to decline and the US economy ceased to be self-generating (see page 71: the Cycle of Prosperity).

Overproduction and underconsumption

Many historians agree that the main problems in the American economy by the end of the 1920s were overproduction (which flooded the market and reduced prices and therefore profits) and underconsumption (which reduced sales and therefore profits).

By the end of the 1920s, therefore, the American economy was in trouble. The boom began to slow down. The construction industry stopped growing in 1926. In 1929, car sales slowed and sales of consumer goods fell (despite $3 billion having been spent on advertising).

There would not have been so much of a problem if American firms had been able to export their products overseas. But European industry had recovered after the First World War (helped by US loans) and was competing with US firms. And, meanwhile, other countries had retaliated against high US tariffs by raising their own tariffs – which made it more difficult for American firms to export. This in turn, therefore, increased oversupply at home, and further reduced prices and profits.

Activities

1 What is meant by 'unequal distribution of wealth'?
2 What was underconsumption?
3 Create a spider diagram showing all the ways in which government policy and actions affected the economy.
4 Why did some groups in society not prosper in the 1920s?

Practice questions

1 Describe two ways in which problems in agriculture contributed to the economic problems of the 1920s.
2 'The biggest problem for the 'older industries' in the 1920s was overproduction'. Do you agree? Explain your answer.

Revision tip

Note that, where it says 'some groups' in Activity 4, you need to be able also to write an answer for ANY specific group (such as black Americans, unemployed people, coal miners, textile workers and workers in rural areas).

This page provides guidance on how to answer question 4 in the exam.

Question 4

Why did American industry face problems in the 1920s? **[8]**

Guidance

You have 10 minutes to complete this answer, so that means quite a lot of writing! You must be able to outline problems facing American industry, describe the types of problems, and analyse clearly the impact on American industry. Your answer needs to be well informed, and provide an accurate, well-developed explanation and analysis of the impact.

Follow the steps below for each part of the answer.

STEP 1
Start with an introductory sentence stating the whole question.

Example
There were many reasons why American industry faced problems in the 1920s.

STEP 2a
Take a point, and explain the impact on American industry.

Example
One reason was over production: because the supply of goods was greater than demand, prices fell. This led to falling profits, and mines and factories failed. The number of miners fell from 700,000 in 1919 to 450,000 in 1929.

STEP 2b
Repeat for another point.

Example
Another reason was poor industrial relations. In 1921, 10,000 West Virginia coal workers fought the 'Battle of Blair Mountain' with the police and a private army of coal company guards; this led to many strikes on the textiles industry. This reduced productivity.

STEP 2c
Repeat for a third point.

Example
Government tariffs also caused problems. Although these helped American industry at first, other countries then raised their own tariffs — which made it more difficult for American firms to export. This in turn increased over-supply and further reduced prices and profits in the USA.

STEP 2d
Repeat for a fourth point.

Example
Another reason was the unequal distribution of wealth. By 1929 the top five per cent of the population owned one third of the wealth. The increasing number of millionaires had little to do with their money but save it, whilst those who would have spent it did not have any.

The Wall Street Crash of October 1929

The basic idea of shares is that the investors buy 'shares' of the firm. The firm gets the money to use to develop its business, and in return it gives a yearly share of the profits (called a 'dividend') to its shareholders.

Later, however, some of the shareholders might decide to sell their shares on the Stock Exchange. If the firm is doing well and delivering a good dividend, they might find that those shares are popular, and they can sell them for more than they bought them and thus make a profit.

As a result, some people, therefore, buy shares, not to invest in the firm and get the dividends, but hoping to try to sell at a profit later. These people are called 'speculators'.

In the United States, between 1924 and 1929, the economy was booming, firms were growing, confidence was high and the price of shares on the New York Stock Exchange on Wall Street rose by 500 per cent.

Causes of the Crash

People came to believe prices would go on rising forever, and they began to take greater risks in buying shares. Many people borrowed money to buy shares, hoping to pay back the loan with the profit they made on the sale when the price of their shares went up. American banks were so confident in the market that they were prepared to lend speculators as much as 90 per cent of the share value to buy the shares (this was called 'buying on the margin').

As a result, share prices rose far beyond the value of the firms they represented – what was causing prices to rise was not the success of the firms, but the overconfidence of speculators.

There were other problems in the financial markets which suffered corruption and 'insider trading' (where businessmen use confidential information to buy or sell shares before anybody else finds out). Some firms were total frauds – for example a South American mining company which did not exist.

Behind it all lay the reckless willingness of the banks to lend their customers' savings to speculators. By 1929 there were 600,000 people speculating in shares – Americans borrowed $9 billion for speculating in 1929.

Some people warned that the Stock Exchange was 'overheating'. In 1928, some economists said that the market could not last for ever and predicted a crash. They were criticised for damaging confidence and ignored. If anything, the speculation became even wilder.

▲ A depiction of the Wall Street Crash in an Italian newspaper. What impression of the event is the artist trying to convey?

Events of the Crash

In March 1929, share prices fell steeply and investors began to panic. However, Charles Mitchell, President of National Citibank – nicknamed 'Sunshine Charlie' because of his confidence that everything would be fine – offered to lend $25 million more to speculators so they could continue to buy shares. This not only prevented a crash, it bolstered confidence that any stock market problems were solvable and encouraged even wilder speculation.

In early September, there were repeated warnings of a crash and prices began to fall again. The more prices fell, the more confidence fell, so people wanted to sell even more, and so prices fell faster.

▲ Share prices on the New York Stock Exchange, 1920–1933.

Company	3 Mar 1928	3 Sept 1928	3 Sept 1929	13 Nov 1929
Montgomery Ward (retailer)	132	466	137	49
Union Carbide (industrial chemicals)	145	413	137	59
New York Central Railroad Co.	160	256	256	160
Anaconda Copper Mining Co.	54	162	131	70
Westinghouse (generators, electrical goods)	91	313	289	102

Table 1 Share prices (in dollars) of leading US companies, 1928–1929.

The Wall Street Crash

Thursday 24 October ('Black Thursday')	Nearly 13 million shares were sold; nobody wanted to buy when prices were falling, so prices crashed.
Friday 25 October	A group of bankers spent nearly $250 million buying shares; they hoped thereby to restore confidence, as they had in March (see above).
Monday 28 October	Nine million shares were sold at falling prices
Tuesday 29 October	Shareholders sold 6 million shares in a panic for anything they could get.
November	Share prices continued to fall until mid-November.

Revision tip

Make sure that you can explain the causes of the Wall Street Crash.

Activities

1 What are shares and dividends?
2 Discuss why the Crash occurred so that you are completely sure you understand, then present your ideas in different ways:
   - a wall chart – for example a spider diagram, flow diagram or Venn diagram
   - a cartoon
3 Use your presentation to show how the different factors causing the Crash (speculators, borrowing on the margin, frauds, corruption, overheating, bank lending, economists' predictions) were linked to each other.
4 Looking at Table 1 and the graph, explain to a partner what the figures show about:
   a individual companies
   b the stock market.

The immediate effects of the Crash

First of all, of course, the Crash ruined the speculators; shareholders lost $8 billion in one day on 29 October.

Was that such a disaster? There were only 600,000 speculators in a population of 122 million and only 15 per cent of households held any shares at all.

However, the Crash created a ripple of economic effects which ended up creating a world-wide depression which caused untold human misery (see Chapter 7).

Spreading effects: the banks

You will remember that much of the speculation in shares had been financed with $9 billion of money lent by the banks. So, when the speculators went bankrupt and failed to pay back their loans, many banks went bankrupt too – 659 in 1929; 1,352 in 1930; 2,294 in 1931.

By 1933, 5,000 American banks had failed. When the Bank of the United States went bankrupt, 400,000 depositors lost their money. In this way, the fall in share prices translated into massive human misery.

Spreading effects: the economy

People do not respond to a financial crisis by spending more. They stop spending. Sales of essentials – food, gasoline and tobacco – did not fall by so much (people could not live without them), but sales of things that people could do without plummeted.

- In the years 1929–33 sales of new cars dropped by 75 per cent (so that automobile companies – which had made a $413 million profit in 1929 – lost $191 million in 1932).
- 'Durable' goods (roads, iron and steel) suffered a huge decline; building contracts fell by 90 per cent, 1929–33.
- Department store sales fell by 50 per cent in the same period.

Source A Part of a BBC radio interview with American film-maker Roger Graef (2008). There were 23,000 suicides in 1932 alone.

My grandfather was in insurance. He had investments that all went south and he committed suicide by jumping off a roof . . .

My grandfather was not a captain of industry . . . He was a sad man who was trying to make his way, support his family, [and] had invested in Wall Street with the hope and belief that that was going to do what he wanted to do which was create a safe and better future for his children.

My father always regarded his father in a way that was so contemptuous [disrespectful] of him . . . Suddenly when his father committed suicide he was left having to look after his mother . . . That was part of what he resented about the suicide.

△ A photograph showing a man trying to sell his car, 1929.

The Cycle of Depression

This would have been disastrous enough if the American economy had been healthy but – as you saw on pages 76-78 – the US economy was already showing signs of overproduction and contraction. Firms, faced by falling sales, closed down factories and laid off workers. In this way, the 'cycle of prosperity' which you learned about on page 71 was replaced by the 'cycle of depression' (see diagram), where falling demand created reductions in production, which increased unemployment, which decreased the amount of money available and reduced demand further.

The government made things worse

You will study in Chapter 7 how the government's policies of 'rugged individualism' and laissez faire led to huge human suffering, but its lack of economic understanding also helped to make the country's economic problems worse.

1 The US Federal Reserve ('the Fed') raised interest rates; it thought it was protecting the nation's finances, but all it did was stop borrowing and make it more difficult for firms to survive.

2 Also, the government held onto the 'Gold Standard' – the formula which tied the amount of money in circulation to the amount of gold in the Fed. This actually, by restricting the amount of money in people's pockets, stopped them spending and worsened the depression.

3 Worst of all, in 1930, the government passed the *Hawley–Smoot Act* which increased tariffs even further. The government thought it was protecting American industry. In the event, however, 60 countries passed harsh tariffs in response, world trade slumped and US exporters (especially farmers) were ruined.

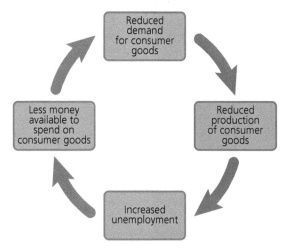

▲ The 'cycle of depression'.

The end of confidence

Above all, the Crash damaged America psychologically. 'People walked round like zombies,' remembered one businessman. The confidence of the boom had gone forever; people had learned to be careful. But when you want people to buy products to get the economy going again, that carefulness is the very thing that stops growth.

Spreading effects: the world

By 1931, the crisis had crossed to Europe. Faced with financial problems at home, American banks began calling in their huge international loans (especially to Germany), which caused bank bankruptcies and financial crises in Europe. Europeans stopped buying too: international trade fell by 40 per cent, 1929–32. This damaged American exports and made the position of American companies even worse.

Source B International Loans by American Banks

International Loans by American Banks			
$_millions	1924	1928	1929
Europe	527	598	142
Asia	100	137	58
Latin America	191	331	176

Activities

1 The photograph and Source A describe a 'human side' to the results of the Crash which is different from the facts and figures in the text. Which is more useful for historians? Explain your answer.
2 Define the term 'cycle of depression'.
3 What was the Hawley–Smoot Act?

Practice questions

1 Explain how the Crash developed into the Great Depression.
2 Describe **two** ways the American economy was affected in the years following the crash.

The effects on industry, agriculture and people's lives

Closures and unemployment

As you saw in Chapter 6, the Wall Street Crash of 1929 spilled over into the economy and, in a series of linked effects, caused a worldwide depression.

Banks – the first victims of the Crash – struggled to recover. By the end of the 1930s, some 10,000 banks had failed (with all that meant for the human misery of their depositors). There were 'runs on the banks' (where everybody tried to get out their money, fearing that the banks were about to go bankrupt) in 1930, 1931 (twice) and 1932. In March 1933, the government was forced to declare a four-day 'Bank Holiday', during which government inspectors looked at each bank's financial situation and only allowed it to open for trading if it was financially stable. The fact that the entire banking industry had to be, in effect, turned off and re-booted, shows how broken it was.

▶ **American industry** was also performing very poorly. Industrial production in the United States fell by 46 per cent and more than 100,000 businesses shut down in the period 1929–32. The number of unemployed rose to almost 13 million (a quarter of the working population) in 1933; women and unskilled workers were very badly affected, and up to three-quarters of black workers were unemployed in some southern towns. Average wages fell by 60 per cent.

▶ **The 'old industries'** were particularly badly hit. Textiles production fell by 16 per cent, cement by 62 per cent, automobiles by 64 per cent, iron and steel production fell by 59 per cent. In the steel town of Cleveland, half the workers were unemployed; in nearby Toledo, 80 per cent of the working-age population were unemployed.

Effects on people's lives

The 'new industries'

It was not 'all-doom-and-gloom', because some areas of the American economy continued to thrive throughout the period.

Prices roughly halved, so people in a job were better off during the Depression. The 'new industries' (electrical goods, chemicals) continued to expand. Sales of refrigerators grew, even in the worst of the Depression in 1929–33, and most people who bought them did so on credit.

So it is not true that the economy ground to a halt. One of the features of the economy was that, whilst the 'old industries' closed down and went into decline, the 'new industries' invested and innovated so that they could cut costs and reduce prices. The 1930s saw 'nylons', the first TV channels, popular air travel and the first beer cans.

Poverty and hunger

For millions of people, however, the Great Depression was a disaster. The Republican government believed in 'rugged individualism' and America had only a very limited welfare system, which the poverty of the Depression overwhelmed. In June 1932, for example, the city of Philadelphia – which was handing out weekly groceries ($5 for a family of six) to 57,000 families – declared that the money had run out, and stopped all relief for ten weeks.

So the economic depression created poverty. Soup kitchens (one was provided by Al Capone), long 'breadlines' of people waiting for a food parcel, and men wearing placards begging for a job, became common features of American towns.

In 1931, 45 people in New York starved to death and in the next two years there were hunger marches all over the United States. The marchers were met with force. In March 1932, a peaceful march of 5,000 people in Detroit was attacked by police and security guards from the Ford Automobile Company (three marchers were killed). In 1933, a march in Seattle was met by an army of 700 vigilantes, armed with machine guns.

Hoovervilles

Hoovervilles were shanty towns, built of packing boxes and corrugated iron sheets, named after President Hoover (1929–33), whom people blamed for their situation (see page 90). There were hundreds of Hoovervilles. The Hooverville in Seattle (some 500 shacks with up to 1,200 residents) lasted from 1932 to 1941.

Residents of the Hoovervilles worked together to provide support services which the government did not. The Hooverville in St Louis had 600 shacks, four churches, a labourer (called Gus Smith) whom they elected as 'mayor' and a soup kitchen called the *Welcome Inn* which fed 4,000 people a day.

It is worth noting that the Hoovervilles were the top end of the homelessness market – the residents, mainly single men, bought and sold the tiny shacks. Millions of other homeless people had to sleep rough.

The Bonus Army

In 1924, Congress had voted to give every soldier who fought in the First World War a bonus based on length of service, up to a maximum of $625, due to be paid in 1944.

Faced with unemployment, many former soldiers asked to receive their bonus immediately, and in January 1932 a 'Bonus Army' of 25,000 men marched on Washington. They set up a Hooverville, military-style, with strict hygiene rules and a daily parade.

On 28 July, President Hoover sent in 600 troops, who attacked with fixed bayonets, supported by six tanks. At first the veterans, thinking the soldiers were marching in support of them, cheered; then they fled. In the day's fighting, two veterans were killed, a baby died from gas inhalation and 54 people were injured.

The veterans were given their bonuses in 1936.

> **Activities**
>
> 1 What were Hoovervilles?
> 2 What does the photograph below tell you about:
>   ● Hoovervilles
>   ● the government's attitude to protest
>   ● the events of July 1932?

▼ US Soldiers burn the Bonus Army's Hooverville in Washington, July 1932 – Senator Hiram Johnson called it 'one of the blackest pages in our history'. Notice the Capitol in the background. Why do you think Hoover was so hostile to this Hooverville?

Effects of tariffs and overproduction

Agriculture (see page 77) struggled during the 1920s as a result of overproduction, prohibition, tariffs and disease.

The hard times of 1929–33, therefore, caused a collapse. The price of wheat dropped to $14 a tonne – it was cheaper to burn the wheat as fuel than transport it to market. Cotton prices fell by 70 per cent.

This would have been disastrous enough, but many farmers, who were being encouraged to modernise and mechanise, had taken out large loans. When the Wall Street Crash occurred in 1929, some farmers who had bought shares were ruined. In the crisis that followed, so many rural banks failed that some historians believe that this financial crisis in farming caused the Depression, not the other way round.

The government made things worse:

▶ It raised tariffs to record levels in 1930. Other countries responded by raising their tariffs, which reduced American exports and made the overproduction problem worse.

▶ It raised interest rates – the rate paid by farmers on a loan, which had been about 6 per cent in 1929, had risen to 36 per cent in 1931.

Hardships of farmers and sharecroppers

Many farmers went bankrupt; 750,000 farms were foreclosed in 1930–35, and a tenth of all farms were sold in the one year, 1933–34. Farmer-owners began to give way to large 'industrial' farms with paid labourers.

Sharecroppers (see page 47), who lived in debt, were particularly hard-hit, especially in the 'cotton belt' states of Mississippi, Alabama and Georgia. A further pressure black sharecroppers faced in these states was white workers pressurising the landowners to give them the work instead. Landowners reduced their rates to force black sharecroppers off the land and into the factories. In Georgia, more than half of black farmers lost their land.

Farming problems in the Midwest

Nature made things worse for the farmers on the Great Plains of the Midwest. The 1930s saw record summer temperatures and the worst drought in 300 years. In 1935, the one year it did rain, it rained at harvest time and ruined the crop. Pests thrived and bred in the dry conditions – there was a plague of chinch bugs in 1933 and a plague of grasshoppers in 1936. It was said that the only thing a farm could raise was weeds.

During the hard times of the 1920s, farmers in the Midwest had been tempted to overcrop the fields – trying to counter the low prices by growing more. As a result, in many places, the soil had been robbed of nutrients. In the dry drought conditions, when the crops failed, this created huge dust storms. During 'the Dust Bowl' of 1933–36, clouds of dust occasionally blew 1,500 miles to New York. On 'Black Sunday' in Oklahoma, 14 April 1935, 300 million tonnes of topsoil were whipped up by winds of 100mph, leaving dead cattle, at least one person blinded, blocked wells and everything covered in a thick layer of dust.

Many people in these areas simply packed up and left. One modern writer refers to them as 'refugees', as though they were fleeing a war.

▶ A Colorado dust storm in the 1930s. What were the possible psychological effects of a storm like this?

The impact and hardships of the Great Depression

Okies and hobos

Those who stayed on their farms often lived in grinding poverty on what they could grow on the farm. Many farmers and labourers, however, were driven off the land.

Many families migrated to California to do back-breaking work on the fruit farms there. They were called 'Okies' because many of them came from Oklahoma. They lived in filthy shanty towns by irrigation ditches, which they used for their sewage, and for drinking water. Without a free health service, many of them died from disease.

Others became hobos, seeking work from farm to farm by 'padding the hoof' (walking) or 'riding the rails' (jumping into a wagon on a slow-moving train). It is estimated that there were one and a half million hobos in the 1930s, including 200,000 children.

Hobos developed their own culture and language. In work, they might live in a shared 'bunkhouse' (like George and Lennie in John Steinbeck's 1937 novel *Of Mice and Men*), but at other times they slept in a 'flophouse' (cheap hotel), or 'with the moon', with nothing but a 'tokay blanket' (alcohol) to keep them warm.

Source A Wallace Farmer, an American who grew up on a farm in Missouri in the 1930s, remembered:

I didn't know there was any other way but to be hard up all the time.

Source B The novel by John Steinbeck, *The Grapes of Wrath* (1939) described the lives of the Okies.

Tom said, 'Okie? What's that?'

'Well, Okie use' ta mean you was from Oklahoma. Now it means you're a dirty son-of-a-b*tch. Okie means you're scum. Don't mean nothing itself, it's the way they say it ... I hear there's three hunderd thousan' of our people there – an' livin' like hogs ...

'You ain't gonna get no steady work. Gonna scrabble for your dinner ever' day ...'

▲ *Towards Los Angeles*, a photograph taken in 1937. What is the message of this photograph?

The farmers fight back

Some farmers tried to resist the developments.

▶ During the Iowa Farm War of 1932, farmers tried to force up prices by declaring a 'farmers' holiday', when farmers would sell nothing to drive up prices. Led by a union activist called Milo Reno, they built road blocks to try to prevent food reaching the towns and poured milk into ditches.

▶ Farmers in Nebraska had another idea – 'Penny Auctions'. In 1931, they turned up at a foreclosure auction of a local farmer. The first bid was for 5 cents. Nobody else was allowed to bid and the auction raised $5.35 in total. The state government was forced to stop foreclosure auctions in the state.

▶ In 1931, Alabama sharecroppers formed the communist Croppers and Farm Workers Union (CFWU), which demanded a better rate for cotton. It had 800 members, but its meetings were attacked by police, and white mobs attacked black neighbourhoods in retaliation.

In other places, the state governments tried to persuade farmers to 'Live at Home'. Governor Max Gardner was horrified that North Carolina, a rural state, imported large amounts of food. He tried to reduce the amount of land given over to tobacco and cotton by encouraging farmers to grow their own food on their farms.

▲ A photograph of a camp for fruit labourers in California.

▲ *California Agriculture* – a fresco by American artist Maxine Albro (1934).

Activities

1 What was the Dust Bowl?
2 What is meant by foreclosure?
3 Compare the illustrations on this page to Source B on page 87. Which better reflects the hopes of the Okies, and which reflects the reality of their lives?
4 Create a spider diagram of all the ways in which the Great Depression affected life in rural America from 1929–33.

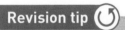
Revision tip

Always begin thinking about a 'Do you agree' question by making a list of all the other possible answers. For example, in answering 'The collapse of business was the most serious effect of the Great Depression. Do you agree?', you could list bank failures, agriculture, poverty, Hoovervilles, the Bonus Army, riots and so on, which will then allow you to decide if the collapse of business was the most serious effect.

Republican beliefs and policies

Presidents Harding (1921–23), Coolidge (1923–29) and Hoover (1929–33) were all Republicans. They believed in:

▶ laissez faire (leaving the economy alone)

▶ 'rugged individualism' (self-reliance)

▶ 'voluntarism' (i.e. that helping the poor was a task for charity, not for government).

These principles were maybe not so damaging when the economy was booming but – as you have seen – when the economy fell into the Great Depression, they plunged people into poverty, homelessness and starvation.

President Hoover and the Great Depression

It is not true that Hoover did nothing to try to end the Depression. However, many historians have claimed that the actions he took not only failed, but actually made things worse.

The impact and effectiveness of Hoover's policies and actions

In 1929, Hoover set up the **Federal Farm Board**, with a fund of $500 million, to support farm prices by buying surplus wheat and cotton.

Effect: this failed because there were no plans to reduce production – so farmers simply produced even more, and the fund ran out.

Hoover refused to abandon the **gold standard**.

Effect: this restricted the money supply and made the Depression worse (see page 83).

Hoover increased **interest rates**.

Effect: this made borrowing more expensive and made the Depression worse (see page 86).

In 1930, Hoover introduced the **Hawley-Smoot Act**, which set a tariff of 60 per cent on 3,200 imported products. This reduced imports by two thirds.

Effect: in return, 60 countries imposed tariffs on American products, which reduced America's exports by 61 per cent. Farming and industries which depended on exports were hit the hardest.

In 1931 Hoover set up the **President's Organization on Unemployment Relief (POUR)**. It advised charities how to help the unemployed, and encouraged fund-raising.

Effect: the amount of charity donations almost doubled in 1931. However, because the government did not give the charities any financial help, they were overwhelmed by the huge demand, and the programme ended in 1932.

▲ Herbert Hoover, president of the USA from 1929 to 1933.

In 1932, the government offered $300 million in loans to the states to provide **unemployment pay**.

Effect: this failed because the states did not want to increase their debt by borrowing more money from the government.

In March 1932, Hoover signed the **Norris-La Guardia Act**, allowing strikes and banning "yellow dog" contracts (which stopped workers joining a Union).

Effect: it had little effect in the Depression, as few workers felt in a strong enough position to insist on their rights.

Also in 1932, Hoover set up the **Reconstruction Finance Corporation (RFC)**, which offered $2 billion in loans to banks and companies which were struggling. He also spent $1.3 billion for road-building, public buildings and the Hoover Dam. In Hoover's four years of office he started more **public work schemes** than in the previous 40.

Effect: in some ways these policies anticipated the 'New Deal' of the 1930s (see 'The 1932 Presidential election' on page 90), but they were not enough to end the Depression.

Hoover's unpopularity

As the Depression continued, Hoover became increasingly hated.

As a Republican, Hoover believed in a 'balanced budget', so he believed he had to increase taxes to pay for his public works. He suggested two ways, and both made him hugely unpopular:

▶ The **Revenue Act** (1932) introduced a progressive table of income tax, rising to 63 per cent for people on incomes of more than $1 million a year. This made him hugely unpopular with the rich, who previously had only paid 25 per cent.

▶ A **Sales Tax**. This caused great anger amongst the poor, because a tax on purchases hits the incomes of the poor relatively more than the rich. Hoover eventually withdrew the idea … but not before the damage to his reputation had been done.

The Democratic Party was very successful in blaming Hoover for the Depression, with slogans such as 'In Hoover we trusted, now we are busted'. Hoovervilles (see page 85) were named after him, but the Democrats invented a whole series of 'Hoover' terms which further ruined his reputation: for example, 'Hoover blanket' (newspaper used as blanketing), 'Hoover leather' (cardboard used to cover a hole in a shoe) and 'Hoover stew' (soup from the soup kitchens). Meanwhile, the attack on the Bonus Army in 1932 (see page 85) was portrayed as a cowardly attack on war heroes.

PHIA RECORD, FRIDAY, MARCH 3, 1933

FINIS.

▲ This cartoon of 1933 shows Roosevelt 'putting out the trash' of the Hoover administration – including his broken promises.

The 1932 Presidential election

During the 1932 elections, cinemas refused to show Hoover's picture because people booed, and his campaign train was pelted with eggs. The Secret Service had to stop a number of attempts to assassinate Hoover, including a suicide bomber.

By contrast, Hoover's opponent Franklin D. Roosevelt was immensely popular. As Governor of New York State, Roosevelt had tried many ideas to combat the Depression. He caught the public mood by blaming the bankers and the rich (which appealed to poor people) and, perhaps most importantly of all, he promised 'a New Deal for the American people' (including public works programmes, welfare, support for industry and agriculture, and banking reform) which offered people a hope for the future.

In the election of 1932, Roosevelt won by a landslide, winning 23 million votes (42 states) against Hoover's 16 million votes (six states).

The history of Roosevelt's New Deal is a story beyond this textbook, but it was a salvation for many poor Americans:

Source C Letter from an old man and his wife to President Roosevelt, summer 1933.

Dear Mr. President: This is just to tell you that everything is all right now. The man you sent found our house all right, and we went down to the bank with him and the mortgage can go on for a while longer. You remember I wrote you about losing the furniture too. Well, your man got it back for us. I never heard of a President like you.

Practice question

1 Why were the economic policies of Republican presidents significant during the 1920s in America?

2 'The Great Depression had more impact on the lives of workers than on the lives of farmers in the period 1929-1933'. Do you agree? Explain your answer.

Activities

1 Describe two ways Hoover's policies harmed people during the Depression.

2 Create two spider diagrams to show all the reasons why Hoover was unpopular, and all the reasons Roosevelt was popular.

3 Use the two diagrams to explain why Roosevelt won the 1932 election.

This page provides guidance on how to answer question 5 in the exam.

Question 5

'The Great Depression had more impact on the lives of workers than on the lives of farmers in the period 1929-1933'. Do you agree? Explain your answer. [16]

Guidance

You should be looking to spend about 20 minutes on this question. This is the longest answer that you have to provide in this section of the examination. It needs to be twice the length of your answer for Question 4. The question type is different too; you are being presented with a statement and are asked to consider whether or not you agree with it. To be able to get the highest marks for your answer you will need to show that you have considered the arguments for and against the statement – before coming to a judgement which is supported by appropriate historical evidence. You can either agree or disagree with the statement – just make sure that the evidence is there to support what you say!

Follow the steps below for each part of the answer.

STEP 1
Introduce the first idea, stating the whole question.

Example
There is a strong case to be made for the idea that the Great Depression had more impact on the lives of workers, from 1929 to 1933.

STEP 2a
Explain how this is so, supporting your ideas with facts and reasoning. For this question, introduce each way the Great Depression had an impact on the lives of workers, then explain how they did this.

Example
The Great Depression affected the lives of workers in several ways. For example, thousands of factories had to close down ... This meant that the millions of people now unemployed...

STEP 2b
Measure how significant this is and explain why you think this. Remember to support your explanation with facts. For example, you could say that there was no benefit or welfare for the newly unemployed and many of them became homeless because they could not pay their mortgages.

Example
The impact of the Great Depression on workers was <very/mildly/not very> powerful because ... This is shown by ...

STEP 3
Introduce the opposing idea, again stating the whole question.

Example
However, there is a strong case to be made for the idea that the Great Depression had more of an impact on farmers.

STEP 4a
Explain how this is so, supporting your ideas with facts and reasoning.

Example
For example, the problems caused by over-production and under-consumption affected farmers by ... Additionally, the Hawley-Smoot Act of 1930 meant that ...

STEP 4b
Measure how significant this is and explain why you think this. Remember to support your explanation with facts. For example, you could say that many farmers went bankrupt partly because the government raised interest rates on loans, from around 6 per cent in 1929 to 36 per cent in 1931.

Example
The impact on farmers was <very/mildly/not at all> powerful because ... This is shown by ...

STEP 5
Make a justified judgement and relate it back to the question.

Example
Therefore, we can see that the impact of the Great Depression <was/was not> greater on the lives of workers rather than farmers.

Option 1 Changing Relations: Northern Ireland and its Neighbours, 1920–49

This option focuses on how relationships between Northern Ireland and its neighbours changed and developed between 1920 and 1949.

During this period the relationship between both parts of the newly-partitioned island of Ireland and Great Britain both changed and matured. At the same time, the lives of those citizens living north or south of the newly-created border were affected by how their respective governments dealt with the main issues that they faced – political, economic and diplomatic.

Particular emphasis is placed on how both parts of the island of Ireland dealt with the social, economic and military impacts of the Second World War.

Towards the end of this period, we focus on the post-war period, looking in particular at the social and diplomatic 'earthquakes' of the years 1945–1949 – not least the fall-out surrounding the creation of the Republic of Ireland. This option examines the following key areas of content:

▶ The partitioning of Ireland

▶ From Irish Free State to Éire

▶ The Economic War

▶ Northern Ireland and World War II

▶ Éire's neutrality and its impact on relationships during the war

▶ German attacks and their impact on Britain, Northern Ireland and Éire

▶ Life in post-war Northern Ireland and Éire, 1945–49

▶ Constitutional changes and effects on relationships.

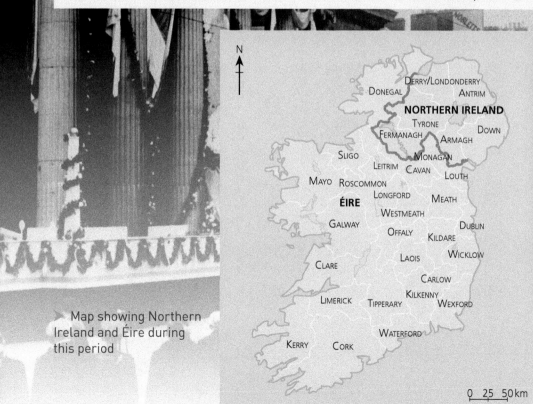

▶ Map showing Northern Ireland and Éire during this period

It is useful to know the history of Ireland's relationship with Britain, as this will help with your understanding of why Ireland was partitioned.

Introduction: Ireland before partition

Between 1801 and 1920, Ireland was ruled by Britain from Westminster. For much of that time, Ireland's nationalist politicians sought the establishment of a home rule Parliament in Dublin. This demand was strongly opposed by Ireland's unionist population, most of whom lived in the north-eastern part of the island.

In 1912, Britain's Liberal government agreed to introduce home rule to Ireland by 1914. In the aftermath of this decision, both nationalists and unionists set up their own private armies. Their intention was to ensure that they got their way, in terms of either getting or stopping home rule. The nationalists set up the Irish Volunteers; the unionists established the Ulster Volunteer Force (UVF). Both armies imported weapons from Germany.

By mid-1914 it seemed as if civil war was about to break out between the two sides; however, with the start of the First World War in August 1914 it was agreed to postpone the introduction of home rule until the conflict had ended. Both sides agreed to send their private armies to fight for the Allies in the war, although a section of the Irish Volunteers refused to fight for Britain and remained at home.

The Easter Rising and its aftermath

Not everyone was prepared to wait for the end of the war. In April 1916, a group of republicans staged a rebellion, which came to be known as the Easter Rising, against British rule and declared Ireland a republic. While the rebellion failed, the harsh way in which the British government reacted to it – executing the leaders and imprisoning many of those involved – meant that many nationalists now demanded that Ireland be given full independence.

Nationalist leader John Redmond is portrayed in this *Punch* cartoon herding a group of pigs (representing the four provinces of Ireland) through a gate (representing Home Rule). One pig (representing the unionist part of the province of Ulster) is trying to get away.

PUNCH, OR THE LONDON CHARIVARI.—October 8, 1913.

SECOND THOUGHTS.

Mr. John Redmond. "FULL SHTEAM AHEAD! (*Aside*) I WONDHER WILL I LAVE THIS CONTRAIRY LITTLE DIVIL LOOSE, THE WAY HE'D COME BACK BY HIMSELF AFTHERWARDS?"

The partitioning of Ireland

In the December 1918 general election, Sinn Féin, led by Éamon de Valera, replaced the more moderate Irish Parliamentary Party as Ireland's largest political party. Rather than send its Members of Parliament (MPs) to Westminster, *Sinn Féin* decided to set up its own parliament in Dublin. This was known as *Dáil Éireann*. With its calls for the creation of an independent Irish Republic, the scene was now set for some sort of clash with the British government.

The conflict was not long in coming. In January 1919, the Irish Republican Army (IRA) began what became known as the Anglo-Irish War against the British forces in Ireland. The IRA had been formed from those members of the Irish Volunteers who had refused to fight in the First World War.

While the Anglo-Irish War was being fought in the south, sectarian violence – involving the revived UVF and the IRA – erupted in the northern counties. The violence was particularly fierce in the cities of Belfast and Derry/Londonderry. Westminster's response was the establishment of the mainly Protestant Ulster Special Constabulary. It had a part-time section called the B Specials who were particularly feared by Catholics. This group was the only remaining part of the three-pronged Ulster Special Constabulary, which had been established in September 1920 to help fight the IRA during the War of Independence.

◁ A painting by Irish artist Sean Keating (1889–1977) showing IRA men during the Anglo-Irish War.

Key terms of the Government of Ireland Act, 1920

While fighting this war, the British government – led by David Lloyd George – began the search for a political solution that it hoped would be acceptable to all sides. The result was the 1920 Government of Ireland Act which partitioned the island. Two new states were set up, Northern Ireland (looking after the six north-eastern counties) and Southern Ireland (governing the remaining 26 counties). Each state would have its own parliament which would have control over areas such as education, health and transport. Each parliament would be made up of two houses, a Commons and a Senate. Proportional representation would be used to ensure that the minorities in both areas would be properly represented. Westminster would keep responsibility for areas such as the crown, defence, foreign policy and taxation. Both jurisdictions would continue to send some MPs to the Westminster parliament whilst the monarch would be represented by a single Viceroy. Later, when the 1921 Treaty (see page 97) was signed, the position of Viceroy was replaced by that of Governor of Northern Ireland.

The Act also established a Council of Ireland as a way of achieving a united Ireland at some future point. Members from both the Belfast and Dublin parliaments (20 from each) would serve as members of this Council and would have the power to impose policies on areas of common concern such as fishing and trade. If both parliaments agreed, the powers of the Council could be increased, thus helping to bring about reunification.

Activities

1 What is Dáil Éireann?
2 Explain the background to the Government of Ireland Act 1920.
3 Create a spider diagram to summarise the key terms of the Government of Ireland Act.
4 What were the unionist and nationalist reactions to the Government of Ireland Act?

Reactions to the Government of Ireland Act in the north and south of Ireland

Whilst never having sought their own Home Rule parliament, the Government of Ireland Act delighted the majority of unionists, ensuring as it did that they would have control over their own affairs (Source A) and would not be subject to Dublin rule. However, the longstanding unionist leader, Sir Edward Carson, was not in favour of a home rule parliament in Belfast. He decided that the time was now right to stand down as unionist leader. Unionists lost no time in holding elections for their new parliament, winning 40 of the available 52 seats. As a result, Sir James Craig (Lord Craigavon from 1927), who had replaced Carson as unionist leader, became Northern Ireland's first Prime Minister. The new parliament was opened by King George V with great pomp in June 1921.

The creation of Northern Ireland was bitterly opposed by the majority of nationalists living there (Source B). Many of them were convinced that the provision of the Boundary Commission in the 1921 Anglo-Irish Treaty (see page 97) meant that partition would not last and so they refused to give any recognition to the new state. As a result, unionists were convinced that nationalists wanted to destroy Northern Ireland. The doubts and suspicions that were being experienced by both sides were increased by the high levels of sectarian violence in the early months of Northern Ireland's existence.

Source A Protestant attitude to the setting up of the Northern Ireland Parliament.

[they saw safety in] 'Having a parliament of our own, for we believe that once a parliament is … working well … we should fear no one, and we feel that we would then be in a position of absolute security.'

Source B The Catholic attitude to the new Northern Ireland state, as expressed by George Crolly, Parish Priest of St Matthew's, Belfast, April 1921.

This so-called northern parliament is a danger to our liberties and a barrier to the permanent solution of the Irish problem, we [nationalists] can neither give it recognition nor lend it support.

The terms of the Government of Ireland Act were also completely unacceptable to Irish Republicans, who termed it the 'Partition Act'. They wanted much more power than the Government of Ireland Act gave them and so the Anglo-Irish War went on. The only part of the Act that Republicans made use of was the election system set up to elect a parliament for Southern Ireland; instead, however, this mechanism was used to elect a second *Dáil*.

It was not until July 1921 that both sides agreed a ceasefire and began to talk about a political solution. The outcome of these negotiations was the signing, in December 1921, of the Anglo-Irish Treaty. This established the Irish Free State as a dominion of the British Commonwealth.

Although it was still not full independence, the Anglo-Irish Treaty gave Dublin more power than the Government of Ireland Act had done. In the words of Michael Collins, one of the Irish leaders who signed the Treaty, it gave Irish politicians 'freedom, not the ultimate freedom that all nations desire and develop to, but the freedom to achieve it' (Source C).

Not all of Collins' colleagues agreed however, and the Anglo-Irish Treaty divided Irish Republicans.

> **Source C** Seán MacEoin gives a supporter's view of the Treaty, December 1921.
>
> To me this treaty gives me what I and my colleagues fought for; it gives us for the first time in 700 years, the evacuation of Britain's armed forces out of Ireland.

Problem one: the continuation of strong links with the British Commonwealth

By signing the Treaty the Irish accepted that the new Irish Free State would retain links with the UK. This relationship would be symbolised by:

▶ An oath of allegiance to the British monarch, to be sworn by members of the Irish Parliament.

▶ The appointment of an official by the London government who would represent the King or Queen in the Irish Free State. This official would be given the title of Governor General.

▶ The right of citizens of the Irish Free State to appeal judgements of Irish courts to the British Privy Council.

In addition, the British also held on to three military/naval bases in the Irish Free State. These 'treaty ports' were located in Berehaven, Cobh (both in County Cork) and Lough Swilly (County Donegal).

Problem two: the confirmation of the partitioning of Ireland as introduced by the 1920 Government of Ireland Act

During the negotiations leading to the Treaty, the *Sinn Féin* delegation reluctantly accepted the partition of Ireland as a temporary price to pay for political independence. They were helped here by the British Prime Minister's promise to set up a Boundary Commission to examine the location of the border at a future date. The Irish delegation was persuaded by Lloyd George that this commission would take land from Northern Ireland and leave it too small to survive. In this way, they believed, Ireland would be united again.

This promise did not convince all Republicans. The anti-treaty members of *Sinn Féin*, led by Éamon de Valera, attacked the Treaty for its acceptance of partition (as well as for its offer of less than a fully independent republic). They argued that it meant the abandonment of half a million nationalists living inside the new state of Northern Ireland (Source D).

> **Source D** Seán T. O'Kelly provides the view of those members of *Sinn Féin* who were against the Treaty, December 1921.
>
> The two great principles for which so many have died – no partition and no control of Ireland by any foreign power – have gone by the board in this treaty.

Journalist to do?

The Butchery of Ireland.
CARTOON EXECUTED AFTER ATTENDING
REPUBLICAN GATHERING.

 A cartoon from *Dublin Opinion* suggesting that the 1921 Treaty may not be good for Ireland. The cartoon shows Michael Collins (on the left) and Arthur Griffiths (a key *Sinn Féin* leader) about to 'execute' Ireland by agreeing to the terms of the Treaty. What do you think might be represented by the 'head' of Ireland?

Activities

1 Who won the elections held for the first Northern Ireland Parliament?
2 How much power did the new Northern Ireland Parliament have?
3 How did Northern nationalists react to the establishment of Northern Ireland?
4 How did members of *Sinn Féin* react to the 1921 Treaty?
5 Explain the reasons for opposition to the Treaty under the following headings:
   • Partition   • Links with Britain

The setting up of the Irish Free State

The divisions between Republicans were so serious that a civil war was fought between the two sides from 1922 to 1923. In the end, the pro-treaty side was victorious and, under the leadership of *Cumann na nGaedheal* (the pro-treaty party), the Free State set about establishing the new state and increasing its independence from Britain, bit by bit. In doing so, the Free State was proving – as Collins suggested – that the Treaty was providing it with the 'freedom to achieve freedom'. This process ended with the passage of the 1931 Statute of Westminster, which stated that dominions were independent countries that could leave the Commonwealth without Britain's permission.

During this period, Éamon de Valera continued to lead the anti-treaty side. In 1926 he parted from *Sinn Féin* and established a new party, *Fianna Fáil*. It entered the *Dáil* in 1927 and within a year had become the official opposition party.

The Boundary Commission, 1924–25

In the end – and despite British promises – nationalists were to be disappointed with regard to the border. The Boundary Commission finally met in 1925. The delay was due to the Irish Civil War and the refusal of the Northern Ireland government to engage with the process – to the extent of refusing to appoint a representative to sit on the commission. In the end, the Boundary Commission did not lead to any change in the border as the commission chairman – Justice Richard Feetham of the South African Supreme Court – chose to interpret its role quite narrowly (Source E). Feetham decided to pay more attention to economic and geographical conditions rather than the wishes of those living close to the border. The commission's report – leaked to the press in November 1925 – actually recommended handing some of the Irish Free State's land to Northern Ireland, something that Dublin had never considered. Such an eventuality would have resulted in a political crisis in the Irish Free State.

Source E Article XII of the 1921 Treaty stated in relation to the border.

[To decide the boundary] … in accordance with the wishes of the inhabitants, so far as may be compatible with economic and geographical conditions.

Following a hastily convened meeting in London, all sides agreed to shelve the still unpublished commission report in favour of an Anglo-Irish Agreement. This stated that the border would remain unchanged from that fixed by the 1920 Government of Ireland Act. It added that the powers of the Council of Ireland, established by the 1920 Act, would pass to the Belfast parliament. At the same time, the Irish Free State was let off making the contributions to the UK's national debt that it had agreed to pay as part of the 1921 Treaty. Northern Ireland was relieved from paying any more land annuities. Craig was said to have returned home to Belfast 'happy and contented'.

From that point it became clear that partition would be permanent and nationalist MPs – realising that Northern Ireland was there to stay – finally took up their seats in the Northern Ireland Parliament. That said, few nationalists were involved in the running of the new state, whilst jobs tended to stay within the divided communities. In addition, education of young people was delivered along sectarian lines.

⋀ King George V (1865–1936) arriving to open Northern Ireland's first Parliament in June 1921.

Practice questions

1 Give one reason for the creation of the 1921 Treaty.
2 Give the name of one of the political parties set up in the Irish Free State after the Civil War.
3 Describe one reason why the failure of the Boundary Commission was so important for the future of Northern Ireland.
4 How useful is the cartoon on page 98 for an historian studying what relations were like among Irish Republicans in 1921?

Activity

Construct a timeline to show the events that took place over the partitioning of Ireland.

Revision tip ↻

There is a lot for you to understand within this section – from the establishment of partition to the failure of the Boundary Commission. Make sure you are clear about what happens at each stage and how the different parties react to each development.

Source A De Valera outlining his policy aims at a rally commemorating the 1916 Easter Rising, April 1933.

Let it be clear that we yield no willing assent [agreement] to any form or symbol that is out of keeping with Ireland's right as a sovereign nation. Let us remove these forms one by one, so that this state we control may become a republic in fact.

As you will see in this section, Éamon de Valera was instrumental in the creation of Éire.

De Valera and his role in the dismantling of the Anglo-Irish Treaty by 1937

Following a general election in March 1932, *Fianna Fáil*, with the support of the Irish Labour Party, became the Free State's government. The IRA, declared illegal by the previous government, was legalised and began to organise openly again, even attacking *Cumann na nGaedheal* members. That party responded by setting up the Army Comrades Association (ACA) which also became known as the Blueshirts. In 1933, *Cumann na nGaedheal* and the Blueshirts joined together to form a new party, *Fine Gael*.

In the end, de Valera's tolerance of the IRA did not last that long. In 1936 he responded to continuing illegal activities by IRA members by declaring the organisation illegal.

Now in power, de Valera (also serving as the Free State's Minister for External Affairs – or Foreign Minister) began to change parts of the Anglo-Irish Treaty he was most unhappy about (Source A). Bit by bit, and making use of the legal means available to him, de Valera began to remove the Free State's remaining links with Britain, as established by the 1921 Treaty.

In November 1932, the London government recalled Governor General James MacNeill. This was because *Fianna Fáil* ministers were engaged in a policy of snubbing him as he was the King's official representative. MacNeill was replaced by *Fianna Fáil* politician Domhnall O'Buachalla who, instead of being called Governor General, was titled *an seanasca* (Chief Steward). De Valera acted in other ways to undermine the position that O'Buachalla now held, and thus play down the Free State's link with the British crown. O'Buachalla's powers were limited; he never lived in the Governor General's official residence in Dublin's Phoenix Park and he undertook no public duties. O'Buachalla's only function was to sign bills passed by the *Dáil* into law.

THE BRIDGE-BREAKER.

MR. DE VALERA. "IF I CAN SHIFT THIS KEYSTONE, THAT OUGHT TO CLEAR THE WAY FOR SOMETHING DRAMATIC."

◀ Cartoon showing Éamon de Valera destroying the 'Commonwealth Bridge'. De Valera is attempting to remove some of the key elements of the 1921 Treaty (such as the Oath of Allegiance), named on the stones. What does the cartoon suggest might happen to the Commonwealth if he does so?

In May 1933, the Dublin government passed the Removal of the Oath Act, which removed the oath of allegiance that all *Dáil* members had to swear to the King. This action followed on from de Valera's victory in a snap election in January 1933. That election had been called to prove that the government had public support for the policies that it was following.

In May 1933, the Free State constitution was changed to prevent citizens appealing Irish court verdicts to the British Privy Council (as allowed for in the Treaty). In 1935 London challenged these actions before the Privy Council itself, but it ruled that the 1931 Statute of Westminster gave de Valera the power to introduce the changes that he was making. In other words, Westminster had no legal basis for objecting to what de Valera was doing.

De Valera used the December 1936 abdication crisis to pass two new laws. The Constitution (Amendment No. 27) Act removed all reference to the British monarch and the Governor General from the constitution. Through the External Relations Act, the monarch's official role within the Free State came to an end, even though in legal terms Ireland remained a member of the Commonwealth – whose symbolic head was the British monarch.

Nothing could be done to stop these proposals passing into law; earlier that same year the Irish Senate had also ceased to exist, as de Valera saw it as too keen to delay his plans to change radically the constitution of the Irish Free State.

Activities

1 Why was de Valera so opposed to the oath of allegiance?
2 Make a copy of the following table and fill it in, showing the steps de Valera took to weaken the terms of the 1921 Treaty.

Area	Date	Action taken	Result
Oath of allegiance			
Governor General			
Privy Council			
Position of monarch			

3 How did de Valera ensure that it would be difficult for the British government to oppose the actions that he took?

Revision tip

Some very important changes to the constitutional position of the Irish Free State took place between 1932 and 1936. You need to be able to explain why de Valera wanted to make these changes and how the 1931 Statute of Westminster had made it possible for him to do so.

The reasons for and terms of the 1937 Constitution

All of the changes introduced by de Valera since coming to power in 1932 more or less made the first Constitution of the Irish Free State – written in 1922 – rather out of date. The Senate no longer existed and to all intents and purposes the Irish Free State no longer had a Head of State. The 1922 Constitution was also a document that de Valera saw as having been very much imposed by the 1921 Treaty and, therefore, less appealing to Republicans. In 1937, therefore, de Valera made an important break with the Irish Free State by introducing a new constitution, known as *Bunreacht na hÉireann* (Source B). Starting anew, he argued, would allow him to create a nation that reflected his ideal of what Ireland should be. That ideal did not include any constitutional links with the United Kingdom.

> **Source B** Extracts from *Bunreacht na hÉireann* (the Irish Constitution), 1937.
>
> Article II   The national territory consists of the whole island of Ireland, its islands and territorial seas.
>
> Article III   While maintaining the right to rule all 32 counties in Ireland, the laws passed by the Dublin Parliament will apply only to the 26 counties until Ireland is reunified.
>
> Article XLIV   The state recognises the special position of the Holy Catholic Apostolic and Roman Church as the guardian of the faith professed by the great majority of the citizens.

The new constitution included three significant changes from the Irish Free State's Constitution of 1922:

1 The Irish Free State would henceforth be known as Éire.
2 The title of the head of government would be *Taoiseach*.
3 The head of state, whose duties would be mainly ceremonial, would have the title of President. The position would be decided by an election, held every seven years. In 1938, Douglas Hyde, a well-known Gaelic scholar, was elected as the first President of Éire.

The Constitution recognised Irish as the official language of the state. It also said that the Catholic Church would have a 'special position … as the guardian of the faith professed by the great majority of the citizens' although 'freedom of conscience and the free profession and practice of religion' was granted to other faiths. Article II claimed that Dublin had the right to rule over the whole island. However, Article III added that until the end of partition, Éire's laws would only apply to the 26 counties that were currently controlled by the Dublin government.

Nowhere in the new constitution could any reference to the King be found. Éire had become a republic in all but name, yet despite this, de Valera did not declare Éire a republic and the country still remained part of the Commonwealth. Speaking in the *Dáil* on the passage of the new constitution, de Valera suggested that breaking the link with the Commonwealth completely would make partition even harder to end.

Activities

1 Create a spider diagram to summarise the key terms of the 1937 Constitution.
2 Why did de Valera not declare that the Free State was now a republic?

The impact of the 1937 Constitution on relations between Britain, Northern Ireland and Éire

Unsure whether Éire remained in the Commonwealth or not, London decided that the changes introduced by the new constitution were relatively unimportant and so did not alter its existing relationship with Dublin (Source C). Unionists were not so calm. *Bunreacht na hÉireann* reinforced their fears and suspicions of their neighbours and strengthened their determination to remain within the UK.

The unionist government – located at Stormont since 1932 – strongly criticised *Bunreacht na hÉireann* (Source D). In particular, it condemned Éire's territorial claim over Northern Ireland (contained in Article II) and denounced the new constitution's particular mention of the position of the Catholic Church and the Irish language. Lord Craigavon used the opportunity presented by the new constitution to call a snap general election in 1938. The result was an increased unionist majority at Stormont.

Some historians believe that northern nationalists also had a lot to be dissatisfied with following the introduction of *Bunreacht na hÉireann*. In many ways, despite the inclusion of Articles II and III, it could be argued that by removing almost all links with Britain and the Commonwealth, *Bunreacht na hÉireann* had actually strengthened partition and so had made the eventual reunification of the island even more unlikely. The realisation of this fact made northern nationalists feel even more cut off.

Source C London's response to *Bunreacht na hÉireann*.

His Majesty's government … [is] prepared to treat the new constitution as not effecting a great change in the position of the Irish Free State.

Source D Stormont's attitude towards the new Irish constitution.

The effect of … this new constitution … will be to strengthen … the determination of Ulster to resist attacks from there [Éire] and make the links between Britain and ourselves stronger.

Activities

1 Why was *Bunreacht na hÉireann* introduced?
2 What impact did *Bunreacht na hÉireann* have on the Free State's relationship with Britain?
3 Identify and explain the different reactions to the new constitution.

Practice questions

1 Give **one** term of the 1937 Constitution.
2 Using **Source D** and **your contextual knowledge**, give one reason that explains why unionists did not support the 1937 Constitution.

Revision tip

The 1937 constitution marks an important stage in the development of Ireland as a republic. You should be able to explain the reasons why de Valera made the changes that he did.

3 The Economic War

Land reform was one of the biggest issues in Irish history in the nineteenth century. It was an issue in terms of who owned the land – the landlords or those who worked it. The 1870 Land Act had tried to resolve the issue by giving tenants the chance to buy the land they were farming from the landowners. To make this happen, the British Government had loaned tenants the necessary funds. Each year the farmers had paid back part of these loans, in payments known as land annuities, worth an estimated £5 million per year to the British Government. Disagreements over these annuities became one of the main causes of the Economic War.

The causes of the Economic War

Between 1922 and 1932 the Irish Government collected the payments and sent them to London. However, Irish farmers, believing that they owned the land, disliked paying annuities. De Valera stopped the payments, arguing that:

▶ The Irish economy was suffering from the consequences of a global depression and could not spare the money.

▶ The British Government had abolished land annuities for Northern Ireland's farmers (in the aftermath of the failure of the 1925 Boundary Commission) (see page 97). It was only fair, therefore, that the same concession should be extended to farmers in the Free State.

Britain, angry that de Valera's government refused to pay monies that the previous government had paid, responded by imposing duties of 20 per cent on Free State imports. The Irish government reacted in two ways:

1 In January 1933, de Valera called the snap general election, as mentioned above (see page 101), which gave him enough seats to rule without the Labour Party. Thus there would be no other party threatening to leave the government during the crisis, strengthening his position.

2 The Dublin Government imposed similar duties on imports from all over the UK, including Northern Ireland. De Valera may have hoped that making British goods more expensive would encourage Irish people to set up their own businesses and produce similar goods more cheaply. If there were any complaints

about the harshness of the economic situation, de Valera could simply blame the British for starting it (Source A).

Source A De Valera commenting on the importance of the Economic War, November 1932.

If the British government should succeed in beating us in this fight then we could have no freedom, but at every step they could threaten you . . . and force you again to obey the British. What is involved is whether the Irish nation is going to be free or not.

This Economic War continued for six years, although in 1935 both sides seemed to want to improve relations. They agreed a Coal–Cattle Pact that made trade in these goods much easier. Some historians believe that de Valera's threat to source coal from Poland and/or Germany played a key part in securing this deal.

▲ Trade between the Irish Free State, Britain and Northern Ireland, 1932–38.

The effects of the Economic War

Given that 90 per cent of Irish exports went to Britain (see above), the Economic War had a significant impact. While the Dublin government benefited from keeping the £5 million-worth of annuities, Irish farmers probably suffered most, with a 35 per cent reduction in cattle exports (from 1929 levels) resulting in massive overproduction of beef and many Irish farmers going bankrupt. Much of this reduction came as a result of a decrease in trade with Britain; however, it partly also resulted from the loss of cross-border trade with Northern Ireland. Alternative markets were unavailable due to the impact of the ongoing global Depression. Subsistence farmers in Éire probably suffered less as they benefited from the reduction in their annuities.

The Dublin government attempted to encourage Irish farmers to explore new markets by offering subsidies to increase production of crops such as sugar beet and wheat. However, this was unsuccessful as only the bigger farmers switched. Small-scale farmers kept on growing traditional crops such as barley and so did not benefit. As a result, living standards fell even though taxes were raised to compensate farmers. As noted already, small-scale farmers did benefit from the reduction of the land annuities (Interpretation B).

While the industrial sector was not quite as badly hit as agriculture, it was not a massive success either. De Valera hoped that increasing the price of British goods in the Irish Free State would stop people buying those products and encourage the development of new Irish industries. Despite the appointment of the talented Sean Lemass as Minister for Industry and Commerce, this did not happen in any significant way, due mainly to a lack of investment. To make matters worse, any new Irish industries that did emerge were unable to sell their products abroad, as they were not prepared for the export market. The economy experienced a trade deficit as well as cutbacks in electricity generation and rail transport. The lack of coal imports from the UK did result in coal shortages, which particularly impacted upon the poor, but which also saw the local peat industry grow. Additionally, cement factories were established in Drogheda and Limerick, while the Dublin government spent £1 million on improving bridges and rural cottages.

The impact on relations between Northern Ireland and Britain

Undoubtedly the Economic War led to a deterioration in Dublin's relations with both London and Belfast (Interpretation C). Some evidence suggests that unemployment in Britain did increase somewhat because of the Economic War, not least in those ports that had previously handled Free State trade. Welsh coalmine owners were also scared of losing the Irish market to other coal exporters. That said, while Britain had

many other markets, much of Northern Ireland's economic prosperity was due to strong cross-border trade with the Free State. This prosperity was hit by the import duties de Valera imposed. All such trade stopped during the Economic War, although smuggling increased. On the other hand, Northern Ireland's farmers were helped by being able to provide Britain with produce no longer supplied by the Irish Free State.

Interpretation B Historian M.E. Collins writing about the Economic War in Ireland, 1868–1966.

The attempt to get self-sufficiency had failed. Agricultural exports to Britain were still the mainstay of the economy.

Interpretation C Historian D. Kennedy describes Northern Ireland's reaction to the Economic War.

De Valera's confrontation policy ... was seen in the north as a strategy to destroy the treaty settlement and reopen the question of unity.

"On the other hand, it's quite possible his story of taking a wrong turning could be perfectly true."

⬆ A cartoon published during the Anglo-Irish Economic War comments humorously on the increase in cross-border smuggling.

Activities

1 In what ways did de Valera hope the Economic War would benefit the Free State's economy? Was he correct?

2 Explain the impact of the Economic War under the following headings:
- the Irish economy
- the British economy
- the Northern Irish economy.

The end of the Economic War

The British Prime Minister Neville Chamberlain decided that relations between London and Dublin would have to improve. This would mean:
▶ ending the Economic War
▶ resolving the issue of the treaty ports.

Chamberlain recognised the strategic value of the ports, but also knew they were out of date as they had not had any investment since the time of the Treaty. He therefore decided that returning them would help end the Economic War and would, as a consequence of de Valera's gratitude, result in Éire's assistance if war broke out (Source D).

Keen to get the ports back, de Valera believed that Britain's continued control would weaken Éire's claims to neutrality and leave it open to attack.

> **Source D** British Deputy Chiefs of Staff report on the importance of the treaty ports to Britain's defence, April 1936.
>
> The present time seems a suitable one for [returning the treaty ports to Ireland] since [their importance] has somewhat decreased in view of the recent changes of defence policy of this country.

The terms of the Anglo-Irish Agreements of 1938 and their significance for relations between Britain, Northern Ireland and Éire

Representatives of the two governments began to talk in January 1938. On 25 April 1938, the British and Irish delegations signed three separate agreements on defence, finance and trade. As a result, the Economic War was ended and the three treaty ports were returned to Éire. This meant that another symbolic link between the two countries was broken, the terms of the 1921 Anglo-Irish Treaty were further undermined and Éire's independence was further reinforced.

▶ British forces preparing to leave the military facility at Cobh, County Cork, in 1938.

Éire agreed to pay Britain £10 million to resolve the annuities question (see page 105), while all duties imposed by both countries during the Economic War were removed.

The end to the trade war between Éire and Britain did not apply to cross-border trade with Northern Ireland, which was subject to a long-running boycott. Both sides also approved a three-year trade agreement. Overall, de Valera was delighted with the outcome of the agreements (Source E) which, historians agree, were much more favourable to Éire.

While the agreements received a positive response from most people, the return of the treaty ports was criticised sharply by British politicians such as Winston Churchill who had described the returned facilities as the 'sentinel towers of the western approaches'. By this Churchill meant that the ports were like 'look out' posts by which Britain could see danger approaching and respond to it. He did not share Chamberlain's belief that Éire would allow Britain to use the ports during a future war.

Unionists were less than pleased with the outcome of the Anglo-Irish negotiations. Craigavon also agreed with Churchill's view that the return of the treaty ports would weaken the security of both the UK and Éire. He feared the improvement in Anglo-Irish relations might lead to the reunification of Ireland. Chamberlain attempted to calm Craigavon by making concessions on agricultural subsidies and the promise of an increased share of weapons manufacture.

Source E De Valera's reaction to the return of the ports, April 1938.

Handing over the treaty ports recognises and finally establishes Irish sovereignty over the 26 counties.

Activities

1   Why did Chamberlain want to improve Britain's relationship with Éire?
2   What benefits did Chamberlain see in returning the treaty ports to Éire?
3   Why would de Valera have been so pleased at the return of the treaty ports?
4   Which side gained most economically from the 1938 agreements?
5   Explain the different reactions to the agreements.

Practice questions

1   Explain two of the following:
    a   The reasons for the 1937 Constitution
    b   The impact of the Economic War on Northern Ireland
    c   The significance of the terms of the Anglo-Irish agreements of 1938
2   Look back at Source D on page 107. Using Source D and your contextual knowledge, give two reasons that explain the importance of the treaty ports in ending the Economic War.

Revision tip

You should be prepared to write not only about the economic terms of the 1938 Anglo-Irish agreements, but also the agreements' implications for both British and Irish foreign policy.

Revision tip

You need to be able to explain the reasons why the Economic War started and the impact that it had on the economies of both islands.

This page provides guidance on how to answer question 1 in the exam.

Question 1

Study Source A below and answer the question which follows:

> **Source A** Protestant attitude to the setting up of the Northern Ireland Parliament.
>
> '[they saw safety in] Having a parliament of our own, for we believe that once a parliament is ... working well ... we should fear no one, and we feel that we would then be in a position of absolute security.'

Using Source A and your contextual knowledge, give **one** reason which explains why Protestants supported the creation of a parliament for Northern Ireland. **[2]**

Guidance

You should be looking to spend a maximum of two–three minutes on this question. To access both marks you need to give one clear point from the source that provide the information required.

Step 1

Read the source carefully (line by line). By doing this you should find at least one reason for the explanation the question is asking for.

Example

In Source A the Protestants or unionists say they will 'fear no one' once they have their own parliament.

Step 2

Use your knowledge of this topic to develop what you have said about the source, including detail where possible.

Example

This is because they were aware that they would hold a majority of seats in this parliament and this majority would allow them to have control over all aspects of their lives.

On 1 September 1939, German forces invaded Poland. The Second World War began two days later – on 3 September 1939 – when Germany refused to abide by Britain and France's ultimatum to withdraw from Poland.

Northern Ireland's reaction to the outbreak of war

The Northern Ireland Parliament met on 4 September to discuss the declaration of war. The war provided the Stormont government with the opportunity to declare and demonstrate its loyalty to Great Britain. In this way, it was believed, the union with Great Britain could be strengthened. Speaking during the debate, Craigavon reassured the London government of Northern Ireland's readiness to play its part in the forthcoming war effort (Source A). Just how ready Northern Ireland was remained to be seen.

> **Source A** Lord Craigavon, speaking in the Northern Ireland Parliament on 4 September 1939.
>
> [There will be] no slackening in [Ulster's] loyalty. There is no falling off in our determination to place the whole of our resources at the command of the [Westminster] government … anything we can do to facilitate [help] them … they have only just got to let us know.

Differing attitudes towards conscription

Some months earlier (in April 1939) the British government had announced the introduction of conscription in Great Britain. However, the fear of a negative nationalist reaction and the desire not to worsen relations with Dublin, meant that conscription was not extended to Northern Ireland. At the time, an angry Craigavon demanded that this decision be reversed as a demonstration of Northern Ireland's unity with Britain.

Craigavon's demand annoyed nationalists and Catholic bishops issued a statement opposing his appeal. Cardinal Joseph MacRory, the Archbishop of Armagh and the head of the Irish Catholic Church, stated that resisting the introduction of conscription would be morally justified. De Valera also voiced his concerns, as did a range of other groups and individuals.

▼ War is declared, September 1939.

109

In May 1939, Chamberlain met Craigavon to explain that the reason for the decision not to introduce conscription was Northern Ireland's 'special difficulties'. Craigavon was unhappy but accepted the decision (Source B).

To compensate for the refusal to extend conscription, Northern Ireland was awarded over £6 million in defence contracts. Particularly involved were the Short & Harland aircraft factory and the Harland & Wolff shipyard. While this investment resulted in a fall of over 30,000 in the number listed as unemployed during 1939, it also meant that Belfast might be a target for enemy bombers if war broke out.

In May 1940, a series of rallies in favour of conscription was held across Northern Ireland; however, the response was not as positive as Craigavon might have hoped. The memories of the carnage of the Battle of the Somme may have contributed to this, as well as the fact that the Minister of Agriculture, Sir Basil Brooke, was chosen to lead the recruitment drive. Many still remembered Brooke's 1933 speech when he had urged unionist employers to 'employ good Protestant lads and lassies'.

Source B Lady Craigavon, writing about how Chamberlain persuaded Craig not to push for the extension of conscription to Northern Ireland, May 1939.

J. [James] was asked flat out by Chamberlain, 'is Ulster out to help Britain in her war effort?' To which, of course, he answered, 'you know we are. I have offered personally all the resources at our disposal to help you, and we have passed resolutions [laws] in our Parliament to the same effect.' Chamberlain said, 'if you really want to help us, don't press for conscription, it will only be an embarrassment'. What else could J. do than say, 'Very well then, I won't!'

In the aftermath of the 1941 Belfast Blitz (pages 122–124), the British Labour Minister, Ernest Bevin, again raised the possibility of conscription being introduced in Northern Ireland. Again most nationalists opposed the move, seeing this as Britain's war, not theirs. Aside from de Valera again condemning the proposal, thousands of nationalists took to the streets of Belfast in protest, supported by local Catholic bishops and nationalist politicians.

The strength of nationalist opposition meant that the unionist leadership, after initially welcoming the prospect of conscription, now decided that introducing it would create more problems than it would solve. Moreover, the Royal Ulster Constabulary (RUC) Inspector-General informed the government of his fear that any attempt to introduce conscription could lead to serious public disorder. Once more London announced that conscription would not be extended to Northern Ireland.

Activities

1 How did Belfast react to the start of the Second World War?
2 Why was Lord Craigavon so keen to offer Northern Ireland's support and assistance to Great Britain during the war?
3 How successful was the Northern Ireland Government's May 1940 recruitment drive? Why was this?
4 Construct a timeline to show what happened with conscription. Add notes to your timeline about who supported and opposed conscription and why.

Revision tip

Be prepared to explain the reasons for the refusal of the British government to extend conscription to Northern Ireland in 1939 – and in 1941.

The war effort in Northern Ireland: complacency?

Northern Ireland was not ready for war when it started on 3 September 1939. While the Stormont government was quick to promise its support to London, there is less evidence that it had really thought through what being at war would mean for the people of Northern Ireland. For example, the administration continued to believe that the province was beyond the range of enemy aircraft and so appropriate defence measures (both aerial and ground based) were not put in place (Source E).

Even with the war underway, the government still remained slow to act, in terms of putting adequate defence measures in place. It was not until well into 1941 that the majority of Northern Ireland was covered by radar and steps had been taken to establish a number of anti-aircraft batteries. Even then some feared that enemy planes could still approach Northern Ireland without being picked up, while others suggested that far too few anti-aircraft defences (including anti-aircraft guns, night-fighters and searchlights) were in place.

Source E The view of Edmond Warnock (Parliamentary Secretary at the Ministry of Home Affairs), on the possibility of a *Luftwaffe* attack on Belfast, June 1939.

An attack on Northern Ireland would involve a flight of over 1,000 miles. For aeroplanes of the bombing type, loaded, this is a very big undertaking ... the enemy aeroplanes must twice pass through the active gun, searchlight and aeroplane defences of Great Britain ... it is possible that we might escape attack.

Northern Ireland's industrial, agricultural, military and strategic contributions to the war

The people and location of Northern Ireland made a large contribution to the war.

Military service

It is estimated that close to 40,000 people from Northern Ireland joined one of the services. Just over 10 per cent of this number died. It is probable that more of Northern Ireland's unionist population would have joined up were it not for the fact that they were employed in reserved occupations. Many of those who joined up served with considerable distinction. One such individual was James Magennis, a Royal Navy sailor who was awarded the Victoria Cross for the part he played in sinking a Japanese cruiser off the coast of Borneo.

In excess of 43,000 Éire citizens fought for the Allies. Their reasons for doing so ranged from support of the Allied cause to desperation to escape from poverty. However, the recent history of poor Anglo-Irish relations meant that their contribution was not recognised at home.

The Home Guard

Northern Ireland's experience of the Home Guard differed noticeably from Britain's. Craigavon's fear of Republican infiltration if the force was created through open enrolment, meant that the B Specials (see page 95) formed the core of the Northern Ireland Home Guard. Unlike Britain, the RUC rather than the army controlled this force.

As a result, Catholic membership was limited and the Home Guard was seen as little more than a sectarian force (Interpretation F). Although some members of the British government expressed unease with this, in the end nothing was done to change the situation.

Much of the focus of the Northern Ireland Home Guard was on counteracting the IRA threat. Pro-German ideas were held in some Republican circles and in September 1939 the government had responded to the declaration of war by introducing internment to deal with IRA activists. After several additional moves against Republican suspects – including the arrest of IRA Chief of Staff Hugh McAteer in 1942 – IRA activity dropped off.

Interpretation F Historian Brian Barton comments on the sectarian nature of the Home Guard in Northern Ireland (adapted).

There was obvious justification [reason] in the view that the government had succeeded in transforming the Home Guard into a sectarian body. MacDermott (Minister of Public Security) recalled that a few Catholics did enlist but that 'virtually all left because they hated the B Specials'.

Strategic significance

Northern Ireland's geographical location ensured that it played a key role in the war, particularly after the return of the treaty ports to Éire (1938) and Éire's declaration of neutrality in September 1939 (see page 117). Once France fell to the Germans in 1940, Allied shipping went north of Ireland and thus Northern Ireland's strategic significance increased.

▶ Naval bases, such as Lisahally outside Derry/Londonderry, provided vital support and services for those vessels involved in the Battle of the Atlantic and acted as bases for ships and submarines, keeping sea lanes open (Interpretation G). The port at Derry/Londonderry was the biggest such base in Britain for warships protecting merchant ships.

▶ Derry/Londonderry itself became an important base for service personnel, including large numbers from the USA and other Allied countries. By mid-1943 there were nearly 150 ships based at the port, whilst by the end of the same year there was an estimated 40,000 military personnel stationed in and around the city.

▶ Natural inlets such as Lough Foyle provided refuge from U-boat attack for merchant shipping on their trans-Atlantic journeys.

▶ Air bases at locations such as Aldergrove, Ballykelly, Eglinton, Limavady, Nutts Corner, Long Kesh and Castle Archdale (for Coastal Command) provided much needed cover for convoys. Aircraft from Castle Archdale sank 18 U-boats in 1943.

▶ A variety of US forces based themselves in Northern Ireland between 1942 and 1944. Apart from training troops, bases to service aircraft and shipping were established. Most notable among these service bases was Langford Lodge, on the shores of Lough Neagh. Magee College in Derry/Londonderry served as the main communication base for US forces across Europe.

▶ Northern Ireland was also used as a base for preparations for operations in North Africa and southern Italy and for D-Day. By 1943, there were close to 300,000 military personnel stationed in various locations throughout the province. One unforeseen consequence of such huge numbers was that there was sometimes friction with the local male population, unhappy at the 'challenge' of those in uniform!

> **Interpretation G** Historian Patrick Buckland reflects on the strategic role that Northern Ireland played during the Second World War.
>
> With its ports [Northern Ireland] stood as 'a faithful sentinel' helping to protect the sea lanes between Britain and America, particularly the north-west approaches to Merseyside and Clydeside.

Was Northern Ireland really prepared for enemy attack?

Northern Ireland did not compare well to the wide-ranging evacuation and air raid protection schemes that had been implemented across Britain prior to the outbreak of war.

▶ The Stormont government introduced an Air Raid Precautions Act in 1938; however, unlike the rest of the UK, it did not make local council provision of civil defence measures compulsory. As a result, Northern Ireland's population was not as well prepared for enemy attacks.

▶ It was not until July 1940 that a local evacuation plan was launched, and even this only resulted in 7,000 out of a possible 70,000 children being evacuated from Belfast.

▶ Public responses to the dangers of air attack were almost as incompetent as those of the government. Air Raid Protection or ARP wardens and blackouts were routinely ignored. By early 1941, recorded blackout offences in Belfast alone had reached nearly 1,000 per month. That said, the blackout of the headlights of cars, buses and bicycles was obeyed by the public, even though it made travel at night-time very difficult!

▶ When people were offered the chance to be evacuated from Belfast, few did so.

▶ When Belfast was bombed in 1941 (pages 122–123) there were insufficient recruits for the various civil defence services.

▶ In spite of constant government advice and warnings, the majority of people did not carry gas masks (issued at the start of the war) until after the Belfast Blitz.

▶ Nearly a year after the declaration of war, only 15 per cent of the Belfast households entitled to an Anderson air raid shelter had taken delivery of one.

Activities

1 Why had the Stormont government not prepared Northern Ireland effectively for war?
2 How well were Northern Ireland's people prepared for enemy attack?
3 Explain the steps taken to prepare Northern Ireland for war, under the following headings:
   ● air defence
   ● precaution against air raids.
4 What part did the people of Éire play in the fighting of the war?
5 Why did the Northern Irish Home Guard become an issue of controversy?

ISSUE OF RESPIRATORS
CITY OF BELFAST
FOR ONE WEEK ONLY

THE following DISTRIBUTING CENTRES will be open each evening from 7-30 p.m. to 9-30 p.m., FROM MONDAY, 4th SEPTEMBER, to FRIDAY, 8th SEPTEMBER, AND FROM 10 a.m. to 9-30 p.m. ON SATURDAY, 9th SEPTEMBER.

Residents of the city of over school age who have not yet received their respirators should attend at the centres for their Wards.

NIGHT WORKERS SHOULD ATTEND ON SATURDAY, 9th SEPTEMBER.

AGED AND INVALID PERSONS WHO ARE UNABLE TO ATTEND. Names and addresses should be sent or given in to the Ward Centres. Wardens will then visit these addresses.

CHILDREN.

ALL SCHOOL CHILDREN are dealt with in the schools.

CHILDREN NOT YET AT SCHOOL. Names and addresses should be given in at the distributing centres or to the A.R.P. Office, 40 Academy Street.

RESPIRATORS WILL NOT BE ISSUED TO THE PUBLIC AT A.R.P. HEADQUARTERS, ACADEMY STREET.

A.R.P. VOLUNTEERS AND OTHERS WHO KINDLY ASSISTED AT THE PREVIOUS ISSUE ARE REQUESTED TO GIVE THEIR HELP AGAIN AT THE CENTRES.

WARDS.			DISTRIBUTING CENTRES.
COURT	...	...	ST. ENOCH'S P.E.S., Carlisle Circus.
CROMAC	...	...	McQUISTON MEMORIAL P.E.S., Oak Street/Donegall Pass.
DOCK	...	...	HILLMAN P.E.S., Upper Meadow Street, and EARL STREET P.E.S., 3/5 Earl Street.
DUNCAIRN	...	...	MOUNTCOLLYER P.E.S., Limestone Road.
GREENCASTLE	...	...	WHITEHOUSE P.E.S (Tram Terminus), Shore Road
FALLS	...	...	ST. PAUL'S P.E.S., Cavendish Square.
ORMEAU	...	...	PARK PARADE P.E.S., Ormeau Embankment.
POTTINGER	...	...	AVONIEL P.E.S., Avoniel Road.
SHANKILL	...	...	GLENWOOD P.E.S. Upper Riga Street.
LIGONIEL	...	...	ST. MARK'S P.E.S., Ballysillan.
SMITHFIELD	...	...	ST. COMGALL'S P.E.S., Divis Street.
ST. ANNE'S	...	...	GROSVENOR P.E.S., Roden Street.
ST. GEORGE'S	...	...	LINFIELD (Sen.) P.E.S., Blythe Street (Sandy Row).
VICTORIA	...	...	TEMPLEMORE P.E.S., Templemore Avenue.
WINDSOR	...	...	FANE STREET P.E.S., Ashley Avenue (Lisburn Road).
WOODVALE	...	...	ARGYLE P.E.S., North Howard Street.
CLIFTON	...	...	In this Ward no Centre will be opened, as there are sufficient numbers of Trained Wardens to complete the issue by house-to-house visits.

▼ Allied shipping moored in Derry/Londonderry during the Battle of the Atlantic.

▲ An official notice from 1940.

Agriculture

The best-performing section of the Northern Ireland wartime economy was agriculture.

▶ With increasing demand from Britain for food, the amount of land used for growing crops increased by 60 per cent as farmers switched from livestock to arable farming.

▶ Particularly significant were the increases in the production of flax, wheat and potatoes.

▶ The number of allotments increased fourfold in the war years. Careful planning by the government ensured that sufficient artificial fertilisers were made available to support this increase, which became known as the 'Dig for Victory'.

▶ The numbers of cattle and poultry increased significantly. Northern Ireland's chickens were responsible for providing Britain with 20 per cent of its egg consumption.

▶ Along with eggs, Britain received sheep, cattle and dairy produce from Northern Ireland (£3 million-worth per year); Scotland received 100,000 litres of Northern Ireland milk each day.

As a result of this Ulster's farmers grew wealthy.

There were two main reasons for this impressive performance:

▶ the continued availability of fertilisers

▶ the more than 100-fold increase in tractor numbers.

Much of the credit for the agricultural sector's success belongs to the Minister for Agriculture, Basil Brooke. He took to the countryside to persuade Northern Ireland's farmers to increase production. Brooke's success contributed to his appointment as Prime Minister in 1943.

Rationing

The war resulted in the introduction of rationing to discourage waste and encourage self-reliance. Although shortages did not bite as quickly in Northern Ireland as they did in Britain, by 1941 goods such as fresh meat and dairy produce became much more difficult to source, particularly in towns. Fuel shortages had a massive impact on the use of cars and as a result the use of public transport increased. For some, particularly those living close to the border, smuggling eased the shortages; for others, the solution was to buy goods on the black market.

Industry

The fortunes of Northern Ireland's industrial economy were not quite as impressive as those of the agricultural sector. For the first two years of the war output was hit by:

▶ Bad management.

▶ A lack of planning. For example, a year and a half into the war, no new factories had been built.

▶ A shortage of skilled workers coupled with poor working conditions.

▶ A series of strikes (even though strikes were supposed to be illegal).

Year	Number of unemployed people
1941	70,000
1942	50,000
1943	19,000
1944	10,000

Table 1 Unemployment levels 1941–44.

Although things began to improve in late 1941, it was 1943 before any real improvement could be seen in Northern Ireland's industrial output. By the time the war ended, much of this industrial unrest had disappeared. After initially increasing, unemployment had dropped from a high of 70,000 (late 1941) to just 10,000. Production figures had begun an upward climb and both wages and the standard of living had improved. A variety of Northern Ireland firms produced significant numbers of tanks, ships, aircraft and munitions.

This performance is best illustrated by examining the performance of two of Northern Ireland's largest companies during the war years:

Harland & Wolff:
▶ 140 warships (including three destroyers and six carriers)
▶ 123 merchant ships (10 per cent of Britain's total wartime production)
▶ 3,000 ships repaired or converted to other uses
▶ 500 tanks
▶ over 13 million aircraft components.

Short & Harland:
▶ 1,500 Stirling bombers
▶ 125 Sunderland flying boats
▶ 150 Hereford bombers
▶ over 3,000 aircraft repairs.

Between 1939 and 1945, other local companies (especially James Mackie & Sons) produced other wartime essentials, including weapons and ammunition, nets and ropes as well as uniforms and parachutes. In total, local factories produced close to 75 million shells, 180 million bullets, 50,000 bayonets, 50,000 camouflage/cargo nets, 30,000 shirts, 200,000 yards of cloth (used for uniforms), two million cloth parachutes and 250,000 tonnes of rope (one third of the entire total used by the British Army). While these figures are impressive, historical research would suggest that Northern Ireland's economic performance might still have been better (Interpretations H and I).

Activities

After reading pages 111–115, work in a group of 3 or 4: each group takes a different contribution that Northern Ireland made to the war (industrial, agricultural, military and strategic).

- Use a spider diagram to map out the ways your chosen contribution was important.
- Share your ideas with other groups, who have been analysing other contributions.
- Compare/weigh up the importance of your chosen contribution against the other contributions.
- How significant is your chosen contribution?

Practice questions

1 Describe one reason why there was opposition to conscription in Northern Ireland.
2 Explain two of the following:
▶ The impact of rationing on Northern Ireland during World War II.
▶ The different attitudes towards conscription during World War II.
▶ The impact of World War II on Northern Ireland's industrial sector.

Interpretation H
Historian Brian Barton comments on the performance of Northern Ireland's wartime economy.

Despite Northern Ireland's impressive wartime output, production levels were consistently lower in the region than in any other part of Britain.

Interpretation I
Historian M.E. Collins reflects on the less impressive aspects of Northern Ireland's economic performance during the war.

The Northern economy boomed during the war [but] wartime expansion was marred by bad management, poor productivity rates and bad work practices. Industrial unrest flared up from time to time with several strikes, in spite of the fact that they were illegal.

Revision tip

There were both positive and negative aspects of Northern Ireland's contribution to the war effort. Make sure that you know what they were and the reasons for them.

This page provides guidance on how to answer question 2 in the exam.

Question 2

Study **Source B** below and answer the question which follows:

> **Source B** The Catholic attitude to the new Northern Ireland state as expressed by Mgr George Crolly, Parish Priest of St Matthew's, Belfast, April 1921.
>
> This so-called northern parliament is a danger to our liberties and a barrier to the permanent solution of the Irish problem, we [nationalists] can neither give it recognition nor lend it support.

Give **two** reasons from **Source B** to explain why nationalists were opposed to the creation of a parliament for Northern Ireland. [4]

Guidance

You should be looking to spend a maximum of six minutes on this question. To access all the available marks, you need to provide an explanation of each reason that you identify.

Step 1

Read the source carefully (line by line). By doing this you should find at least two reasons for the explanation the question is asking for.

Example

In Source B the nationalists say the new parliament is a 'danger to our liberties' …

Also, the nationalists say the new parliament is 'a barrier to the permanent solution of the Irish problem' …

Step 2

Use your knowledge of this topic to develop what you have said about the source, including detail where possible.

Example

In Source B the nationalists say the new parliament is a 'danger to our liberties'; this is because lots of nationalists were afraid that the new unionist parliament would discriminate against them.

Also, the nationalists say the new parliament is 'a barrier to the permanent solution of the Irish problem'. A 'permanent solution' would be a united Ireland under its own rule, and so nationalists thought that having a new parliament in Northern Ireland would mean that partition was going to make the creation of a united Ireland much more difficult, if not impossible.

The reaction to the start of the war was somewhat different south of the border. The day after Britain declared war on Germany, de Valera announced Éire's neutrality (Interpretation A).

Interpretation A Historian F.S.L. Lyons on the meaning of Éire's neutrality (adapted).

Neutrality ... was the outward and visible sign of absolute sovereignty. To be free to choose between peace and war was the mark of independence, to be free to choose between peace and a British war demonstrated to all of the world just how complete that independence really was.

The reasons for de Valera's policy of neutrality

There were several reasons for the Éire government's decision to introduce this policy:

▶ De Valera correctly assumed that people would support neutrality to reinforce Éire's independence from Britain (Interpretation B).

▶ The continued existence of partition ruled out Éire's involvement in the war.

▶ Éire was divided over whether or not to support the British war effort; some citizens may even have sympathised with Germany.

▶ Many in Éire believed Germany posed no threat to Éire – and if there was a threat, they believed that Britain would protect Éire, as a member of the Commonwealth.

▶ Éire was not equipped to fight a war, economically or militarily.

▶ The Dublin government wanted to unite its people against invasion and protect them against the hardships of war.

The Irish Government also introduced the Emergency Powers Act, increasing its control over the country. This gave it extensive powers to ensure that the policy of neutrality was maintained. For example, censorship was introduced and strictly enforced.

Interpretation B Sir John Maffey, the British government's representative in Dublin, commenting on Irish attitudes to neutrality.

The policy of neutrality commands widespread approval among all classes and interests in Éire.

Attitude of the people of Éire towards neutrality

By and large neutrality was a popular policy, though many people remained largely sympathetic to the Allied cause. The main reasons for popular support for neutrality included the belief that it helped reinforce Ireland's position as an independent nation, able to make its own decisions. At a more basic level, many were relieved that a policy of neutrality would hopefully save Ireland and its people from the horrors of modern warfare. Even Ireland's minority unionist population supported de Valera's approach, whilst continuing to lend their support to the Allied war effort.

The response of Northern Ireland and Britain to Éire's neutrality, and impact on relations

Great Britain accepted Éire's declaration of neutrality only grudgingly. Some viewed it as potentially damaging to the war effort, while fears were expressed that Germany might use Éire as a base from which to invade Great Britain. Particular opposition came from Winston Churchill, soon to be appointed Prime Minister. At the same time, realising the importance of maintaining communication between London and Dublin, Sir John Maffey was appointed as representative of the British Government to Éire. He had a good knowledge of Ireland and soon developed a positive relationship with de Valera and as a result working relations remained effective and a diplomatic breakdown was prevented. That said, Britain never recognised Éire's neutrality and pressure on Éire to end the policy remained strong, particularly after Churchill became Prime Minister in May 1940.

Reactions in Northern Ireland were even less positive than Churchill's. There was strong resentment at Éire's declaration of neutrality, which was viewed as an act of betrayal and a threat to the security of the entire United Kingdom. Not surprisingly, it was condemned publicly in Stormont where Craigavon condemned neutrality as disloyal.

Benevolent neutrality

Éire asserted its neutrality during the war in several ways:

▶ It refused military assistance to both sides.

▶ The Allies were denied use of Éire's ports and airfields.

▶ News bulletins gave purely factual reports about the war.

▶ Weather forecasts ceased to be broadcast in case they helped either side.

▶ When the US entered the war in late 1941, de Valera resisted US pressure to end neutrality.

On occasion, de Valera went to extraordinary lengths to display even-handedness. He irritated the US government by protesting at the arrival of US troops in 1942. He further annoyed Allied opinion when, in April 1945, he visited the German ambassador to express sympathy over Hitler's death. Earlier the same month, however, he had carried out a similar visit to the US embassy to pay respects to the late US President, Franklin D. Roosevelt.

Yet Dublin's actions made it appear that their neutrality was biased in favour of the Allies:

▶ The German ambassador's radio transmitter was confiscated.

▶ German pilots who bailed out of their planes over Éire were imprisoned, whilst similar Allied airmen were secretly allowed to cross the border into Northern Ireland.

▶ During the Belfast Blitz (pages 122–124), de Valera sent 13 fire engines (with 71 crew) to help. In its aftermath, Relief Centres were set up close to the border, relief funds were started and officials from both governments met to discuss how best the refugee problem could be handled.

▶ Allied airmen patrolling the Western approaches or refuelling on trans-Atlantic missions were permitted to fly over Irish territory through the 'Donegal air corridor' (from Beleek, County Fermanagh to the coasts, see map). Later in the war, US airmen were also permitted to use this route.

▶ In the final months of the war, de Valera allowed the RAF to establish a number of secret radar bases on Irish territory.

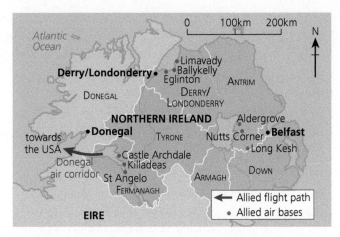

▲ The location of the Donegal air corridor.

It is important, though, to consider the real reasons for Éire's ability to remain neutral:

▶ Éire benefited from the sympathetic attitude of British and German government representatives in Dublin, and their recommendations to not compromise neutrality.

▶ If the Allies had found it strategically necessary to invade the South, there is little doubt that they would have done so. That they did not was due mainly to Northern Ireland's significant strategic role (see pages 107–108).

The possibility of such an Allied invasion was revealed by Churchill when he condemned de Valera's role and praised Northern Ireland's role (Source C). De Valera used his response to score a few points of his own (Source D).

Source C Excerpt from Churchill's end of war broadcast, May 1945.

Owing to the action of Mr de Valera ... the approaches which the southern Irish ports and airfields could so easily have guarded were closed by hostile aircraft and U-boats. This was indeed a deadly moment in our life, and had it not been for the loyalty and friendship of Northern Ireland, we should have been forced to come to close quarters with Mr de Valera, or perish forever from the earth.

Source D De Valera's response, May 1945.

Mr Churchill is proud of Britain's stand alone ... Could he not find in his heart the generosity to acknowledge that there is a small nation [Ireland] that stood alone, not for one year or two, but for several hundred years against aggression; a small nation that could never be got to accept defeat and has never surrendered her soul?

Reaction to Britain's offer to end partition

Britain made two main attempts to encourage Ireland on to its side:

▶ In June 1940, a month after Churchill became Prime Minister, London proposed the reunification of Ireland if Éire joined the Allies (Source E). In return it was suggested that the Dublin government would allow British forces to be stationed in Éire and use Éire's naval facilities. However, de Valera rejected the offer on the strength of Éire's 'unpreparedness' for war, the negative impact it would have on Éire's independence, and that there was no guarantee that Northern Ireland would agree to reunification since its government had not even been consulted (Source F). Indeed, when he became aware of the British offer, Lord Craigavon indignantly informed the British government 'to such treachery to loyal Ulster I will never be party'.

▶ Following the Japanese attack on Pearl Harbor (7 December 1941), Churchill telegrammed de Valera. His offer of 'Now is your chance. Now or never "A nation once again" ' was understood by de Valera to refer to the possibility of Irish unity if he joined the Allies. Again, he declined.

In 1942 Churchill yet again attempted to regain the use of the treaty ports. Once more de Valera rejected this.

▲ A 1940 cartoon from Britain's *Daily Mail* showing the dangers for Éire if it continued with its policy of neutrality.

Source E Extract from Britain's proposal of a united Ireland if Éire helped Britain in the Second World War, June 1940.

There should be a declaration of a United Ireland in principle … Ulster to remain involved in the war, Éire to remain neutral … for the time being … A joint defence council to be set up at once … British naval ships to be allowed into Éire's ports, British troops and aeroplanes to be stationed at certain agreed points in the territory, the British government to provide additional equipment for Éire's forces.

Source F De Valera's response to the British offer.

[This] plan would commit us definitely to an immediate abandonment of our neutrality. [However] it gives no guarantee that in the end we would have a united Ireland.

Activities

1 What evidence is there that Britain was keen to get Éire involved in the war?
2 What evidence is there to indicate that Éire was not totally neutral during the Second World War?
3 What problems did Éire's neutrality pose for the British?

Practice question

1 How reliable is the Daily Mail cartoon for an historian studying what relations were like between Britain and Éire in 1940? Explain your answer, using the cartoon and your contextual knowledge.
2 How useful is the Daily Mail cartoon for an historian studying what relations were like between Britain and Éire in 1940? Explain your answer, using the cartoon and your contextual knowledge.

Revision tip

You will also be expected to be able to explain just how neutral Éire was during the war.

119

The Battle of Britain

By the end of June 1940 all of Western Europe had been conquered by Hitler's armies; Britain now stood alone against Germany. However, its army was low in numbers and – following its evacuation from Dunkirk - did not have the equipment needed to fight a war; things looked hopeless. To deal with this desperate situation:

▶ Factories worked multiple shifts to produce aircraft, tanks and heavy weapons and a government campaign began for scrap metal from Britain's households.

▶ Over 500,000 rifles were ordered from the USA.

▶ The Local Defence Volunteers (later renamed the Home Guard) was established in May 1940. In just over a year it had over a million members.

Although the Royal Navy had begun a blockade of the North Sea and was patrolling the Channel to defend against German warships and U-boats, the RAF was in a stronger position than other branches of the military due to its ongoing improvements since 1935. The provision of radar, as well as providing early warning of the approach of enemy aircraft, also enabled RAF fighters to be directed accurately to intercept enemy planes. The RAF was also reorganised into three sections:

▶ Fighter Command

▶ Bomber Command

▶ Coastal Command.

The events of the Battle

In July 1940, Great Britain rejected Hitler's attempts to negotiate a peaceful conclusion to the war – in return for Britain recognising Nazi domination of Western Europe. The German leader responded by ordering the implementation of Operation Sealion, the invasion of Britain. Before this could take place, however, the RAF would have to be destroyed. This was because its control of the skies over the English Channel would prevent a successful sea invasion being launched from northern France (Source A).

Source A Churchill's speech to the House of Commons, 18 June 1940.

The Battle of France is over. I expect that the Battle of Britain is about to begin … Hitler knows that he will have to break us in this island or lose the war … Let us therefore brace ourselves to our duty and so bear ourselves that if the British Commonwealth and Empire lasts for a thousand years, men will still say, 'This was their finest hour.'

On 12 August 1940 the Luftwaffe launched Operation Eagle, its attack on the RAF. The plan was to gain air supremacy by bombing RAF airfields and destroying planes on the ground. If any aircraft were able to take off, they would be shot down by German fighters. Although initial Luftwaffe losses were greater (225 aircraft losses against the RAF's 117), it had significantly more aircraft and so it is likely that if these attacks had continued the RAF would eventually have been worn down. However, on 7 September the Luftwaffe switched tactics; instead of continuing to attack RAF bases it started to bomb London. This was in response to recent RAF raids on Berlin. The bombing raids continued for months and were quickly extended to include other British cities (such as Coventry, Liverpool and Glasgow). While the nightly blitz caused massive devastation to cities and Britain's civilian population, the change of tactics allowed the RAF to reorganise and obtain newly manufactured aircraft. This meant that the RAF continued to control the skies over Britain, and for this reason Operation Sealion was finally called off in October 1940 (Interpretation B). Apart from the decision to stop bombing RAF bases, historians believe that the RAF's victory was ultimately due largely to its use of radar and the superiority of the Spitfire as an aircraft.

Interpretation B Historian Jack Watson explains the reasons for the RAF's victory in the Battle of Britain.

The pre-war development of the RAF proved to have been just adequate. Under the command of Air Chief Marshal Dowding, with Beaverbrook in charge of aircraft production, with the valuable help of radar and, above all, with the heroism of the 'few' fighter pilots who flew the Hurricanes and Spitfires, the RAF defied the might of Göring's Luftwaffe.

The significance of the Battle of Britain

The Battle of Britain was significant for a number of reasons. It was the first important military campaign to be fought entirely by aircraft, showing how technology was changing the nature of war. It was also the largest and most continuous aerial bombing campaign to have been undertaken. Most significantly, perhaps, the Battle of Britain also marked the first time that Hitler's military forces had tasted defeat since the start of the Second World War in September 1939. The German leader now made the decision to switch his attention to the invasion of the USSR, a decision that would ultimately play a significant part in the defeat of the Nazis. Of course, the failure of Hitler's invasion plans were also a significant morale boost to the people of Great Britain, playing no small part in reinforcing their decision to keep going in their fight against Germany.

Activities

1 Why was Britain in such a vulnerable position after June 1940?
2 What steps were taken to prepare Britain for war?
3 Why did Germany need to gain control of the skies over Britain and the English Channel?
4 Explain the different stages of the Battle of Britain.
5 Why was the RAF's victory in the Battle of Britain so important?

Revision tip

You need to be able to explain the important part that the RAF played during the Battle of Britain, as well as why Germany lost this battle when it had such superiority in numbers.

MacDermott's reforms

In June 1940, John MacDermott was appointed to the new post of Minister of Public Security. He organised:

▶ the rapid erection of public air-raid shelters
▶ the reinforcement of the emergency services
▶ efforts to evacuate children from Belfast.

At the same time, blackout curtains were used to stop lights alerting *Luftwaffe* pilots to the locations of towns and cities across Northern Ireland.

MR. DE VALERA'S SYMPATHY

Wholehearted Help for Belfast

MR. DE VALERA, speaking at Castlebar on Saturday, expressed sympathy with the victims of the air attack on Belfast, and promised " any help we can give them."

" This is the first time I have spoken in public since the disaster in Belfast," he said, " and I know you will wish me to express, on your behalf and on behalf of the Government, our sympathy with the people who are suffering there.

" In the past, and probably in the present, too, a number of them did not see eye to eye with us politically," Mr. de Valera continued, " but they are all our people, they are one and the same people, and their sorrows in the present instance are also our sorrows.

" I want to say that any help we can give them in the present time we will give to them wholeheartedly.— (applause)—believing that were the circumstances reversed they would also give us their help wholeheartedly."

▲ Newspaper report on de Valera's reaction to the Belfast Blitz.

The events of the Belfast Blitz

However, it was too little too late. When over 150 *Luftwaffe* aircraft bombed Belfast in April and May 1941, the city still only had 22 anti-aircraft guns, insufficient air cover from fighter aircraft and public shelters capable of housing no more than a quarter of the city's population.

The *Luftwaffe* bombed Belfast four times in 1941 (7–8 April, 15–16 April, 4–5 May and 5–6 May). Belfast was targeted for a number of reasons:

▶ Germany was aware of the key role that the city's industries were playing in the war effort.
▶ Northern Ireland was important strategically.

As a result of these attacks:

▶ The city's most densely populated areas were bombed: 955 civilians were killed and 2,436 were injured.
▶ Almost 57,000 homes were damaged or destroyed, leaving in excess of 100,000 people temporarily homeless and 15,000 permanently affected.
▶ In the short term, many thousands fled Belfast to the rest of Northern Ireland and even to Éire, enduring harsh conditions.
▶ Belfast's industrial infrastructure, the bombers' main target, suffered extensive damage. It took six months for industrial production to recover.

The impact of the *Luftwaffe* raids

Belfast suffered more, relatively speaking, from *Luftwaffe* attacks than other British cities had, at least up to that point (Source A). The 745 deaths that resulted from the raid of 15–16 April was greater than the number of deaths resulting from a single raid elsewhere in the UK.

Source A Ernst von Kuhren, a German journalist, reporting his impressions of the Blitz of 4–5 May 1941 (adapted).

I can really say that I could not believe my eyes. When we approached the target ... we stared silently into a sea of flames such as none of us had seen before ... In Belfast there was not a large number of fires, but just one enormous fire which spread over the entire harbour and industrial area.

Other parts of Northern Ireland also suffered, although not on the same scale. Derry/Londonderry was also raided in April 1941 and, although it is probable that the intended target was military, the bombs fell on civilian housing, killing 15 people. Also attacked were Bangor (where five civilians lost their lives) and Newtownards Airport (where ten guards died).

◀ Luftwaffe map from 1940 showing key targets in Belfast.

An unexpected impact of the Blitz

What the *Luftwaffe* attacks exposed clearly was the poverty, poor housing and levels of health being endured by many in Northern Ireland, particularly its urban areas. Only 50,000 houses had been built in the interwar years. In addition, housing standards were significantly lower than those in Britain and it is estimated that up to 5,000 existing houses were uninhabitable even before the war. Indeed in the aftermath of the air raids, the Home Affairs Minister, Dawson Bates, described those living in Belfast's slums as 'nearly sub-human'. Contemporary reports would appear to support this, showing that children were infested with lice and many were suffering from illnesses such as tuberculosis (responsible for half the deaths of 15–25-year-olds).

Activities

1 How effective were preparations for war in Northern Ireland?
2 Why did German bombers see Northern Ireland as a target?
3 What did the Blitz reveal about living conditions for many of Belfast's citizens?

Revision tip

You must be able to explain the impact that the Blitz had on Belfast and Derry/Londonderry.

A review of housing needs concluded that there needed to be massive improvements to existing housing, including rural housing, alongside a substantial programme of house building. It also recommended improvements to the health and educational sectors.

In many ways the foundations for the reforms that were introduced in the years following the end of the war were laid in the destruction caused – and revealed – by the Belfast Blitz. In light of the appalling health of many of its poorest citizens, the Stormont government established a new Ministry of Health and Local Government in 1944.

Éire and the Blitz

Despite de Valera's declaration of neutrality, there remained the possibility that Ireland might be invaded by Germany as the first stage of an invasion of Britain. This possibility was discussed by representatives of both governments. The outcome of their talks was the agreement that members of the British Army based in Northern Ireland could move back into Éire to secure its vulnerable western flanks.

Well aware of the limitations in its armed forces (Interpretation D), the government increased Éire's military capacity by:

► Increasing the size of the army to over 40,000.
► Creating a reserve force in the shape of the Local Defence Force. However, this force was poorly equipped.
► Extending the size of the navy.
► Establishing an air force.

De Valera moved against the IRA as a result of that organisation's rather clumsy efforts to conspire with the Third Reich against the British and because its members had stolen a million rounds of ammunition from Dublin. Using the Offences Against the State Act, the government introduced internment without trial against suspected IRA members. At least 1,000 individuals were targeted in this way. Six IRA members were hanged and when a further three went on hunger strike, nothing was done to prevent their deaths. De Valera's stance was supported by the vast majority of the population. In the event, the government's onslaught left the IRA broken (Interpretation E).

▲ Irish Army on manoeuvres during the war. Note the German Army-style helmets that the soldiers are wearing; soon after these were changed.

Interpretation D Historian M.E. Collins comments on the Éire Army's ability to defend the country from invasion.

These men had no decent equipment. Little had been spent on defence during the 1930s and there was no native arms industry.

Interpretation E Historian M.E. Collins reflects on de Valera's attitude to the IRA during the emergency.

Once war broke out, IRA activity became a threat to neutrality … De Valera struck ruthlessly against this threat [and] by 1943 the IRA had almost ceased to exist.

Activity

Create a table to show the events of the Blitz in and the impact of the Blitz on both Northern Ireland and Éire.

The effects of the war on Éire

The war – or 'Emergency' as it was called – had an impact on Ireland in a number of ways:

▶ Poor *Luftwaffe* navigation resulted in Dublin being bombed several times. In one attack in May 1941, 28 people died (some historians put the fatalities at 34 while a recent account puts the death-toll at over 40), at least 90 were injured (again, estimates vary) and several hundred houses were damaged or destroyed.

▶ The Ministry of Supplies was set up under Sean Lemass to ensure that Ireland was not left totally without essential materials. Lemass established the Irish Shipping Company to carry supplies previously brought by British ships. However, factories still had to close because they could not get hold of sufficient natural resources or manufacturing equipment. Petrol and coal were particularly in short supply. As a result of the lack of the former, usage of public transport increased. As a result of the lack of the latter, the use of turf as fuel increased many times over.

▶ Ireland benefited from a food surplus. However, the lack of available artificial fertilisers damaged productivity even though over one and a half times more land was being used to grow crops. In addition, other imports such as tea and sugar had to be rationed due to the lack of imports. Attempts were made to increase wheat production to support the production of bread. Unfortunately the Irish climate was not best suited to this crop and so rationing had to be introduced.

▶ The lack of maize meant that home-grown grain had to be used to feed livestock.

▶ Other goods that were rationed included butter, while fruit and chocolate became unavailable. As a result, cross-border smuggling increased. However, the availability of most meat and dairy produce, in addition to the potato, meant that most people were able to survive without having to tighten their belts too much.

▶ The closure of factories had an impact on employment levels and many Irish people began to seek their fortunes in Britain. It is estimated that between 1939 and 1945 about 200,000 (estimates vary) Irish people crossed the Irish Sea. Many of these emigrants worked in British munitions factories.

At the same time there were no wartime blackouts in Éire and the state's cinemas and theatres remained open for business. As a consequence, large numbers of servicemen and better-off northerners crossed the border for entertainment and nights out.

Despite the general support for neutrality among the Éire population, the harsh economic situation meant that *Fianna Fáil* still lost 10 seats in the 1943 general election. Within a year, all but one of these seats had been regained in another election. This snap poll was called by de Valera to take advantage of the increased popularity of his government as a result of the Allies' decision to isolate Ireland in advance of D-Day. The reason for the Allies' action was de Valera's refusal of an American request to shut down the German and Japanese embassies in Dublin to prevent leaks of the Allied invasion plans.

Activities

1 What changes did the Dublin government make to Éire's military forces at the start of the war?
2 What steps did the Dublin government take against the IRA during the war? How effective were these measures?
3 What impact did the war have on Éire? Use the following headings in your answer:
   ● *Luftwaffe* bombing raids
   ● the supplies
   ● foodstuffs and rationing
   ● emigration
   ● politics.

Revision tip

You must be able to explain the steps that Dublin took to prepare itself against invasion, and the impact of the war and the 'Emergency' on Éire.

Practice question

Describe one reason why the Irish Republican Army (IRA) was banned towards the end of World War II.

This page provides guidance on how to answer questions 3 and 4 in the exam.

Question 3

Study **Source C** and answer the question which follows:

How **useful** is **Source C** for an historian studying de Valera's attitude to the Irish Free State's membership of the British Commonwealth and the actions that he took once in power?

Explain your answer, using **Source C and your contextual knowledge**. [5]

Guidance

You should be looking to spend about seven minutes on this question. To access all the available marks your answer needs to address fully the issue of the source's utility: its usefulness.

Useful means **what do we learn from the source**: what does it tell us about the event in question? What kind of source is it? Where is it from, why was it produced and who was seeing it at the time? Most importantly, remember to comment – considering your own knowledge – on what the source does **not** tell us (its limitations), which may reduce its usefulness.

Source C Cartoon showing Éamon de Valera destroying the 'Commonwealth Bridge'. De Valera is attempting to remove some of the key elements of the 1921 treaty (such as the Oath of Allegiance), named on the stones

THE BRIDGE-BREAKER.

MR. DE VALERA. "IF I CAN SHIFT THIS KEYSTONE, THAT OUGHT TO CLEAR THE WAY FOR SOMETHING DRAMATIC."

Example

Step 1

Look carefully at the source and caption and see if you can recognise any figures or phrases in it. Say how the source is useful, and include details from your own knowledge.

→ Source C is a primary source and it is useful because it shows de Valera being called a 'bridge-breaker' and wanting to destroy the Governor Generalship, Oath of Allegiance and Annuities. The 'bridge' may refer to the existing links between the Irish Free State and the Commonwealth. The date is useful because it is the year de Valera came to power. The cartoon also outlines the main areas that de Valera wanted to deal with in terms of his relationship with the Commonwealth. It also suggests that there may be dangers for the Irish Free State in destroying the 'bridge', and that de Valera may not understand the potential dangers of the action he is planning to take.

Example

> However, the usefulness of the source is limited because it is from a British magazine and therefore only shows one perspective [the British one]. For example, it does not show that de Valera had a lot of support for his policies within the Irish Free State. Also, it is a cartoon, so there are questions about how usefully it can explain what was a complicated issue.

Question 4

Study **Source C** again and answer the question below:

How **reliable** is **Source C** for an historian studying de Valera's attitude to the Irish Free State's membership of the British Commonwealth and the actions that he took once in power?

Explain your answer, **using Source C and your contextual knowledge**.   [6]

Guidance

You should be looking to spend about eight minutes on this question. To access all the available marks, your answer needs to address fully the issue of the source's reliability.

Reliability means **whether or not we can take what the source says to be true**. Keep in mind issues such as the source's **type**, its **author**, **when** it was written, **who** it was written for (its **audience**), **why** it was written (**motive**) and its **tone and content**.

When discussing reliability the issue of **bias** will more than likely appear. Remember, just because a source is **biased** – and all sources are biased in some way or other – does not mean that it is not useful.

Step 1

Look carefully at the source and caption and see if you can recognise any figures or phrases in it. Say how the source is reliable or not reliable.

Example

> Source C may not be reliable because it is a cartoon from a British magazine. Cartoons are usually meant to make a point visually or to send a message and so they can be seen as biased. It is from a British magazine so it has been created from that point of view and was intended mainly for a British audience.

Step 2

Use details from your own knowledge.

Example

> The source is showing de Valera as a 'bridge-breaker', wanting to destroy the link to the Commonwealth through removing key parts of the Irish Free State's relationship with the Commonwealth, including the Governor Generalship, the Oath of Allegiance and the Land Annuities. It shows him as destructive when actually he had a lot of support in 1932 when he came to power.

In May 1945, the Second World War ended in Europe; two months later the Labour Party led by Clement Attlee won the British general election. Although Churchill and the Conservatives had led Great Britain to victory, voters were more attracted by Labour's promises of jobs for all, government ownership of Britain's industries and, most importantly of all, the introduction of a free health care, education and benefits system available to all British citizens (Source A). This system was based on ideas first developed by Lord Beveridge in 1942 – when he published a report that recommended wholesale reforms within the existing United Kingdom's health, social services and education systems. The changes that Beveridge proposed would become known as the Welfare State.

> **Source A** Extract from the Labour Party's manifesto for the 1945 general election. The manifesto was entitled *Let us Face the Future*.
>
> The nation wants food, work and homes. It wants more than that – it wants good food in plenty, useful work for all, and comfortable, labour-saving homes … It wants a high and rising standard of living, security for all against a rainy day, an educational system that will give every boy and every girl a chance to develop the best that is in them.

▲ A Labour election poster of 1945.

The new Labour government's policies in Britain

Taking up office just after six years of total war, the new government faced a very difficult situation:

▶ The country was almost broke.

▶ Poverty was widespread.

▶ Most of the goods being made in Britain were being sold abroad so that food could be bought in from other countries.

▶ Coal, bread and potato supplies had almost run out. In 1946, rationing of bread was introduced. A year later potatoes were also rationed.

As a result the immediate post-war period in Britain was known as the 'age of austerity'.

The Labour Party believed that the government should control Britain's key industries and service providers. This policy of nationalisation was implemented as follows:

▶ 1947: coal mines and electricity.

▶ 1948: railways.

▶ 1949: iron and steel.

The Labour government began to construct large numbers of houses in order to eliminate Britain's slums and as a response to the damage caused by German bombs. A massive 680,000 houses were erected between 1947 and 1950.

The reaction at Stormont to Labour's victory in Westminster

In the past, the Labour Party had been strongly critical of the Northern Ireland state. Some unionists were so worried about the new Labour government at Westminster, and its plans for social reform, that there were calls for Northern Ireland to seek dominion status, as had been granted to the Irish Free State in 1921. Some unionists were particularly worried about how much the reforms would cost. In the end, however, it was felt that Northern Ireland's best chance of staying economically stable was to keep its close relationship with the rest of the United Kingdom.

The establishment of the Welfare State in Britain and Northern Ireland

The issues already outlined reinforced the need for a new approach to issues of social policy and so a National Health Service (NHS) came into operation in July 1948. At first it faced opposition from those in the middle and upper classes concerned about the costs in terms of increased taxation and from doctors fearing that it would limit their freedoms, restrict their ability to earn money and turn them into civil servants. In the end, however, the NHS was joined by 90 per cent of doctors and was hugely successful, even if it was massively expensive, and it greatly benefited public health in Britain and in Northern Ireland.

Reasons for the introduction of the Welfare State in Northern Ireland

The destruction left by the Blitz (see pages 123–24) showed how there was an urgent need to change social policy and look after the people who needed help the most, such as the poor and sick who lived in slums or houses that were not fit to be lived in.

Attitudes to the Welfare State in Northern Ireland

Despite the need for massive reforms in health care and housing following years of poverty and deprivation, many in Northern Ireland were worried about what Labour's reforming policies might mean for them. The middle classes and doctors voiced the same objections as their equivalents had done across the Irish Sea. Unionist business leaders feared the implications of nationalisation. Meanwhile, apart from its suspicions of what it saw as the Labour government's socialism, the Stormont administration feared the loss of power to a centralising government and wondered how it was to finance the introduction of similar reforms (Interpretation B). Not surprisingly, those less well-off welcomed the Welfare State as it promised improvements in their quality of life, while nationalists welcomed the initiative as they viewed a Labour government as potentially more sympathetic to their situation.

Stormont need not have worried; the Labour government demonstrated its gratitude for Northern Ireland's contribution to the war effort by helping to cover the costs of the introduction of the Welfare State through the provision of generous subsidies (Interpretation C). As a result improvements were effected in a range of areas.

Interpretation B Historian J.J. Lee explains Stormont's attitude to the prospect of a Welfare State.

The unionist cabinet contemplated with distaste the election of a Labour government in Britain … [however] it decided it had no option but to adhere to the existing constitutional arrangement and do its best to modify the more repellent features of Labour's welfare legislation.

Interpretation C Historian M.E. Collins explains how the Welfare State was financed in Northern Ireland.

Since the North could not afford [the Welfare State reforms] out of its own resources, the unionist government made an agreement with London that Britain would subsidise [help to fund] them … This subsidy allowed the Northern government to give its citizens a far higher level of health care, social service and education than they could otherwise have afforded.

Activities

1. Why did the Labour Party win the 1945 general election?
2. Why was this period known as an 'age of austerity' in Britain?
3. Make a copy of the following table and fill it in:

Area	Aims	Actions taken
Industry		
Housing		
NHS		

4. How did the Stormont government react to Labour's plans? How did Labour overcome this opposition?

The impact of the Welfare State in Northern Ireland

The biggest development was the introduction of the health service, similar to the new programme in Britain. The new system began in 1948 and took root quickly, fighting against diseases such as polio and tuberculosis. By 1962, Northern Ireland's death rate was the lowest in the UK; in 1939 it had had the highest. Northern Ireland's population was also assisted through the introduction of a range of other welfare initiatives, including family allowance, national assistance and non-contributing pensions. These changes came in the aftermath of a restructured health system too, with the establishment – under the terms of the 1948 Health Services Act – of a General Health Services Board and a Hospitals Authority.

As already discussed, an already serious housing shortage in Northern Ireland was made worse by the impact of the war. A report commissioned by Brooke soon after he became Prime Minister was published in 1944. It estimated that 37 per cent of homes (43,000) in Belfast were unsuitable for living in and more than 100,000 new homes were required for the whole of Northern Ireland. In 1945, the Northern Ireland Housing Trust was established to oversee their construction. This was a massive undertaking that took two decades to complete. Local councils were also encouraged to construct dwellings through the provision of generous subsidies, however they were not as successful. Also, the way in which those council houses were given to people meant that not all benefited equally.

The Stormont government also made efforts to improve Northern Ireland's economy, particularly given the long-term decline in some of Northern Ireland's traditional industries such as linen and shipbuilding. The 1945 Industrial Development Act provided the land and incentives for the building of new factories.

At the same time, while living standards undoubtedly improved, the reforms did mean that Stormont came to rely more and more on the British government for money. This fact was resented by some unionist politicians.

The 1947 (Northern Ireland) Education Act and its impact

Radical changes were also introduced to the education sector by the 1947 Education Act when the school-leaving age was raised to 15 (with transfer to post-primary education at the age of 11). For the first time, children could stay at school free of charge until they were 15, and children who passed the 11+ examination could attend grammar schools, again without payment. As a result, the numbers of students in post-primary education doubled over the following eight years. In addition, local education authorities were required to provide free services to all schools, including transport, milk, meals, books, stationery and health care.

New secondary schools were constructed to cope with the massively increased numbers in education, while funding for the voluntary sector increased from 50 to 65 per cent (much higher than equivalent grants in England). Scholarships were also provided to allow more people to access third level education. Teacher training provision was also improved in both Catholic and Protestant sectors and soon had a positive impact in the classroom.

Activity

Describe the steps the Northern Ireland government took in the following areas:
- health and welfare
- education
- housing
- economy.

Revision tip

The introduction of the Welfare State in Northern Ireland was a development of great significance. Make sure that you can identify and explain its different elements, the variety of reactions to it and its overall impact.

The reforms greatly helped the Catholic population. As a consequence of the 1947 Education Act, the educational system in Northern Ireland changed to become more modern, even if the old religious divisions remained. In spite of their poor backgrounds, now more Catholic children could go to secondary schools and universities. But as the Catholic population became more educated, some of its members began to speak out against what they saw as the inequality and discrimination within Northern Ireland.

▲ A cartoon showing Labour's socialist medicine: a bitter medicine for the Stormont government. On the right we see Basil Brooke unwillingly swallowing a dose of medicine that is being given by a representative of the Westminster government. Why does Brooke not want to take it?

Activities

Work in groups of three or four. Each group takes one of the following topics:
- The establishment of the Welfare State in Britain
- The establishment of the Welfare State in Northern Ireland
- The 1947 (Northern Ireland) Education Act.

Using pages 128–131, discuss and note for your topic:
- Why it happened
- What happened
- The impact on Northern Ireland.

Share your ideas with the rest of the class, presenting them in an appropriate way:
- as a wall chart – for example a spider diagram or Venn diagram
- as a cartoon.

Revision tip

It is important that you understand how important it was for Attlee's government to fulfil its promises to the British people.

Practice question

Explain two of the following:
a The reaction at Stormont to the election of a Labour government at Westminster.
b The different attitudes of people in Northern Ireland to the Welfare State.
c The social impact of the 1947 Education Act on Northern Ireland.

This page provides guidance on how to answer question 5 in the exam.

Question 5

(a) Name the British Prime Minister at the time of the Anglo-Irish Agreements in 1938. [1]

(b) Give **one** reason for the introduction of the Welfare State. [1]

(c) Give **one** term of the Irish Constitution of 1937. [1]

(d) Describe **one** reason why there was nationalist opposition to the introduction of conscription. [2]

Guidance

You should be looking to spend a maximum of four minutes on this question. To access all marks you need to give clear answers and, with reference to Parts (b) and (d), a clear reason for the issue/event in question.

Whilst being accurate, make sure that you do this question as quickly as you can. Example answers for parts b and d are below.

> **Example for part 5b**
>
> The war highlighted the very poor conditions in which people were living across Britain and Northern Ireland.

> **Example for part 5d**
>
> One reason for nationalist opposition to the introduction of conscription was that members of the nationalist community did not believe that the British government had the right to introduce conscription in Northern Ireland.

8 Constitutional changes and effects on relationships

After 1945, Éire found itself isolated economically, particularly by its nearest neighbour, Britain, and its allies. The reason was London's dissatisfaction with Éire's decision to remain neutral during the Second World War. The result was a severe economic depression, which was made worse by poor weather in 1946 and 1947 (Interpretation A):

▶ The number of people unemployed shot up.

▶ Building materials, particularly timber, became almost unobtainable.

▶ The lack of fertilisers during the war meant that the land was short of essential nutrients, thus limiting productivity. Poor weather in summer 1946 had a further impact on crop production.

▶ Britain withheld coal imports.

▶ Éire experienced severe fuel shortages in 1947 as a result of increased demand during the harsh winter weather.

▶ Wartime rationing remained in force and was extended to include bread from the start of 1947.

▶ Inflation began to rise and, as workers failed to achieve sufficient wage increases, a wave of strikes broke out.

▶ Emigration rates remained high, with as many as 24,000 leaving Éire each year. This in itself had a significant economic impact.

A State of Emergency

By 1947 the situation had deteriorated to the point where de Valera declared that Éire remained in a State of Emergency.

Unlike Northern Ireland, which was now beginning to benefit from Labour's modernising policies, state benefits (unemployment, family allowance) in Éire were almost non-existent and there was no welfare state to look after people. Instead people had to pay for their own medical care.

The end result was increased unpopularity for the *Fianna Fáil* government; as a consequence it lost the 1948 general election.

As a result of *Fianna Fáil*'s defeat, a coalition government took power in Éire. This was made up of a range of political parties:

▶ *Fine Gael* was the largest of the parties. It was set up in 1933 as a union of a number of parties/groups including *Cumann na nGaedheal*. It was led by General Richard Mulcahy.

▶ Two different Labour parties, each opposed to the other.

▶ Farmers were represented by *Clann na Talmhan*.

▶ *Clann na Poblachta* was a Republican and socialist party. It was led by Seán MacBride, former Chief of Staff of the IRA, 1936–38.

▶ The government also had the support of 12 independent TDs (*Teachta Dála* – Deputy to the *Dáil*, Member of *Dáil Éireann*).

As leader of the largest party, Mulcahy should have become *Taoiseach*. However, he was unacceptable to MacBride because of his involvement in the Irish Civil War. For this reason, senior *Fine Gael* politician John A. Costello was appointed as *Taoiseach* (Interpretation B).

Interpretation A An assessment of Éire's economic situation after 1945 by Dermot Keogh in his book *Twentieth Century Ireland*.

It was a case of wartime conditions without a war.

Interpretation B Historian M.E. Collins assesses the reasons for the inter-party government's survival.

The new government looked weak and unlikely to last. It contained an uneasy blend of old and young, of Republicans and Free Staters, of conservatives and socialists. In practice, however, it worked well. Costello was an excellent *Taoiseach*. He gave each minister a good deal of freedom to pursue his own policies.

▲ The grass is greener on the other side of the fence!

The new government introduced a range of policies that were designed to modernise the Irish economy. These measures included:

▶ The establishment in 1949 of the Industrial Development Authority (IDA). Its purpose was to revitalise Éire's economy.

▶ The creation of *Córas Tráchtála*, a government body set up to increase the country's trade with North America.

▶ A house-building programme which resulted in the erection of close to 12,000 new houses annually by 1950.

▶ The initiation of huge land reclamation projects and the extension of electrification schemes.

▶ The signing of a trade agreement with Britain in 1948. This improved profit margins for Irish agricultural exports.

As a result of these measures, the Irish economy entered into a slow, if steady, period of improvement; however, the government's failure to engage in longer-term economic planning meant that the economy did not develop as quickly as it might. At the same time, the problem of emigration continued to bleed away the potential of the Irish population.

Revision tip ↻

North–South differences were made worse by the impact of the Second World War. Make sure that you understand all of the reasons why this was the case.

Activities

1 How well did the Éire economy perform in the post-war period? Why was this?
2 How did this situation differ from Northern Ireland, both economically and socially?
3 Why did de Valera lose power in 1948?
4 What type of government took over from *Fianna Fáil* in 1948?
5 What economic policies did the inter-party government introduce during its term of office?

Éire intends to become a Republic

The members of the inter-party government – particularly *Clann na Poblachta* – felt that the 1937 constitution had made Éire a republic in all but name and had left the country's relationship with Britain in a confused state, neither fully in nor fully out of the Commonwealth. Therefore, in November 1948 the Republic of Ireland Bill was introduced into the *Dáil*. It came into effect on Easter Monday 1949 (Interpretation C).

Reaction among the people of Northern Ireland to Éire's intention

Reactions to developments in Dublin were mixed in Northern Ireland:

▶ Northern nationalists unsuccessfully demanded seats in the *Dáil* so that their views could be heard. Many of them felt abandoned by Dublin and objected to the inter-party government's claim that it represented the whole island. Some continued to call the Republic the Irish Free State, believing that the former term should be reserved for a 32-county Irish Republic.

▶ Unionists felt threatened by the declaration of the Republic. Fearing – correctly – that the Republic would now make a determined effort to reunite Ireland, unionists rejected Dublin's offer of any reasonable guarantees to respect their rights if they were to agree to end partition.

The significance of the Anti-Partition League and the 'chapel gate election'

The Stormont government, therefore, pledged its defiance to the declaration of the Republic and used the border issue as the justification for calling a general election for February 1949. Brooke urged unionists to vote in support of Northern Ireland's continued membership of the UK (Source D).

Nationalists, not surprisingly, were urged to vote in favour of a united Ireland. In this election they were represented by the Anti-Partition League which had been established in 1945 to unite 'all those opposed to partition into a solid block' and in response to the Dublin government's seeming inability to make any progress in terms of securing the removal of the border. Indeed, the League had proved remarkably successful in gaining support across the island of Ireland and amongst Irish communities living abroad.

Once the election was called, the Anti-Partition League called for the support of its backers in the Republic of Ireland. As a result, it was agreed to set up an 'anti-partition fund' to help finance the election campaign. Indeed the election became known as the 'chapel gate election' as much of the money used to fund the nationalists' campaign was raised mainly through collections outside churches in the South. This fact alone caused great resentment within the unionist community and more than likely helped strengthen unionist support for the Stormont government. No doubt Brooke also benefited from being able to point to southern political interference in the election campaign – as well as substantial church support for the Anti-Partition League.

The outcome – after a bitter campaign spoiled by sectarian violence – was an increased share of votes and seats for both unionists and nationalists, although it was the former who still controlled Stormont once the votes had been counted. Brooke used his increased support as justification for demanding a British guarantee of Northern Ireland's future within the UK.

Interpretation C
Historian M.E. Collins assesses the significance of the Declaration of a Republic in 1949.

Ireland at last cut the few tenuous [weak] links which had bound her to the British Commonwealth. This changed nothing of the reality of independence which had existed since 1937–8. But it did mark a final end to the old quarrel over the treaty. The question of Irish independence was finally laid to rest. As evidence of its new-asserted independence, the Dublin government declined the invitation to join NATO in 1949, arguing that membership would compromise its neutrality and recognise the partition of Ireland.

Source D Extract from an election speech delivered by Brooke, 1949.

Our country is in danger ... we fight to defend our very existence and the heritage of our Ulster children ... Loyalists must stand united, pledging themselves ... that, come what may, we shall maintain our province as part and parcel of the United Kingdom.

Declaration of the Republic of Ireland, 1949

As Éire was the first country to leave the Commonwealth, there was concern about how Britain would react. If London responded negatively it could have a major impact on the Irish economy and on the position of Irish people living and working in Great Britain. The British Government was annoyed at what Costello's government had done (Source E), however, Australia and Canada supported Éire, stating that there was no reason why an Irish Republic could not continue to work closely with the members of the Commonwealth. As a consequence, London decided not to overreact.

> **Source E** Attlee's view of Éire's decision to leave the British Commonwealth, 1948.
>
> The government of Éire considered the cutting of the last tie which united Éire to the British Commonwealth as a more important objective than ending partition.

At the same time, London – probably due to pressure from other Commonwealth countries such as Australia and Canada – decided that it would not treat Éire as a foreign country but as a near neighbour with which it enjoyed a special relationship. Therefore, the Ireland Act provided for the rights and privileges of Irish citizens travelling to, living in and working in Great Britain. It stated that:

▶ Passports were not needed for travel between the two countries.

▶ Working permits were not required for Irish workers in the UK or British workers in the Republic of Ireland.

▶ Citizens of both nations had voting rights in each other's elections if they were living in the other country.

▶ Éire would continue to enjoy preferential treatment compared to non-Commonwealth countries when it came to trade.

▲ The Republic is declared. Crowds gather outside Dublin's General Post Office, 1949.

Reactions and effects, and the impact on relations

Westminster's response to the declaration of the Republic was the Ireland Act of June 1949. It stated that: 'In no event will Northern Ireland … cease to be part of … the United Kingdom without the consent of the Parliament of Northern Ireland'. Put simply, the Northern Ireland Parliament had been given the final word in any future debate about the ending of partition. Not surprisingly, unionists felt reassured by these guarantees – the strongest guarantee they had ever received from a British Government. As a consequence Unionist control of Northern Ireland was confirmed and partition made much more difficult to end. That said, Westminster still had the power to change its mind in the future, should it choose. A royal visit to Northern Ireland in 1949 further cemented its sense of union with the other parts of the UK. Therefore, relations between the governments did not deteriorate as much as might initially have been expected.

Dublin and the nationalists in Northern Ireland, on the other hand, were outraged and strongly expressed their displeasure with the Act, particularly the guarantees regarding partition. While this reaction is understandable, it is difficult to see what else the Irish Government might have expected. Its foreign policy focus became persuading London to remove the border. However, nothing was changed; Attlee felt that, as Dublin had not consulted him about the declaration of the Republic, he was free to give whatever guarantees he wanted to Northern Ireland.

Activities

1 For what reasons did the inter-party government declare Ireland a republic?
2 How did the following react to this declaration?
   - Commonwealth countries
   - Britain
   - the different groups in Northern Ireland.
3 What was the purpose of the Ireland Act, 1949?
4 Explain how the following groups responded to the Ireland Act:
   - unionists
   - The Dublin Government
   - nationalists in Northern Ireland
5 Attlee claimed that 'The government of Éire considered the cutting of the last tie which united Éire to the British Commonwealth as a more important objective than ending partition.' Do you agree?

Practice questions

1 Give one of the policies introduced by the 1948 coalition government of Éire.
2 Describe one reason why the Fianna Fáil government lost the Éire general election in 1948.

Revision tip

The passage of the 1949 Ireland Act was of huge importance to Northern Ireland's unionist population. Make sure you are able to explain what the Act stated and why Westminster was prepared to pass it.

This page provides guidance on how to answer question 6 in the exam.

Question 6

Explain **two** of the following:

A The impact of the 1941 Belfast Blitz on Northern Ireland.

B The reasons for the Economic War.

C The different reactions to the impact of the Declaration of Independence in 1948.

Explanation One: (A, B or C)

Explanation Two: (B or C if you chose A; A or B if you chose C; A or C if you chose B)   [9+9]

Guidance

You should be looking to spend about ten minutes on **each part** of this question.

To access all the available marks, your answer needs to 'demonstrate knowledge and understanding to explain and analyse historical events and periods'. You will need to ensure that there is sufficient (relevant) detail in your answer and show – through what you write – that you understand the issue that you are attempting to explain.

Remember that the quality of written communication will be assessed in this question.

Step 1

You have a choice here – spend a little time considering each answer option, and then choose the two you are most familiar with. Start with your first option and state your point clearly.

> The 1941 Blitz had a significant impact on Northern Ireland in general and on Belfast in particular …

Step 2

Use accurate detail in your answer and remember that you are trying to explain an event as fully as you can: **do not** write a story of what happened. Remember to keep your points relevant to the question.

> Belfast was a great strategic significance due to the number of industries that were supporting the Allied war effort. These industries included Short and Harland, and Harland and Wolff.
>
> Belfast was bombed four times in April/May 1941. The different Luftwaffe raids had a number of impacts including: deaths [give detail], destruction of property [give detail], dislocation of people [give detail], and damage to industrial production …
>
> Even though Belfast was the Luftwaffe's main target, other areas of Northern Ireland also came under attack. These included …

Step 3

Do the same for your second option.

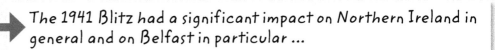

> The Economic War began because of a variety of reasons …

This option focuses on how relationships between Northern Ireland and its neighbours changed and developed between 1965 and 1998.

During this period the relationship between both parts of the island of Ireland and with Great Britain changed significantly.

At the start of this period, unionist control was assured; following the appointment of Terence O'Neill as Prime Minister of Northern Ireland, the situation became somewhat delicate – given the unionist and nationalist reactions to his attempts to modernise Northern Ireland.

In the context of a broader – international – drive for equality, the demands of NICRA and People's Democracy came up against the desire of many unionists to maintain the status quo.

Increasing tensions resulted in the emergence of paramilitary groups, the deployment of the British Army, and a number of terrible tragedies. Attempts at a political solution failed and resulted in the implementation of direct rule from Westminster.

Thereafter, the history of Northern Ireland became one of desperately seeking a political solution – against the background of very different political ambitions. Through Hunger Strikes, local party negotiations, Inter-Governmental Conferences, bombings, shootings and more negotiations, the conflict seemed almost beyond resolve. Then, in 1998, a workable solution did emerge in the form of the Good Friday Agreement.

This option examines the following key areas of content:

▶ The O'Neill years
▶ The campaign for civil rights
▶ A deteriorating situation, 1969–72
▶ The search for a political solution – attempt at power-sharing, 1973–74
▶ Changing Republican strategy
▶ Changing relations – towards closer co-operation
▶ The Downing Street Declaration, 1993
▶ The Good Friday Agreement, 1998

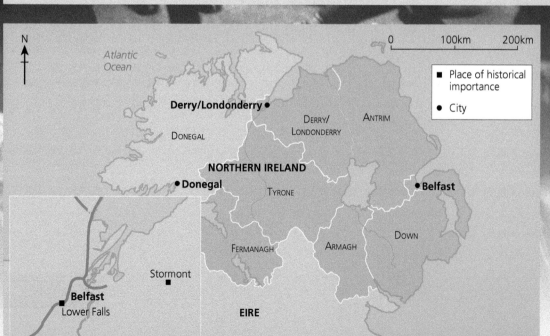

◀ Map showing Northern Ireland during this period

Introduction

The state of Northern Ireland was established by the 1920 Government of Ireland Act. This Act partitioned Ireland into two parts:

1 A 26-county Southern Ireland (which after the 1921 Anglo-Irish Treaty became the Irish Free State).
2 A six-county Northern Ireland.

The first elections for the new Northern Ireland Parliament were held in May 1921 and it met for the first time the following month.

Reactions to the new state

The population of Northern Ireland reacted to the new arrangements rather differently:

▶ Unionists – who were mostly Protestant – were delighted. The new state had a substantial Protestant majority and so their control of the new state's government was more or less guaranteed. Indeed, in the May 1921 elections unionists won 40 out of the 52 seats available.
▶ Nationalists – most of whom were Catholic – were deeply upset; they wanted to be part of the rest of Ireland and governed by a parliament in Dublin.

Violence and discrimination

As a result of this desire, most unionists felt that nationalists could not be trusted and in this atmosphere of distrust the number of sectarian murders rocketed. The London government had already responded to increasing tensions by establishing the Ulster Special Constabulary (populated mainly by former members of the UVF). The new Northern Ireland government added to its powers by passing the Special Powers Act (1922), which allowed them to arrest and detain suspects without holding a trial.

Other political responses to the seeming threat of nationalism included:

▶ The abolition of proportional representation (despite its inclusion in the Government of Ireland Act) for local elections. This meant that fewer nationalists would be elected to councils.
▶ The redrawing of the boundaries of local council areas to ensure unionist control even where there was a nationalist majority. This was known as gerrymandering.
▶ Allowing only those who paid rates to vote in local elections. For every £10 paid in rates, one vote was given, up to a maximum of seven votes. This usually resulted in extra votes for the wealthy – who tended to be Protestant – and no votes for the poor – who were mostly, but not always, Catholic.

Discrimination was also practised against Catholics in other ways:

▶ They were allocated fewer houses than Protestants by the unionist-controlled councils, since ownership of a house gave a vote in local elections.
▶ The quality of much Catholic housing was inferior.
▶ They were less likely to have a job than those who were Protestant.

Developments up to 1963

The political, economic and social conditions created in the early 1920s remained largely unchanged until the 1960s. Northern Ireland played a valuable part in the Allied war effort 1939–45, and in the late 1940s the Welfare State was introduced to improve living conditions.

However, relations with the South (the Republic of Ireland since 1949) remained tense, particularly as Articles II and III of the Republic of Ireland's 1937 constitution laid claim to all of the island. Furthermore, an IRA campaign between 1956 and 1962 opposing the border, reinforced the northern government's view that nationalists were untrustworthy, though that campaign actually failed due to a lack of nationalist support.

In March 1963, the hard-line Lord Brookeborough resigned as Prime Minister of Northern Ireland. His replacement was the Minister of Finance, Captain Terence O'Neill.

O'Neill's policies and actions

Right from the start, O'Neill's leadership was weak, as most of the Official Unionist Party's (OUP) MPs had wanted another minister, Brian Faulkner, to get the job. However, at that time the party's leader was decided by a group of senior party members, not by election. This lack of widespread support within his party would undermine O'Neill throughout his premiership.

O'Neill's early statements suggested the prospect of change and progress in Northern Ireland. He believed that 'the face of Ulster' had to be transformed if it was to prosper. To achieve this goal, O'Neill promised to introduce 'bold and imaginative measures'.

O'Neill's main concern lay with improving the economy (Source A). To this end a number of key economic measures were either proposed or introduced during his time as Prime Minister:

▶ £900 million of investment and the creation of five economic zones to update existing industries and attract new ones.

▶ Modernisation of the road and railway network (including closing seemingly unprofitable railway lines).

▶ Co-operation with the Dublin-based Irish Trades Union Congress, whose support was important for economic development.

▶ The establishment of an economic council under Brian Faulkner to drive forward the modernisation of the economy.

▶ The creation of a Ministry of Development to drive economic revival.

▶ The establishment of a new city based on the existing towns of Lurgan and Portadown. The new city was to be called Craigavon.

▶ The development of a new university in the market town of Coleraine to help develop a skilled workforce.

Revision tip ↻

O'Neill never had the total loyalty of his party. Make sure you can explain how this would have weakened his position as Prime Minister.

Source A Terence O'Neill, sketching out his economic vision in 1963 (adapted).

It is a new motorway driving deeper into the province. It is a new airport worthy of our position as the busiest air centre in Britain outside London. It is a new hospital in Londonderry – the most modern in the British Isles. It is new laboratories and research facilities at Queen's to carry us to the frontiers of existing knowledge and beyond. It is the replacement of derelict slums by modern housing estates.

Successes and failures

It was soon clear that these policies were having a positive impact:

▶ A number of multinational firms such as Michelin, DuPont, Goodyear, ICI and Grundig took advantage of generous investment grants and tax allowances to open factories in Northern Ireland.

▶ The construction of a motorway system was started.

▶ An oil refinery was opened in Belfast.

▶ A new airport was under development.

▶ Links with the Republic of Ireland resulted in the signing of an agreement on the supply of electricity from the Republic of Ireland.

In total over 35,000 new jobs were created during the 1960s, but at the same time over 20,000 were lost in the ailing traditional industries such as linen manufacturing.

This was not the only bad economic news:

▶ Between 1963 and 1969 the government had to give money to shipbuilders Harland & Wolff to keep it afloat.

▶ Unemployment averaged between seven and eight per cent.

▶ Several companies refused government grants to open factories west of the River Bann, seeing the area as too remote from their export markets.

This last fact alone had significant implications, not only for unemployment in the west (over 12.5 per cent) but also for feeding allegations of bias in government policy. This was because the majority of the population in the west was nationalist.

Activities

1 What weakness did O'Neill face in his position right from the time of his appointment as Prime Minister of Northern Ireland?

2 Describe two measures taken by O'Neill to improve the economy of Northern Ireland.

3 Construct a spider diagram showing the economic policies introduced by O'Neill.

4 Explain what O'Neill hoped to achieve with his economic policies.

5 Make a copy of the following table. Using the information on the left, fill in the table as appropriate. Now look at your results; would you say that O'Neill's economic policies were a success or a failure? Provide evidence to support your answer.

Economic successes	Economic failures

Revision tip

Make sure that you are able to explain the successes and failures of O'Neill's economic policies.

O'Neill's attempts to improve community relations and differing responses

Within Northern Ireland, O'Neill tried to improve relations with the nationalist community by:

▶ Visiting Cardinal William Conway, Archbishop of Armagh, and spiritual leader of Ireland's Catholic population.

▶ Offering official condolences to the Catholic Church on Pope John XXIII's death (June 1963).

▶ Visiting schools and hospitals run by the Catholic Church.

▶ Increasing the financial support provided for Catholic schools and hospitals (such as Belfast's Mater Infirmorum Hospital) and schools.

These steps were courageous and were well received by the nationalist community. However, whether in the end they would go far enough for one community or be seen as too much for another remained to be seen.

▲ Terence O'Neill (left) and his wife (middle) leaving St Anne's Cathedral, Belfast, where they heard the Dean of Belfast, Cuthbert Peacocke (right), preach about the political situation in Ulster.

Revision tip ↻

O'Neill's actions with regard to reaching out to Northern Ireland's nationalist community were unheard of in terms of the history of the state. Make sure you can explain what he did and why he did it.

Activities

1 What actions did O'Neill take to improve relations between the communities in Northern Ireland?

2 Construct a spider diagram showing all of the policies introduced by O'Neill to improve relations within Northern Ireland.

3 What do you think could have been the benefits and dangers for O'Neill in holding out the hand of friendship within Northern Ireland?

O'Neill's attempts to improve relations

O'Neill realised that his economic policies would not change Northern Ireland on their own. There would also have to be social and political modernisation within Northern Ireland – to end discrimination and help nationalists to identify more strongly with the state. There would also have to be improvements in relations with the Republic of Ireland – to benefit the economy. As someone with both Gaelic and planter ancestry, O'Neill believed that he was the right man for the job. However, introducing such changes would increase the chances of division within unionism.

The Hand of Friendship: Dublin

On 14 January 1965, the first face-to-face meeting of Ireland's main leaders since 1925 took place at Stormont when O'Neill met with the *Taoiseach* Sean Lemass. That this was the first such meeting in 40 years was an indication of the tensions that had existed between the two parts of the island (Source B). Speaking later on television, O'Neill defended the meeting by arguing that both systems shared 'the same rivers, the same mountains and some of the same problems'.

O'Neill made a return visit to Dublin four weeks later. Both meetings focused on areas of economic co-operation and did not consider political issues.

Discussions also took place between northern and southern ministers on issues such as tourism and electrical link-ups.

There was both support and opposition within the unionist community for O'Neill's attempts to change Northern Ireland. The mixed reaction was due to the desire of many moderate unionists for reform and the fear among others of the changes that such reform might bring to their own position.

O'Neill's support among ordinary members of the OUP had never been total. Indeed, O'Neill did not even inform his own cabinet colleagues of Sean Lemass' January 1965 visit in advance (Interpretation C). This indicated his concerns about their possible reaction and also suggests that the idea for the visit was his alone.

Evidence of the divisions within the OUP over the visit was clear when Brian Faulkner condemned O'Neill's failure to consult his cabinet. That said, when Lemass' successor as *Taoiseach*, Jack Lynch, visited Northern Ireland in December 1967, the visit was agreed in cabinet, implying that by then such a visit had become more acceptable to its members.

> **Source B** Terence O'Neill reflecting on the likely fallout of the visit of Sean Lemass in Ulster at the Crossroads.
>
> [Lemass] suddenly said, 'I shall get into terrible trouble for this.' 'No, Mr Lemass,' I replied, 'it is I who will get into trouble for this.'

> **Interpretation C** The views of historian Jonathan Bardon, on Lemass' visit to Stormont. From his book *A History of Ulster* (1992).
>
> Some members of the Northern Ireland government did not easily forgive O'Neill's willingness to discuss the visit with senior civil servants without mentioning it in cabinet.

> **Revision tip** ↺
>
> O'Neill's meetings with Lemass were a significant development in the relationship between Northern Ireland and the Republic of Ireland. Make sure you can explain why this was.

▲ Terence O'Neill (1914–90) meeting Sean Lemass (1899–1971) at Stormont on 14 January 1965.

The emergence of Reverend Ian Paisley

While there was no widespread hostile public reaction to the Lemass visit, there was strong objection from the Moderator of the Free Presbyterian Church, Reverend Ian Paisley. Apart from longstanding Protestant concerns about the influence of the Catholic Church in the Republic, Paisley objected to any links with the Republic of Ireland, especially as Articles II and III of its constitution laid claim to the whole island of Ireland. When Lynch visited in 1967, Paisley illustrated his continuing opposition by snowballing the *Taoiseach*'s car. On the same day, Paisley and his supporters also carried placards describing O'Neill as a 'Lundy'.

Throughout the rest of the decade, Paisley's support grew as many unionists came to fear the implications of O'Neill's new policies and to resent the failure of such policies to improve their own lives. In the short term, however, O'Neill was delighted with the success the OUP enjoyed in the November 1965 general election when it won 38 out of 52 seats. This result seemed to suggest that many people were satisfied with his policies.

Violence and division

Before long, however, the situation in Northern Ireland deteriorated. Tensions increased in 1966 with the commemorations for the fiftieth anniversaries of the Easter Rising and the Battle of the Somme, and rioting broke out. Yet this was not the worst of the violence: two Catholics died in May and June 1966, the result of a series of gun attacks by the re-emerging UVF. O'Neill responded by banning the organisation.

As the situation worsened, O'Neill found that support within his own party was weakening. In September 1966, he revealed a plot by OUP backbenchers to get rid of him as leader. There were also growing rumours of opposition within his own cabinet from Deputy Prime Minister Brian Faulkner and Agriculture Minister Harry West.

By late 1967, the levels of O'Neill's support within unionism in general and the OUP in particular were dwindling. The ruling party was divided over strategy while opinion polls indicated increasing support within the unionist population for Paisley's policies.

Nationalist reactions: satisfaction and disappointment

O'Neill's policies received similarly mixed reactions from the nationalist community. Initial support for his policies soon gave way to frustration as the better future that seemed to have been promised failed to materialise. This annoyance was particularly felt among a new generation of Catholics.

▲ Ian Paisley (1926–2014) leading a protest march against ecumenism.

At first Catholic leaders, both political and religious, reacted warmly to O'Neill's attempts to hold out the hand of friendship. The visit of Lemass to Stormont was followed by the decision of the Nationalist Party to take up the role of official opposition in Stormont for the first time in its history.

However, O'Neill's policies also raised expectations, some of which were unlikely to be met given the growing tensions within unionism. There was outrage within nationalist circles at the decision of the Minister of Development, William Craig, to name the new city linking Portadown and Lurgan, Craigavon, after Northern Ireland's first Prime Minister.

There were also continued accusations that O'Neill's economic policies favoured the Protestant east at the expense of the Catholic west (Interpretation D). As evidence of this a number of points were made:

▶ With the exception of Derry/Londonderry, all the places earmarked for economic development were in Protestant areas.

▶ Unemployment was at a higher level west of the Bann.

▶ Despite significant cross-community protest, Northern Ireland's second university was sited in the mainly Protestant town of Coleraine rather than in the mainly nationalist Derry/Londonderry, Northern Ireland's second city.

▶ No significant attempts were made to increase Catholic membership of various health and education bodies. This fact alone even led the pro-O'Neill *Belfast Telegraph* to argue that a 'nonsense' was being made of attempts at bridge building.

Interpretation D Irish historian Professor J.J. Lee, writing in *Ireland 1912–1985: Politics and Society* (1989), (adapted).

Catholics could not be convinced that Craigavon and Coleraine were anything but sectarian decisions, designed to deprive the mainly Catholic west from ever catching up with the mainly Protestant east.

Activities

1 What did O'Neill hope to achieve by meeting with his Republic of Ireland counterparts?
2 What do you think could have been the benefits and dangers for O'Neill in holding out the hand of friendship towards the Republic of Ireland?
3 Explain how and why the following groups differed in their initial reaction to O'Neill's policies:
   ● moderate unionists
   ● OUP MPs
   ● supporters of Rev. Ian Paisley.
4 How had the unionist reaction to O'Neill's policies changed by 1967?
5 How did nationalists react at first to O'Neill's policies? Why did this reaction to O'Neill's policies change as time went on?

Practice questions

1 Give one reason why O'Neill wanted to improve the Northern Ireland economy.
2 Name the two leaders who met at Stormont in 1965.

It was not difficult to see why the US civil rights movement would have appeared attractive to reformers in Northern Ireland. Martin Luther King Jr's campaign had employed non-violent methods of civil disobedience in an effort to achieve equal opportunities for black people. Most importantly, by 1967 a series of marches and protests had led the US Congress to pass laws outlawing public discrimination and guaranteeing voting rights. These successes were widely reported in Europe.

The influence on Northern Ireland

The Northern Ireland Civil Rights Association (NICRA) was established at the start of 1967. One of its founder members, Paddy Devlin, later wrote that NICRA was 'inspired by the civil rights campaign to get justice and equality for blacks in the USA'. At the same time there were other sources of encouragement in the period following NICRA's establishment, notably the student demonstrations that took place in France during 1968.

Reasons for the emergence of NICRA

Set up as a non-sectarian movement, NICRA did not seek to end partition; rather it hoped to end what it saw as a number of serious abuses in the existing political system (Source A).

In particular it sought to:

▶ Achieve 'one man, one vote'. This would allow a vote to all people over 18 years old. It would also remove the right of business owners to cast multiple votes.

▶ Ensure the fair allocation of council houses. Being able to vote in council elections depended on being a ratepayer (householder). The fewer the number of Catholics who possessed a property, the fewer the number of Catholics who could vote.

▶ End gerrymandering. Perhaps the most infamous example of the practice was in the city of Derry/Londonderry, 1966, where the unionist-dominated council ruled over a Catholic population of 20,102 compared with a Protestant population of 10,274.

▶ Prevent discrimination in the allocation of government jobs. The Cameron Commission found widespread evidence of favouritism towards Protestants in the allocation of jobs (Source B). There was similar evidence of under-representation of Catholics in other areas of government employment, including the senior civil service and Northern Ireland's judges.

▶ Remove the operation of the Civil Authorities (Special Powers) Act, 1922, which allowed the government to arrest and detain people without trial.

▶ Disband the B Specials (see page 95).

▶ Establish a formal complaints procedure against local authorities to report breaches in the above areas.

Source A Political activist Eamon McCann reflects on NICRA's aims.

NICRA was a reformist organisation, out for limited change within the North, not an end to the northern state.

Source B An extract from the report of the Cameron Commission into disturbances in Northern Ireland, published on 12 September 1969.

The conclusion at which we arrived ... that certain at least of the grievances fastened upon by NICRA ... were justified in fact is confirmed by decisions already taken by the Northern Ireland government since these disturbances began.

Attitudes towards NICRA

Support for NICRA came from across the community, particularly from a new generation of Catholics, the first to have benefited from free education in the late 1940s. They had seen the growing self-confidence of Catholics elsewhere, not least in the USA where John F. Kennedy had been elected President in 1960. They were also unhappy with their own Nationalist Party, led by Eddie McAteer. Its only policy seemed to be the ending of partition.

Liberal Protestants sympathised with some of NICRA's demands and believed that making Northern Ireland fairer would undermine demands for a united Ireland. Support also came from communists, academics and trade unionists.

There was much suspicion about the emerging movement from within the unionist population. Some felt that it was simply intent on causing trouble and was just a front for the IRA; others believed it was only interested in Catholic rights (rather than rights for all) and would undermine the position of Protestants (Source C). Others thought that NICRA wanted a united Ireland, thus threatening the continued existence of Northern Ireland.

> **Source C** A Protestant housewife's view of NICRA.
>
> It was all the Catholics this, the Catholics that, living in poverty and us lording it over them. People looked around and said 'What, are they talking about us? With the damp running down the walls and the houses not fit to live in.'

▲ Crowds gather for a NICRA march under the watchful eye of the RUC.

Activities

1 Explain where NICRA borrowed some of its tactics and ideas from.
2 Construct a spider diagram showing NICRA's main demands.
3 Explain why a new generation of Catholics was emerging at this time and why it was unhappy with its current political leadership.
4 Why did many unionists react negatively to NICRA? Was this a reasonable interpretation? Explain your answer.

Revision tip

Many unionists saw NICRA as a front for Republicans. Make sure that you are able to explain how this would have had an impact on unionist attitudes to their demands.

Early civil rights marches and responses

The US civil rights movement's tactic of organising peaceful marches was first used in Northern Ireland on 24 August 1968. The occasion was a march between the County Tyrone towns of Coalisland and Dungannon. This demonstration took place because of the decision of the Dungannon rural district council to give a council house in the County Tyrone village of Caledon to a 19-year-old Protestant woman, rather than to a nationalist family. In response, Austin Currie, nationalist MP for East Tyrone, squatted in the house. After he was evicted, Currie suggested holding a protest march to highlight the situation. Although the demonstration was prevented by the police from reaching its intended destination of Dungannon town square, an alternative rally was organised at the police barricade and the event passed off without incident.

House allocation was also the issue that led to NICRA's second march. To highlight seeming inequalities in Londonderry Corporation's housing policy, a march was organised for 5 October 1968. In response the unionist apprentice boys organisation threatened to hold a rival march. The Stormont government responded by banning the holding of any march east of the River Foyle or within the historic city walls. The NICRA march's organisers rejected this ban.

Although the crowd that turned up on 5 October was relatively small, it was accompanied by powerful allies: four Westminster MPs (including Gerry Fitt, MP for West Belfast) and, even more importantly, an RTE (Irish television) camera crew. That night, television pictures beamed across the world showed more clearly than any words the heavy-handed tactics of the police to break up the rally. It became clear that Northern Ireland was on the verge of a crisis that would prove difficult to resolve (Interpretation D).

Further NICRA marches, including in Newry in January 1969, worsened the situation. Quite often, violence resulted. There were several reasons for this:

▶ NICRA had been going ahead with marches that the government had banned.

▶ Marches were seen as provocative, especially ones through Protestant areas.

▶ NICRA marches were coming into contact with unionist counter-demonstrations.

▲ The RUC moves to break up the NICRA march in Derry/Londonderry on 5 October 1968.

Interpretation D Extract from an article in the October 1988 edition of current affairs magazine *Fortnight* commenting on the NICRA march of 20 years earlier.

The whole affair was a series of blunders. The violence resulted from inadequate planning and leadership by the organisers of the march, and from stupidity and breakdown of control on the part of the authorities. But the greater share of the blame lies with those who had the greater power – the Minister of Home Affairs and the Royal Ulster Constabulary.

The Five-Point Reform Programme

As a result, O'Neill, Faulkner and Craig were summoned to Westminster on 4 November to meet the British Labour Prime Minister Harold Wilson. The outcome was the announcement, on 22 November, of a reform programme which included five main proposals, all of which were to be in place by the end of 1971:

▶ The allocation of council housing on a points system.

▶ The replacement of Londonderry Corporation by a Development Commission.

▶ The removal of parts of the Special Powers Act.

▶ Reforms within local government, including the ending of extra votes for business owners.

▶ The appointment of an ombudsman to investigate complaints.

Calm before the storm?

Although O'Neill himself later dismissed this package as too timid, at the time it seemed to point the way towards a better future, even if it failed to deliver all of NICRA's demands. However, in the short-term, protests and counter-protests continued and so on 9 December, O'Neill appeared on television to highlight to people the starkness of the position Northern Ireland now found itself in. In particular, he appealed to NICRA's leaders to help to restore calm to the province (Source E).

At first, all further street protests were called off. However, the breathing space O'Neill had won would prove to be very short-lived. While he might have managed to calm the civil rights movement, there were additional problems to deal with:

▶ The reforms had caused dismay among unionists, who opposed concessions to the threat of violence and who now felt that their position was under threat.

▶ O'Neill faced further opposition from within his own party, with Home Affairs Minister William Craig condemning his speech and arguing that the Prime Minister was acting under pressure from the British. Craig was sacked, but this did not deter opposition.

Source E Terence O'Neill, broadcasting on television on 9 December 1968.

Ulster stands at the crossroads ... our conduct over the coming days and weeks will decide our future ... I have made it clear that a Northern Ireland based on the interests of any one section rather than upon the interests of all could have no long-term future ... What kind of Ulster do you want? A happy and respected province in good standing with the rest of the United Kingdom? Or a place continually torn apart by riots and demonstrations and regarded by the rest of Britain as a political outcast?

The effectiveness of NICRA

A conclusion as to how effective NICRA had been by the end of 1968 might depend upon the political viewpoint of the individual being asked that question. The announcement of the Five-Point Reform Programme would certainly suggest that some of NICRA's aims had been fully – or partially – achieved. And yet, the subsequent emergence of People's Democracy (see page 152) would suggest that not all were satisfied.

Activities

1 Which issue led NICRA to hold its first two marches?
2 How did the Northern Ireland Government react to the events of 5 October 1968?
3 Explain why the issue of housing was so prominent in the earliest NICRA marches.
4 If the Derry/Londonderry march was illegal, why was it that the authorities came out of the events of 5 October worst?
5 Make a copy of the following table. On the left-hand side list NICRA's demands (see page 148). On the right-hand side match O'Neill's reforms (see page 150) with the appropriate demand. Which of NICRA's demands had not been granted?

NICRA demands	Five-point reform programme

Revision tip

O'Neill thought the five-point reform programme was not enough. Many nationalists would have agreed, but many unionists would have believed that they were too much. Are you able to explain why these reforms led to such different reactions?

Reasons for the emergence of the People's Democracy

Although NICRA had called for a halt to its campaign of marching, its decision was ignored by the recently formed People's Democracy. This group, mainly university students, had emerged out of anger at the violence NICRA had faced in October 1968 and the desire to disrupt the Stormont administration. Its leading figures were Michael Farrell and Bernadette Devlin (who was elected Westminster MP for Mid Ulster in April 1969). People's Democracy had developed demands broadly similar to those of NICRA, namely:

▶ one man, one vote
▶ fair boundaries
▶ houses on need
▶ jobs on merit
▶ free speech
▶ repeal of the Special Powers Act (Source F).

Unhappy with the limited nature of O'Neill's five-point reform programme, People's Democracy announced that they were holding a march between Belfast and Derry/Londonderry, from 1 to 4 January 1969. The march was condemned by NICRA and nationalist leaders, fearing its impact on an already tense situation.

◀ People's Democracy marchers come under attack at Burntollet on 4 January 1969.

Source G An extract from the report of the Cameron Commission into disturbances in Northern Ireland, published on 12 September 1969.

A number of policemen were guilty of misconduct which involved assault and battery, malicious damage to property … and the use of provocative, sectarian and political slogans.

Source F The aims of the People's Democracy march by Michael Farrell, a People's Democracy leader.

The march would be the acid test of the government's intentions. Either [it] would face up to the extreme right of its own OUP and protect the march … or it would be exposed as impotent in the face of sectarian thuggery, and Westminster would be forced to intervene, re-opening the whole Irish question for the first time in 50 years.

Ambush at Burntollet

The condemnations were ignored and the demonstration began on schedule. Much of the march was to go through Protestant areas, forcing the police to enforce different routes to avoid confrontation. However, on the third day confrontation took place; the marchers were the target of a violent ambush at Burntollet Bridge, an attack that the police seemed to do little to deflect. Later on the same night, tensions were further raised in Derry/Londonderry when police rampaged through nationalist areas of the city (Source G). Such events did little to endear the RUC to members of the nationalist community.

Reactions to Burntollet

NICRA had called off its marches in response to O'Neill's reforms; believing now that the events in the north-west indicated that nothing had changed, it started to march again. The first march was held in Newry and again violence resulted. In response, O'Neill established the Cameron Commission to investigate the increasing violence. This led two cabinet members, one of whom was Brian Faulkner, to resign from the government. Faulkner argued that O'Neill was not strong enough to control the situation.

Faulkner's opinion of O'Neill seemed to be gaining support within the OUP, with 12 MPs calling for his resignation on 30 January 1969. Instead, O'Neill called a general election, which he termed the 'crossroads election', in an attempt to prove that public opinion was behind his efforts to modernise Northern Ireland.

Activities

1 Explain the origins of the People's Democracy movement.
2 Explain what happened at Burntollet Bridge.
3 Using the information in the text, explain:
   • the reasons for the People's Democracy march
   • why People's Democracy was not prepared to stop marching if NICRA was.
4 Explain why the events of January 1969 might be seen as having been disastrous for the police.

Revision tip

You must be able to explain clearly the differences between People's Democracy and NICRA.

Reasons for the downfall of O'Neill

The election took place on 24 February 1969; however, the result was not what O'Neill had wanted:

▶ There was a reduction in unionist support and increased divisions of loyalty among the OUP MPs elected.

▶ There was little or no evidence of the hoped for support from Catholic voters.

▶ O'Neill, who had never before had to face a challenger in his own Bannside constituency, only polled 1,400 votes more than his opponent, Rev. Ian Paisley.

O'Neill struggled on for another two months, but with his party now hopelessly divided and with a further deterioration in the political situation caused by increasing violence and confrontation, he resigned on 28 April 1969 (Source H).

The final nail in his coffin was a series of bombings, which at the time appeared to be the work of the IRA but which were actually carried out by loyalists (extreme unionists) in an attempt to force O'Neill to go. Writing later in his autobiography, O'Neill reflected that the bombs 'quite literally blew me out of office' (Interpretation I). Some historians believe, however, that O'Neill became a victim of the hopes that he raised but was unable to fulfil.

In the resulting leadership election, O'Neill was succeeded by his cousin, Major James Chichester-Clark. Chichester-Clark had resigned from the government less than a week earlier in protest at O'Neill's decision to introduce one man, one vote in time for the next council elections. Then Chichester-Clark had argued that the timing of the measure was wrong; now he declared he would continue with O'Neill's reform programme.

Source H Terence O'Neill, speaking on television on 28 April 1969.

I have tried to break the chains of ancient hatreds. I have been unable to realise [achieve] during my period of office all that I had sought to achieve.

Activities

1 Construct a timeline showing the main times and issues of division 1963–69.

2 Using all that you have learnt about O'Neill so far, explain whether you believe that his premiership was either a success or a failure. Provide reasons for your answer.

▲ James Chichester-Clark (1923–2002).

Interpretation I Terence O'Neill, writing in his autobiography.

As the party would never stand for change, I was really reduced to trying to improve relations between North and South; and in the North itself between the two sections of the community. In this respect I think I can truthfully say that I succeeded. During the period between 1965 and 1968 the Catholics came to realise that I was interested in their welfare, while the South began to take an interest in the North.

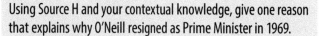
Practice question ❓

Using Source H and your contextual knowledge, give one reason that explains why O'Neill resigned as Prime Minister in 1969.

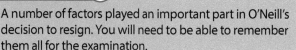
Revision tip 🔄

A number of factors played an important part in O'Neill's decision to resign. You will need to be able to remember them all for the examination.

This page provides guidance on how to answer question 1 in the exam.

Question 1

Study Source A below and answer the question which follows:

> **Source A** Terence O'Neill sketching out his economic vision in 1963 (adapted)
>
> It is a new motorway driving deeper into the province. It is a new airport worthy of our position as the busiest air centre in Britain outside London. It is a new hospital in Londonderry – the most modern in the British Isles. It is new laboratories and research facilities at Queen's to carry us to the frontiers of existing knowledge and beyond. It is replacement of derelict slums by modern housing estates.

Using **Source A and your contextual knowledge,** give one improvement that O'Neill was attempting to achieve through his economic policies. [2]

Guidance

You should be looking to spend a maximum of 2–3 minutes on this question. To access both marks you need to give one clear point from the source that provides the information required.

STEP 1
Read the source carefully (line by line). By doing this you should find at least one reason for the explanation the question is asking for.

Example
In Source A O'Neill provides a number of improvements or developments that would result from his new economic policies ...

STEP 2
Use your knowledge of this topic to develop what you have said about the source, including detail where possible.

Example
One such development was the improvement of transport links within and across Northern Ireland. To avoid increasing unemployment O'Neill wanted to attract industries from abroad and to do so would require good transport links.

A change of leadership did not reduce tensions in Northern Ireland. Continuing civil rights protests – now more confrontational than before, in the aftermath of Burntollet – were followed by serious rioting in Belfast. As the July–August marching season approached, grave concerns were raised over the likely impact of marches on an already tense situation.

Increasing tensions and violence, summer 1969

Concerns were evident both within and outside Northern Ireland:

▶ The Stormont government was worried if the already stretched security forces would be able to cope with a further increase in violence.

▶ After more or less ignoring Northern Ireland since 1921, the London government had become concerned enough to establish a cabinet committee on Northern Ireland.

▶ The Dublin government was anxious about the safety of the minority community and sent an intelligence officer to Northern Ireland to watch what was happening.

To make matters worse, armed groups seemed to be emerging:

▶ among loyalists angry at what they saw as concession after concession to nationalists

▶ among Republicans who were apprehensive at their own seeming inability to protect nationalists.

A Long Hot Summer

In July, violence broke out in Belfast, but soon spread to Derry/Londonderry. In Belfast, the violence mainly took the form of house burning, mostly by loyalists, forcing many to leave their homes. However, seven people also lost their lives, while 100 were wounded. In Derry/Londonderry the conflict began after the annual apprentice boys parade on 12 August. In the middle of intense and frightening violence, centred on the Bogside area, the *Taoiseach*, Jack Lynch, issued a statement outlining his concerns (Source A) – which, with the accompanying movement of Irish troops and field hospitals to the border, did little to ease tension.

▲ The aftermath of the Battle of the Bogside, August 1969.

Source A *Taoiseach* Jack Lynch, speaking on television on 13 August 1969.

It is clear now that the present situation cannot be allowed to continue. It is evident that the Stormont government is no longer in control of the situation … it is clear also that the Irish government can no longer stand by and see innocent people injured and perhaps worse.

In total the rioting, during what became known as the Battle of the Bogside, lasted for 50 hours. Finally, an uneasy calm was restored by using a small number of troops, as requested by nationalist politicians, among others. However, violence flared up in several provincial towns and more particularly in Belfast where sectarian conflict was particularly intense (Interpretation B).

The events of August 1969 were later to be seen as a turning point in the development of what became known as 'the Troubles'. They were seen as directly responsible for:

▶ the deployment of the British Army on the streets of Northern Ireland on 14 and 15 August in an attempt to restore law and order

▶ the eventual re-emergence of the IRA.

Interpretation B The views of historian Jonathan Bardon, from his book *A History of Ulster* (1992).

Except for the middle-class suburbs, Belfast had become a war zone.

The reasons for and consequences of government intervention

Using the army might help to stop violence, but it would not solve Northern Ireland's problems; new political ideas were also needed. The question now was whether such ideas would come from Stormont or Westminster. London had left the government of the province to the local parliament for decades without interference; could that now be allowed to continue? More importantly, could Westminster introduce policies that would reconcile nationalists and reassure unionists?

On 19 August, Chichester-Clark travelled to London to meet the British Prime Minister, Harold Wilson. The outcome of this meeting was the publication of the Downing Street Declaration. This declaration aimed to reassure both communities:

▶ Nationalists were told that 'every citizen of Northern Ireland is entitled to the same equality of treatment and freedom from discrimination as [exists] in the rest of the UK irrespective of political views or religion'.

▶ Unionists were told that 'Northern Ireland should not cease to be part of the UK without the consent of the people of Northern Ireland'.

Additional reforms

Further reforms were announced or introduced in the following weeks:

▶ The introduction of one man, one vote and an end to gerrymandering.

▶ A committee on policing was established under Lord Hunt (a British official who had the distinction of leading the first British team to climb Mount Everest).

▶ Following pressure from the British Home Secretary James Callaghan during a visit to Northern Ireland, the Stormont government announced that it was setting up the Scarman Tribunal to investigate recent disturbances (Interpretation C).

▶ A single housing authority was established, taking over from local councils.

▶ Measures to prevent discrimination in public employment were announced.

▶ A Ministry of Community Relations was created.

> **Interpretation C** The views of historian Jonathan Bardon, from his book *A History of Ulster* (1992).
>
> The Scarman Tribunal ... reported that in Belfast alone 1,820 families fled their homes during and immediately after [the riots]; 1,505 of these families were Catholic, making up more than three per cent of all Catholic households in the city.

Activities

1 Why did violence break out in the summer of 1969?
2 Describe two impacts of the violence.
3 Explain the reasons for the introduction of troops on to the streets of Northern Ireland in August 1969.

▶ British troops on the streets of Belfast, August 1969.

There were also moves to improve the economy:

▶ a £2 million programme of work-creating schemes

▶ increases in investment grants.

However, everyone did not welcome these initiatives. Despite the reassurances of the Downing Street Declaration, many unionists were concerned at what they saw as continuing concessions to nationalists. The final straw came when the Hunt Report was published. It recommended:

▶ disarming the RUC

▶ disbanding the B Specials and replacing them with the Ulster Defence Regiment, a part-time force under army control.

Angered at the proposals, extreme loyalist violence erupted on Belfast's Shankill Road.

Nationalists reacted positively to the reforms, believing that an improved future involving a reformed political system was now within their grasp.

Activities

1. The situation in Northern Ireland by mid-1969 has been described as a 'time bomb'. What evidence can you find to support this view?
2. Explain two reforms introduced by the British Prime Minister in August 1969.
3. Give two reasons for unionists' angry reaction to these reforms.
4. Make a copy of the following table. Using the information on page 155–157, fill in the table as appropriate. Now look at your results; would you say that nationalists or unionists would have been more satisfied by the Downing Street Declaration? Explain your answer.

Proposals aimed at nationalists	Proposals aimed at unionists

5. How would nationalists and unionists have felt about the conclusions of the Cameron Report and the Hunt Report? Use the information in the text to help you with your answer.

Practice question

Using Source A on page 155 and your contextual knowledge, give two reasons that explain why British troops were deployed to Northern Ireland in August 1969.

Revision tip

Are you able to understand why August 1969 was such an important month in the emergence of 'the Troubles'?

Revision tip

The Downing Street Declaration was one aspect of the Westminster government's attempt to create stability within Northern Ireland. You need to be able to explain how it was viewed by both unionists and nationalists.

The re-emergence of paramilitary organisations

'I Ran Away' was the accusation most frequently levelled at the IRA because of its seeming failure to defend the Catholic population during the violence of 1969. Since the ending of its border campaign in 1962, the IRA seemed to have become more interested in Marxism. However, some of its younger members were unhappy with this inaction and wanted to take matters into their own hands, particularly the defence of nationalist areas.

The split in the IRA and the objectives of the Provisional IRA

In the final days of 1969, the IRA split into two parts:

▶ The Official IRA, which continued to focus on establishing a socialist Ireland. At the same time violence was still used until a ceasefire was called in May 1972. In 1974, the movement split again, with the emergence of the Irish Republican Socialist Party and the militant Irish Nationalist Liberation Army (INLA).

▶ The Provisional IRA, which claimed for itself the traditional role of defender of the nationalist community.

By Easter 1970, the new Provisional movement had declared its objectives; these were:

▶ achieving civil rights
▶ defending the Catholic population
▶ destroying the Stormont government
▶ removing 'British imperialism' from Ireland.

The IRA and the British Army

The last aim meant that the IRA would come into conflict with the British Army. Ironically, up to this point, the Army had been more acceptable to nationalists – as a source of protection – than to the unionists. However, although initially welcomed by the Catholic community as preferable to the distrusted RUC, the Army now found itself in an impossible situation, trying to maintain order while a political solution was imposed (Interpretation D).

> **Interpretation D** Irish historian Professor J.J. Lee, writing in *Ireland 1912–1985: Politics and Society* (1989).
>
> If the Army did nothing but wait, the IRA might gradually acquire the resources to mount an aggressive campaign against it. If it seized the initiative through 'arms searches' it would inevitably foster IRA recruitment among outraged Catholics whose homes it had vandalised … The 'arms searches' came as a godsend to the IRA.

The Falls Road curfew

As the IRA's campaign began to take off in the middle of 1970, the British Army moved to protect itself. In July it responded by imposing a 34-hour curfew on the Lower Falls area of Belfast while a house-to-house search for weapons was carried out. Although a number of weapons – as well as ammunition and explosives – were discovered, politically the search was a disaster. It damaged the Army's previously good relationship with the nationalist community and helped increase IRA membership (Interpretation E).

> **Interpretation E** Irish historian Professor J.J. Lee, writing in *Ireland 1912–1985: Politics and Society* (1989).
>
> If there was a decisive turning point in Catholic attitudes to the army … it was probably the 34-hour curfew … 'In political terms it was a disaster', and Provisional influence increased enormously … Membership mushroomed from about 100 to about 800 in the second half of 1970.

▶ British troops search for hidden arms as they frisk suspects in Newry, as a build up to expected disorder in the area in 1972.

The re-emergence of the Ulster Volunteer Force (UVF) and its objectives, and the setting up of the Ulster Defence Association (UDA)

The loyalist paramilitaries also wanted to see an end to the current Stormont regime, although for different reasons. They sought a return to the old days of unionist domination. The UVF re-emerged in the mid-1960s and had grown and prospered against the background of NICRA's campaign and what was seen as O'Neill's appeasement of Catholics. It sought to oppose the actions of Republican paramilitaries and to ensure that Northern Ireland remained a part of the United Kingdom.

September 1971 saw the formation of the Ulster Defence Association (UDA) to fill a gap in the defences of the loyalist community. For most of its existence the UDA remained a legal organisation. It viewed itself as a defensive grouping that would protect protestant areas and resist Republican aggression, particularly the actions of the PIRA. With over 30,000 members within a year, it was viewed by the authorities as too large to ban. However, within the UDA a group known as the Ulster Freedom Fighters (UFF) existed. The members of this group were involved in the organisation of and carrying out of paramilitary attacks. The UFF was outlawed in 1973.

Faulkner replaces Chichester-Clark

The levels of violence and destruction shot up during the remaining months of 1970 and on into 1971. The Stormont government demanded a stronger response from Britain's new Conservative government; however, little happened, as Westminster did not want to alienate the nationalist community even more. In despair at London's inaction, Chichester-Clark resigned as Prime Minister on 20 March, to be replaced by Brian Faulkner.

While Faulkner appeared to have a better grasp of the situation than his predecessor, he too was unable to reduce the levels of violence or the growth of the Provisional IRA. By the time the marching season arrived in July–August 1971, violence was at an all-time high, particularly in Derry/Londonderry. The government's response – in the face of few other options – was the reintroduction of internment: the arrest and detention without trial of those suspected of working for the destruction of the state.

> **Revision tip**
>
> There are a lot of important issues in this section. You need to understand why the IRA split and how the aims of the two IRA groups differed. You will also need to be able to explain how and why nationalist attitudes to the British Army changed.

◄ Brian Faulkner (1921–77).

> **Activities**
>
> 1 Explain how nationalist attitudes towards the British Army changed in the early years of the 1970s.
> 2 Why did the Provisional IRA emerge in 1970?
> 3 Explain why the Army found itself in a no-win situation in 1970.
> 4 Explain who benefited most from the arms searches of July 1970.
> 5 Explain the reasons for the growth in loyalist paramilitary groups.

Internment

Brian Faulkner was unable to reduce the levels of violence and, facing strong unionist pressure for firm action to be taken, he reintroduced the previously successful policy of internment – through Operation Demetrius – on 9 August 1971.

Reasons for and effects of internment

Internment failed spectacularly (Interpretation A). The intelligence was entirely out of date. Not one of the 452 men arrested was a leading member of the Provisional IRA. Those individuals the government really wanted to arrest, Faulkner himself later admitted, had 'escaped the net'. Moreover, despite the high levels of loyalist violence, all those targeted for internment were nationalists or civil rights supporters. The first loyalists were not interned until February 1973.

Unionists were happy with the introduction of internment at first, although their support decreased when the policy failed to reduce levels of violence. They believed that it had worked in the past and saw it as essential in ending IRA violence, particularly against Protestant businesses. They also believed that internees could help with the location of IRA weapons, something that Faulkner believed did happen. Nationalists, however, saw internment as one-sided in its application and open to substantial abuse. As a result, IRA membership increased. In addition, as the British Army was involved in the implementation of internment, its increasingly poor relations with the nationalist community deteriorated even further.

> **Interpretation F** Historian Sabine Wichert, writing in her book *Northern Ireland Since 1945* (1991), (adapted).
>
> The political consequences of internment were serious; the unionist government could be seen to have acted with the army against the Catholic population at large, breaking any remaining good will of Catholics towards unionism.

Violence and destruction followed the introduction of internment in 1971, leaving many dead and thousands from both communities homeless. From then until the end of the year, 143 people lost their lives through bombings and shootings. This was nearly five times as many as died in the first eight months of 1971. Nor was the violence all from the one side; the increasing Republican violence resulted in the establishment of the paramilitary UVF in September 1971. It was responsible for the bombing, on 4 December, of McGurk's Bar in Belfast. Fifteen people lost their lives in this attack, the worst single atrocity of the year.

Violence was not the only response to the introduction of internment. Along with other nationalist and Republican Labour representatives, the SDLP called for people to withhold payment of rents and rates and for a withdrawal from local government in protest at the policy. Civil rights marches were also organised in protest at the introduction of internment, but the army's response also seemed to be hardening. A protest held at Magilligan Internment Camp on 22 January 1972 was met with baton charges and CS gas from the army.

Bloody Sunday, 1972, and responses to it

In the aftermath of another march in Derry/Londonderry eight days later, a riot developed. In response, troops from the Parachute Regiment were ordered into the Bogside and shot thirteen men dead. Thirteen more were injured, one of whom subsequently died of his wounds. An official inquiry headed by Lord Widgery failed to provide a satisfactory explanation, although it did establish that none of those who died had been carrying a weapon when shot (Source G).

> **Source G** An extract from the Widgery Report into the events of Bloody Sunday.
>
> There would have been no deaths in Londonderry ... if those who organised the illegal march had not thereby created a highly dangerous situation in which a clash between demonstrators and the security forces was almost inevitable ... At one end of the scale some soldiers showed a high degree of responsibility; at the other ... firing bordered on the reckless ... None of the deceased or wounded is proved to have been shot whilst handling a firearm or bomb.

Apart from the immediate outpourings of grief and anger, the events of 30 January 1972 had a number of results:

Unionist responses

▶ Continued support for the government from the unionist community, which, while regretting the deaths, saw the march as both illegal and provocative. Some unionists believed that the IRA was involved in the organisation of the march and that some of those killed had been armed.

▶ The resulting increase in violence and the government's failure to end it led to the formation in February 1972 of the Ulster Vanguard. Headed by William Craig, the former Stormont minister, Vanguard was described as a coordinating body for traditional Loyalist groups. One of its largest meetings, in Belfast's Ormeau Park, attracted 70,000 people, a powerful symbol of the levels of unionist discontent.

Nationalist responses

▶ Given the belief that all of the victims were innocent and the Parachute Regiment attack unprovoked, nationalist hostility to the state was increased. This was symbolised by rioting in nationalist areas and by the burning down of the British Embassy in Dublin.

▶ IRA membership grew – particularly in Derry/Londonderry – and its bombing campaign intensified (Source H).

▶ Additionally, Britain faced international condemnation for the role it was playing in Northern Ireland.

By now Westminster had concluded the Northern Ireland Government was no longer capable of maintaining law and order. It was also becoming increasingly difficult to justify unionist domination. After 50 years of devolved rule it looked as if the writing was on the wall for Stormont.

▲ The NICRA march which preceded the events of Bloody Sunday, 30 January 1972.

Source H An extract from the Irish Press, commenting on the events of Bloody Sunday.

If there was an able-bodied man with Republican sympathies within the Derry area who was not in the IRA before yesterday's butchery there will be none tonight.

Activities

1 What were the effects of the introduction of internment?
2 What were the effects of Bloody Sunday?
3 Explain why internment was always likely to fail.

Revision tip

It is important that you are able to explain why the British government decided to end the Stormont Parliament. You also need to be able to identify the differences in the nationalist and unionist reactions to the suspension.

Practice questions

1 How useful is Source J for an historian studying the reasons for the fall of Stormont and direct rule in 1972?
2 How reliable is Source J for an historian studying the reasons for the fall of Stormont and direct rule in 1972?

Direct rule

After the escalation of violence in the late 1960s and early 1970s, Britain now demanded control.

Reasons for the fall of Stormont

Faulkner now demanded the power to rearm the RUC and re-establish the B Specials. Conservative Prime Minister Edward Heath responded by demanding control of law and order and justice; however Faulkner refused. On 22 March 1972 senior Stormont members travelled to London for what they believed would be top-level talks with the British government about the situation in Northern Ireland. Once there, Heath informed them of proposed changes:

▶ the transfer of security control to Westminster
▶ a referendum on the future of the border
▶ the gradual removal of internment
▶ a Secretary of State for Northern Ireland
▶ talks with other parties in Northern Ireland to establish a 'community government'.

The introduction of direct rule

After lengthy negotiations, the entire Northern Ireland government resigned, unable to accept the loss of control over security policy (Source I). On 24 March, Heath responded by suspending Stormont for a year (later extended) and introducing direct rule (Source J). From now on, Northern Ireland was to be governed directly by the British Government in London, with a team of ministers, led by a Secretary of State (William Whitelaw), taking over the functions of the Stormont cabinet.

> **Source I** An extract from Brian Faulkner's letter of resignation.
>
> [The transfer of security powers to London] is not justifiable and cannot be supported or accepted by us. It would wholly undermine the powers, authority and standing of this government.

> **Source J** Edward Heath, speaking on 24 March 1972.
>
> The United Kingdom government [believes] that the transfer of [law and order] to Westminster is [vital] for progress in finding a political solution in Northern Ireland. The Northern Ireland government's decision therefore leaves us with no alternative to assuming full and direct responsibility for the administration of Northern Ireland until a political solution to the problems of the province can be worked out.

Reaction in Northern Ireland and in the Republic of Ireland

Reactions to the end of 50 years of local government were predictable. Most unionists were horrified at the removal of Stormont, which they had seen as a barrier against a united Ireland. The last hours of the Parliament were played out on 28 March before a crowd estimated at 100,000. This came in the midst of a series of massive strikes and shutdowns, organised by Ulster Vanguard in protest at the suspension. The strikes were successful at shutting down much of life in Northern Ireland for a two-day period, but they were unable to open Stormont up again. There was also an increase in support for loyalist paramilitaries and a spate of sectarian killings, particularly in Belfast. Meanwhile, support for the DUP and other strongly unionist parties also increased in the aftermath of the introduction of direct rule.

Few tears were shed for Stormont on the nationalist side, with the SDLP and the Dublin government welcoming the chances for a new beginning. The IRA, although it had achieved one of its aims, stated its opposition to direct rule and announced its determination to continue its struggle to achieve a united Ireland. NICRA stated that its campaign for civil rights would continue.

> **Activity** 🖉
>
> Compare and contrast the attitudes of the Northern Irish and British Prime Ministers (Sources I and J) in terms of who should control law and order.

This page provides guidance on how to answer question 2 in the exam.

Question 2

Study **Source B** below and answer the question which follows:

> **Source B** Taoiseach Jack Lynch, speaking on television on 13 August 1969 about the deteriorating situation in Northern Ireland
>
> It is clear now that the present situation cannot be allowed to continue. It is evident that the Stormont government is no longer in control of the situation … it is clear also that the Irish government can no longer stand by and see innocent people injured and perhaps worse.

Give **two** reasons from **Source B** that explain why the Dublin Government was so concerned about the political situation in Northern Ireland   [4]

Guidance

You should be looking to spend a maximum of six minutes on this question. To access all the available you need to provide an explanation of each reason that you identify.

Step 1

Read the source carefully (line by line). By doing this you should find at least two reasons for the explanation the question is asking for. Use your knowledge to develop the first reason.

Example

Source B states the view of the Irish Taoiseach that the Northern Ireland government has lost control of the situation in the North …

In other words, Mr Lynch was stating that the political situation had become so bad — and the violence on the streets so serious — that the Northern Ireland government was no longer able to run the country properly.

Step 2

Use your knowledge of this topic to then develop the second reason, including detail where possible.

Example

Also, the Taoiseach speaks of his belief that his government 'can no longer stand by and see innocent people injured and perhaps worse' … By stating this, Mr Lynch was suggesting that the Republic of Ireland might try to become more directly involved in what was happening in Northern Ireland. He seemed to be suggesting that nationalists were in danger of their lives and was also suggesting that the only government that might look after them was the Irish government. Lynch might have been making this 'threat' to try to force the British government to become more involved in running Northern Ireland.

Despite the introduction of internment and direct rule and the existence of a two-week IRA ceasefire, 1972 turned out to be the worst year of the Troubles. By the end of the year, 496 people had lost their lives in a series of appalling atrocities including:

▶ 21 July when the IRA detonated 20 bombs around Belfast in just over one hour. Nine civilians died on a day that became known as Bloody Friday.

▶ 31 July when, without warning, an IRA bomb exploded in the village of Claudy in County Derry/Londonderry. In total, nine civilians lost their lives.

The reasons for and responses to the introduction of a power-sharing Executive

The British government responded on 31 July with Operation Motorman. This aimed to allow the army and police to reclaim control of the paramilitary-controlled no-go areas, which had sprung up in Belfast, Derry/Londonderry and elsewhere. The success of this operation encouraged the British government to make moves towards a political settlement and, by late 1972, it was holding discussions aimed at establishing a government which could enjoy cross-community support.

The year 1973 began as 1972 had ended, with increased levels of violence. Constant loyalist violence led to their internment in early February. Clearly some form of political progress was crucial but it was not until 20 March 1973 that the British government published its proposals for the future of Northern Ireland.

The plans proposed a new law-making assembly (parliament) elected by proportional representation, but not given control over security or justice.

▲ The aftermath of one of the bombs detonated on Bloody Friday, 21 July 1972.

There would also be an executive, or government. For the plan to work, the British insisted on two other conditions:

▶ the sharing of power between Catholics and Protestants
▶ the formal recognition of an 'Irish dimension' – a role for the Republic of Ireland – through the creation of a Council of Ireland, allowing for the discussion of interests common to Belfast, Dublin and London.

Early problems

While nationalist reactions were broadly supportive, unionism was divided in its reaction to the plans. While some of the OUP remained loyal to Brian Faulkner (who was supporting Secretary of State William Whitelaw's plans), other unionists – the remainder of the OUP, the DUP and the new Vanguard Unionist Progressive Party (set up by William Craig to oppose power-sharing) – joined together to form the United Ulster Unionist Council (UUUC) to oppose the plans. Apart from their opposition to the 'Irish dimension', they saw the proposals as undemocratic and believed that power should not be shared with those disloyal to the Union.

The extent of these splits became clear when the outcome of the assembly elections were announced at the end of June 1973. The results (see Table 1) revealed that the number of anti-power-sharing unionists elected was greater than the number of unionists elected who supported power-sharing (Interpretation A).

It was clear that the prospects for the success of the new venture were already far from certain (Interpretation B).

Party	Pro- or anti-power-sharing	Percentage of vote	Number of seats won
Faulkner unionists	Pro	29.3	24
UUUC unionists	Anti	32.1	26
SDLP	Pro	22.1	19
APNI	Pro	9.2	8
Northern Ireland Labour Party (NILP)	Pro	2.6	1

Table 1 Assembly election results.

Activities

1 What was the power-sharing assembly?
2 Who won the elections to the new power-sharing assembly?
3 What were the attitudes of Northern Ireland's voters to the British government's proposals? Use the text and the information in Table 1 to help you with your answer.

Interpretation A Dr Duncan Morrow, writing in *Northern Ireland Politics* (1996).

For unionists, every attempt to bring anti-unionists into power, whether in the form of Northern Irish nationalists or through the formal involvement of the Republic of Ireland, diluted and threatened the Union itself.

Interpretation B Dr Duncan Morrow, writing in *Northern Ireland Politics* (1996).

While there was support in all places for some of the proposals, it was enormously difficult to maintain cross-community support for the package as a whole.

Revision tip

The most important thing that you need to understand about the power-sharing assembly is the reaction of unionist voters to it and how this weakened its chances of success.

A Council of Ireland

Nearly five months later, on 21 November 1973, Whitelaw announced that the membership of a power-sharing executive had been agreed. There would be 11 ministries, all of which would go to supporters of power-sharing. Six were to be held by unionists, four by the SDLP and one by the Alliance Party. There would also be four non-voting members of the executive: two SDLP, one unionist and one Alliance. The OUP's Brian Faulkner would head the executive while the SDLP's Gerry Fitt would be his deputy. Table 2 lists the names and positions of the other ministers.

Two of the three elements of the new system were now in place. All that remained was to reach agreement on the form and powers of the Council of Ireland.

The discussions about the Council of Ireland began on 6 December 1973 at Sunningdale in Berkshire. The meeting brought together a powerful assortment of politicians from Britain, Ireland and Northern Ireland, as Table 3 shows.

There were, however, no anti-power-sharing politicians present; the Irish government and other local parties had argued that they would disrupt the negotiations. At one stage Rev. Ian Paisley (DUP leader) and William Craig (Vanguard Unionist Progressive Party leader) were asked to attend but only to give their views. Unsurprisingly this offer was rejected.

Name	Party	Voting/non-voting member	Portfolio
Herbie Kirk	OUP	Voting member	Finance
Roy Bradford	OUP	Voting member	Environment
Basil McIvor	OUP	Voting member	Education
Leslie Morrell	OUP	Voting member	Agriculture
John Baxter	OUP	Voting member	Information
Lloyd Hall-Thompson	OUP	Non-voting member	Chief Whip
John Hume	SDLP	Voting member	Commerce
Austin Currie	SDLP	Voting member	Housing, Development and Local Government
Paddy Devlin	SDLP	Voting member	Social Security
Ivan Cooper	SDLP	Non-voting member	Community Relations
Eddie McGrady	SDLP	Non-voting member	Planning and Co-ordination
Oliver Napier	APNI	Voting member	Office of Law Reform
Bob Cooper	APNI	Non-voting member	Manpower Services

Table 2 Ministers in the new assembly.

Representing	Politicians	Position	Politicians	Position
UK	Edward Heath	Prime Minister	Francis Pym	Secretary of State
Republic of Ireland	Liam Cosgrave	*Taoiseach*	Garret FitzGerald	Foreign Minister
OUP	Brian Faulkner	Chief Executive Designate		
SDLP	Gerry Fitt	Deputy Chief Executive Designate		
Alliance	Oliver Napier	Office of Law Reform		

Table 3 The Sunningdale participants.

Terms of the Agreement

After several days of negotiations, agreement between the parties was finally secured on 9 December. The Sunningdale Agreement contained the following elements:

▶ London agreed not to oppose Irish unification if a majority of the Northern Ireland population desired it.

▶ Dublin accepted that Irish unity could only ever be achieved peacefully and with the consent of the majority of the people of Northern Ireland.

▶ A Council of Ministers with 14 members was to be established. The powers were vague but it was agreed it would help with the development of co-operation between Northern Ireland and the Republic of Ireland and would eventually be given decision-making powers.

▶ A 60-member Consultative Assembly would be elected by the *Dáil* and the assembly at some future date.

▶ Also at some future date, control over internal security issues would be returned to the assembly at Stormont.

▶ Approval of the decisions made at Sunningdale was to take place at a future conference.

Problems for the future

On the surface the agreement looked promising; the problem was, however, that the unionist and nationalist representatives involved believed that they had agreed to something entirely different Interpretation C:

▽ The discussions at Sunningdale, December 1973.

▶ The SDLP saw the agreement as paving the way towards the creation of closer ties between Northern Ireland and the Republic of Ireland.

▶ Faulkner saw it as a mere token, which he had agreed to as a means of getting Dublin to accept the position of Northern Ireland as part of the UK.

When these different interpretations became clear, they would have a significant impact on the chances of success for power-sharing. Republicans were also lukewarm in their response, seeing the new system as proposing substantially less than what they sought.

In the shorter term, however, Faulkner faced more serious problems. On 10 December 1973, loyalist paramilitaries announced the formation of an Ulster Army Council to resist any significant 'Irish dimension'. Nor did the IRA seem any more satisfied, setting off a series of bombs in London in the week before Christmas. It seemed as if the power-sharing experiment was facing a very uncertain future as the date for the handover of power approached.

Interpretation C Comment by Paul Bew and Gordon Gillespie, from *Northern Ireland, A Chronology of the Troubles* (1993), (adapted).

The flaw in the Sunningdale Agreement was that those involved in it had completely different views of what it involved. Faulkner saw the Council of Ireland as an advisory body. Some members of the SDLP had a different opinion of what the Council of Ireland would mean. The British government failed to define clearly the areas which the Council of Ireland would control and which it would not.

The Executive took up office on 1 January 1974, but almost immediately its future was plunged into doubt (Interpretation D). A meeting of the OUP's ruling body, the Ulster Unionist Council, on 4 January voted to reject the Sunningdale Agreement (Interpretation E). Faulkner immediately resigned as party leader and was replaced by Harry West. However, Faulkner retained the support of 19 of the 21 OUP Assembly members and so was able to remain as Chief Executive of the power-sharing executive. It was clear, however, that he was isolated within unionism.

> **Interpretation D** Historian Sabine Wichert, writing in her book *Northern Ireland Since 1945* (1991).
>
> When the new power-sharing executive took office … it looked on the surface as if … the Protestants appeared to have accepted a compromise, the Catholics seemed to have voted for constitutional politics, violence had declined considerably … and there appeared to be a prospect of working out a political solution.
>
> Almost a third of the electorate, however, had given its vote to non-Faulknerite unionism … Neither Protestant or Catholic paramilitaries had been nor could be defeated, and new fuel was added to the sectarian smouldering by the introduction of the 'Irish dimension', which enraged Loyalists but did not appease extremist Nationalists.

> **Interpretation E** The judgement of historian Patrick Buckland, from *A History of Northern Ireland* (1989).
>
> The insistence on the Irish dimension ruined whatever chance Faulkner had of persuading a majority even of official unionists to accept the executive as a genuine attempt to achieve a lasting settlement in the North.

The general election of 1974

Unfortunately for the new system, events in Great Britain provided further problems. A general election for the Westminster Parliament was called for 28 February. A struggle for the hearts and minds of unionist voters followed between the pro-Faulkner candidates and the anti-Sunningdale UUUC.

The outcome was almost a landslide for the UUUC. With 80 per cent of the vote, 11 of the 12 Northern Ireland constituencies were won by anti-Sunningdale candidates. The only exception was Gerry Fitt, who retained his West Belfast seat for the SDLP.

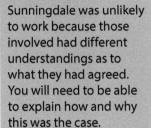

Revision tip

Sunningdale was unlikely to work because those involved had different understandings as to what they had agreed. You will need to be able to explain how and why this was the case.

Activities

1 Explain why the main Northern Ireland politicians went to Sunningdale in December 1973.

2 Construct a spider diagram showing the main points agreed at Sunningdale.

3 How did the paramilitaries react to the Sunningdale Agreement?

4 Explain the reasons for the resignation of Brian Faulkner as leader of the OUP in January 1974.

> ➤ Members of the power-sharing executive meeting *Taoiseach* Liam Cosgrave (1920–) (third from left) and other members of the Irish government.

Closer examination of the results revealed that pro-agreement unionists won just over 94,000 votes compared to just under 367,000 for their UUUC opponents. Naturally enough there were calls from the UUUC for new assembly elections but none took place.

The UUUC had portrayed the election as a referendum on the Sunningdale Agreement. The results clearly indicated that a majority of the population of the province were opposed to what had been agreed. It could justifiably be argued that the Assembly was no longer a true reflection of public opinion in Northern Ireland.

More impacts of the 1974 general election

The election also resulted in a change in government in London with Labour returning to power under Harold Wilson. In local terms, Merlyn Rees replaced Francis Pym (who had replaced William Whitelaw) as Secretary of State, but a small Labour majority in Westminster meant that he was forced to spend more time in London than was good for the already ailing Northern Ireland system.

These political developments took place against a background of continuing violence coupled with regular public protests against the Sunningdale Agreement. Although the British Government continued to insist that there was no alternative to the agreement, it was clear that within unionism there was a determination that the system would fail. Since nothing else attempted seemed to have worked, the weapon chosen to destroy Sunningdale would be a massive strike.

The UWC strike and its effects

On the evening of Tuesday 14 May 1974, shortly after the Assembly had voted to continue its support for the Sunningdale Agreement, a general strike began. The strike was organised by the Ulster Workers' Council (UWC), a group of Protestant trade unionists who had gained substantial amounts of political and paramilitary support. Its aim was to show the levels of unionist opposition to the Sunningdale Agreement.

Initially support for the strike was limited, but UDA intimidation and improved co-ordination by the UWC ensured that by the end of the week much of Northern Ireland had come to a standstill. Industries had closed down, there were regular electricity blackouts, fuel supplies were strictly controlled and there were hundreds of roadblocks – making travel almost impossible. Attempts by some of Northern Ireland's trade unions to organise a back-to-work demonstration on 21 May met with little support – only 200 people turned up.

The tension in the province was further heightened by the news on 17 May that car bombs, believed to have been planted by loyalists, in Dublin and Monaghan, had claimed 27 lives (five more of those injured later died of their wounds). This was the worst single day's death toll during the entire period of the Troubles.

Although there were by now 17,500 soldiers in the province, the army was hesitant about taking on the strikers, arguing that the strike was political and not a terrorist action. The British Prime Minister however, was losing patience with the situation and appeared on television on 25 May to denounce the strike and call its organisers 'spongers' (Source F). This speech infuriated unionists and more than anything else, ensured that the strike continued.

> **Source F** Adapted excerpt from British Prime Minister Harold Wilson, speaking about the 1974 UWC strike in a speech broadcast on television, 25 May 1974.
>
> [The strike is] a deliberate attempt to bring down the whole constitution of Northern Ireland ... The people on this side of the water ... have seen their sons spat upon and murdered. They have seen the taxes ... going into Northern Ireland. They see property destroyed by evil violence and are asked to pick up the bill for rebuilding it. Yet people who benefit from this now defy Westminster, claiming to act as though they were an elected government, spending their lives sponging on Westminster and British democracy and then fighting democratic methods. Who do these people think they are?

Source G Brian Faulkner, speaking on 28 May 1974.

It is ... apparent to us from the extent of support for the present stoppage that the degree of consent needed to sustain the executive does not at present exist.

The re-introduction of direct rule

Although the British Government was not prepared to use the army to break the strike, it was prepared to use it to maintain fuel supplies. When the army was ordered in to take over fuel supplies, the UWC ordered a total shutdown across Northern Ireland. Seeing no obvious solution and with the British and SDLP still refusing to negotiate with the UWC, Faulkner resigned as Chief Executive on 28 May (Source G). The other unionist members of the executive resigned with him, thus ending power-sharing. Having achieved its goal, the UWC ended the strike on 29 May. The Assembly was suspended on 30 May and, after five months' absence, direct rule was reintroduced.

It is impossible to know if power-sharing could have worked if it had been given more time to establish firm roots. It seems clear that many of those involved in the power-sharing initiative were not as fully committed to its success as was needed. This lack of commitment – coupled with intense opposition from some quarters – was enough to ensure the failure of this attempted solution – and the continuation of political unrest.

Practice questions

1 Give one of the points agreed at the power-sharing agreement in 1973.
2 Name two of the groups involved in the UWC strike in 1974.
3 Describe one reason why the Prime Minister's speech had a large impact on the UWC strikers in 1974.

▲ British troops keeping a petrol station open during the UWC strike.

Revision tip

There are a number of reasons for the failure of the power-sharing system of 1973–74; make sure you can identify these.

Activities

1 What did the results of the 1974 general election to the Westminster Parliament show?
2 Explain why the executive collapsed at the end of May 1974.
3 Construct a spider diagram showing the reasons for the success of the strike.

5 Changing Republican strategy

During the rest of the 1970s and the early years of the 1980s, successive British governments attempted, without success, to solve the Northern Ireland problem. At the same time, although the levels of violence lessened due to improved security measures, the IRA launched a campaign of violence in Britain, exploding bombs in towns and cities such as Guildford and Birmingham.

The reasons for the hunger strikes: new security policies

Following the collapse of the power-sharing executive, the Secretary of State Merlyn Rees and his successor Roy Mason pursued policies of Ulsterisation and criminalisation. The former involved reducing the strength of the army in Northern Ireland while increasing the size of the RUC and UDR. The latter saw the end of special category status for those convicted of terrorist offences.

Introduced in 1972, special category status had allowed those who claimed that they had broken the law for political reasons to live as prisoners of war (POWs). Its removal meant that those convicted after March 1976 would be treated in the same way as other criminals. They would be housed in a new prison consisting of H-shaped blocks, which had been built at the Maze outside Belfast.

Although the numbers of deaths as a result of violence began to decrease in the latter years of the 1970s, there were still some appalling incidents, such as the IRA firebombing of the La Mon House Hotel outside Belfast, resulting in the deaths of 12 people.

IRA prisoners – who saw themselves as soldiers fighting for Ireland's freedom – detested the policy of criminalisation. From the time of the ending of special category status in 1976, the scene was set for a confrontation between prisoners and the British Government. That confrontation was to reach its climax with the 1981 hunger strikes.

The initial reaction of Republican prisoners to the removal of special category status was to refuse to wear prison clothes, instead covering themselves with blankets. This blanket protest was followed in 1978 by the dirty protest, when prisoners smeared their cell walls with excrement rather than having to slop out. By late 1980, over 340 of the 837 Republican prisoners were involved in the protest.

▲ The H blocks.

Public demonstrations in support of the protests met with little success. Even a series of attacks on prison wardens proved ineffective, as the new Conservative Secretary of State, Humphrey Atkins, refused to compromise with the prisoners. Therefore, in late 1980, the IRA began a group hunger strike as a last method of achieving its demands. This historically successful tactic was called off in December, however, without anything having been achieved, although the prisoners had believed that they had agreed a deal on the wearing of their own clothes.

On 1 March 1981, a second hunger strike began, led by Bobby Sands, the IRA inmates' Commanding Officer. Unlike the previous strike, this time prisoners would join the protest at intervals. This would make the strike last longer and so maximise its impact. However, although the hunger strike gained huge publicity and the sympathy of many in the nationalist community, it did not change government policy (Source A). Therefore, when Frank Maguire, the Independent MP for Fermanagh–South Tyrone died, Republicans saw their chance to increase pressure on the British and put Sands up as a candidate. On the fortieth day of his strike, Sands, standing as an anti-H-block candidate, was elected to Westminster.

> **Source A** Prime Minister Margaret Thatcher, speaking about the hunger strikes in the House of Commons on 20 November 1980.
>
> Let me make one point about the hunger strike in the Maze Prison … There can be no political justification for murder or any other crime. The government will never concede political status to the hunger strikers.

> **Revision tip** ↻
>
> The new security policies introduced in the late 1970s would prove important later on. Make sure you know what these policies were.

The impact of the hunger strikes, 1980–81

Despite huge amounts of international pressure on both sides, neither side would compromise and on 5 May, Sands died. His funeral was attended by an estimated 100,000 mourners. The strike continued until 3 October 1981, by which time nine other prisoners had died. In the same period, 61 people died as a result of the violence that erupted in reaction to the deaths inside the prison.

Concessions granted

No concessions were made during the hunger strike. However, within a week of the strike's end, James Prior, the new Secretary of State, announced that a number of the concessions that the prisoners had sought would be granted. These included:

▶ Prisoners would be allowed to wear their own clothes at all times.

▶ The 50 per cent reduction in length of sentence lost by those involved in protests would be restored.

▶ More prison visits would be permitted.

▶ More association among prisoners would be allowed.

These concessions resulted in the protests in favour of special category status all but ending by late October 1981.

Politically this was a difficult time for the British government. In the aftermath of the hunger strikes new problems were emerging:

▶ Increased nationalist alienation from the state, resulting from what they saw as Prime Minister Margaret Thatcher's heavy-handed approach to the hunger strikers whose cause they saw as reasonable (Interpretation B).

▶ Rising support for Republicans.

▶ Unionists, while glad that the government had not given into the demands of the hunger strikers, who they saw as murderers and criminals, were increasingly voicing their anxieties at the growth in support for the IRA (as demonstrated by the huge numbers attending the funerals of Bobby Sands and other hunger-strikers) and seeming weaknesses of the province's security provisions which allowed IRA violence to continue (Interpretation C).

▶ The Irish government was pushing for the introduction of a new political initiative to end the Troubles.

Interpretation B Irish historian Professor J.J. Lee, writing in *Ireland 1912–1985: Politics and Society* (1989).

The British handling of the whole H-block situation was inept … the hunger strike and the authorities' response did more to unite Catholic opinion than any other single event since internment in 1971 or Bloody Sunday in 1972.

Interpretation C Politics lecturer Paul Dixon, writing in *Northern Ireland, The Politics of War and Peace* (2001).

Unionists tended to interpret the election of Sands and the turnout at his funeral as implying widespread Catholic support for terrorists who had murdered members of their community.

▲ The funeral of Bobby Sands, 7 May 1981.

Activity

Construct a timeline of the hunger strikes, beginning with the introduction of special category status. Annotate the timeline with key events, reasons for the hunger strikes and their impact.

Revision tip

Make sure that you understand and can explain why the hunger strikes began and what they achieved.

Sands' victory in Fermanagh–South Tyrone was hugely significant. It showed the Republican movement that there was much to gain from involvement in the political process at a time when the British Government was enjoying increasing success in its undercover campaign against Republicans. That Sands' victory was not a fluke was proved when his election agent, Owen Carron, won the seat at the by-election following Sands' death.

The official adoption of this policy came at the 1981 *Sinn Féin Ard Fheis*. At this the delegates approved the movement's plan of contesting elections while also continuing to use extra-constitutional methods to achieve its aims (Source D).

The effect of Sinn Féin's electoral success on the SDLP

The results of following elections clearly revealed the growth in support for *Sinn Féin* among nationalist voters. The party was soon winning an increasing number of local council seats. Then in the June 1983 Westminster general election, the party's President, Gerry Adams, defeated Gerry Fitt for the West Belfast seat. The British government was growing increasingly concerned that *Sinn Féin* might even replace the SDLP as the main nationalist party in the province. This prospect also worried the SDLP. The party, led since 1979 by John Hume, was looking more and more to Dublin for support.

Now, with both governments co-operating ever more closely in the face of *Sinn Féin*'s growth, there was the possibility that the SDLP might again have a significant input into the future direction of the province.

At the same time, the levels of violence – while lower than the 1970s – still gave considerable cause for concern. On 6 December 1982, 17 people, 11 of whom were soldiers, died when an INLA bomb exploded in Ballykelly. The INLA had emerged in 1975 from a split in the Official IRA (see page 158).

Source D Danny Morrison, speaking at the Sinn Féin *Ard Fheis*, 31 October 1981.

Who here really believes we can win the war through the ballot box? But will anyone here object if, with a ballot box in one hand and the Armalite [gun] in the other, we take power in Ireland?

▲ Gerry Adams (1948–).

Activities

1 Why did Sinn Féin decide to become involved in the political process?
2 Explain the reasons for the growth in support for Sinn Féin in the 1982 and 1983 elections.
3 How did the SDLP react to the political growth of the Republican movement?

Revision tip

You need to be able to explain how and why nationalist politics began to change in the aftermath of the 1981 hunger strike.

Practice question

Explain two of the following:
a The re-emergence of the Irish Republican Army (IRA) in 1970.
b The reasons for the fall of Stormont and the introduction of direct rule in 1972.
c The reasons for the hunger strikes in 1980-81.

This page provides guidance on how to answer questions 3 and 4 in the exam.

Question 3

Study **Source F** and answer the question which follows:

> **Source F** Adapted excerpt from British Prime Minister Harold Wilson, speaking about the 1974 UWC strike in a speech broadcast on television, 25 May 1974.
>
> [The strike is] a deliberate attempt to bring down the whole constitution of Northern Ireland ... The people on this side of the water ... have seen their sons spat upon and murdered. They have seen the taxes ... going into Northern Ireland. They see property destroyed by evil violence and are asked to pick up the bill for rebuilding it. Yet people who benefit from this now defy Westminster, claiming to act as though they were an elected government, spending their lives sponging on Westminster and British democracy and then fighting democratic methods. Who do these people think they are?

How **useful** is **Source F** for an historian studying the 1974 Ulster Workers' Council Strike?

Explain your answer, **using Source F and your contextual knowledge**. [5]

Guidance

You should be looking to spend about seven minutes on this question. To access all the available marks, your answer needs to address fully the issue of the source's utility: its usefulness.

Useful means **what do we learn from the source**: what does it tell us about the event in question? What kind of source is it? Where is it from, why was it produced and who was seeing it at the time? Most importantly, remember to comment – considering your own knowledge – on what the source does **not** tell us (its limitations), which may reduce its usefulness.

Step 1

Look carefully at the source and caption and see if you can recognise any figures or phrases in it. Say how the source is useful, and include details from your own knowledge.

Example

Source C is a primary source, and extremely useful because it gives us the viewpoint of the British Government at the time. The Prime Minister's speech was made just a few days before the strike resulted in the collapse of the power-sharing executive. The source outlines the British Government's opinion of the strikers and condemns their aims and actions. It claims that they have mistreated British soldiers. It strongly condemns the strikers as being against democracy.

Step 2

Say how the source is not useful, again using details from your own knowledge.

Example

However, the source's usefulness may be limited because it only gives one viewpoint: it does not tell us about what the other groups involved in the strike felt, nor does it tell us anything about how nationalists in Northern Ireland felt. In addition, the source seems to be very emotional, so it may not even be the real views of all members of the British government.

Question 4

Study **Source F** again and answer the question below:

How **reliable** is **Source F** for an historian studying the 1974 Ulster Workers'
Council Strike?

Explain your answer, using **Source F and your contextual knowledge**.   [6]

Guidance

You should be looking to spend about eight minutes on this question. To
access all the available marks your answer needs to address fully the issue
of the source's reliability.

Reliability means **whether or not we can take what it says to be true**. Keep in
mind issues such as the source's **type**, its **author**, **when** it was written, **who**
it was written for (its **audience**), **why** it was written (**motive**) and its **tone
and content**.

Step 1

Look carefully at the source
and caption and see if you
can recognise any figures
or phrases in it. Say how
the source is reliable or not
reliable.

Example

Source C dates from 1974, the year that the Ulster Workers'
Council organised a strike in an attempt to destroy the
power-sharing executive which took power on 1 January
1974. The date of the source — 25 May 1974 — was just a few
days before the strikers achieved their aims and the Power-
Sharing Executive collapsed. The speaker was the British
Prime Minister, Harold Wilson, so it is reliable in that it gives
us a clear view of what the London Government felt about
events in Northern Ireland at this time. The speech clearly
shows Wilson's anger at what was taking place in Belfast and
elsewhere. It was made on television so he was trying to have
his views heard by as many people as possible.

Step 2

Use details from your own
knowledge.

Example

The speech in the source is designed to get people to turn
against the strikers. It is probably true to say that the main
audience may have been those people living in Northern
Ireland, perhaps even those involved in the strike. By stating
so clearly and publicly how wrong their actions were, Wilson
might have hoped that they would end the strike.

6 Changing relations – towards closer co-operation

Faced with such violence and growing support for *Sinn Féin*, the British and Irish governments decided to work more closely together.

Closer co-operation: the Anglo-Irish Agreement

The outcome of this cooperation was the Anglo-Irish Agreement, signed by Margaret Thatcher and *Taoiseach* Garret FitzGerald on 15 November 1985. Historians have provided different reasons as to why it was signed:

▶ Constitutional nationalists and the British Government were afraid that *Sinn Féin* might overtake the SDLP and become the principal nationalist party in Northern Ireland. This could make agreement within Northern Ireland more difficult, worsen the security situation and threaten the stability of Ireland.

▶ Thatcher's main reason for signing the Anglo-Irish Agreement was security. The IRA's attempt to kill her at the 1984 Conservative Party Conference in Brighton made Thatcher realise that unless she dealt with nationalist alienation in Northern Ireland, she would not be able to improve security.

▶ FitzGerald hoped that reduced nationalist alienation and reform of the security forces in Northern Ireland would undermine the minority's toleration of the IRA.

What was different from earlier attempted solutions, however, was that no assembly or executive was established; it was purely an agreement between the two governments. In this way, it was reasoned, institutions that did not exist could not be pulled down.

What was agreed?

The key terms were:

▶ The establishment of an intergovernmental conference, dealing with issues such as security, legal matters, political questions and improving cross-border co-operation.

▶ A permanent secretariat made up of northern and southern civil servants to provide administrative support to the conference.

▶ Devolution would only occur if there was agreement on the sharing of power.

The agreement clearly recognised that the Republic had a role to play in the Northern Ireland government. At the same time, the Republic accepted that a united Ireland was a long-term goal that would only happen with a majority agreement (Interpretation A). Britain hoped that the agreement would lead to better security and co-operation, while Dublin hoped to persuade nationalists to accept the Northern Ireland state. Dublin believed that if this happened, support for *Sinn Féin* would collapse.

> **Interpretation A** Historian Sabine Wichert, writing in her book *Northern Ireland Since 1945* (1991).
>
> Who had most reason to be satisfied about after the signing of the Anglo-Irish Agreement?
>
> In political terms, the Anglo-Irish Agreement was an extraordinary achievement for Britain.

▲ Garret FitzGerald (1926–2011) and Margaret Thatcher (1925–2013) signing the Anglo-Irish Agreement.

The significance of the agreement

While the agreement passed through both Westminster and the *Dáil* without any real problems, it met with a variety of reactions within Ireland, both in Northern Ireland and the Republic of Ireland.

Unionists of all shades and opinions were appalled by the agreement (Source B). They felt that they had been abandoned by their own government and believed that they were now in a process that would eventually result in a united Ireland. What annoyed them the most, however, was the fact that they had been kept in the dark during the negotiations, while it looked as if the SDLP had been at least consulted in the process. Only the Alliance Party did not condemn the agreement outright.

The SDLP had been given more of a role in the creation of the agreement than any other party in Northern Ireland. It was therefore able to view the accord as an opportunity to create a better way of life for all those living in the province (Source C).

Sinn Féin condemned the agreement, arguing that rather than bringing a united Ireland closer, it actually made the division of Ireland more permanent, since in the agreement the Irish government was recognising the existence of Northern Ireland (Source D) and accepting that a united Ireland was a long-term aim that would only happen with the consent of a majority in Northern Ireland.

While the agreement was clearly acceptable to the *Fine Gael* and Labour parties that made up the Republic's coalition government, the *Fianna Fáil* opposition party led by Charles Haughey condemned it. Like *Sinn Féin*, *Fianna Fáil* was dismayed at Dublin's recognition of Britain's right to be in Northern Ireland. A prominent Irish Labour Party Senator, Mary Robinson, resigned from her party because the agreement was unacceptable to the unionist community (Source E).

The agreement enjoyed overwhelming cross-party support at Westminster but individual members of the British Parliament were not so happy. Ian Gow, the Prime Minister's former Parliamentary Private Secretary and now a Treasury Minister, resigned from his position in the government. He argued that the agreement was won by violence and would make the situation in the province worse rather than better (Source F).

Source B Rev. Ian Paisley, speaking in his church in the aftermath of the Anglo-Irish Agreement.

We pray this night that thou wouldst deal with the Prime Minister of our country … O God, in wrath take vengeance upon this wicked, treacherous lying woman: take vengeance upon her O Lord, and grant that we shall see a demonstration of thy power.

Source C John Hume, speaking in the House of Commons on 26 November 1985.

This is the first time that we have had a real framework within which to address the problem … There is no road towards a solution to this problem that does not contain risks. The road that has been chosen by both governments is the road of maximum consensus and is, therefore, the road of minimum risk.

Source D Gerry Adams, speaking on 16 November 1985.

This deal does not go anywhere near bringing peace to this part of Ireland. On the contrary it reinforces partition because Dublin is recognising Northern Ireland.

Source E The views of Irish Labour Party Senator, Mary Robinson.

I do not believe that [the agreement] can achieve its objective of securing peace and stability within Northern Ireland or on the island as a whole.

Source F Conservative MP Ian Gow, on the agreement.

The involvement of a foreign power in a consultative role in the administration of the province will prolong, and not diminish, Ulster's agony.

Activities

1 What were the main terms of the Anglo-Irish Agreement?
2 Explain the various reasons provided for the signing of the Anglo-Irish Agreement.
3 What did unionists in Northern Ireland think of the Anglo-Irish Agreement?

Revision tip

It is essential that you are able to explain what the main parts of the Anglo-Irish Agreement were.

The campaign against the agreement

Where could unionists look for support in their campaign against the agreement? The two main groups opposing the agreement apart from themselves, *Fianna Fáil* and *Sinn Féin*, would not have been the unionists' first choice for support. It seemed that they would have to look to their own community for ways of making their sense of despair and betrayal clear.

Unionist politicians decided that the best way of opposing the Anglo-Irish Agreement was by a campaign of non-cooperation with the British government. However, they were also keen to demonstrate, by strength of number, the depth and breadth of unionist opposition to what they termed the 'Dublin diktat'.

The campaign against the agreement took a variety of forms:

▶ Bonfires burning models of Margaret Thatcher, Irish Foreign Minister Peter Barry and other members of the Dublin government.

▶ Marches to the headquarters of the new Anglo-Irish Secretariat. On a number of occasions the marches became violent.

▶ A huge protest rally was held at Belfast's City Hall on 23 November 1985, attended by an estimated 100,000 people. (Some historians put the figure as high as 250,000.) The crowd was addressed by the OUP leader, James Molyneaux, and the DUP leader, Rev. Ian Paisley.

▶ All 15 unionist MPs resigned their seats at Westminster on 17 December but then stood for them again in the resulting by-elections. The aim was to show the strength of unionist opposition through the total number of votes the candidates received.

The results of these by-elections, held on 23 January 1986, were extremely interesting. The unionists gained a total of over 420,000 votes but lost one of their seats to the SDLP. Significantly, *Sinn Féin*'s share of the nationalist vote fell from nearly 42 per cent to just over 35 per cent. This suggested that one of the key aims of the architects of the agreement – the destruction of *Sinn Féin* – might be achievable.

▶ A unionist 'day of action' was arranged for 3 March 1986. Although much of the province was brought to a standstill using peaceful protest, in a number of places the protests resulted in violence.

▶ The launching of a campaign of civil disobedience with measures including the shunning of British ministers, the refusal to set rates in unionist council areas and a boycott of Westminster.

At the same time, a more sinister response was becoming evident. Loyalist paramilitaries engaged in a campaign of violence and intimidation against the RUC, who were seen as essential to the success of the agreement. In addition, in November 1986, Ulster Resistance, a paramilitary organisation whose aim was the destruction of the agreement, was formed.

> **Revision tip** ↻
>
> The different responses to the Anglo-Irish Agreement are extremely important. Make sure that you can explain who supported and who opposed the agreement and why this was so.

▼ Aerial view of the crowd protesting against the Anglo-Irish Agreement at the City Hall, Belfast, 23 November 1985.

Results of the campaign

By and large, however, these tactics failed to have any impact on the British government's determination to stick by the agreement. The absence of 14 MPs out of over 650 was not noticed at Westminster and since local councils had little power as it was, the refusal to use this power made little or no difference. By September 1987, when the unionist leaders agreed to talk to British ministers again, it was clear that the campaign to destroy the agreement had failed (Interpretation G and H).

Interpretation G The views of historian Jonathan Bardon, from his book *A History of Ulster* (1992).

In most respects the unionist plan was a miserable failure. The absence of Unionist MPs from Westminster was hardly noticed … Local authorities in Northern Ireland exercised very limited powers … [And] many unionists were uncomfortable with abstention tactics, which seemed rather too similar to those applied by *Sinn Féin* for decades.

Interpretation H Historian Sabine Wichert, writing in her book *Northern Ireland Since 1945* (1991).

The unionist protest … gradually modified its demands from scrapping the agreement to suspending it, after which, they said, they would be willing to talk to the SDLP about devolution and power sharing.

Activities

1 Using the information provided, explain the reaction of the following groups to the Anglo-Irish Agreement:
   - unionists
   - northern nationalists
   - republicans.
2 Make a copy of the following table. Using the information on pages 176–178, fill in the table as appropriate.

Supporters of the Anglo-Irish Agreement	Opponents of the Anglo-Irish Agreement

   Now look at your results; what strikes you as surprising about the people who opposed the agreement?
3 How did unionists show their opposition to the Anglo-Irish Agreement?
4 Make a copy of the following table. Using the information on pages 176–178, fill in the table as appropriate.

Unionist tactics against the Anglo-Irish Agreement	Reasons tactics were successful	Reasons tactics were unsuccessful

   Now look at your results. Using the information in your table and in the text, decide whether or not the unionists' campaign against the agreement was a success or a failure. Provide evidence to support your answer.

Revision tip

It is important that you are able to explain the ways in which unionists opposed the Anglo-Irish Agreement and why their campaign was a failure in the end.

Practice question

Give one reason for the signing of the Anglo-Irish agreement of 1985.

▲ John Hume (1937–).

By the latter part of the 1980s, SDLP leader John Hume believed that much could be gained from talking to Republicans, something no other party or government seemed prepared to do. In early 1988, therefore, he began secret talks with *Sinn Féin* President, Gerry Adams.

The Hume–Adams initiative

The Hume–Adams talks lasted eight months, ending in August 1988. They remained secret until April 1993, when their existence was revealed by a newspaper, the *Sunday Tribune*. By that point both politicians had started meeting again. The talks in general and John Hume in particular were severely criticised by other politicians. Indeed, recently revealed British Government papers reveal the level of opposition from within his own party that Hume faced whilst the talks were taking place with both South Down MP Eddie McGrady and Deputy Leader Seamus Mallon. (Source A and Interpretation B).

Interpretation B
Seamus Mallon, speaking on BBC *Talkback*, 28 December 2015.

They [*Sinn Féin*] used John – John Hume – like you'd play a 3lb trout. And he gave them the thing they were looking for. And that was a respectable image in the United States. They used him – oh, yeah, I think so, there's nothing new, I've said this. I said it to John. I've said it within the party.

Source A Extract from a memo on a meeting held between British Government officials and Eddie McGrady, September 1988, as reported in the *Belfast Telegraph*, 25 August 2016. (Mr McGrady was a founding member of the SDLP. He was MP for South Down from 1987 until his retirement in 2010. He died in November 2013.)

McGrady was clearly relieved that the SDLP/*Sinn Féin* talks had come to an end. He made clear that he never had any faith in this exercise and had refused to be part of the SDLP team for the talks … In his view there had never been any prospect of persuading *Sinn Féin* to abandon the armed struggle … *Sinn Féin*'s lack of sincerity had been demonstrated by the fact that the violence had escalated while the talks were going on.

In 1992, *Sinn Féin* published *Towards a Lasting Peace*. This document revealed a considerable reduction in the Republican movement's emphasis on armed struggle. Instead, considerable weight was placed on developing the concept of self-determination. At the same time, the Republican leadership suggested that it was Britain's responsibility to persuade unionists that their interests would best be served within a united Ireland.

Towards a Lasting Peace also argued that all Irish nationalist parties needed to join together to achieve constitutional change in Ireland. Such an all-Ireland coalition would, in turn, reduce the unionist majority within Northern Ireland to a minority within the whole island and, it was reasoned, when Britain realised that they would be unable to continue to prop up unionism, it would be prepared to deal with the Republican movement.

Source C Secretary of State, Peter Brooke, speaking on 9 November 1990.

It is not the aspiration to a sovereign, united Ireland against which we set our face, but its violent expression.

That this wasn't just wishful thinking on *Sinn Féin*'s part, had been proven by the Secretary of State, Peter Brooke. In 1989, Brooke suggested that if the PIRA called a ceasefire the British Government would react in an imaginative manner. Perhaps even more significantly, Brooke stated in November 1990 that his government had no 'selfish strategic or economic interest' in remaining in Northern Ireland (Source C).

Of course, not all the exchanges were happening in the public eye. While speaking out in public, Brooke had also approved the establishment of the 'Back Channel'. This was a private line of communication with the republican leadership. The very fact that both sides were prepared to talk at some level was an indication that there was new thinking emerging.

Brooke also attempted to kick-start discussions between the main constitutional parties regarding a political settlement. However, the main stumbling block with regard to unionist engagement remained the Anglo-Irish Agreement. To assist the process, the Intergovernmental Conference element of the 1985 Agreement was temporarily suspended to allow talks to begin.

Progress?

Some progress was made. It was agreed that any settlement of the Northern Ireland question would have to involve three elements or 'strands'. These were intercommunity relations, North–South co-operation and intergovernmental negotiations. Final agreement would only be recognised when consensus was reached in each of these areas.

That was about as far as the negotiations got; by the middle of 1991 the whole initiative was dead and buried. The discussions collapsed over the agreement of a timetable for each strand and over the issue of who would chair North-South co-operation element.

By the middle of 1992, the British General Election had taken place and Sir Patrick Mayhew had replaced Brooke as Secretary of State. Significantly, that election saw a reduction in *Sinn Féin*'s share of the vote and the loss – to the SDLP's Joe Hendron – of Adams' trophy seat in West Belfast. Mayhew also started a talks process utilising the same broad three-stranded framework introduced by his predecessor. However, these discussions also collapsed within a matter of months.

The Downing Street Declaration

While all of this was taking place, discussions between Hume and Adams recommenced. In April 1993, the two leaders issued a joint statement in which they reaffirmed their intention of achieving self-determination for the people of Ireland. The discussions gave birth to a draft document in which *Sinn Féin* stated that it was prepared to acknowledge the necessity of unionist consent with regard to the future constitutional development of Northern Ireland.

Despite the change in Republican thinking evident in the Hume–Adams statement, the British and Irish governments found themselves unable to accept it as a basis for peace given Gerry Adams' involvement with it. Instead, London and Dublin began to draw up their own document and in December 1993 they jointly produced the *Downing Street Declaration*, which outlined their approach to the removal of conflict.

In the Declaration the British undertook to 'uphold the democratic wish of a greater number of the people of Northern Ireland on the issue of whether they wish to support the Union or establish a sovereign united Ireland.' At the same time they reaffirmed Brooke's 1990 declaration that they had no 'selfish strategic or economic interest in Northern Ireland.'

▲ Peter Brooke (1934–).

▲ Sir Patrick Mayhew (1929–2016).

Activities

1 Which two nationalist leaders began secret talks in early 1988?
2 What evidence is there that the approaches of both *Sinn Féin* and the British Government were changing by the early 1990s?

Source D Excerpt from the Downing Street Declaration, 1993.

[The British concluded that] it is for the people of the island of Ireland alone, by agreement between the two parts respectively, to exercise their right of self-determination on the basis of consent, freely and concurrently given, north and south, to bring about a united Ireland.

Meanwhile, Dublin accepted that a united Ireland had to be the result of majority consent within Northern Ireland. Significantly, it accepted that important elements of the 1937 Constitution were unacceptable to unionists and in light of this undertook – in the context of an overall settlement – to make changes to that document.

Just in case people got carried away with what was being suggested, the British Government put a number of important qualifications on its position. London stated that it would not persuade unionists to join such a new union. Also, just in case anyone thought that they had gone soft on the issue, the British also reaffirmed that they still held sovereignty over Northern Ireland and did not contemplate sharing this with Dublin.

The key terms and responses

The Declaration was a significant development (Source D). Not least in terms of importance was the British acceptance that the desire to see a united Ireland was a legitimate aspiration to hold. Yet the above qualifications were still too much for Republicans. *Sinn Féin* argued that even if it was glad to see that Britain was at least accepting the concept of self-determination, the document's language allowed unionists a veto over its exercise.

The response from the different unionist parties was equally cautious. While the Ulster Unionist Party (UUP) was comforted by the British Government's qualifications, it was less than happy with what they termed the Declaration's 'green tinge'. It was a similar reaction from the DUP, although it argued that, more than having a green tinge, the Declaration was yet another step towards a united Ireland.

On the whole, the unionist parties remained unpersuaded by key elements of the Declaration. In particular, they were concerned at the vague nature of the Republic's pledges to change its Constitution. They argued that the language used would permit Dublin to decline to change the Constitution if it was dissatisfied with the 'overall settlement'. Moreover, they argued that if the Republic was satisfied it would be an indication that its long-standing constitutional claim over Northern Ireland had been achieved. That would not exactly be a cause for celebration either.

Source E Former BBC Correspondent, Denis Murray, reflecting on the Downing Street Declaration 20 years on (as reported on the BBC News website in an article dated 15 December 2013).

In that live broadcast, I felt I had to say the following: 'Albert Reynolds has said this is a historic opportunity. Whether this declaration turns out to be a historic occasion depends on four things – this is intended to produce an IRA ceasefire; which will, in turn, produce a ceasefire by the loyalist paramilitary groups; and then will follow all-party talks, and then, hopefully, a new political agreement. And any of those will be a really good trick to pull off.' And despite all the odds against it, they all happened … Astonishing.

The significance of the Declaration: ceasefire

At first glance, the Declaration might not have been the political answer to all that the Provisional IRA (PIRA) was looking for. In the end, however, careful explanation of the thinking behind the Declaration – provided by Irish Government representatives – enabled the Republican movement to use the document as a basis for its 'complete cessation of military operations' as of 31 August 1994. The months between the Declaration and the cessation had been taken up with discussions and negotiations between the main players at home, and providing reassurances for Republicans at home and abroad.

Activities

1 What were the main terms of the *Downing Street Declaration*?
2 Why was the *Downing Street Declaration* significant?

The PIRA statement

The PIRA statement recognised the 'potential of the current situation' but warned that 'a solution will only be found as a result of inclusive negotiations'. In other words, *Sinn Féin* would have to be fully included in any talks process.

If *Sinn Féin* had hoped that the PIRA's cessation would provide its passport for entry into real talks, it was to be sorely disappointed. The British Government announced that it wanted to hear the PIRA use the word 'permanent' in connection with its cessation and it added that it would also require a period of time to test the Republican movement's actions rather than its words. *Sinn Féin* argued that the silence of the PIRA weapons and its own electoral support provided more than enough justification for its immediate inclusion in talks.

In contrast to London, both Dublin and Washington reacted more positively to the PIRA statement. Just a week after the cessation took effect, *Taoiseach* Albert Reynolds shook hands with Gerry Adams when the two of them appeared publicly on the steps of Government Buildings along with John Hume. Just over a month later, Dublin announced the establishment of a Forum for Peace and Reconciliation, to be attended by representatives of all Irish parties, while in early December, nine PIRA inmates were released on licence. Meanwhile, President Bill Clinton allowed Adams into the United States and organised numerous conferences aimed at supporting the peace process with economic investment.

Within four months, however, the Dublin part of this support network had crumbled. In December 1994, Reynolds' *Fianna Fáil* administration was replaced by a *Fine Gael*–Labour–Democratic Left coalition. Neither the new *Taoiseach*, John Bruton, nor Proinsias de Rossa, the leader of Democratic Left, were known for their love of Republicanism.

Meanwhile, the loyalist paramilitaries waited a further six weeks after the PIRA declaration before they announced their own ceasefire on 13 October 1994. The loyalist statement warned that the continuation of their ceasefire would be 'completely dependent upon the continued cessation of all nationalist/Republican violence' (Source F).

▲ Left to right: Gerry Adams, Albert Reynolds (1932–2014), and John Hume join hands following their meeting at Government Buildings on 6 September, 1994.

The loyalists' ceasefire also began to pay political dividends for their political representatives, the Progressive Unionist Party (PUP) and the Ulster Democratic Party (UDP). By the close of the year, both groups were engaged in exploratory discussions with representatives of the London government.

The Framework Documents

In February 1995, the London and Dublin governments put two further progress papers forward. The aim of the *Framework Documents* was, not surprisingly, to provide a framework for taking the peace process forward. They stressed that the two governments wanted to see a 'comprehensive settlement' that would return greater 'power, authority and responsibility to all the Northern Ireland people'.

Source F Combined Loyalist Military Command (CLMC) Ceasefire Statement, 13 October 1994.

After a widespread consultative process … and after having received confirmation and guarantees in relation to Northern Ireland's constitutional position within the United Kingdom, as well as other assurances, and, in the belief that the democratically expressed wishes of the greater number of people in Northern Ireland will be respected and upheld, the CLMC will universally cease all operational hostilities as from 12 midnight on Thursday 13th October 1994.

The first paper, *A Framework for Accountable Government in Northern Ireland*, outlined Britain's proposals for new political institutions for Northern Ireland. These included a 90-strong assembly that would exercise powers similar to its 1974 power-sharing predecessor. A range of mechanisms was also suggested to provide protection for the nationalist minority.

The second Framework Document, *A New Framework for Agreement*, was produced jointly by London and Dublin. It was based around the principles of self-determination, consent, non-violence and parity of esteem. To help develop relationships within Ireland, it proposed the establishment of some form of Northern Ireland – Republic of Ireland body while relations between Britain and Ireland would be underpinned by structures similar to those established by the Anglo-Irish Agreement.

As usual, reactions from the local parties were mixed. Unionists saw too many similarities with Sunningdale and hated the possibility of the development of Northern Ireland – Republic of Ireland links into some form of institutions with executive powers (Source G).

Not long afterwards, the UUP leader, James Molyneaux, resigned to be replaced by Upper Bann MP David Trimble. Molyneaux had always claimed to have the ear of the British; the Anglo-Irish Agreement and the *Framework Documents* seemed to have proved this assertion to be somewhat misplaced. He left behind a divided and demoralised party.

Sinn Féin also had issues with the *Framework Documents* but these went in the opposite direction from those of the unionists. They argued that the *Documents* provided mechanisms by which unionists would be able to veto progress. Only the SDLP and Alliance reacted positively to what had been proposed.

> **Source G** DUP Deputy Leader Peter Robinson, MP, reflecting on the Framework Documents in an article published in the *Independent*, 24 February 1995.
>
> The people I represent, more than any others, deserve peace and stability. They are the most wronged, persecuted and vilified [lied about] people in the civilised world. For a quarter of a century, they have refused to bow to terrorism and many have paid for it with their life's blood. They have been bombed and shot at, bullied and blackmailed, yet even in their darkest hour, they held on to their cherished membership of the British family.
>
> Being British, for them, was no nominal condition. Their citizenship was under attack, but that danger only caused them to cling more tightly to their Britishness. A dagger wielded by the hand of a friend is the cruellest cut of all and they now see, once again, a Tory Prime Minister betraying loyal Ulster.
>
> The process is clear. It is to bring about a United Ireland, incrementally [little by little] and by stealth. This week's published *Framework Document* offers no Union-strengthening option. It is entirely a nationalist agenda for bringing about a united Ireland. We are told rejection of this proposal could end the peace process. As if we, who have been the victims of violence, would be responsible for the terrorists starting up again because we refuse to surrender.

▲ David Trimble (1944–).

Activities

1 Explain the PIRA and loyalist paramilitary ceasefires using the following:
   - reasons
   - reactions.
2 What were the main elements of the *Framework Documents*?
3 How did the different parties/groups respond to the *Framework Documents*?

The collapse of the ceasefire

Meanwhile, the continuing absence of face-to-face talks between the British Government and Republicans began to impact severely on the stability of the peace process. The main problem for the British was the absence of PIRA decommissioning. The British and unionists were demanding this before entering into negotiations. For the PIRA, such a demand was as good as an admission of defeat and surrender; two things which they were unlikely to ever sign up to. Its frustration boiled over and instead of continuing to follow the lead of the *Sinn Féin* leadership, the PIRA began to plan for a return to military operations.

Unaware of what was being planned, London attempted to find a way around the standstill by establishing a commission, chaired by former US Senate Majority Leader George Mitchell, to look into the issue of decommissioning. The Mitchell Commission reported its findings in early 1996. Its solution to the deadlock was christened the twin track approach or parallel decommissioning. It suggested the handover of weapons in parallel with talks taking place, but not before. The Commission also put forward proposals or principles of non-violence, to which all parties would have to sign up in order to demonstrate their commitment to peace (Source H).

Source H The Mitchell Principles of Non-Violence.

1 To use democratic and exclusively peaceful means of resolving political issues.
2 To seek the total disarmament of all paramilitary organisations.
3 To agree that such disarmament must be verifiable [shown to be true] to the satisfaction of an independent commission.
4 To renounce [say no to] for themselves and to oppose any effort by others to use force, or threaten to use force to influence the course or the outcome of all-party negotiations.
5 To agree to abide by the terms of any agreement reached in all-party negotiations and to resort to democratic and exclusively peaceful methods in trying to alter any aspect of that outcome with which they may disagree.
6 To urge that 'punishment' killings and beatings stop and to take effective steps to prevent such actions.

Obstacles to peace

Mitchell's work should have provided a way out of the impasse, but before long there were yet more obstacles to overcome. One was the decision to hold elections to a Peace Forum – an idea first raised by the Mitchell Commission – as a way of providing a mandate for the participants. The other was the collapse of the PIRA cessation in February 1996 when it exploded a bomb at London's Canary Wharf. This was proof enough for all of the doubters that the Republican movement had never seen its cessation as anything more than a tactic.

▼ Canary Wharf following the PIRA bomb, February 1996.

The PIRA placed the blame for its decision to return to violence on the British Government's continued reluctance to move the peace process forward (Source I). It has been suggested that one of the main reasons for this was the position that the Conservative Government found itself in by that time. John Major – who had succeeded Margaret Thatcher as British Prime Minister in 1990 – had been returned to power in 1992 with a small majority. Within a few years, the loss of several by-elections and the withdrawal of the whip from a number of Conservative MPs over their opposition to the government's policy on Europe had left the Prime Minister reliant on the support of UUP MPs to stay in office. He could only push the process forward at a pace with which the unionists were comfortable.

Unionists supported the Forum plan but nationalists were furious. They simply did not see the need for participants in the peace process to have to prove their mandate further. In their view, the plan was yet another stalling exercise, an example of the influence that the unionist parties in general and the UUP in particular were exercising over the Conservative Government.

▲ George Mitchell (1933–).

Source I Irish Republican Army (PIRA) Statement ending the Ceasefire, 9 February 1996.

It is with great reluctance that the leadership of the IRA announces that the complete cessation of military operations will end at 6pm on February 9.

As we stated on August 31, 1994, the basis for the cessation was to enhance the democratic peace process and to underline our definitive [complete] commitment to its success.

We also made it clear that we believed that an opportunity to create a just and lasting settlement had been created.

The cessation presented an historic challenge for everyone and the IRA commends [praises] the leaderships of nationalist Ireland at home and abroad. They rose to the challenge. The British Prime Minister did not.

Instead of embracing the peace process, the British government acted in bad faith with Mr Major and the unionist leaders squandering this unprecedented [wasting this unexpected chance] opportunity to resolve the conflict.

Time and again, over the last 18 months, selfish party political and sectional [group] interests in the London parliament have been placed before the rights of the people of Ireland.

We take this opportunity to re-iterate [repeat] our total commitment to our republican objectives.

The resolution of the conflict in our country demands justice. It demands an inclusive negotiated settlement. That is not possible unless and until the British government faces up to its responsibilities.

The blame for the failure thus far of the Irish peace process lies squarely with John Major and his government.

In spite of their hostility to the plan, both the SDLP and *Sinn Féin* put forward candidates for the Forum elections. However, as far as *Sinn Féin* was concerned, that was as far as its involvement would go. It announced that it would boycott the resulting assembly. The SDLP announced that it would make up its minds to attend the Forum on a day-by-day basis depending on what the agenda was.

Election results

The election results revealed that support for the DUP and *Sinn Féin* had increased. The UDP and PUP were also successful in winning seats, which meant that they would be able to attend any future peace talks. This was probably one of the most positive outcomes of the decision to hold elections. It provided for broadly based negotiations that at least had the potential to bring all the key players in the process along.

The peace talks finally began in June 1996. However, the Canary Wharf bomb and the continuing absence of a PIRA ceasefire ensured that *Sinn Féin* was not present. Moreover, it did not have the same voices to plead its case as earlier in the process because the end of the cessation and the change of government in Dublin had weakened the so-called pan-nationalist front that had been built up by Hume, Adams and Reynolds.

The entire peace process was in some form of limbo throughout 1996 and during the first half of 1997. It appeared that no real progress would be possible until a stronger government had been installed in London. As there had to be an election in 1997 and as it seemed more than likely that the Conservatives would be defeated, attention turned to the likely impact that a Labour government would have on the peace process.

Activities

1 Explain the background to the Canary Wharf bomb of February 1996.
2 What was the role of Senator George Mitchell in the Northern Ireland Peace Process in 1996?
3 What did the PIRA blame for the collapse of the ceasefire?

Revision tip

The main things for you to understand when studying this period is how the governments, paramilitaries and parties began to move closer to a position where a genuine peace process could begin. Of course, there were many ups and downs within this process. You need to be able to explain the approaches of the different groups and individuals involved.

Practice question

Describe one consequence of the Downing Street Declaration in 1993.

This page provides guidance on how to answer question 5 in the exam.

Question 5

(a) Name the British Prime Minister 1990–1997.   [1]

(b) Give **one** reason for the introduction of Direct Rule in 1972.   [1]

(c) Give **one** term of the Anglo-Irish Agreement of 1985.   [1]

(d) Describe **one** reason why there was unionist opposition to the
    Good Friday Agreement.   [2]

Guidance

You should be looking to spend a maximum of four minutes on this
question. To access all marks you need to give clear answers and, with
reference to Parts (b) and (d), a clear reason for the issue/event in question.

Whilst being accurate, do this question as quickly as you can.

Example answers for parts b and d are below.

Example for part 5b

One reason was that there was a need to restore law and order
within Northern Ireland.

Example for part 5d

There was unionist opposition to the Good Friday Agreement
because the Agreement had republican involvement.

The May 1997 Westminster General Election transformed the political map in Britain and provided the stimulus for developments in Ireland. The new Labour government – led by Tony Blair – wasted no time in getting things moving again in Northern Ireland by announcing that if the PIRA renewed its ceasefire, *Sinn Féin* would be allowed to enter talks.

The same election had proven successful for *Sinn Féin* too; Martin McGuinness had won a Westminster seat in Mid Ulster, thus doubling the Party's potential representation in Parliament (given that party leader Gerry Adams had retaken the Belfast West seat that he had lost to the SDLP's Joe Hendron in 1992). These results seemed to suggest that electoral support for the Republican movement was again growing.

▲ Bertie Ahern with Tony Blair meeting for a crisis talk on the future of Northern Ireland, 3 February 1998.

At the same time a poll in the Republic of Ireland (June 1997) had seen the electorate's rejection of the current *Fine Gael*–Democratic Left administration and a return to power of *Fianna Fáil*, partnered by the Progressive Democrats. As a result *Fianna Fáil* leader Bertie Ahern became *Taoiseach*.

The creation of the Good Friday Agreement

Having been assured that it would be included in talks, the PIRA ceasefire was renewed on 20 July 1997 (Source A). Then, having signed up to the Mitchell Principles of Non-Violence (see page 185), *Sinn Féin* entered the talks in September 1997.

Source A Extract from PIRA Ceasefire Statement, 19 July 1997.

The IRA … [wants] a permanent peace and therefore we are prepared to enhance the search for a democratic peace settlement through real and inclusive negotiations.

So having assessed the current political situation, the leadership … are announcing a complete cessation of military operations from 12 midday on Sunday 20 July, 1997.

We have ordered the unequivocal [complete] restoration of the ceasefire of August 1994. All IRA units have been instructed accordingly.

Sinn Féin's entry was the signal for some unionist parties to absent themselves from the process. Both the DUP – and the minority United Kingdom Unionist Party (UKUP) – refused to even consider proximity negotiations, a position that was not shared by the UUP nor indeed by the parties representing the loyalist paramilitaries.

Sinn Féin's entry also caused problems within the Republican movement. It was important that the party's leadership would be able to negotiate without the PIRA beginning its campaign again – as had happened at Canary Wharf in February 1996. A General Army Convention was therefore called to agree a change to the PIRA's constitution that would allow its Army Council (which the *Sinn Féin* leadership allegedly controlled) to decide on possible concessions. The leadership's victory at this Convention resulted in a section of the Republican movement leaving to form a new paramilitary grouping, the Real IRA.

▲ President Bill Clinton (1946–).

Source B British Prime Minister Tony Blair, 8 April 1998, arriving in Belfast for the talks which produced the Good Friday Agreement.

A day like today is not a day for soundbites, really. But I feel the hand of history upon our shoulders. I really do.

Source C Statement by Senator George Mitchell, Friday 10 April 1998.

I am pleased to announce that the two governments and the political parties in Northern Ireland have reached agreement.

It had already been decided that the negotiations would be based around three strands. Strand One would concentrate on establishing a suitable internal governmental structure for Northern Ireland; Strand Two would be concerned with relationships between the two parts of Ireland, while Strand Three would deal with British–Irish relations. At the same time, an Independent International Commission on Decommissioning was launched under the chairmanship of Canadian General John de Chastelain.

Having decided that a deadline would help concentrate minds in terms of reaching agreement, Senator Mitchell stated that midnight on Holy Thursday, 9 April, would be the final deadline for the talks. In the event, that deadline was overrun – even though both Blair and Ahern had joined the negotiators in an effort to reach agreement (Source B). Then, just when it seemed that UUP objections to decommissioning and the release of paramilitary prisoners might lead to the collapse of the process, Tony Blair called on the persuasive powers of US President, Bill Clinton, to keep the negotiations going. On the evening of Friday 10 April 1997, Good Friday, it was announced that a deal was finally done (Source C).

The key terms of the Good Friday Agreement

As with the negotiations, the Agreement was divided into three strands.

Strand One	Dealt with the internal political settlement. It established a 108-member Assembly that was to be elected by proportional representation (PR). This body would enjoy full legislative and executive authority over areas previously administered by the Northern Ireland Office (the government department that ran Northern Ireland).
Strand Two	Focused on relations within the island of Ireland. It established a North–South Ministerial Council that would be responsible for cross-border co-operation in a range of areas including language, agriculture, health, tourism and trade. Meetings of the Council would include the relevant ministers from both jurisdictions depending on the issues under discussion.
Strand Three	Centred on East–West relations, namely those between Ireland and Britain. As part of this aspect there would be a Council of the Isles or British–Irish Council comprising members from all parliaments and devolved assemblies within the British Isles. Its purpose was to enable consultation and co-operation in a range of areas including drugs, agriculture, energy and regional issues. There would also be a British–Irish Intergovernmental Conference with responsibilities similar to the institutions established between London and Dublin by the 1985 Anglo-Irish Agreement.

Activities

1 What political changes resulted from the 1997 UK and Irish General Elections?
2 Create a spider diagram to show the key elements of the 1998 Good Friday Agreement.
3 What were the main responses to the 1998 Good Friday Agreement?

Other elements of the Good Friday Agreement

There were other significant elements. The Irish government undertook to renounce its constitutional claims to Northern Ireland as contained within Articles II and III of the 1937 Irish Constitution (Source D). Meanwhile, London agreed to replace the 1920 Government of Ireland Act (see page 96). There were also to be prisoner releases, coupled with the decommissioning of paramilitary weapons.

Policing would be one of the key elements in the creation of a new political beginning and a police force that could attract the support of both communities was, therefore, essential. The Agreement provided a roadmap for reform of policing. Under its terms, an Independent Commission on Policing in Northern Ireland was established under the chairmanship of Chris Patten, former Conservative Party Chairman and last Governor of Hong Kong.

Source D Extracts from *Bunreacht na hÉireann* (the Irish Constitution), 1937.

Article II	The national territory consists of the whole island of Ireland, its islands and territorial seas.
Article III	While maintaining the right to rule all 32 counties in Ireland, the laws passed by the Dublin Parliament will apply only to the 26 counties until Ireland is reunified.
Article XLIV	The state recognises the special position of the Holy Catholic Apostolic and Roman Church as the guardian of the faith professed by the great majority of the citizens.

The responses to the Good Friday Agreement

Even before the Agreement was signed it was clear that there were going to be difficulties in selling it, particularly within the unionist community. The absence of the DUP and the UKUP from the negotiations has already been noted; however, public divisions were now beginning to emerge within the ranks of the majority UUP. The first sense of this came when Jeffrey Donaldson – one of the members of the UUP negotiating team – walked out of the negotiations just as the deal was nearing completion.

Six of the UUP's ten MPs had set their faces against the deal, creating a very difficult situation for David Trimble. In May, all the unionists opposed to the Agreement – including UUP dissidents – set up the United Unionist Campaign to co-ordinate their campaign of opposition. Their slogan became 'It's Right to say No.'

Initially, somewhat contradictory reactions from within Republican ranks provided further cause for concern. On the last day of April, the PIRA issued a statement suggesting that the Agreement fell somewhat 'short of presenting a solid basis for a lasting settlement', and added that it would not decommission any of its weapons.

However, a few days later, the *Sinn Féin* leadership advised its supporters to back the Agreement. At the Party's *Ard Fheis*, members voted to change their constitution so as to allow members to take seats in the Northern Ireland Assembly. This was an historic moment in the history of the Party. For the first time it was prepared to take up seats in what it itself might have previously termed a 'partitionist parliament'.

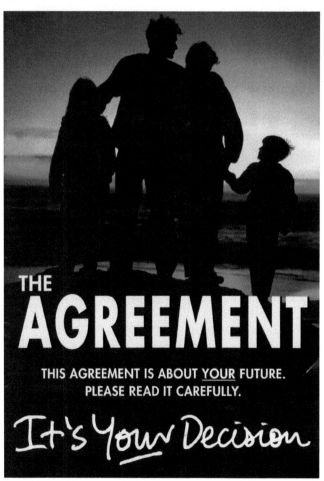

▲ The Cover of the Good Friday Agreement.

The referendums

The first real test of the Good Friday Agreement would be how the voting public would react to it. Referendums were held on both sides of the border on 22 May 1998 to ascertain the electorate's reactions. These were preceded by a pro-Agreement campaign that enjoyed almost overwhelming cross-party support in all political jurisdictions within the British Isles. Of course there were notable exceptions: the DUP, UKUP, a number of senior UUP members and a number of prominent individuals including former Prime Minister Margaret (now known as Baroness) Thatcher.

Within Northern Ireland, 71.12 per cent of those who voted indicated their support for the Agreement. The overall turnout was 80.98 per cent, a figure significantly higher than that produced at most election times.

As the vote was carried out on the basis of Northern Ireland as a single constituency, it was impossible to give an accurate breakdown of support levels within the two communities. Insofar as estimates can be relied upon, it seemed that close to 97 per cent of nationalists gave the Agreement their support while the comparable figure within unionism stood at about 52 per cent. This limited majority (for the latter), while better than the figures achieved at the time of the 1973 power-sharing elections, still gave significant cause for concern in terms of the prospects of success for the current deal.

The figures for the referendum in the Republic were even clearer. There, 94.4 per cent agreed with the Dublin government's plans to amend Articles II and III of the Irish Constitution as agreed at the peace talks.

Revision tip

It is important that you can fully describe the background to, terms of and reactions to the 1998 Good Friday Agreement. It is a complicated topic, so make sure that you are clear about the Agreement's terms – and how the different parties and populations responded to these same terms.

The new Assembly

Elections for the new Assembly were held in late June. On the surface it seemed that there was a clear majority of members elected in favour of power-sharing (75 per cent of the votes resulting in 80 out of 108 Assembly seats); however this failed to take account of two important qualifications. First, not all of the 28 UUP members elected were in favour of the Agreement – even though the UUP was meant to be a pro-Agreement Party. Second, and more important, the Agreement dictated that certain decisions (called key decisions) called for majority support from both nationalist and unionist communities. Given the fine balance between pro- and anti-Agreement unionist support, that was going to be easier said than done.

The new Assembly gathered for the first time on 15 July 1998 with the Alliance Party's Lord John Alderdice having been appointed Presiding Officer by the Secretary of State. David Trimble, UUP Leader, and Seamus Mallon, SDLP Deputy-Leader, were elected as First and deputy First Ministers (Designate).

Activities

1 How did the different parties/organisations react to the Good Friday Agreement?
2 What did the results of the May 1998 referendums reveal about the different attitudes within the island of Ireland to the Good Friday Agreement?
3 What did the results of the 1998 Assembly elections reveal about attitudes to the Good Friday Agreement within Northern Ireland?

Practice question

Explain two of the following:
a The reasons for the Anglo-Irish Agreement in 1985.
b The responses to the Downing Street Declaration in 1993.
c The significance of the Agreement for relations between Britain, Northern Ireland and the Republic of Ireland.

This page provides guidance on how to answer question 6 in the exam.

Question 6

Explain **two** of the following:

A The reasons for NICRA's campaign in the 1960s.

B The effects of the introduction of internment in 1971.

C The different reactions to the Hunger Strike in 1981.   [9+9]

Explanation One: (A, B or C)

Explanation Two: (B or C if you chose A; A or B if you chose C; A or C if you chose B)

Guidance

You should be looking to spend about ten minutes on **each part** of this question.

To access all the available marks your answer needs to 'demonstrate knowledge and understanding to explain and analyse historical events and periods'. You will need to ensure that there is sufficient (relevant) detail in your answer and show – through what you write – that you understand the issue that you are attempting to explain.

Remember that the quality of written communication will be assessed in this question.

Step 1

You have a little choice here – spend a little time considering each option, and then choose the two you are most familiar with. Start with your first option and state your point clearly.

Example

There were a number of different reactions to the 1981 Hunger Strike.

Step 2

Use detail in your answer and remember that you are trying to explain an event as fully as you can: do not write a story of what happened. Remember to keep your points relevant to the question.

Example

There were a number of different reactions to the Hunger Strike: the nationalist/republican reaction [give detail], the unionist reaction [give detail], the British Government reaction [give detail], the Irish Government reaction [give detail] ...

Step 3

Do the same for your second option.

Example

There were many effects of the introduction of internment in 1971 ...

Outline study: International Relations, 1945–2003

This unit focuses on the developments in international relations between the superpowers in the years after the Second World War.

Most of the period was taken up with a 'Cold War'; an ideological power struggle between the United States and the Soviet Union. This involved a number of 'flashpoints' – both in Europe and in the wider world – which could have caused a nuclear war resulting in the destruction of all life on earth.

The Cold War ended in 1989 and the Soviet Union collapsed soon after, but the world did not become a safe place. Superpower interference – notably in Afghanistan – had sown the seeds of *jihadism*, and the West soon found itself engaged in a so-called 'War on Terror'. This option examines the following key areas of content:

▶ Co-operation ends and the Cold War begins
▶ Emerging superpower rivalry and its consequences, 1945–49
▶ Flashpoints in Europe and the impact on international relations
▶ Flashpoints outside Europe and the impact on international relations
▶ The end of the Cold War, 1985–91
▶ New tensions emerge, 1991–2003

The breakdown of the wartime alliance between the USA and USSR

The Second World War took place from 1939 to 1945 and was fought between two general groups:

Allied Powers (Allies)

▶ Britain (led by Winston Churchill)
▶ The USA (led by Franklin D Roosevelt)
▶ The Soviet Union or USSR (led by Josef Stalin)
▶ China (mainly led by Chiang Kai-shek's Nationalist Kuomintang (KMT), although Mao Zedong's communists were gaining power)
▶ France (led by Charles de Gaulle)

Axis Powers

▶ Germany (led by Adolf Hitler)
▶ Italy (led by Benito Mussolini)
▶ Japan (led by Emperor Hirohito)

By the end of the war in 1945, the power of Germany and Japan had been broken, and the USA and USSR were established as the two main superpowers in the world. Far from bringing peace, however, within months of the end of the Second World War, the USA and the USSR had become engaged in a new struggle for power, as the allies of 1945 became enemies. This struggle came to be called 'the Cold War'.

Ideological differences: the origins of the Cold War

To understand how the alliance between the USA and the USSR broke down, it is best to look at the ideological differences between the two countries.

Although historians usually date the beginning of the Cold War to 1945, its origins actually go back much further. In October 1917, Bolsheviks (or the 'Reds'), led by V.I. Lenin, seized power in Russia. This revolution greatly worried most Western countries, which were capitalist democracies. This was because Bolsheviks believed in communism and wanted to destroy the capitalist system that they operated (Source A). Table 1 outlines the main differences between the two systems.

	Capitalist democracies	Communist countries
Political system	Free and regular elections where people vote for candidates	Elections – if they are held at all – have no choice; all candidates are for the same party. Only the government party's ideas are heard.
Media	Freedom of the press and of speech is protected. People are free to disagree with the political system.	Restrictions on freedom of speech. The media is only allowed to print and say what the government allows it to.
Wealth	Individuals own the different industries. They are free to keep the profits that they make.	All industry is under the control of the government. Individuals are not allowed to make a profit.

Table 1 The main difference between capitalist and communist systems.

Mutual fear and distrust grew in the years that followed:

▶ Britain, France, Japan and the USA helped the Bolsheviks' opponents (the 'Whites') when civil war broke out in Russia in 1917 during the Russian Revolution
▶ Britain refused to recognise the communist regime as Russia's government until 1924
▶ The USA also refused to recognise the communist government until 1933
▶ During the 1930s, Britain and France refused to form an alliance with Russia against Nazi Germany.

Source A Josef Stalin, speaking in November 1920 after the defeat of the last 'White' army.

Here I stand on the border line between the old, capitalist world and the new, socialist world. Here, on this border line, I unite the efforts of the proletarians of the West and of the peasants of the East in order to shatter the old world.

Meanwhile, Josef Stalin (who succeeded Lenin as leader of Russia, now called the USSR or the Soviet Union) was well aware of the West's hostility to communism. He began a series of Five-Year Plans to ensure that the Soviet economy would be ready to fight a war against the West – which he believed wanted to destroy the USSR. When it became clear in the 1930s that Britain and France did not intend to help him against the growing power of Nazi Germany, Stalin instead signed a Non-Aggression Pact with Hitler in August 1939. This meant the USSR did not go to war against the Nazis a month later, when the Second World War began. This was mainly because the USSR was not ready to go to war.

Fighting a common enemy (before 1945)

When Germany invaded the Soviet Union in June 1941, Stalin and the Allies joined together. It was, however, not an easy alliance. The Soviets suffered terribly during the Nazi invasion with perhaps as many as 20 million people killed during the war, yet Britain and America ignored Stalin's pleas to open up 'a second front' (an attack from the west to distract the Nazis) until the D-Day invasion of June 1944.

Stalin remained suspicious of the West, believing that Britain and the USA had delayed D-Day in the hope that Nazi Germany and the communist USSR would destroy each other.

Meanwhile, as the Soviets first stopped the Nazis' advance and then began to drive them back into Germany, the British Prime Minister Winston Churchill viewed their progress with alarm and tried to persuade the Americans to advance faster into Germany to stop it.

Nevertheless, mainly because of the willingness of the US President Franklin D. Roosevelt (1933–45) to trust Stalin, and also because of the shared need to defeat Hitler and the Nazis, the alliance of the USA, the USSR and Britain held together until it was clear that the war was coming to an end.

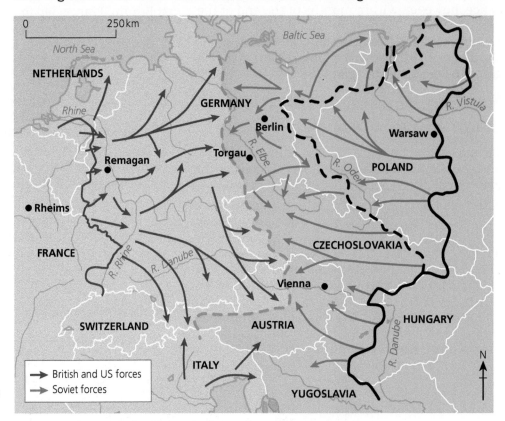

➤ Allied forces advance into Germany in 1945: the Red Army from the east and the British, Americans and Canadians from the west.

Yalta, February 1945

In February 1945, the leaders of Britain (Winston Churchill), the USA (Franklin D. Roosevelt) and the USSR (Stalin) – known as the 'Big Three' – met at Yalta in the Ukraine. Although the war was not yet over, it was clear that the Allies were going to win. The aim of the meeting was to reach agreement on what would happen in post-war Europe.

Each leader was hoping to achieve something different from the meeting:

▶ Churchill wanted to ensure the survival of the British Empire; however, he also saw the USSR as a danger to the West that had to be stopped. This was because as the USSR or Red Army was pushing the Germans back into Western Europe, it was gaining control of countries such as Poland and Hungary.

▶ Roosevelt was not so keen on a revival of the British Empire. He sought the creation of a free world that would be protected by the United Nations (UN), a new peace-keeping organisation. The Americans wanted the USSR to join the UN and were prepared to work with Stalin to ensure that this happened (Source C).

▶ Stalin sought the creation of a buffer zone between Western Europe and the USSR as a way of protecting the USSR from attack. To ensure that the countries making up this zone would be friendly towards the USSR, Stalin wanted them to be controlled by communist governments (see Source D).

Decisions made at Yalta

Despite these differences, the following agreements were reached at Yalta:

▶ Germany and Berlin would be divided into four zones, to be occupied by the armies of Britain, France, the USSR and the USA.

▶ Germany would pay reparations.

▶ The UN would be established to help keep the peace.

▶ The USSR would declare war on Japan in August, three months after Germany's surrender.

▶ There would be new borders for Poland (although no agreement was reached on the type of government Poland would have).

▶ Eastern Europe would come under the influence of the USSR. However, it was also agreed that there would be democratic elections in these countries to allow the people of Eastern Europe to choose their own governments.

Source C The views of Harry Hopkins, Roosevelt's closest aide, speaking after the Yalta conference.

We really believed in our hearts that this was the dawn of the new day we had all been praying for … There wasn't any doubt in the minds of the President or any of us that we could live with [the Soviets] and get along with them peacefully for as far into the future as any of us could imagine.

Source D The views of historian Allan Todd, in his book *Democracies and Dictatorships: Europe and the World 1919–1989* (2001).

Stalin was determined to ensure his country could never be invaded again. He therefore sought the creation of a buffer zone of communist countries between Western Europe and Russia as a way of protecting the Soviet Union from attack.

▼ The 'Big Three' (left to right: Churchill. Roosevelt and Stalin) at Yalta. What does this photo say about their relationship with each other? Can you think why this is?

Potsdam, July 1945

By the time the 'Big Three' met again at Potsdam in Germany in July 1945, several important changes had taken place:

▶ Hitler was dead and the war in Europe had ended with the surrender of Germany (May 1945); plans were being made for most US troops to return home.

▶ Soviet troops were spread throughout Eastern Europe.

▶ Roosevelt had died in April 1945 and was replaced as President by Harry Truman (1945–53). Truman did not like Stalin and was suspicious of the USSR's aims. Truman's advisers were also urging him to take a harsh line against Stalin.

▶ Labour's Clement Attlee replaced Churchill as Britain's Prime Minister during the conference at Potsdam.

▶ US and British attitudes towards the USSR were hardening as they watched Germany being stripped of resources and saw puppet governments being set up in several of the countries in Eastern Europe now under Soviet control.

Source E President Truman, writing about the Potsdam Conference in his memoirs in 1955.

Our experience with them was such that I decided to take no chances in a joint setup with the Russians ... Force is the only thing the Russians understand.

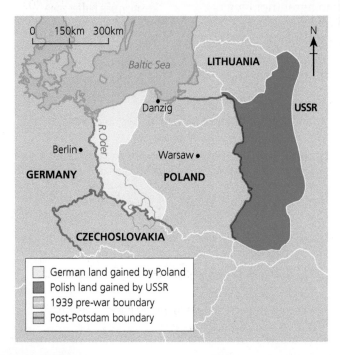

Legend:
- German land gained by Poland
- Polish land gained by USSR
- 1939 pre-war boundary
- Post-Potsdam boundary

Decisions made at Potsdam

The meeting at Potsdam was, therefore, much less friendly (Source E). Nevertheless, the following was agreed:

▶ How Germany was to be divided and occupied. Each power could take reparations from its own zone, although not so much as to endanger the lives of ordinary Germans. The USSR could also take some reparations from the British and US zones in return for providing supplies of food, fuel and raw materials.

▶ How Austria was to be divided and occupied.

▶ Changes to Germany's border with Poland. This border was moved westwards to the Oder river. This created a natural border between the two countries. All former German territory to the east of the new border became part of Poland and all Germans still living within this area were made to leave. At the same time, the USSR's border with Poland was also moved to the west.

In general, however, there was considerable disagreement about the future shape of Europe. Now that the common enemy of Nazism was defeated, the wartime alliance was breaking up. The suspicions and tensions of Potsdam marked the first 'drop in temperature' of what would become the Cold War.

Revision tip

The role of personalities is important in explaining the origins of the Cold War. You need to be able to explain how and why the changes within the 'Big Three' had an impact on events and attitudes.

Activities

1 What does Source E reveal about Truman's attitude at Potsdam?
2 Create two spider diagrams showing the key decisions made at Yalta and Potsdam.
3 Which side would have been happier after the two conferences? Explain your answer.

◀ The new borders for Germany and Poland after the Potsdam Agreement.

Hiroshima and Nagasaki

Although the war in Europe was over, even while the Potsdam Conference was taking place, the war in the Pacific against Japan was continuing, and it was proving very difficult. During the capture of the islands of Iwo Jima (February–March 1945) and Okinawa (April–June 1945), the Japanese fought so much that American generals feared the invasion and conquest of Japan itself might cost perhaps a million American soldiers' lives.

President Truman was also alarmed by the idea of Soviet intervention in the Pacific, as had been agreed at Yalta (see page 197). He feared that the USSR would try to establish Communism in the Pacific as they had already done in Eastern Europe.

Then, on 21 July 1945, during the Potsdam conference, Truman received confirmation that an atomic bomb test had been successful. He did not directly inform Stalin that the USA had developed an atomic bomb, but observers at the conference noted that Truman's attitude towards the Soviets became more assertive from that moment.

The Atomic Age

On 6 August 1945, the American B29 bomber *Enola Gay* dropped an atomic bomb (nicknamed 'Little Boy') on the Japanese city of Hiroshima. Everything within a two-mile radius was flattened. People at 'ground zero' – the point closest to the detonation – were vaporised. Overall, perhaps a quarter of a million people were killed. Three days later, on 9 August, the Americans dropped another bomb on Nagasaki. The Japanese surrendered on 14 August.

When he realised that the Americans had the atomic bomb, Stalin was furious that his allies had not shared the technology with him. Indeed, he regarded the bombing of Hiroshima more as an act of intimidation aimed at the Soviet Union than a way to force Japan to surrender. In a speech made in Moscow in February 1946, he accused the USA of using its atomic advantage to build an empire. Many historians believe that, in this way, the atomic bomb caused the final breakdown of US–Soviet relations.

▲ Hiroshima after the dropping of the atomic bomb, 1945. Why did the Cold War begin in 1945?

The start of the Cold War

Thereafter, things just got worse. Stalin told his scientists to build an atomic bomb, which they achieved by 1949. Consequently, by the mid-1950s, the two world superpowers had built enough weapons to destroy all life on earth many times over.

Thus the USA and the USSR found themselves engaged in a war – but in a war which could never be allowed to descend into fighting. In the expression of the time, they dared not have a 'hot war', they had to fight a 'cold war'.

Practice questions ❓

1 What does Source E on page 198 tell us about American foreign policy in 1945?

2 How convincing is the view of Harry Hopkins in Source C on page 197 about the reasons for the USA trusting the USSR at Yalta in 1945? Explain your answer using Source C and your contextual knowledge.

3 Describe two consequences of the dropping of the atomic bomb on Hiroshima in August 1945.

This page provides guidance on how to answer question 1 in the exam.

Question 1

Study Source E below and answer the question which follows.

> **Source E** President Truman writing about the Potsdam Conference of 1945 in his memoirs (1955).
>
> Our experience with them was such that I decided to take no chances in a joint setup with the Russians ... Force is the only thing the Russians understand.

What does Source E tell us about American foreign policy in 1945? [4]

Guidance

You should be looking to spend five minutes at most on this question.

You need to spot two inferences – what the Source is 'getting at'/ its underlying point – which you must justify with arguments and evidence from the Sources.

Although your contextual knowledge will help you understand and interpret the Source, do not spend time writing it into your answer – it will earn you no marks.

Follow the steps below for each part of the answer.

STEP 1a
See an inference.

Example
One thing the Source tells us is that the Americans did not trust the Soviets.

STEP 1b
Justify your inference with arguments and evidence from the Source.

Example
We can see this in the way Truman refers to 'our experience with them' (which has clearly been a bad experience in the past). He goes on to say that he is going to 'take NO chances' — which proves that he does not trust them at all.

STEP 2a
Find a second inference.

Example
A second thing the Source tells us is that the USA took a tough line in its negotiations with the USSR.

STEP 2b
Justify your second inference with arguments and evidence from the Source.

Example
We see this expressed openly in Truman's statement that 'force is the only thing the Russians understand' — implying that he was prepared to use force if necessary.

2 Emerging superpower rivalry and its consequences, 1945–49

The Soviet takeover of Eastern Europe

The world at the end of 1945 was very different than it had been just six years earlier:

▶ The USSR and the USA were now superpowers.
▶ Each feared that the other wanted to spread its influence.
▶ Each believed that the other wanted to destroy them. In particular, the USSR feared the atomic bomb. In turn, the USA was concerned at the huge size of the Red Army.
▶ Each was suspicious of the reasons behind the other's actions and began to act defensively against the other.

The actions of the USSR in Eastern Europe, 1945–49

In the closing years of the Second World War, the Soviet Army had taken over most of the countries in Eastern Europe (see page 196); after the war, it stayed in those countries. At Yalta, Stalin had promised democratic elections in these countries and, between 1945 and 1947, elections were held in a number of states. However, every one of these elections resulted in the election of governments friendly to Moscow. The West therefore suspected that the elections were not democratic or fair at all, and had actually been rigged (people had cheated to get a desired result); however, the USSR denied this. Yet, by 1947 the following countries were ruled by communists:

▶ Albania
▶ Bulgaria
▶ Hungary
▶ Poland
▶ Romania.

While the West feared that the Soviets were building a huge empire in Eastern Europe, Stalin saw it only as a reasonable attempt to create a 'buffer zone' to protect the USSR from a future German invasion (see Source A).

Stalin therefore took steps to make sure that all the countries of eastern Europe had governments which were friendly towards, and controlled by, the Soviet Union. Although the takeover of each country differed to some degree, certain trends were common to each. For example:

▶ USSR pressure to ensure that communists, many of whom had been trained in Moscow, obtained key positions (such as control of law and order) in the temporary governments set up after the war.
▶ Suggesting radical changes to help economic recovery. This helped gain the communists popularity.
▶ Controlling elections to ensure a communist victory.
▶ Controlling the population by means of the secret police.

The hard-line Hungarian communist leader Mátyás Rákosi described the gradual takeover of government departments, press, police and army as similar to 'slicing salami': taking power one bit at a time.

In addition, the Soviets controlled the area of eastern Germany they had conquered and occupied during the war, and communists also held power in Yugoslavia (see Figure 1).

By the end of 1947, only Czechoslovakia remained free from communist control in Eastern Europe, though it became communist in February 1948.

> **Source A** Stalin replying on 13 March 1946 to Churchill's Fulton speech (see page 204).
>
> [The USSR's] loss of life has been several times greater than that of Britain and the USA ... So what is surprising about the Soviet Union, anxious for its own future safety, trying to see that loyal governments should exist in these countries?

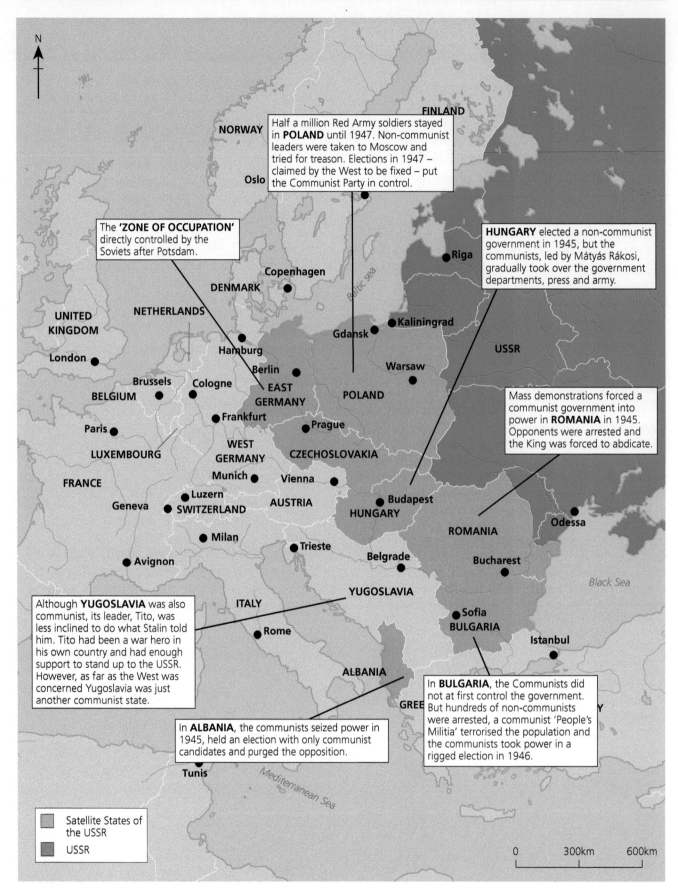

N

Half a million Red Army soldiers stayed in **POLAND** until 1947. Non-communist leaders were taken to Moscow and tried for treason. Elections in 1947 – claimed by the West to be fixed – put the Communist Party in control.

The **'ZONE OF OCCUPATION'** directly controlled by the Soviets after Potsdam.

HUNGARY elected a non-communist government in 1945, but the communists, led by Mátyás Rákosi, gradually took over the government departments, press and army.

Mass demonstrations forced a communist government into power in **ROMANIA** in 1945. Opponents were arrested and the King was forced to abdicate.

Although **YUGOSLAVIA** was also communist, its leader, Tito, was less inclined to do what Stalin told him. Tito had been a war hero in his own country and had enough support to stand up to the USSR. However, as far as the West was concerned Yugoslavia was just another communist state.

In **ALBANIA**, the communists seized power in 1945, held an election with only communist candidates and purged the opposition.

In **BULGARIA**, the Communists did not at first control the government. But hundreds of non-communists were arrested, a communist 'People's Militia' terrorised the population and the communists took power in a rigged election in 1946.

NORWAY
FINLAND
Oslo
DENMARK
Copenhagen
Riga
Baltic sea
UNITED KINGDOM
NETHERLANDS
Hamburg
Kaliningrad
Gdansk
USSR
London
Berlin
Warsaw
Brussels
Cologne
EAST GERMANY
POLAND
BELGIUM
Frankfurt
Paris
Prague
LUXEMBOURG
WEST GERMANY
CZECHOSLOVAKIA
FRANCE
Munich
Vienna
Luzern
AUSTRIA
Budapest
Geneva
SWITZERLAND
HUNGARY
Odessa
Milan
ROMANIA
Trieste
Belgrade
Bucharest
Avignon
Black Sea
YUGOSLAVIA
ITALY
Sofia
BULGARIA
Rome
Istanbul
ALBANIA
GREE
Tunis
Mediterranean Sea

Satellite States of the USSR
USSR

0   300km   600km

▲ **Figure 1** The Iron Curtain in Europe, 1945–1989.

The response of the USA and its allies

Each side viewed these events in different ways. This was one of the main reasons for the huge increase in international tension:

▶ In particular, the USA's view of the USSR's actions was influenced by the ideas of George Kennan, an American diplomat based in Moscow. Kennan argued that communism demanded the spread of revolution worldwide and so the two superpowers could never live in peace. He recommended that the USA would have to act to contain the USSR's aggression in the future (Source B). President Truman took him at his word and the policy of containment was born. Where possible, the USA would act to stop the further spread of communism.

▶ At the same time, the USA failed to understand that the USSR was obsessed with its own security. By seeing everything that the USSR did as evidence of the communists' desire to control Europe, the suspicion, fear and hostility that were characteristic of the Cold War were increased.

Revision tip

Both sides in the Cold War blamed the other for starting it; this is because each side viewed the actions of the other as aggressive and their own actions as defensive. A good examination answer will be able to explain why each side felt that they were in the right.

> **Source B** Adapted extract from an article, *The Sources of Soviet Conduct*, written by George Kennan, US ambassador to the USSR, in July 1947.
>
> The United States … must continue to regard the Soviet Union as a rival. It must continue to expect that Soviet policies will reflect no real faith in the possibility of a permanent happy coexistence [state of living together] of the Socialist and Capitalist worlds, but rather a cautious, persistent pressure toward the breaking and weakening of all rival influence and rival power…
>
> Balanced against this is the fact that Russia [the USSR] is still by far the weaker party. This would of itself justify the United States entering with reasonable confidence upon a policy of firm containment, designed to confront the Russians [Soviets] … at every point where they show signs of attacking the interests of a peaceful and stable world.

Activities

1 Make a timeline of the key events of 1945–47. For each event, present them:
   - as a Soviet would have done
   - as an American would have done.
2 Were Eastern European countries as free to determine their own future as Stalin had promised at Yalta? Use Source A (page 201) and Figure 1 (page 202) to help explain your answer.
3 Explain the policy of containment. Use Source B on this page to help you.
4 Explain two ways in which Source A (page 201) is different from Source B (on this page).
5 'The USSR was more to blame than the USA for the increases in post-war tension.' Do you agree?

Revision tip

To find out why sources differ you need to look at their provenance, that is, who wrote or said them. This will help you understand why they said what they said – what motivated them/ where they were 'coming from'.

The emergence of the Cold War and the impact on relations, 1946–47

Churchill's Iron Curtain speech

It was Winston Churchill who most clearly expressed the West's suspicion of the USSR in a speech he gave in Fulton, Missouri, USA in March 1946 (Source C). In this speech, Churchill condemned Stalin's attempts to control Eastern Europe and demanded an Anglo-American alliance to stop the spread of communism. It was in this speech that the phrase 'Iron Curtain' was used.

Stalin reacted angrily to the speech (Source D; see also Source A on page 201). He felt that his actions were necessary; he argued that the way in which the USSR suffered during the war made it only natural that he should want to protect his country from invasion

▲ A British cartoon showing Churchill peeping under the Iron Curtain. Explain the meaning of the cartoon; what does it tell us about Britain's attitude to the USSR?

Source C Churchill speaking at Fulton, 5 March 1946.

An iron curtain has descended across the continent … and all are subject in one form or another … to a very high and increasing measure of control from Moscow.

Source D Stalin, writing in the Soviet newspaper *Pravda* in March 1946.

Mr Churchill has called for a war on the USSR.

Activities

1 Study Source C. Using your knowledge of the historical context of the situation in 1946, explain why Churchill's speech played so significant a part in the development of the Cold War.
2 Why, do you think, did Churchill choose to give his speech in America, rather than in Britain?
3 Who do you believe was responsible for the Cold War? Use the information in the text and in the sources to help you fill in a copy of the following table:

Reasons why the Cold War was the fault of the USA	Reasons why the Cold War was the fault of the USSR

4 'Winston Churchill caused the Cold War.' How far do you agree?

The Truman Doctrine and Marshall Plan

Events in Greece

After the end of the Second World War, the Allies had agreed to help train and equip the Greek army, which was engaged in a civil war with Greek communists. In March 1947, the British Government announced that it could no longer afford to continue funding the Greek forces. This worried Truman, who feared that if Greece became communist, so too would neighbouring countries and the oil-rich Middle East.

The Truman Doctrine

Truman decided to ask the US Congress for help (Source E). He told Congress that rather than remain isolated – as it had done between the First and Second World Wars – it would now be the USA's policy to use military or economic means to stop countries falling to communism either from external invasion or internal revolution. This policy became known as the Truman Doctrine and remained one of the main parts of US foreign policy. Congress released $400 million, which provided enough support and equipment to end the communist threat in Greece.

The Marshall Plan

Truman believed that communism spread more easily if countries were poor. He thought that if economic recovery took place in such countries:

▶ communism would fail to take control
▶ these countries would be able to trade with the USA, helping its economy.

US Secretary of State, General George Marshall, agreed. He had toured Europe in April 1947 and had seen that many countries were in danger of economic collapse and a communist takeover. Marshall proposed a massive investment of $13.3 billion into Europe over a four-year period (Source F). The money would be offered to all countries as long as they opened their markets to Western goods and made their economic records available for inspection. The investment became known as the Marshall Plan or Marshall Aid. Large amounts of the money were spent on defence and armaments, as well as roads, machinery and factories.

Activities

1 Explain the part events in Greece played in the emergence of the Truman Doctrine.
2 What was Truman's explanation for increasing the USA's involvement in European affairs? Use the text and the information in Source E to help you with your answer.
3 Why, do you think, was some Marshall Aid spent on weapons?
4 'The USA was more to blame than the USSR for the increase in post-war tension.' Have you changed your opinion since you considered this on page 203?

Revision tip

The introduction of the Truman Doctrine and the Marshall Plan was an important turning point in the development of the Cold War. You need to be able to explain why these policies were introduced and what impact they had.

Source E Extract from a speech delivered by President Truman to the US Congress, 12 March 1947.

I believe it must be the policy of the US to support free peoples who are resisting attempted subjugation [conquest] by armed minorities or by outside pressures ... The seeds of totalitarian [dictatorial] regimes are nurtured [fed] by misery and want. They spread and grow in the evil soil of poverty and strife. They reach their full growth when the hope of a people for a better life has died. We must keep that hope alive ... If we falter in our leadership we may endanger the peace of the world – and we shall surely endanger the welfare of our own nation.

Source F Extract from a speech by US Secretary of State, George Marshall, 5 June 1947.

It is logical that the United States should do whatever it is able to do to assist in the return of normal economic health in the world, without which there can be no political stability and no assured peace. Our policy is directed not against any country or doctrine but against hunger, poverty, desperation and chaos.

Reactions to the Marshall Plan

At first, Congress was unconvinced by the Marshall Plan. However, events in Czechoslovakia – the only country in Eastern Europe not to fall under communist control – made Congress change its mind. Most Czechoslovakians did not want a communist government. However, in February 1948, in a planned coup, communist 'Action Committees' organised armed demonstrations and threatened a general strike. The Czech President, Edvard Beneš, gave way and appointed a communist government. Finally, on 10 March, the only non-communist minister – Foreign Minister Jan Masaryk – was thrown to his death from a window. So, on 31 March, the US Congress approved the Marshall Plan.

Sixteen countries, particularly Britain and the Allied parts of Germany, benefited from the Marshall Plan, which was overseen by the Organisation for European Economic Co-operation (OEEC).

Stalin described the Marshall Plan as 'dollar diplomacy'. He argued that the USA was using its investment to gain influence over countries by controlling their economies (Source G). He rejected the offer of finance and made sure that all the countries he controlled did the same by:

▶ Establishing the Communist Information Bureau (Cominform) in 1947. This aimed to ensure communist nations worked together more effectively.

▶ Setting up the Council for Mutual Economic Assistance (Comecon) in 1949. A Soviet version of the Marshall Plan, encouraging economic co-operation among Iron Curtain states.

NEIGHBOURS

"Come on, Sam! It's up to us again."

▲ A cartoon from Punch magazine commenting on the importance of Marshall Aid for Western European recovery. What does the cartoon tell us about how America saw its role in international relations?

Source G Extract from a speech delivered at the United Nations, 18 September 1947, by the USSR's Deputy Foreign Minister, Andrei Vyshinsky.

It is becoming more and more clear to everyone that ... the Marshall Plan will mean placing European countries under the economic and political control of the United States ... This plan is an attempt ... to complete the formation of a bloc of several European countries hostile to the interests of the democratic countries of Eastern Europe and most particularly to the interests of the Soviet Union.

Impact of the Truman Doctrine and Marshall Plan

Both the Truman Doctrine and Marshall Plan mark a significant development in the Cold War, in both a positive and negative sense (see Table 1).

The Marshall Plan played a vital part in the economic reconstruction of Europe. However, it might also be seen to have played a central part in the ongoing destruction of East–West relations (Source I). It is interesting that 1947 was the year in which the phrase 'Cold War' was first used to describe the relationship that now existed between East and West.

Positive	Negative
The USA was indicating its intent to remain involved in European affairs.	Political and economic divisions between East and West were deepened.
The economies of many European countries recovered rapidly.	The USSR strengthened its grip over the Iron Curtain countries with the establishment of Cominform and Comecon.
The US economy developed rapidly.	

Table 1 Impact of US involvement in Europe after the Second World War.

Source H Extract by the British historian John W. Mason, in his book *The Cold War, 1945–1991*, (1996).

The Marshall Plan was an obvious economic success … To humanitarians [people who care about other people] the Marshall Plan brought long-term aid to a Europe in economic chaos. To those in the United States … it offered a way to revive world trade. To those who feared communist subversion [rebellion] in Western Europe it [helped] to create healthy national economies … The very success of the Marshall Plan caused a crisis in Soviet–Western relations.

Source I Extract from an article by Russian historian Mikhail Narinsky on the Marshall Plan (1994)

The Marshall Plan was designed to stabilize Western Europe, to [bring back] western Germany into the Western bloc, and to reduce Soviet influence … The Marshall Plan and the sharply negative Soviet reaction to it marked an important turning point on the way to the split of Europe.

▲ The Kromhaut Manufacturing Company in Amsterdam was one of the factories which received Marshall Aid. The revamped and modernised factory produced diesel engines, which in turn helped the recovery of the Dutch fishing industry.

Practice questions ?

1 What does Source F on page 205 tell us about the USA's attitude to the USSR in 1947?

2 What does Source G on page 206 tell us about the USSR's attitude to the USA in 1947?

3 Study Sources H and I. Source H and Source I give different views about the impact of the Marshall Plan in 1947.

(a) Explain two ways in which these views differ.

(b) Explain one reason why the views in Source H and Source I are different.

Examination practice: International Relations, 1945–2003

This page provides guidance on how to answer question 2 in the exam.

Question 2

Study **Source H and Source I below** and answer the questions which follow:

Source H Extract by historian John W. Mason, in his book *The Cold War, 1945–1991* (1996)

The Marshall Plan was an obvious economic success ... To humanitarians [people who care about other people] the Marshall Plan brought long-term aid to a Europe in economic chaos. To those in the United States ... it offered a way to revive world trade. To those who feared communist subversion [rebellion] in Western Europe it [helped] to create healthy national economies ... The very success of the Marshall Plan caused a crisis in Soviet–Western relations.

Source I Extract from an article by Russian historian Mikhail Narinsky on the Marshall Plan (1994)

The Marshall Plan was designed to stabilize Western Europe, to [bring back] western Germany into the Western bloc, and to reduce Soviet influence ... The Marshall Plan and the sharply negative Soviet reaction to it marked an important turning point on the way to the split of Europe.

(a) **Source H and Source I** give different views about impact of the Marshall Plan in 1947.
Explain **two** ways in which these views differ. [4]

(b) Explain **one** reason why the views in Source H and Source I are different. [2]

Guidance for 2(a)

You should be looking to spend five minutes at most on this question.

As in Question 1, you need to spot contrasting inferences – which you must support with arguments and evidence from the Sources. You must mention both Sources both times.

Again, although your contextual knowledge will help you understand and interpret the Source, do not spend time writing it into your answer – it will earn you no marks.

Follow the steps below for each part of the answer.

2(a) Explain **two** ways in which these views differ. [4]

Step 1
See (and support) one inferred difference

Example

One difference is that, where Mason said good things about the Marshall Plan – how it was 'long-term' and 'a way to revive world trade', Narinsky looked at it with suspicion as a way to help western Germany 'to reduce Soviet influence'.

Step 2
Repeat (and support) for a second inferred difference

Example

A second difference is that, where Mason talks about the economic benefits – trade and 'healthy economies', Narinsky stresses its political aims, concluding it damaged international relations and caused 'the split of Europe'.

Guidance for 2(b)

You should be looking to spend three minutes at most on this question.

Your answer will probably come from the provenance of the sources (who wrote it and when), which will reveal the different motivations of the authors. Support your suggested reason with arguments and evidence from both the Sources, and make sure your explanation connects the reason to the outcome.

Follow the steps below for each part of the answer.

2(b) Explain **one** reason why the views in Source H and Source I are different.   [2]

Step 1

State and support the reason, mentioning both Sources.

→

Example

The reason Sources H and I are different is that Narinsky is a Russian historian, whereas Mason is a British historian.

Step 2

Explain the reason.

→

Example

This explains their different views because they are different interpretations. Narisnky is looking at the Marshall Plan from the Russian point of view, so he sees the Marshall Plan as a plan to benefit Western Europe and the United States. Mason, looking at the Marshall Plan from a British point of view, seems more prepared to credit the USA with good motives such as humanitarian aid and reviving world trade.

The actions of the USSR in Eastern Europe

In the years following the American decision to 'contain' communism, there were four significant confrontations between the superpowers in Europe.

The Berlin Blockade and Airlift, 1948–49

More than two years after the end of the Second World War, the former Allies still had not agreed on the long-term future of Germany. This issue caused the first major crisis of the Cold War.

At the Allied conferences held at Yalta and Potsdam (see pages 197–198) it had been agreed that Germany would be divided into four zones, each to be controlled separately by the British, Americans, Soviets and French. Berlin was also divided, but as it was located over 100 miles inside the Soviet zone, the Allies had to travel through the Soviet area to get to the city.

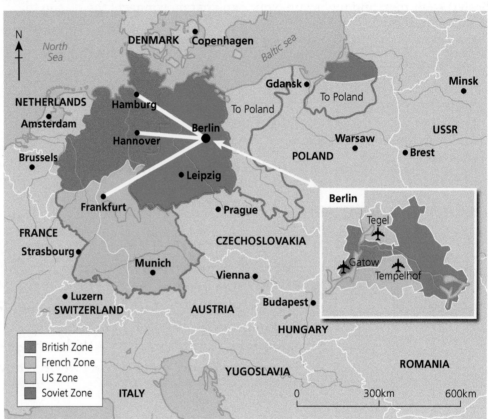

▲ The division of Germany and Berlin.

However, that was all that they had agreed on.

Causes of the Berlin Blockade and Airlift

Different aims

Both sides had completely different opinions about Germany's future:

▶ The USSR wanted Germany to remain weak, since Germany had invaded them twice since 1914.

▶ The Western powers wanted Germany to recover so it could be both a barrier against the further spread of communism and an important part of European economic recovery. Therefore, significant resources were invested in Germany, including over $1,300 million of Marshall Aid.

Different economies

By 1948, the Western zones of Germany were on the road to economic recovery, mainly because of Marshall Aid. The same could not be said of the Soviet zone; during the same period the USSR had removed a significant amount of resources from the eastern zones to compensate for war damage. As a result, living conditions were much poorer there than those in the Western zones.

A new currency

In March 1948, hoping to strengthen the economy of the Western zones of Germany, the USA, Britain and France united their zones in Germany into a single economic unit (called 'Trizonia'). In June 1948, the Allies decided to introduce a new currency, the Deutschmark, into the region. They believed that this was essential for economic recovery. Stalin was not consulted about this decision and was unhappy about it:

▶ He saw it as the first stage in the reconstruction of a Germany that would again threaten the USSR.

▶ Even worse, this recovery would be obvious to the poor people of East Berlin who were living so close to their western neighbours. This could cause problems as people may come to resent the lower living standards in the communist zone.

The events of the Berlin Blockade

Therefore, on 24 June 1948, and ignoring what had been agreed at Potsdam, Stalin ordered the closure of all road, rail and canal links with West Berlin. The official reason given for the closures was 'technical difficulties'; in fact, the Soviets believed that the whole affair was an attempt by the West to destroy the East German economy (Source A).

Why did Stalin take this risk? It is unlikely that he expected his actions to lead to war; instead he probably hoped that he could force the West to abandon Berlin and thus leave it under Soviet control. Berlin only had enough supplies to last it for a maximum of six weeks.

Of course, there was no way that the USA could allow this to happen; Berlin had become a powerful symbol of the struggle for power in Europe between capitalism and communism. Any sign of weakness might result in the collapse of American influence over the rest of Europe. Action had to be taken (Source B).

Source A A Soviet viewpoint on the Berlin Blockade.

The crisis was planned in Washington, behind a smokescreen [veil] of anti-Soviet propaganda ... The conduct of the Western powers risked bloody incidents.

Source B President Truman, writing in his memoirs (1955).

When we refused to be forced out of Berlin, we demonstrated to Europe that we would act when freedom was threatened.

The events of the Berlin Airlift

General Lucius Clay, the Governor of the US zone, pushed for breaking the blockade by force, but Truman rejected the idea. It was decided that airlifting supplies to West Berlin would be the best way of breaking the blockade: Stalin was unlikely to shoot planes down, as that would be seen as an act of war.

For almost a year, therefore, up to 13,000 tonnes of supplies were flown in each day with planes landing, on occasion, at two-minute intervals. The two million citizens of West Berlin had to endure severe rationing. By mid-1949, Stalin was forced to admit defeat. On 12 May, the blockade was lifted. Over two million tonnes of supplies had been airlifted in; 101 men had died, mostly as a result of plane crashes, but war had been avoided and Berlin, for now, had been saved from communism.

THE BIRD WATCHER

▲ A cartoon from the British magazine *Punch*. Use your knowledge to explain the different parts of the cartoon.

The consequences and impact on relations

The breaking of the Berlin Blockade was a huge propaganda triumph for the West and a setback for the USSR. It was also a turning point in the Cold War, and had significant consequences and impacts on relations:

▶ Tensions increased between the superpowers (Source C)

▶ The policy of containment could be seen to have worked, as communism had failed to spread into West Berlin.

▶ In April 1949, even before the end of the blockade, 12 Western nations set up the North Atlantic Treaty Organisation (NATO). The reason was to ensure that the West could co-operate to prevent future Soviet aggression. NATO was based around the principle that an attack on one of its members would be considered as an attack on all.

▶ All hopes for the reunification of Germany were now gone. In May 1949, the Federal Republic of Germany (known as West Germany) was established. In October, the USSR renamed its zone the German Democratic Republic (East Germany).

▶ Although NATO was established as a defensive organisation, the Soviets refused to accept that it was anything other than an aggressive alliance. This opinion seemed to be confirmed when West Germany was allowed to join NATO in 1955. Again, the Soviet fear of a strong Germany was revived. In response, the Warsaw Pact was established in May 1955. It was basically a communist version of NATO with all countries in the Soviet sphere of influence agreeing to defend each other if one was attacked. The pact was dominated by the USSR, however.

> **Source C** Extract from Steve Phillips, *The Cold War: Conflict in Europe and Asia* (2001).
>
> The Berlin crisis … marked the first major flashpoint of the Cold War. Relations between the USA and the USSR … reached such a low position of distrust and suspicion that it became difficult to have any meaningful dialogue, let alone agreement.

Revision tip

When you are judging a source or an opinion, remember to look at two factors:

● Do the facts of the matter as you know them justify such an opinion?

● How does the provenance of the author affect your opinion of the source's reliability – how impartial or trustworthy do you consider its author to be?

Activities

1 Explain how the former allies differed in their ideas about what should happen to Germany and Berlin.
2 Create a timeline of the events of the Berlin Blockade and Airlift.
3 Study Sources A and B. Using the information in the text and in these sources, explain how and why the US and Soviet explanations for the blockade were different.
4 Were Stalin's policies concerning Germany and Berlin a mistake?
5 Using the information you have read and Source C, assess the impact of the Berlin Blockade and Airlift on the development of the Cold War.

Hungary, 1956

Causes of the uprising

Background to the uprising: 'The Thaw'

Josef Stalin died in March 1953. By 1955, Nikita Khrushchev had emerged as the country's leader. For a time the policies pursued by Khrushchev suggested that this would mean a thaw in the Cold War.

In 1955–56, Khrushchev:

▶ Visited Yugoslavia and apologised for how Stalin had treated the country.

▶ Met with leaders of the West in Geneva, the first such meeting for over a decade.

▶ In a speech known as the Secret Speech, denounced the policies that Stalin had followed and urged the development of peaceful co-existence with non-communist nations.

▶ Began a policy of de-Stalinisation to end Stalin's influence over the USSR.

▶ Ordered the breaking up of Cominform (see page 206).

Khrushchev's Secret Speech was listened to with great interest by other Iron Curtain countries (satellite states), which began to hope that a more relaxed system of government might emerge in their countries, one that would provide economic prosperity and a better standard of living. Indeed Khrushchev himself spoke of there being 'different roads to socialism'.

However, these changes did not happen straight away. As a result, in July 1956 there were riots and demonstrations in Poland and Czechoslovakia.

Then, in Hungary in October–November 1956, years of bitterness at the hardships of communist rule spilled over into a full-blown rebellion.

The main causes

> **Revision Tip** 🔄
>
> When you are studying any major event, make sure that you understand and can explain its Causes, Course and Consequences.

> **Source D** US Secretary of State, John F. Dulles, commenting on events in Hungary, October 1956.
>
> To all those suffering under communist slavery, let us say: you can count on us.

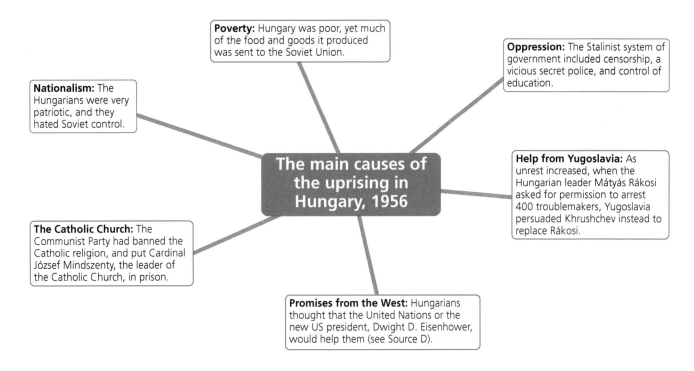

Poverty: Hungary was poor, yet much of the food and goods it produced was sent to the Soviet Union.

Oppression: The Stalinist system of government included censorship, a vicious secret police, and control of education.

Nationalism: The Hungarians were very patriotic, and they hated Soviet control.

The main causes of the uprising in Hungary, 1956

Help from Yugoslavia: As unrest increased, when the Hungarian leader Mátyás Rákosi asked for permission to arrest 400 troublemakers, Yugoslavia persuaded Khrushchev instead to replace Rákosi.

The Catholic Church: The Communist Party had banned the Catholic religion, and put Cardinal József Mindszenty, the leader of the Catholic Church, in prison.

Promises from the West: Hungarians thought that the United Nations or the new US president, Dwight D. Eisenhower, would help them (see Source D).

The crushing of dissent

The rebellion developed as follows:

Timeline

23 October	Hungarian students followed the Polish example and took to the streets demanding reforms.
24 October	As unrest grew Imre Nagy, a moderate communist, was appointed as leader.
1 November	Nagy announced that Hungary would hold free multi-party elections and would withdraw from the Warsaw Pact (see page 212).
4 November	More than 6000 Soviet tanks crossed the border to put down the revolt. Pleas were made for the West and UN to intervene.

In the fierce fighting that followed the invasion, 30,000 died and a quarter of a million fled westward. Nagy fled to the Yugoslav Embassy but was later arrested and executed. He was replaced by Janos Kadar and communist control was reasserted. At that stage some reforms were introduced.

The consequences and impact on relations

The USSR's response

The USSR's response indicated that it could not take the risk of a member of the Warsaw Pact (see page 212) leaving the organisation, since it might result in:

▶ The opening of a gap in the Iron Curtain leaving the USSR exposed to attack.

▶ The collapse of the Iron Curtain; if one country was allowed to break free then all the others might follow suit.

The West backs down

Throughout the crisis the people of Hungary had hoped for assistance from the West; however, nothing arrived except words of support. The West decided that it would be too risky to confront the USSR in Eastern Europe, which it now accepted as a Soviet sphere of influence, and decided instead to confront communism in Asia.

The end of the 'thaw'

More than anything, the events of 1956 suggested that Khrushchev's criticism of Stalin did not mean any change in the USSR's attitude to its defence and control of Eastern Europe. Khrushchev might speak of peaceful co-existence, but this seemed to mean keeping things as they were.

Activities

1 Explain the background to events in Hungary in 1956.
2 Make notes on the uprising under three headings:
   ● causes
   ● events
   ● consequences
3 Was Khrushchev any different than Stalin?

Berlin, 1959–61

Reasons for growing tension

The Hungarian experience confirmed that it was impossible for Eastern European nations to break free from communist control. In Berlin, however, the same was not true for individuals. Although a divided city, it was still possible for people to flee to the West using West Berlin as their point of exit.

Why did they want to go? Due to a lot of US investment, West Berlin was a living advertisement for the benefits of capitalism and many Eastern Europeans wanted to buy into the lifestyle that it seemed to promise. It is estimated that by 1962 more than two million people – many of whom were highly skilled – had slipped through the Iron Curtain in this way. Even when barbed wire and other barriers were erected, the flow of people still continued. This was a source of embarrassment to the USSR (Source E).

Khrushchev was also concerned because West Berlin was a centre for western espionage, enabling the West to gather information about activities behind the Iron Curtain (Source F).

Khrushchev hoped to pressure the West into leaving Berlin; in 1958 he attempted to force the West to withdraw by threatening to give East Germany control of access points to the city; however, he failed. In 1960, he attended a summit meeting in Paris, again hoping to persuade the West to leave, but the meeting collapsed when Khrushchev revealed that the USSR had shot down a U2 spy plane flying over its territory.

Source E From a modern school textbook, *GCSE Modern World History* (Ben Walsh, 2009).

The communist government could not afford to lose these high-quality people. More importantly, the sight of thousands of Germans fleeing communist rule for a better life under capitalism undermined Communism generally.

Source F Soviet explanation for the Wall (1961).

The Western powers use Berlin as a centre of rebellious activity against East Germany.

The building of the Berlin Wall

The events during the 1960 meeting increased tensions even further and a new wave of people fled through West Berlin, causing labour shortages in the east of the city.

At the Vienna meeting of June 1961, with the new US President John F. Kennedy (1961–63), Khrushchev demanded that the West hand over West Berlin to the Soviets. Kennedy refused to do so, and in fact in the next month increased US spending on weapons by $6.4 billion.

Khrushchev decided that he could not allow this to continue and so in August 1961 he ordered the erection of a massive wall that made permanent the division of the city. Armed guards patrolled the wall and those attempting to cross it without permission ran the risk of being shot. The river of defections dwindled to a trickle.

▲ Berlin divided. The Berlin Wall snakes its way through the divided city. In the background can be seen the famous Brandenburg Gate.

The response of the West

The USA protested but did nothing, unwilling to risk war. Although in public the Americans complained about the Wall, in private they were relieved (Source G).

The Berlin border had been a source of tension between the superpowers and by closing it the Soviets had removed the problem.

The consequences and impact on relations

Meanwhile, anti-communist sentiment in the West increased, and this 'Concrete Curtain' became a powerful symbol of the ideological, social and economic divisions that existed between East and West. Over the years, as hundreds of people died trying to get across the wall, the view of the Iron Curtain as something holding people back increased. Thus – although the building of the Wall had initially seemed to be a Soviet victory – the West was able to use the Berlin Wall as a propaganda vehicle (Source H).

> **Source G** President Kennedy speaking in private about the permanent division of Berlin, August 1961.
>
> If the Russians wanted to attack us … they wouldn't be putting up barbed wire … I'm not going to get het up [annoyed] about it.

> **Source H** In June 1963, President Kennedy made a speech close to the Berlin Wall. He was listened to by large crowds on both sides of the Wall.
>
> There are many people in the world who really don't understand what is the great issue between the free world and the communist world. Let them come to Berlin!
>
> There are some who say in Europe and elsewhere we can work with the communists. Let them come to Berlin!

Activities

1 Create two spider diagrams:
   - one showing the reasons for the Berlin Wall
   - one showing the consequences of the Berlin Wall
2 What evidence is there to suggest that at the start Khrushchev seemed to be a different style of leader from Stalin?
3 Explain the reasons why the USA offered only words of support during the Hungarian and Berlin crises.
4 By 1961, who do you think was winning the Cold War: the USA or the USSR?

Revision tip

Events in Hungary and Berlin were the first main internal challenges that the USSR faced to its control of Eastern Europe. Make sure you understand why these events happened and why Khrushchev responded in the way that he did.

◀ West Germans wave to family members trapped behind the Wall, whom they thought they would never see again.

Czechoslovakia, 1968

Causes of the 'Prague Spring'

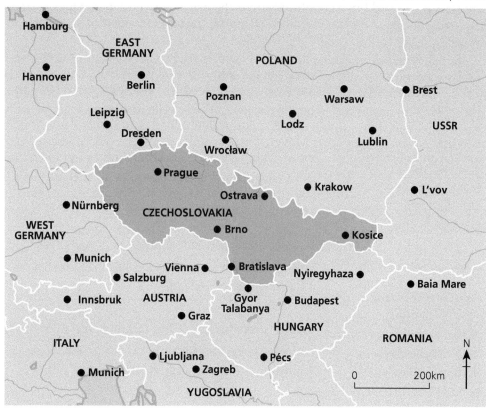

▼ Czechoslovakia, 1960s

The communist leadership in Moscow removed Khrushchev in 1964 due to dissatisfaction with parts of his domestic and foreign policies. He was replaced by the more hardline Leonid Brezhnev. The first major test of his leadership came with the Czech crisis of 1968.

In January 1968, Czechoslovakia's hardline leader Antonin Novotny, was replaced by the more moderate Alexander Dubček. The immediate cause of Novotny's resignation was a series of demonstrations. These were directed against the lack of civil rights and the appalling standard of living that had resulted from two decades of communist rule.

The Czechoslovak economy was in recession and the Czechs resented the fact that industrial products were being exported to the USSR whilst they were in poverty. Czechoslovak students were resentful of the restrictions on freedom; the Union of Czechoslovak Writers wanted freedom of the press.

Dubček wanted Czechoslovakia to remain communist but he also knew that if that were to happen reforms would have to be carried out (Source I). To achieve 'socialism with a human face' he introduced an 'Action Programme' of political and economic reforms that included:

▶ freedom of speech and of the press
▶ less centralised economic control
▶ development of international trade
▶ removal of restrictions on travel abroad
▶ reduction in the powers of the secret police.

These reforms were greeted with widespread public approval. The new atmosphere produced by the reforms was christened the 'Prague Spring'.

The Soviet response

Dubček's reforms were less enthusiastically greeted in Moscow. Brezhnev feared that the reforms would be copied by other Eastern European countries and would ultimately result in the destruction of the Iron Curtain. The communist leaders of Poland and East Germany expressed similar fears. In July, the leaders of these two countries along with Hungary, Bulgaria and the USSR wrote to Czechoslovakia to express their concern. Dubček assured them of his commitment to socialism and guaranteed that Czechoslovakia would remain in the Warsaw Pact.

Despite Dubček's guarantees, Brezhnev ordered 400,000 troops into the country on 20 August 1968, in response to a letter from four Czechoslovak communists asking for help (Source J). Although the invasion was officially a Warsaw Pact operation with troops from Bulgaria, East Germany, Hungary, Poland and the USSR, in reality it was mainly a Soviet force.

Dubček realised that continued opposition would be pointless and urged his people not to resist the invasion with violence. Instead he urged the people to show their opposition through passive resistance. By and large this was the case, although there were isolated examples of violent resistance to the Soviet forces.

Dubček was summoned to Moscow; on his return to Prague he announced to the people that the 'Prague Spring' had ended. He resigned a few months later and was replaced by the much more hardline Gustav Husak.

The repression of the Prague Spring was not as violent as in Hungary in 1956 (about 80 people were killed, and Dubček was demoted rather than executed). However, it was relentless. People who had supported the reforms lost their jobs and homes and found themselves under constant observation.

There was little violent resistance to the Soviet invasion, but on 19 January 1969, Jan Palach was the first of a number of students who burned themselves to death in protest.

Revision tip

There are many similarities between what happened in Czechoslovakia in 1968 and what took place in Hungary in 1956. Make sure that you are able to explain the similarities and differences between these two attempts to introduce reforms to communist rule.

Source L Extract from Steve Phillips, *The Cold War: Conflict in Europe and Asia* (2001).

The Soviet invasion was justified by the Brezhnev Doctrine ... There was no doubt that the USSR was willing to take action when it felt the interests of socialism were threatened ... From a Soviet viewpoint their actions were successful ... There was to be little serious unrest in the region until the early 1980s.

Source I Alexander Dubček, speaking in early 1968.

We want to set new forces of socialist life in motion in this country, allowing a fuller application of the advantages of socialism.

Source J Statement issued by *Tass* (the official Soviet news agency), 21 August 1968.

The leaders of the Czechoslovak Socialist Republic have asked the Soviet Union and allied states to give the Czechoslovak people urgent assistance.

Source K Alexander Dubček, speaking after the Warsaw Pact invasion.

How could they do this to me? My entire life has been devoted to the Soviet Union.

Activities

1 How and why did Dubček try to reform Czechoslovakia?
2 Using the information in Sources I and J, explain whether or not it was Dubček's intention to break free from communism.
3 Why was the USSR so concerned about Dubček's actions?

▲ Protest in Czechoslovakia in 1968. How – and why – does this differ from the photograph of the 1956 Hungarian uprising on page 214?

The response of the West and the impact on relations

The invasion prompted thousands of Communist Party members in Western Europe to resign their membership. However, as with Hungary 12 years earlier, the West responded to the events of 1968 with little more than words of sympathy, and the invasion did not damage relations very much. The USA in particular was too caught up with its own problems in a war in Vietnam and – as with Hungary in 1956 – accepted that there was no point in trying to intervene in events behind the Iron Curtain. It was also keen not to damage the recent improvement in relations between East and West that became known as détente (after the French word for relaxation).

The Brezhnev Doctrine, 1968

Late in 1968, Brezhnev justified the actions that he took in Czechoslovakia. He argued that it was the duty of communist countries to act together to prevent another communist state from turning to capitalism. This became known as the Brezhnev Doctrine (Source L). It was a declaration that the USSR intended always to control the communist countries behind the Iron Curtain.

The weakening of the communist bloc

However, surprisingly, the suppression of the Prague Spring weakened the Soviet Union more *behind* the Iron Curtain, where it alarmed Soviet allies. Albania left the Warsaw Pact (see page 212) less than a month later, and the Romanian leader Nicolae Ceaușescu called the invasion 'a day of shame' and 'a grave error'.

 Activities

1 Should Dubček have realised that the USSR would not allow his reforms to go ahead?
2 How reliable and useful would Source J on page 218 be as evidence to an historian investigating why the USSR invaded Czechoslovakia? Use the information in the text to help you with your answer.
3 Make a copy of the following table and fill it in to show the similarities and differences between the Hungarian and Czechoslovakian risings:

Area:	Hungary	Czechoslovakia
Origins		
Events		
Reaction of USSR		
Results		

4 Were the USSR's actions in Czechoslovakia worthwhile? Use the information in the text and in Source L on page 218 to help you with your answer.

 Practice questions

1 What does Source D on page 213 tell us about the USA's view of the Hungary uprising in 1956?
2 Describe two effects the Hungary uprising in 1956 had on relations between the USA and the USSR.
3 What does Source I on page 218 tell us about the reasons for the Prague Spring in 1968?
4 How convincing is the view in Source L on page 218 about the reasons for the Soviet response to the Prague Spring in 1968? Explain your answer using Source L and your contextual knowledge.

 Revision tip

Make sure you understand (and are able to back up your points with arguments and factual information) how each of the four 'flashpoints' – the Berlin Blockade, the Hungarian Uprising, the Berlin Wall and the Prague Spring – impacted on international relations.

◀ A Warsaw Pact tank ablaze in Prague, 1968. How does this photo affect our understanding of the Czechoslovak response to the Soviet invasion?

Examination practice: International Relations, 1945–2003

This page provides guidance on how to answer question 3 in the exam.

Question 3

Study **Source L on page 218** and answer the question which follows:

How convincing is the view in **Source L** about the reasons for the Soviet response to the Prague Spring in 1968?

Explain your answer using **Source L** and **your contextual knowledge**. [8]

Guidance

You should spend about 10 minutes on this question.

Your answer must demonstrate that you can explain how the author supports his claim, and that you can make an argument using facts from your own knowledge.

You must finish with a weighed judgement about whether the author's view is convincing or not, supporting this with arguments and facts.

Step 1
Start by stating what you think the source is saying.

Example
Steve Phillips says that the Soviets invaded Czechoslovakia because of the Brezhnev Doctrine, because they felt 'the interests of socialism' were threatened. I do not find this convincing.

Step 2
Find any evidence in the source which the author uses to support his view.

Example
Phillips says 'there was no doubt' about this, and he argues that the lack of any more unrest in the region proves the USSR was successful in this aim.

Step 3
Cite any evidence from your contextual knowledge of the events which support the author's claims.

Example
On the one hand, it is true that the communist leaders of eastern Europe feared that the Prague Spring would destroy communism. This supports Phillips's view that they felt the interests of socialism were threatened.

Step 4
Cite any evidence from your contextual knowledge of the events which do not support them.

Example
On the other hand, there is lots of evidence that the Prague Spring was not a danger to socialism. Dubček wanted Czechoslovakia to remain communist, only 'with a human face'. He promised to stay in the Warsaw Pact. Later, he said: 'My entire life has been devoted to the Soviet Union.'

Step 5
Weigh the two sides and come to a substantiated judgement which directly answers the question.

Example
Phillips' argument that the Soviets were right because they won is weak. Although Brezhnev claimed he felt the interests of socialism were threatened, he said this after he had invaded. Against this is a lot of evidence that the Prague Spring did not threaten socialism. Therefore I do not find the argument convincing. It seems more that Brezhnev felt the interests of the Soviet Union were threatened.

Actions of the USA and USSR outside Europe

Chapter 3 looked at the Cold War clashes between the superpowers in Europe. But the USA and the USSR both had global influence, and their conflict came to involve clashes world-wide. This chapter studies four of those confrontations.

The Korean War, 1950–53

The rule of the USSR

Since the 1920s, Chinese communists led by Mao Zedong had been fighting a civil war with Chiang Kai-Shek's Nationalist Kuomintang (KMT). The USA supported the KMT. However, in October 1949, Mao's communists won control, and established the People's Republic of China. The USA saw this as a setback for democracy.

The USSR was delighted that China was now communist, and in 1950 Stalin agreed a Treaty of Friendship which committed the USSR to supporting China's economic, technological and military development. Later, the USSR would take part in aerial battles during the Korean War (see page 223).

The reasons for US involvement in Korea

By contrast, unsurprisingly, the USA was severely concerned by these developments; China was a vast country with a massive population and huge resources. The USA (wrongly) suspected that the fall of China was part of Stalin's scheme to spread communism across the world. Even more worryingly, China's fall to communism came shortly after the USSR successfully exploded its first atomic bomb. The American President Harry Truman came under massive pressure at home to stand up to the communists more forcefully.

Korea had been freed from Japanese control in 1945 by Soviet soldiers who moved into the north of the country and by US troops who landed in the south. The country was partitioned along the 38th parallel of latitude until elections could be held and the country reunited.

Unfortunately, the two superpowers could not agree what kind of a country Korea should become:

▶ The USSR was keen to see the election of a government sympathetic to communism.
▶ The USA sought the establishment of a regime that would ensure the introduction of a capitalist democracy.

The key events of the war

By the time the Soviet and US forces had left Korea in 1949, two separate governments had been established to run the country:

▶ In the north, a communist regime was set up under Kim Il-sung. The new state was called the Korean People's Democratic Republic but was more commonly known as North Korea.
▶ In the south, a capitalist dictatorship was established led by Syngman Rhee. Officially this state was christened the Republic of Korea; more commonly it was called South Korea.

The invasion of South Korea

Both states sought the reunification of the country, but it was Kim Il-sung who acted. After securing the support of both Mao Zedong and Stalin, he invaded South Korea on 25 June 1950. Within days the capital Seoul had been captured by North Korean forces (see Figure 1).

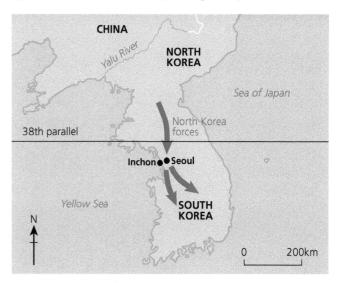

▲ **Figure 1** Korea, June 1950.

Continuing US involvement

The USA believed that Stalin had encouraged the invasion. They also feared that a 'domino effect' would soon begin by which one country after another would fall to communism (Source A). With the UN, the USA changed its policy of containment (see page 203) to rollback: the belief that communism could and should be attacked and pushed back.

For these reasons the USA asked the United Nations to intervene to stop the attack.

In fact, evidence shows that the driving force behind the invasion was Kim himself; Kim believed that Rhee was unpopular because of the dictatorial manner in which Rhee was running the country, and believed that the people of South Korea would welcome the North Koreans. The UN however, agreed with the US interpretation: first it condemned the attack, then it began to put together a military force to stop the invasion.

The UN response

The USSR was unable to object to the UN's actions as it was then boycotting the UN. This was in protest at the USA's refusal to allow communist China to sit on the UN Security Council.

By this time the North Korean army had driven the South Korean forces back to the south-east of the country and were about to defeat them altogether. The UN force – which was mainly US and led by American General Douglas MacArthur – landed at Inchon in September 1950 (Figure 2). Before long it had pushed the North Korean forces back to the 38th parallel (Figure 3).

Source A President Truman, commenting on events in Korea, 1950.

The attack upon Korea makes it plain beyond all doubt that communism has passed beyond the use of subversion [plotting] to conquer independent nations and will now use armed invasion and war.

▲ The UN air-dropped propaganda leaflets at night into enemy areas. The hammer and sickle image is the symbol of communism. What is the leaflet's message to the Koreans?

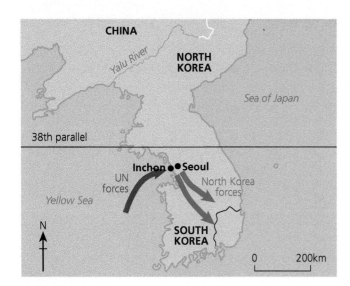

▲ **Figure 2** Korea, September 1950.

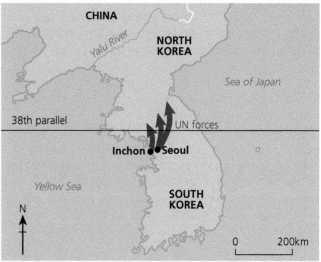

▲ **Figure 3** Korea, September–October 1950.

The invasion of North Korea

On 9 October 1950, American and South Korean forces crossed the 38th parallel and pushed into North Korea as far as the Yalu river, North Korea's border with China (Figure 4). This meant that the UN force was now exceeding its UN orders. However, following the policy of rollback, MacArthur's intention (with Truman's agreement) was to reunite the whole country.

The role of the USSR

The USSR did not enter the war directly, for fear of provoking a world war, but secretly helped the North Koreans and the Chinese throughout the conflict by providing 'advisers', weapons and doctors.

The USSR also sent 63 fighter planes, which had Chinese markings and were flown by Soviet pilots dressed in Chinese uniforms.

The role of China

MacArthur's invasion greatly worried North Korea's neighbour, China, which feared that the USA would take the opportunity to invade China. As a result, in November 1950, more than 250,000 Chinese troops (called 'volunteers' rather than soldiers so that war would not have to be declared) invaded North Korea in November 1950 and pushed the UN forces back over the 38th parallel. (Figure 5).

What had begun as a war between North and South Koreans was turning into an open conflict between the USA and China. MacArthur now pleaded with Truman to allow an attack that would lead to the destruction of communism in China; he even urged the use of the atomic bomb (Source B).

Truman, however, now decided on containment rather than rollback; he refused to consent to an increase in the conflict, fearing direct Soviet intervention. Furthermore, in April 1951 he sacked MacArthur after the General had openly criticised the President's policies.

The war dragged on back and forth across the 38th parallel until the middle of 1951 when both sides dug in. The war then took to the skies for a further two years, with the loss of over 6,000 planes. The aerial battles were kept secret from the US population in case they demanded all-out war with the USSR.

> **Source B** General MacArthur, speaking about the importance of the Korean War.
>
> Asia is where the communist conspirators [plotters] have elected to make their play for global conquest. If we lose this war to communism in Asia, the fall of Europe is inevitable. There is no substitute for victory.

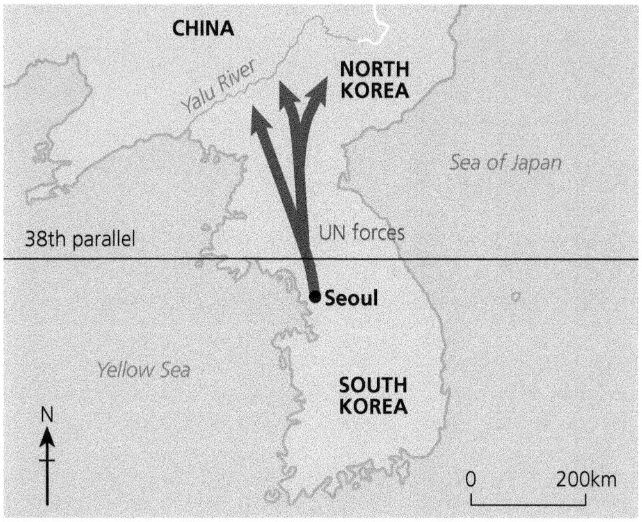

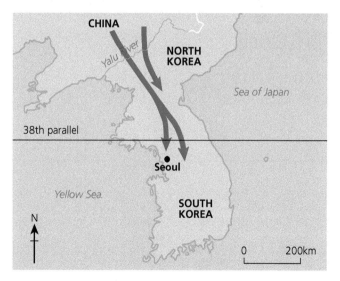

▲ **Figure 4** Korea, October 1950.

▲ **Figure 5** Korea, November 1950.

The end of the war

Peace talks had begun in June 1951 but were unable to find a solution acceptable to all sides. In 1953, a change in the leadership of the USSR and the USA offered the opportunity for an end to the war. President Dwight D. Eisenhower (1953–61) succeeded Truman and Stalin died, eventually leaving Nikita Khrushchev in control. The new leaders sought peace and a ceasefire was agreed at Panmunjom in July 1953. Possibly Eisenhower's threat to use nuclear weapons against China assisted the conclusion of negotiations! Although a peace treaty was never signed, the agreement saw the creation of a permanent border – slightly north of the 38th parallel – and a demilitarised zone (DMZ) between the two states (Figure 6).

The consequences of the Korean War and impact on relations

This was the situation at the end of the war:

▶ More than two million people had died, which resulted in a border little different to where it was before the war began.

▶ Containment had worked – communism had not spread into South Korea – but rollback had failed.

▶ The relationship between North and South Korea remained tense and bitter.

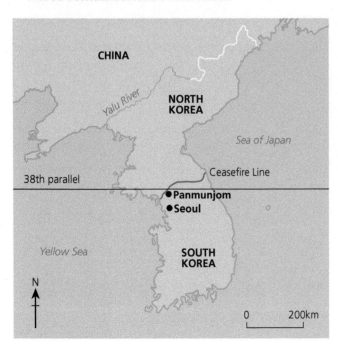

▲ **Figure 6** Korea, July 1953.

▶ US–Chinese relations deteriorated further, particularly as the USA continued to recognise Chiang Kai-shek's Nationalists as China's rightful government.

▶ Realising the importance of preventing Japan falling to communism, the USA signed a peace treaty, ended military occupation and invested heavily in the Japanese economy.

▶ The US signed agreements with the Philippines, Australia and New Zealand, which confirmed its position as the protector of the region.

▶ NATO was changed from a mainly political association into a full-blown military alliance.

Put simply, the Korean War indicated that the USA was now committed to pursuing a policy of containment anywhere in the world if its interests were felt to be under threat, even if this meant committing troops to combat situations.

Activities

1 How and why did the USA get involved in Korea?
2 How did China become involved in the war?
3 Using the information in the text, make a copy of the following table and fill it in.

Positive results of the war	Negative results of the war

Look at your results. Was the Korean War a success or a failure for US foreign policy?

4 'The Korean War was a waste of time for both superpowers.' Do you agree? Explain your answer.

Revision tip

Korea was where the Cold War became hot for the first time. You must be able to explain why fighting broke out and what the main results of the conflict were.

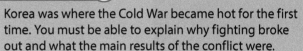

The conflict in Vietnam, 1950–73

Before the Second World War, Indochina (the area of south-east Asia now comprising Vietnam, Cambodia and Laos) had been a French colony, but the French attempt after the war to re-establish its empire there was defeated by the Vietminh – guerrilla forces led by the Vietnamese communist revolutionary Ho Chi Minh.

The Treaty of Geneva (1954) divided Vietnam along the 17th parallel of latitude – the northern part under Vietminh control while the anti-communist Ngo Dinh Diem controlled the South. As in Korea, the USA saw the possibility of the domino theory coming into play; if all of Vietnam fell to communism, then neighbouring countries might follow suit.

The reasons for US involvement, 1950–64

As a result, President Eisenhower provided support for the South Vietnamese government in the form of money, weapons and military advisers. The aim was to contain the spread of communism.

Eisenhower's successor, John F. Kennedy (1917–1963), increased the levels of aid. All this came at a time of increasing guerrilla attacks against the South's army by the National Liberation Front (NLF) or Vietcong. This group had been set up in South Vietnam in 1960 to reunite the country under communist control. It was supported by Ho Chi Minh.

Unfortunately for the USA, Ngo Dinh Diem was not a popular leader. His regime was both brutal and corrupt and the government was made up of mostly Catholic landowners and was out of touch with its people, the majority of whom were Buddhist peasants. The Vietcong gained more and more support and control in the South. In November 1963, Diem was overthrown and assassinated. Shortly after, Kennedy himself was killed; by then there were 16,000 US military advisers in Vietnam.

The Tonkin Resolution

In August 1964, the North Vietnamese attacked a US destroyer, *USS Maddox*, in the Gulf of Tonkin. Kennedy's successor President Lyndon B. Johnson (1963–69) believed that this attack provided the excuse for massive American involvement in Vietnam (Source C). The US Congress agreed and passed the Tonkin Resolution, allowing the President to fight a war as he saw fit.

Johnson took Congress at its word. Over the next three years massive numbers of troops were landed in the country and the US Air Force launched repeated bombing raids (Operation Rolling Thunder) against the Vietcong. In particular, the USA used chemicals such as napalm (a petroleum jelly) and Agent Orange (made up of, among other things, dioxin, which can damage the brain and the central nervous system) in their bombing raids. Napalm burned civilians without reason; Agent Orange cleared the forests of greenery. This enabled the Americans to see their enemy from the air; however it also destroyed the land and wounded countless civilians.

Source C Comment made by President Johnson in 1964.

I am not going to be the President who saw south-east Asia go the way China went.

The actions of the USA, 1965–73

With more than 500,000 troops in Vietnam by 1968, the USA should have had no difficulty in defeating its enemy. The Vietcong was fewer in number and significantly less well equipped.

As the war went on, however, the expected victory did not happen, and some of this may be down to the actions of the USA:

▶ The US generals' 'Search and Destroy' tactics focused on statistics – on the 'body count' (the number of enemy soldiers killed) and the 'kill ratio' (the number of kills per American death) (Source D). This meant they were not focused on the best way of actually defeating the enemy.

▶ US tactics sometimes misfired, for instance, when US bombers dropped napalm on 'friendly' (not communist) villages by mistake.

▶ The US army was made up of many inexperienced soldiers (conscripts) who may have been fighting their first war in another country and did not speak their language – whereas the Vietcong used guerrilla tactics, dressed in the same way as the Vietnamese civilians and knew the country well (Source E).

▶ In its efforts to root out the Vietcong, the US forced the Vietnamese people to move into strategic hamlets. The Vietnamese people saw no benefit to the US troops invading their country, especially because they were prepared to harass and kill civilians. The most notorious US atrocity was the My Lai Massacre of March 1968 when nearly 350 Vietnamese villagers were killed by a company of US troops. The US leader, Lieutenant William Calley, was imprisoned for life but later pardoned by President Richard M Nixon (1969–74).

Additionally, as the war went on, the morale of the American soldiers fell with many running away or going AWOL or taking drugs to cope with the stress of fighting an unwinnable war. In contrast, the Vietcong believed they were fighting a patriotic war of liberation.

Source D Extract from a US soldier's account of the Vietnam War.

Our mission was … simply to kill … The pressure … to produce enemy corpses was intense and led to such practices as counting civilians as Vietcong. 'If it's dead and Vietnamese it's Vietcong' was a rule of thumb in the jungle.

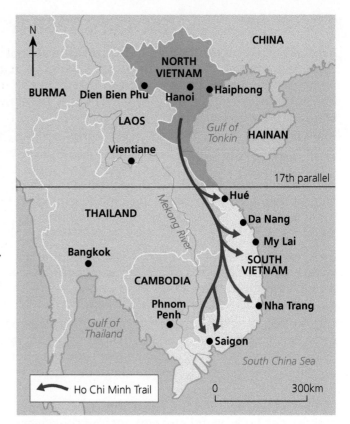

▲ **Figure 7** The Indochina region.

Source E An account of the war by a US marine.

You never knew who was the enemy and who was the friend. They all looked alike. They all dressed alike.

Activities

1 Begin constructing a timeline of the key events of the war, using the information you have read on pages 225 and 226, beginning in 1950 and ending in 1968. Make sure your timeline extends past this date, ready to add events from 1968 up to 1973, as you learn more.

2 Study Source E. What does it tell us about the attitudes of US soldiers in the Vietnam War?

3 Describe two military tactics used by the USA in the Vietnam War.

4 How convincing is Source B on page 223 as a reason for the USA's decision to enter into the Vietnam War?

▶ The Vietcong developed a vast network of tunnels as part of their guerilla campaign. Explain how each feature was designed to make it difficult and dangerous for the US army to dislodge the guerrillas.

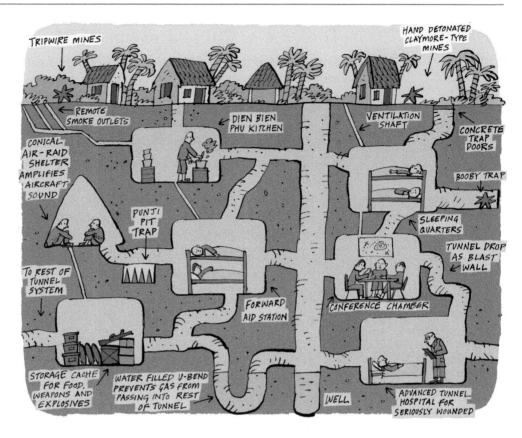

The continuing events of the war

In January 1968, the Vietcong launched a massive counteroffensive (known as the Tet Offensive, as it started at the time of the Vietnamese New Year [Tet] celebrations) against the US forces. Vietcong troops got as far as the South's capital, Saigon, before they were driven back. Although a failure militarily, the Tet Offensive had an even more significant political impact: it made many Americans feel that they could not win this war.

Back in the USA, television pictures showed US atrocities in Vietnam, and young American conscripts being brought home in body bags. There were complaints about the cost of the war. More and more of those being called up burned their draft cards.

President Johnson became hugely unpopular (Source F). Opposition increased after Richard Nixon became President in 1969; during one student protest against the war at Kent State University, Ohio, the National Guard killed four students.

More US actions and the end of the war

Nixon was determined to remove the USA from the Vietnam War, but he wanted to do it in a way that did not make the USA look as if it had lost.

To this end he:

▶ Increased the levels of bombing against North Vietnam and its capital Hanoi.

▶ Ordered secret bombing raids against the neighbouring countries of Cambodia and Laos in 1970. This was because they were being used as supply routes by the Vietcong (the so-called Ho Chi Minh trail). In total up to 10 million tonnes of bombs were dropped by the USA.

▶ Introduced the policy of Vietnamization from 1969. By this US troops would be withdrawn and South Vietnamese forces would do the fighting.

In 1973, after several years of negotiations, a peace treaty was signed in Paris. It agreed the withdrawal of the US forces and the return of US prisoners of war. It allowed the Vietcong to remain in the South and put off a decision on the country's political future until a later date.

Source F Student chant directed against President Lyndon B. Johnson, 1968.

Hey, hey LBJ! How many kids did you kill today?

Source G The view of historian John W. Mason, in his book *The Cold War, 1945–1991* (1996).

The US emerged from the war with a tarnished [disgraced] image abroad and more deeply divided at home than at any time since the civil war [1860–5].

Activities

1 Add to your timeline the key events from 1968 to 1973. Your completed timeline should span 1950 to 1973.
2 Explain the factors that led the USA to support first the French and then the South Vietnamese government. What made the US declare war in 1964?
3 Create a spider diagram showing all the reasons why the US campaign failed in Vietnam.
4 Was the Vietnam War justified?

Revision tip

Identify your opinion on how successful the USA was in Vietnam. Think about what its original reasons were for getting involved and compare these with the situation at the end of the conflict.

The role of China and the USSR

At the start of the war, China sent 170,000 Chinese soldiers as well as military equipment to North Vietnam. The Chinese soldiers helped build and repair roads, railways and airstrips – essential help against US bombing raids. There was less Soviet support at the start of the war, but after 1969, when a border dispute damaged relations between China and the USSR, the USSR took over as the main supplier of the North Vietnamese army:

▶ The Soviets trained North Vietnamese pilots and gave them modern fighter planes.
▶ They supplied medicines, food and oil.
▶ They also supplied tanks, artillery, anti-aircraft guns and deadly surface-to-air missiles (SAMs).
▶ Also, 3,000 Soviet soldiers served in Vietnam as advisers.

Additionally, the Chinese had sent their help as a loan whereas the Soviets provided it as a gift.

The consequences of the war

Nixon claimed he had achieved 'peace with honour'. For many people, however, US involvement seemed to have achieved very little at an immense cost:

▶ There were huge military and civilian losses (see Table 1).
▶ The USA had spent at least $120 billion on the war.
▶ Many of the US veterans (former soldiers) suffered severe psychological damage as a result of their experiences, as well as injuries.
▶ Vietnam was economically and socially devastated by the war.

The impact on relations

1 The war was a humiliation for the United States, and it proved that an enemy that used suitable tactics could defeat the USA. It was many years before the US sent large numbers of troops to a war overseas.
2 The war saw a setback for the US policy of containment in Indochina. Two years after the war, all of Vietnam was in the hands of the communists. Cambodia and Laos also became communist.
3 However, the war did not lead to the total victory of communism in Asia.
4 Also, the war did not increase Soviet power in Asia: although the USSR signed a Treaty of Friendship with Vietnam in 1978, and supplied it with huge amounts of military and economic aid, relations were often strained. Vietnam's relations with China were even worse.
5 Finally, the Vietnam War did not destroy the détente which was developing between the USSR and the USA in the 1970s (see page 219): relations were still relatively relaxed.

Country	Military dead	Military wounded	Civilian dead
North Vietnam	900,000	2,000,000	1,000,000
South Vietnam	250,000	600,000	
USA	58,132	300,000	

Table 1 Deaths during the Vietnam War.

The Cuban Missile Crisis, 1959–62

Perhaps the closest the two superpowers came to all-out war with each other was over the Caribbean island of Cuba, just 90 miles off the Florida coast. For most of the twentieth century, Cuba had exported its main crop, sugar, to the USA, while American companies controlled most of the island's industry.

The causes of the crisis

Since 1959, Cuba had been led by Fidel Castro (1926–2016). Castro had overthrown the previous leader, the dictator Fulgencio Batista.

At first Castro was not a communist; however, he was a nationalist who wished to ensure Cuba's independence from the influence of other countries.

Once in power, Castro began to nationalise industries, many of which were owned by US businesses; naturally this upset the Americans. As US hostility to Cuba grew, trade between the two nations declined. Castro turned elsewhere for assistance; in 1960 the USSR and Cuba agreed to trade oil and sugar for machinery. Before long the USSR had become Cuba's main trading partner. Then, in 1961, Castro announced that he had become a communist.

The Bay of Pigs

In January 1961, John F. Kennedy took over as US President; at 43 years of age he was the youngest man to be elected to the position. Shortly after he took over, the Central Intelligence Agency (CIA) informed Kennedy that it was planning an invasion of Cuba with the assistance of anti-Castro Cuban exiles.

Kennedy approved the invasion but it went totally wrong. It became known as the Bay of Pigs disaster after the bay in Cuba on which the 1,500 invaders landed. The main problem was the bad military intelligence available to the invaders. This had led them to hugely overestimate the amount of support that they would receive from Cubans when they invaded.

The invasion made Kennedy look inexperienced and turned Castro into a hero in Cuba.

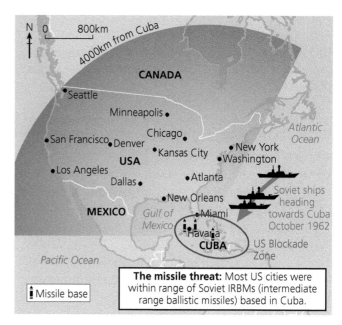

The missile threat: Most US cities were within range of Soviet IRBMs (intermediate range ballistic missiles) based in Cuba.

▲ **Figure 8** The range of missiles located in Cuba.

Key events: USA and USSR actions

Castro was deeply concerned by the American attempts to overthrow him and turned to the USSR for assistance. This resulted, in August 1962, in the arrival of equipment required to establish nuclear missile bases in Cuba. Missiles in Cuba would be able to reach most US cities (Figure 8) and would provide a match for the American missiles that had been installed in countries such as Turkey (because of their proximity to the USSR).

The US intelligence services obtained convincing proof of the missile bases by 14 October 1962. It also revealed that Soviet ships were en route to Cuba with further supplies. Kennedy was determined that he would not be made to look foolish again; he would stand firm against the threat being posed by the USSR.

The USA's options

Throughout the crisis, ExComm, a committee of the National Security Council, advised Kennedy. One of the key members was Attorney General Robert Kennedy, the President's brother. ExComm considered a range of options available to the USA:

▶ an invasion of Cuba
▶ a naval blockade of Cuba
▶ air attacks on the missile bases
▶ a nuclear attack on Cuba
▶ allowing the missile bases to be erected.

Eventually, on 22 October, Kennedy decided on a naval blockade of Cuba. On the same day he revealed the unfolding crisis in a television broadcast (Source H). The remainder of the crisis played out as follows:

23 October The USSR condemned the USA's actions as piracy and argued that it was only helping Cuba to improve its defences.

24 October Beginning of the US naval blockade.

Plans for an American invasion of Cuba were drawn up.

US Air Force planes began to fly over Cuba.

On reaching the naval blockade, the Soviet ships were either stopped or turned away.

Evidence from U2 spy planes suggested that the missile sites were nearing completion.

26 October On the same day that tensions were increased with the shooting down of a U2 spy plane over Cuba, Kennedy received a telegram from Khrushchev, which stated that the USSR would remove the missiles if the USA agreed to end the blockade and undertook not to invade Cuba.

27 October A second telegram arrived from Khrushchev (Source I). This stated that the USSR would only remove its missiles from Cuba if the USA removed its missiles from Turkey.

A U2 spy plane invaded Soviet airspace.

Against a background of advisers recommending an air strike, Kennedy took his brother's advice and decided to ignore Khrushchev's second telegram since he was not prepared to bargain with the USSR. Instead, he would send a reply to the first telegram. In this he agreed to remove the blockade and not invade the island in return for the removal of Soviet missiles. He added that if he did not receive a reply by 29 October an invasion of Cuba would begin.

28 October Khrushchev agreed to Kennedy's offer and the removal of the missiles began.

▲ U2 spy plane photograph of a missile base on Cuba.

Consequences of the crisis and its impact on relations

After 13 days of brinkmanship, nuclear war had been avoided. In public it looked like a great victory for Kennedy; in reality, however, the result was not so clear-cut. Kennedy had agreed secretly, on 27 October, to remove the missiles in Turkey. This was not a great sacrifice as the missiles were old and out of date. Shortly after the crisis ended, the USA began to dismantle some of its missiles from various bases in Europe, including Turkey. Within six months the US missiles were gone; Castro, however, remained in power (Source J).

Several valuable lessons were learnt during the Cuban Missile Crisis. In particular, both sides agreed that such a confrontation should be avoided in the future. To assist with this a telephone hotline between Washington and Moscow was set up. A direct phone line would be much more helpful than other and slower methods of communication. They also agreed to begin talks designed to reduce the number of nuclear weapons each side had. As a result, the Partial Test Ban Treaty was signed in 1963.

Both leaders seemed to have reached an understanding that might have led to a better future. However, within two years both were gone: Kennedy had been assassinated and Khrushchev overthrown.

Activities

1. Explain how and why Fidel Castro annoyed the US government.
2. What made Castro develop closer relations with the USSR?
3. Look at Kennedy's options on page 229; what would be the positive and negative aspects of each option? Why do you think Kennedy chose the option that he did?
4. Using the information in Sources H, I and J and in the text, who do you think won or lost the Cuban missile crisis: Kennedy, Khrushchev or Castro? Explain your answer using the Sources, and your own knowledge.
5. What evidence is there that the Cuban Missile Crisis was a turning point in the relations between the USA and the USSR?

▲ A cartoon showing the battle for supremacy between Khrushchev and Kennedy. What is its message?

Source H President Kennedy speaking on television, 22 October 1962.

Any missile launched from Cuba against any nation in this hemisphere [part of the world] would bring a full retaliatory [revengeful] response upon the USSR.

Source I Extract from Khrushchev's second telegram to Kennedy, 27 October 1962.

Our purpose has been to help Cuba develop as its people desire. You want to relieve your country from danger. Your rockets are stationed in Turkey ... Turkey lies next to us!

Source J Extract from S.R. Gibbons, *The Cold War* (1986).

The Chinese were furious that the Russians [Soviets] had 'backed down' over Cuba ... Castro was also furious: the deal to withdraw the missiles had been made over his head ... Khrushchev later claimed that he had 'won' all he wanted: the American promise not to invade.

The Soviet War in Afghanistan 1979–89

The early 1970s had seen a softening in relations (*détente*) between the superpowers – for example, the US table tennis team visited China in 1971. There was real progress towards peace – in 1972 the Strategic Arms Limitations Talks Agreement (SALT1) limited the number of inter-continental ballistic missiles (ICBMs), with a second round of arms reductions (SALT2) agreed in 1979.

The reasons for USSR involvement

However, *détente* was short-lived because, during the 1970s, the USSR was becoming increasingly nervous about neighbouring Afghanistan.

In 1979, the Shah (king) of Persia (Iran) was deposed by a fundamentalist Muslim revolution. Afghanistan too was a centre of Muslim unrest – Muslim extremists in Afghanistan had rebelled in 1975 and were continually attacking the Afghan government, leading to a violent uprising in March 1979. The Soviets feared that this might unsettle Muslim populations in the USSR.

Although it was a very poor country, Afghanistan had valuable gas fields, which the USSR wished to exploit.

Matters reached a crisis in Afghanistan when, in September 1979, Hafizullah Amin (who was communist, but anti-Soviet) seized power.

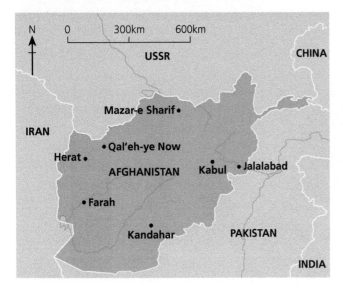

▲ **Figure 9** Map of Afghanistan.

The actions of the USSR

Fearing a hostile Afghanistan on its border, on 25 December 1979, Soviet forces invaded. By New Year they had reached the capital city of Kabul, occupied the President's palace, killed Amin and established a 'puppet ruler', Babrak Karmal, in his place.

The invasion was condemned by the United Nations, the USA (Source K) and also China. Although it did not cause a 'hot' war between the superpowers, instead, between 1981 and 1987 the Americans' funded 'Operation Cyclone' – the supply of $3.2 billion of guns, missiles and money to the *Mujahideen* (Afghan fighters who waged guerrilla warfare against the Soviet invaders). Many of the *Mujahideen* were jihadists – in this book, this is the term used to describe extremists who believed that their religion requires them to go to war for Islam.

The war lasted ten years. The USSR had 125,000 troops, with tanks and helicopter gunships, but soon found itself in the same situation as the Americans had faced in Vietnam. The *Mujahideen* ambushed Soviet supply convoys, shot down their helicopters and then hid in the mountains, in neighbouring Pakistan or amongst the civilian population. The Soviet forces attacked villages, but they could not defeat the guerrilla forces. In 1982, a major Soviet campaign in the Panjshir Valley was defeated by guerrillas.

In 1988, the new Soviet leader Mikhail Gorbachev (1985–1991) decided that the USSR was never going to win the war. He began the process of withdrawal, and in 1989 the last Soviet troops left Afghanistan.

> **Source K** Letter from US President Jimmy Carter to Soviet leader Leonid Brezhnev, 28 December 1979.
>
> The Soviet military intervention in Afghanistan represents an unsettling, dangerous and new stage in your use of military force, which raises deep apprehension [anxiety] … Unless you draw back from your present course of action, this will inevitably jeopardise [cause damage to] the course of US–Soviet relations throughout the world.

> **Source L** Letter from Brezhnev to Carter, 29 December 1979.
>
> The strong tone of certain statements in your message hit us squarely between the eyes. Would it not be better to evaluate the situation more calmly, keeping in mind the supreme interests of the world rather than the relations of our two powers?

The short-term consequences of the war and its impact on relations

The consequences of the war

The war caused terrible suffering in Afghanistan. A million Afghans died, mainly civilians, and some three million refugees fled to Pakistan. The war split Afghan society and created a country dominated by local warlords, ruling over a bitter and war-hardened population.

For the Soviet Union the sheer cost of the war bankrupted the country, eventually leading to its collapse in 1989 and the fall of the Berlin Wall (see page 237) soon after. Within the USSR, for the first time people spoke out against the Soviet government.

At the same time, by mobilising fundamentalist jihadist groups from all over the world to support the *Mujahideen*, the war can be said to have helped create the international terrorism that came to dominate the early twenty-first century.

The impact on relations

The impact of the war on relations was huge. Some of these impacts are explained below.

1 A new Soviet Communism

The cost and criticism of war led to changing policies in terms of Soviet Communism, as examined in the next chapter.

2 A destroyed *détente*

US President Jimmy Carter (1977–81) withdrew from the SALT2 negotiations, stopped trade with the USSR, and the USA boycotted the 1980 Olympics, held in Moscow. In addition, Ronald Reagan, who became president in 1981 and served two terms (1981–89), was already passionately anti-communist. He did not trust Brezhnev and famously called the USSR an 'evil empire' in 1983.

3 More weapons and increased tensions

US nuclear missiles were placed in Britain and Europe from 1979 onwards, and at the same time the USSR was trying to keep up with continuing their arms stockpile. Many people were frightened and angry at this and attended huge protests, held by peace groups such as the Campaign for Nuclear Disarmament (CND), against this threat of war. Reagan went further, supporting the development of the Strategic Defence Initiative (SDI) or 'Star Wars' programme in 1983. This was a laser system that would effectively create a shield around the USA, which would drive away Soviet missiles. The USSR then boycotted the 1984 Olympics, held in Los Angeles, USA.

Source M University teacher and *New York Times* foreign correspondent Stephen Kinzer, writing in the *Guardian*, 2009.

The problems in Afghanistan began with America's decision to intervene in the country following the Soviet invasion in 1979.

Source N Writer Gregory Feifer, former Moscow correspondent for National Public Radio in the US, in his book *The Great Gamble: The Soviet War in Afghanistan* (2009)

... The Soviet leadership indeed ignored the [previous] lessons in its certainty that a quick invasion ... would not only increase its influence in Afghanistan but also send a message to all continents that Moscow remained a vital power.

Source O Extract by Gregory Fremont-Barnes, in *The Soviet-Afghan War 1979–89* (2012)

As the years passed and the casualties [dead and wounded] steadily rose, the war exposed the weaknesses of the Soviets' strategy ... both Soviet tactics and strategy contained fatal flaws.

Practice questions ?

1 Describe two consequences of the Vietnam War, 1950–73.
2 How did the actions of the USSR impact on international relations in the 1950s and 1960s?
   Use the following guidelines in your answer. You must also use information of your own.
   ▸ The Hungarian uprising, 1956
   ▸ The Cuban Missile Crisis, 1959-62
   ▸ The Prague Spring, 1968
3 What does Source H on page 231 tell us about the USA's attitude to the USSR in 1962?
4 How convincing is the view in Source J on page 231 about the reasons for the USSR's agreement with the USA to withdraw missiles?
5 How far do you agree with the view in Source O that the Soviet invasion in Afghanistan in 1979 was a failure because of Soviet 'weaknesses'?
   In your answer, you must use Sources M, N and O and use information of your own.

This page provides guidance on how to answer question 4 in the exam.

Question 4

Study Sources **M, N and O** and answer the question below.

> **Source M** University teacher and New York Times foreign correspondent Stephen Kinzer, writing in the *Guardian*, 2009.
>
> The problems in Afghanistan began with America's decision to intervene in the country following the Soviet invasion in 1979.

> **Source N** Writer Gregory Feifer, former Moscow correspondent for National Public Radio in the US, in his book *The Great Gamble: The Soviet War in Afghanistan* (2009)
>
> ... The Soviet leadership indeed ignored the [previous] lessons in its certainty that a quick invasion ... would not only increase its influence in Afghanistan but also send a message to all continents that Moscow remained a vital power.

> **Source O** Extract by Gregory Fremont-Barnes, in The Soviet-Afghan War 1979–89 (2012)
>
> As the years passed and the casualties (deaths) steadily rose, the war exposed the weaknesses of the Soviets' strategy ... both Soviet tactics and strategy contained fatal flaws.

How far do you agree with the view in Source O that the Soviet invasion in Afghanistan in 1979 was a failure because of Soviet 'weaknesses'?
In your answer, you must use **Sources M, N and O** and use information of your own. **[16]**

Guidance

You should be looking to spend about 20 minutes on this question.

To access all the available marks, your answer must analyse all three named sources, looking at how each supports or contradicts the opinion in question. You will then use these findings PLUS your own knowledge and arguments to reach a 'substantiated judgement' which does not come down on one side or the other, but which — using the language of probability — explains 'how far' the view seems to be correct.

Follow the steps below for each part of the answer.

STEP 1

Introduce the opinion in question.

> **Example**
>
> There is a case to be made for Source O's view that the war failed because of Soviet weaknesses

STEP 2a

Explain how a named Source supports or contradicts this view, justifying your statements with reasoning and evidence from the Source.

> **Example**
>
> Source N somewhat supports this view …

STEP 2b

Explain how another named Source supports or contradicts this view, justifying your statements with reasoning and evidence from the Source.

> **Example**
>
> On the other hand, Source M contradicts the view in Source N …

STEP 3

Sum up the judgement of the three named Sources and decide which seems the strongest case. At this point, use the provenances to judge which Sources/opinions are more trustworthy.

> **Example**
>
> Thus, although the historians in Source N and O … the modern journalist Stephen Kinzer in Source M does not agree …

STEP 4

Introduce your own opinion, based on your own knowledge. Remember that you are evaluating the opinion-in-question and organise your arguments and facts for and against that suggestion.

> **Example**
>
> My own studies of the Soviet invasion show that …

STEP 5

By now, you should have clearly shown that you have considered the different viewpoints in all three sources. In this final step, do not repeat things you have already said, but sum the differences up and end with a justified judgement using evidence and your own knowledge.

> **Example**
>
> Therefore we can see that, although to some degree …, the <overwhelming/ likely> probability seems to be that … and so I <agree/disagree> with Source O because …

The actions of the USA and the USSR in Europe and the impact on international relations

During this period, the Cold War descended to new depths of tension but also reached new heights of co-operation, heights that had been almost unimaginable up to that point.

The role of Reagan

US President Reagan had already made his views on communism clear (Source A). The Soviet response to US policies was equally clear (Source B).

> **Source A** President Reagan's judgement of the USSR, 1983
>
> An evil empire ... the focus of evil in the modern world ... I believe that communism is another sad, bizarre chapter in human history whose last pages even now are being written.

> **Source B** Soviet response to Reagan's policies, 1984
>
> The Reagan administration is pushing mankind to the brink of disaster.

Initially, Reagan denounced the USSR, used the USA's economic superiority to increase US military spending, and announced the 'Star Wars' programme (see page 233).

However, when a new Soviet leader, Mikhail Gorbachev, came to power, withdrew from Afghanistan and announced the end of the Brezhnev Doctrine, Reagan moved from a position of rollback to diplomacy and negotiated the 1987 Intermediate Nuclear Forces Treaty: a reduction in arms on both sides (see page 239). At the same time, he made a speech in Berlin calling on Gorbachev to 'tear down this wall!' Many historians believe that Reagan's combination of bullying and negotiation was important in ending the Cold War and causing the collapse of the USSR.

Mikhail Gorbachev: new leader, new policies

The USA's SDI system (see page 233) was nicknamed 'Star Wars'. It cost billions of dollars and before long the US economy was in difficulty. However, the situation was even worse in the USSR. As Moscow tried to keep up with US technological advances, the already crumbling Soviet economy came close to total collapse. Both countries needed to reduce costs as a matter of urgency.

The state of the Soviet economy particularly concerned Mikhail Gorbachev, who took over the USSR in March 1985. He was the first Soviet leader not to have been politically associated with the Stalinist era. Gorbachev knew that the USSR could not afford to spend money in a vain attempt to keep up with US defence spending. This was because:

▶ Living standards were appallingly low.

▶ There were significant levels of corruption within the Communist Party and as a result money was being wasted.

▶ Millions were on the verge of starvation because of the poor performance of the country's agricultural sector.

▶ Many of the USSR's main industries were in dire need of modernisation.

▶ Technologically, the USSR was decades behind the West.

▶ The war in Afghanistan was draining billions from the economy.

▲ Mikhail Gorbachev (1931–) and Ronald Reagan (1911–2004) meeting in Iceland 1986.

Gorbachev's policies: *Glasnost* and *Perestroika*

Gorbachev knew that the USSR had to change completely, both politically and economically, if it was to survive. The first step was to end the arms race so that money could be invested in the Soviet economy. However, Gorbachev also began to encourage his people to offer constructive criticism of the communist system as a way of helping it to modernise and improve.

Gorbachev stated that his reforms would revolve around the ideas of *glasnost* and *perestroika*:

▶ *Glasnost*: openness. In other words there would be freedom to debate, freedom for the media, freedom from government control.

▶ *Perestroika*: restructuring of the Soviet economy through the introduction of more Western-style policies (Source C).

In 1988, Gorbachev announced the end of the Brezhnev Doctrine (Source D). The thinking behind this was simple: his decision to end the Cold War meant that the Eastern European buffer zone was no longer needed. Now, there would be no attempt to hold countries back if they sought their freedom (Source E). To show that he meant what he said, Gorbachev began to withdraw Soviet troops from Eastern Europe.

Source C Mikhail Gorbachev explaining his new domestic policy ideas in *Perestroika* (1987).

Perestroika means overcoming. *Perestroika* is the development of democracy ... It is a thorough renewal of every aspect of Soviet life.

Source D Mikhail Gorbachev outlining his new foreign policy ideas to the United Nations, December 1988.

Force, or the threat of force, neither can, nor should be instruments of foreign policy ... The principle of freedom of choice is vital.

Source E USSR Foreign Minister Gennady Gerasimov, explaining Moscow's replacement for the Brezhnev Doctrine, 1989 (adapted).

The new doctrine is in place which is the Frank Sinatra doctrine. Frank Sinatra doctrine has a very popular song, 'I did it my way'. So Hungary, Poland, any other country does it its own way. They decide which road to take. It's their business.

The collapse of communism in Eastern Europe

The people of the other Iron Curtain countries – fed up with years of repression and economic decline – had been watching the changes in the USSR with great interest. Gorbachev's decision to loosen the bonds that tied them to the USSR and his refusal to demand that countries remain communist meant that similar freedoms were now within their own grasp. It was in 1989 that most countries broke free. Unlike the experiences of 1956 and 1968, there was no resistance to their freedom.

The iconic event of the collapse of communism was the fall of the Berlin Wall. As it struggled to hold onto power, on 9 November 1989 the communist government of East Germany eased the restrictions on travel between East and West Germany. The East German press announced: 'The gates in the Wall stand open wide'. Crowds of people swarmed to the checkpoints and pushed past the terrified guards. They were welcomed by equally large crowds of cheering West Berliners. Shortly afterwards, people climbed onto the Wall and began to demolish it - at first with pickaxes, later with drills and bulldozers.

▼ East German soldiers greet a West German person through a gap in the Berlin Wall, 1989. How is this photograph a symbol of the time?

The opening of the Iron Curtain

In each country the search for freedom took a slightly different path, as Figure 1 shows.

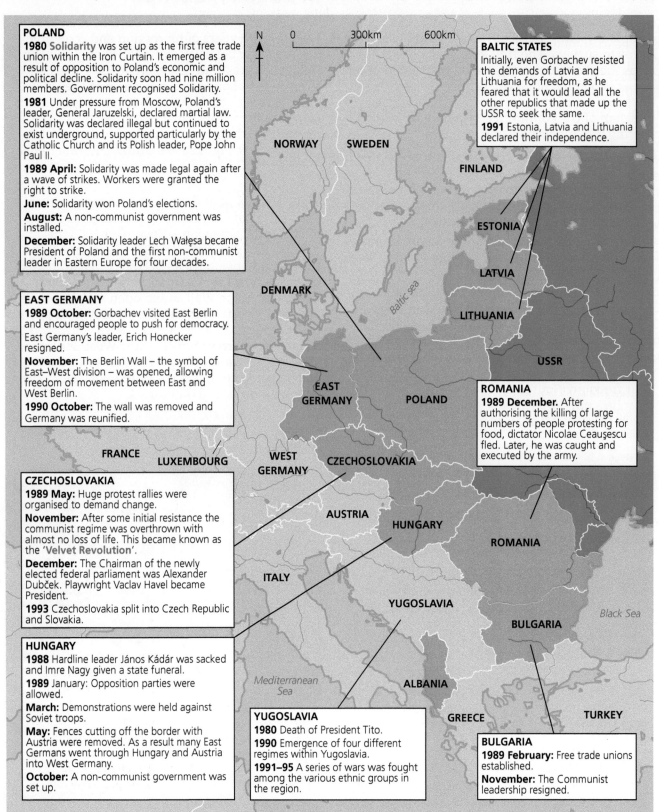

POLAND

1980 Solidarity was set up as the first free trade union within the Iron Curtain. It emerged as a result of opposition to Poland's economic and political decline. Solidarity soon had nine million members. Government recognised Solidarity.

1981 Under pressure from Moscow, Poland's leader, General Jaruzelski, declared martial law. Solidarity was declared illegal but continued to exist underground, supported particularly by the Catholic Church and its Polish leader, Pope John Paul II.

1989 April: Solidarity was made legal again after a wave of strikes. Workers were granted the right to strike.

June: Solidarity won Poland's elections.

August: A non-communist government was installed.

December: Solidarity leader Lech Wałęsa became President of Poland and the first non-communist leader in Eastern Europe for four decades.

BALTIC STATES

Initially, even Gorbachev resisted the demands of Latvia and Lithuania for freedom, as he feared that it would lead all the other republics that made up the USSR to seek the same.

1991 Estonia, Latvia and Lithuania declared their independence.

EAST GERMANY

1989 October: Gorbachev visited East Berlin and encouraged people to push for democracy. East Germany's leader, Erich Honecker resigned.

November: The Berlin Wall – the symbol of East–West division – was opened, allowing freedom of movement between East and West Berlin.

1990 October: The wall was removed and Germany was reunified.

ROMANIA

1989 December. After authorising the killing of large numbers of people protesting for food, dictator Nicolae Ceauşescu fled. Later, he was caught and executed by the army.

CZECHOSLOVAKIA

1989 May: Huge protest rallies were organised to demand change.

November: After some initial resistance the communist regime was overthrown with almost no loss of life. This became known as the 'Velvet Revolution'.

December: The Chairman of the newly elected federal parliament was Alexander Dubček. Playwright Vaclav Havel became President.

1993 Czechoslovakia split into Czech Republic and Slovakia.

HUNGARY

1988 Hardline leader János Kádár was sacked and Imre Nagy given a state funeral.

1989 January: Opposition parties were allowed.

March: Demonstrations were held against Soviet troops.

May: Fences cutting off the border with Austria were removed. As a result many East Germans went through Hungary and Austria into West Germany.

October: A non-communist government was set up.

YUGOSLAVIA

1980 Death of President Tito.

1990 Emergence of four different regimes within Yugoslavia.

1991–95 A series of wars was fought among the various ethnic groups in the region.

BULGARIA

1989 February: Free trade unions established.

November: The Communist leadership resigned.

▲ **Figure 1** The collapse of Communism in Eastern Europe.

The Cold War ends

Gorbachev knew that economic reform in the USSR would have to be preceded by huge cuts in defence spending. Cuts in defence spending would require a better relationship with the West. In 1986, he signalled a major change in Soviet foreign policy when he indicated the USSR's desire to get rid of all nuclear weapons. He also indicated his willingness to abandon previous Cold War policies, such as the Brezhnev Doctrine (page 219), in favour of ensuring the survival of the USSR.

In an attempt to reach agreement, Reagan and Gorbachev held a series of summit meetings. At first little was achieved, but after some intensive negotiations both sides agreed to a reduction in weaponry. Their agreement was contained in the 1987 Intermediate Nuclear Forces (INF) Treaty, which ensured the removal of nearly 4,000 nuclear warheads and the halting of the 'Star Wars' programme. It also allowed teams of inspectors to oversee the destruction of the weapons. A year later, Gorbachev announced the withdrawal of Soviet forces from Afghanistan and a huge reduction in the size of the Soviet armed forces. Troops were also withdrawn from other Iron Curtain countries.

Under Reagan's successor, George H. Bush (Senior) (1989–93), the changes continued. The new President was particularly impressed by the political changes that Gorbachev was introducing behind the Iron Curtain. Bush met Gorbachev in Malta in 1989 and both leaders declared that the Cold War was over (Source F). In July 1991, the Warsaw Pact was dissolved, removing one of the key symbols of East–West divisions (Source G).

> **Source F** Mikhail Gorbachev speaking about the end of the Cold War, 1992
>
> I do not regard the end of the Cold War as a victory for one side. The end of the Cold War is our common victory.

> **Source G** Extract from Steve Phillips, *The Cold War: Conflict in Europe and Asia* (2001).
>
> The Cold War came to an end when the USSR lost its will for empire. It could not sustain the resources needed to pursue an empire it no longer felt it needed to secure itself against its enemies.

Activities

1 Create a timeline showing the developments in relations between the USA and the USSR during the 1980s.
2 Using the information in this chapter and in Source A on page 236, answer these questions:
   • What was Reagan's initial attitude to the USSR?
   • What policies did he introduce because of his attitude?
3 How does Source B on page 236 help to understand the USSR's reaction to the Reagan's policies?
4 Looking at the evidence presented in this chapter, do you think Gorbachev's opinion in Source F is correct?
5 Why did Gorbachev come to seek the end of the Cold War? Give two reasons in your answer.

Revision tip

You need to decide here whether the Cold War began to end because of the influence of individuals, or whether the poor state of the Soviet economy meant that change would have taken place anyway.

Revision tip

Where the 'describe two' question in the exam involves cause or a consequence, make sure you include a brief explanation which connects the cause to its consequence.

Freedom for all?

The USSR's economy was still in crisis and society seemed to be in a state of collapse. The country was divided between those who thought there had been too much change and those who felt that there had not been enough. One of the latter was Boris Yeltsin (1931–2007), who was elected leader of Russia in 1990. Russia was the largest of the different Republics that together made up the USSR.

In August 1991, an attempt was made to overthrow Gorbachev by army hardliners. The coup was defeated by troops loyal to Gorbachev and he was soon reinstated. Yet within four months the Communist Party had been outlawed in Russia and the USSR had ceased to exist; all 15 member Republics had declared their independence. (Three of the largest states, Russia, the Ukraine and Belorussia, formed a new union called the Commonwealth of Independent States).

Gorbachev's decision to end the Cold War and reform the USSR had resulted in the end of communist control. The last leader of the USSR was now a President without a country and he resigned on Christmas Day 1991.

Source H Former US President George H. Bush, speaking in 2009 at the twentieth anniversary celebrations in Germany of the fall of the Berlin Wall.

I have no doubt, zero, that historians will recognize Mikhail for his rare vision and unfailing commitment to reform and openness despite the efforts of those who would resist change and ignore the call of history.

Today we have a fuller appreciation of the tremendous pressure Mikhail faced in that pivotal [key] time. And through it all he stood firm, which is why he'll also stand tall when the history of our time in office is finally written.

Activities

1. Create a timeline showing the key developments in Eastern Europe 1985–91.
2. Create a spider diagram explaining the reasons for the collapse of the USSR in 1991.
3. Create 16 revision flashcards identifying the key facts (two for each country) of the collapse of communism in Eastern Europe.
4. Who deserves the credit for ending the Cold War – Reagan or Gorbachev? Why?
5. Why did the people of Eastern Europe reject communism?

Practice questions

1. What does Source A on page 236 tell us about the response of the USA to the Soviet Union in 1983?
2. Source G on page 239 and Source H on this page give different views about the end of the Cold War in 1989.
   a. Explain two ways in which these sources differ.
   b. Explain one reason why the views in Source G and H are different.
3. How convincing is the view in Source H about the reasons for the end of the Cold War in 1989?
4. Describe two effects of the collapse of Eastern Europe from 1989–91.
5. a. How did the actions of the USA and USSR impact on international relations in the 1970s and 1980s?
   Use the following guidelines in your answer. You must also use information of your own.
   - The Soviet war in Afghanistan, 1979–89
   - The role of President Reagan
   - The policies of glasnost and perestroika
   b. How did the Cold War come to an end from 1985–91?
   Use the following guidelines in your answer. You must also use information of your own.
   - The 'Star Wars' programme
   - Soviet economic problems
   - Gorbachev's policies

This page provides guidance on how to answer question 5 in the exam.

Question 5

Describe two effects of Gorbachev's policies from 1989–91. [4]

Guidance

You should be looking to spend about five minutes on this question.

You will need to know two effects, but to gain full marks you will need to be able to **explain how** Gorbachev's policies led to each effect, using facts and arguments from your own knowledge.

Step 1
See (and explain) one effect

Example

One effect of Gorbachev's policies was the end of the Cold War.

This was because he knew that the USSR could no longer afford to keep up with the USA's Star Wars project, so he realised that the only alternative was a better relationship with the West. He thus held summit meetings with Reagan and agreed the Intermediate Nuclear Forces Treaty of 1987 and the end of the Cold War in 1989.

Step 2
Repeat for a different effect

Example

A second effect of Gorbachev's policies was the collapse of communism in the Soviet Union.

This happened because the USSR became divided between those who wanted more change, and those who thought there had been too much change. In August 1991 a coup by hardliners failed, but within four months the USSR had fallen apart, communist control had ended and Gorbachev had resigned.

The new age of conflict

The end of the Cold War did not bring in a time of peace. Instead, it opened the way for a new kind of conflict: an ideological war between Muslim jihadists (extremists who believed that their religion requires them to go to war for Islam) and Western capitalist democracies. The jihadists used terrorism to scare and weaken the West, and the western powers responded by declaring a 'war on terror'.

> **Source A** After the end of the Cold War in the early 1990s, the Indian Muslim journalist and politician MJ Akbar wrote:
>
> [The West's] next confrontation ... is definitely going to come from the Muslim world. It is in the sweep of the Islamic nations from [North Africa] to Pakistan that the struggle for a new world order will begin.

The consequences of the Soviet War in Afghanistan

The Soviets withdrew from Afghanistan between 1988 and 1989 (see pages 232–33), leaving Afghanistan in chaos. The warlords who took over when the Soviets left were brutally cruel, and the country quickly collapsed into civil war.

At the same time, the *Mujahideen* changed from a collection of disorganised, local guerrilla groups into a powerful international terrorist movement, called the Islamic Unity of Afghanistan Mujahideen. They were supported by jihadist groups from all over the world, including groups such as the Taliban and Al-Qaeda.

The rise of the Taliban

A former *Mujahideen* commander, Mohammed Omar, started a movement to fight against the warlords. Because many of its followers were students educated in the madrassas (Islamic schools) of Pakistan, the new movement was called the 'Taliban' (an Afghan word meaning 'students').

In 1996, the Taliban took control and set up an 'Islamic Emirate', which imposed a strict form of Sharia law on Afghanistan (see Source B). The Taliban's interpretation of Islam is fundamentalist.

Under the Taliban, music, TV, toys and most games were forbidden, and all windows had to be painted black. Women, in particular, lost most of their freedoms – they had to wear a burqa, could not travel in public without a man's permission, and were forbidden an education. Punishments included execution, stoning, flogging and cutting off the hands or feet of thieves. The Taliban have carried out many atrocities and human rights abuses, particularly against women.

> **Source B** Adapted excerpt from *Taliban: Militant Islam, Oil and Fundamentalism in Central Asia*, a book by Pakistani writer and journalist Ahmed Rashid (second edition, 2010).
>
> ... the Taliban had brought relative peace and security to Kandahar [a city in Afghanistan] and neighbouring areas ... but the Taliban had also put in place an extreme interpretation of Sharia or Islamic law that shocked many Afghans and the Muslim world ... They were to inspire a new extremist form of fundamentalism across Pakistan and Central Asia ...

▼ Malala Yousafzai in 2014. Malala was targeted by the Taliban for speaking out against them and saying women and girls need education. A Taliban soldier tried to assassinate her in 2012, when she was 15 years old, but she survived the shooting and is now known around the world as an activist for education.

The origins of Al-Qaeda

Another jihadist group that grew out of the end of the Cold War in Afghanistan was called the 'Afghan Services Bureau' Maktab al-Khidamat (MAK). This group set up charities, supposedly to help refugees, in many countries, including the USA. However, the donations actually went towards recruiting, training and arming fighters for the *Mujahideen*.

Osama bin Laden

One of the founders of MAK was Osama bin Laden, the son of a Saudi Arabian billionaire. He was brought up as a devout Sunni Muslim and became convinced that the Muslim world was being attacked by unbelievers. The only answer was to destroy all outside influences and force a strict form of Sharia law. In 1979, he joined the *Mujahideen* in Pakistan and gained a reputation as a hero of jihad. He was credited with helping to remove the Soviets from Afghanistan in 1988–89. After 1989, MAK grew into the Al-Qaeda organisation, which built an international network of different jihadist terrorist groups and supported many terrorist actions.

The Gulf War, 1991

Saddam Hussein, President of Iraq, 1979–2003, was a tyrant who used violence and abuse to rule his country, particularly against the Kurdish peoples and other minorities in the north of the country.

At first, however, he was an ally of the West, which saw him as a friend against the fundamentalist Muslim government of Iran. When Iraq went to war with Iran in 1980–88, the West supplied him with weapons (including the chemicals from which he made chemical weapons to use on his own people).

That support came to an end in 1990 when Saddam invaded Kuwait, a small oil-rich state south of Iraq. There was outrage among the Western powers. As a result, US President George H. W. Bush Senior organised a coalition of 34 nations which drove the Iraqis out of Kuwait.

Bin Laden's view of the USA

Although US President George H. W. Bush Senior said that all U.S. forces based in Saudi Arabia would be withdrawn once the Iraqi threat had been overcome, American troops stayed there.

▲ Osama bin Laden (1957–2011).

Bin Laden believed Christians and Jewish people controlled the USA and were conspiring against Islam. Also, as Saudi Arabia contains Mecca – the birthplace of the Prophet Muhammad and the holiest of all cities, according to Islam – bin Laden was angered by how it had been turned into 'an American colony'.

In 1998, bin Laden issued a fatwā against the USA: Jihad Against Jews and Crusaders (Source C). Throughout the 1990s, Al-Qaeda carried out many terrorist attacks, the largest of which was the September 11 attacks in 2001, or 9/11.

Source C Al-Qaeda fatwā, 1998

The ruling to kill the Americans and their allies – civilians and military – is an individual duty for every Muslim who can do it in any country in which it is possible to do it, in order to liberate … the holy mosque of Mecca from their grip, and in order for their armies to move out of all the lands of Islam, defeated and unable to threaten Islam.

Activities

1 What are the main differences between the Taliban and Al-Qaeda?
2 Create a spider diagram to summarise the long-term consequences of the Soviet war in Afghanistan.
3 What does Source C tell us about Al-Qaeda's aims?

Reasons for the September 11 attacks

On 11 September 2001, Al-Qaeda carried out terrorist attacks in the United States itself, hijacking commercial planes and flying them into a number of targets such as the World Trade Center and the Pentagon. Because they happened on the eleventh day of the ninth month, the attacks came to be known as the '9/11' attacks.

The new age of conflict

Al-Qaeda grew rapidly among the growth of Muslim fundamentalism and **jihadism** – particularly so in the Middle East, where the weakness and instability of many countries had created a region of chaos (see map below).

After 1989, international *Mujahideen* fighters who had been fighting the Soviets in Afghanistan left to spread jihadism to other countries.

Osama bin Laden's hatred of America

In a 'Letter to America' (2002), bin Laden explained the reasons he had targeted America:

- He condemned US support for Israel – as a fundamentalist Muslim he opposed the creation of the Jewish state of Israel.
- He criticised US interventions in Somalia in 1993-95 (in which US forces fought against jihadist militias), and Iraq (see page 248), both of which he said were 'atrocities against Muslims'.
- He hated that the US was an ally of Saudi Arabia, and that US troops were stationed there, close to the Holy Places of Islam (see page 243).

Why did Al-Qaeda attack the USA on 11 September 2001?

To start a fight

Some historians have suggested that the attack was designed to provoke the USA into attacking the Muslim world. This would then help radicalise Muslims into joining the jihadist movement.

Growing Al-Qaeda activity

During the 1990s, Al-Qaeda had increasingly concentrated its attacks upon the USA:

- In 1993, Al-Qaeda terrorists detonated a truck bomb under the North Tower of the World Trade Center in New York.
- In 1996, they attempted to assassinate US President Bill Clinton during a visit to the Philippines.
- In 1998, Al-Qaeda suicide bombers drove truck bombs into the US embassies in Tanzania and Kenya.
- In 2000, Al-Qaeda terrorists exploded a small boat which they had sailed close to the US destroyer USS Cole.

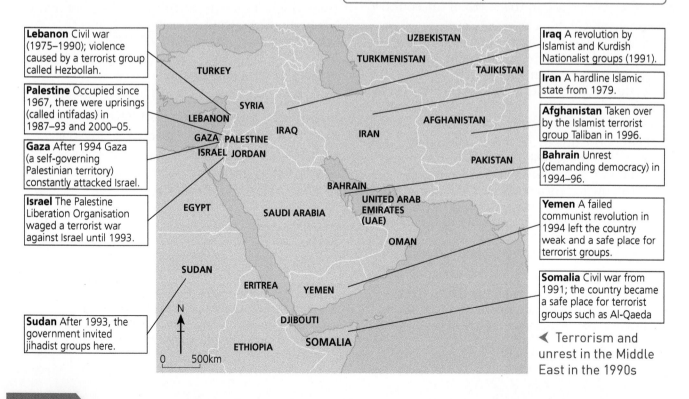

Lebanon Civil war (1975–1990); violence caused by a terrorist group called Hezbollah.

Palestine Occupied since 1967, there were uprisings (called intifadas) in 1987–93 and 2000–05.

Gaza After 1994 Gaza (a self-governing Palestinian territory) constantly attacked Israel.

Israel The Palestine Liberation Organisation waged a terrorist war against Israel until 1993.

Sudan After 1993, the government invited jihadist groups here.

Iraq A revolution by Islamist and Kurdish Nationalist groups (1991).

Iran A hardline Islamic state from 1979.

Afghanistan Taken over by the Islamist terrorist group Taliban in 1996.

Bahrain Unrest (demanding democracy) in 1994–96.

Yemen A failed communist revolution in 1994 left the country weak and a safe place for terrorist groups.

Somalia Civil war from 1991; the country became a safe place for terrorist groups such as Al-Qaeda

◀ Terrorism and unrest in the Middle East in the 1990s

The events of the September 11 attacks

The twin towers of the World Trade Center were chosen for their symbolic significance. They were a sign of the economic power of the United States, and symbolised western capitalism, wealth and love of possessions. They were a huge landmark on the New York skyline, and something that every visitor saw when sailing into New York harbour. They were also a massive target, with 50,000 workers and 200,000 visitors going there every day.

As the CIA and other intelligence discovered later, the attack had been planned from 1996. The team who were to carry out the attacks were recruited in 1998 in Afghanistan and sent to America in 2000. There they planned their attacks, including learning to fly.

The map shows the four attacks the terrorists made on that day:

▶ Two planes were crashed into the twin towers of the New York World Trade Center – a symbol of US economic power.

▶ A third plane nose-dived into the Pentagon, the headquarters of the US Defence Department in Virginia, causing substantial damage and 125 deaths.

▲ This photograph captures the moment Flight 175 hit the second tower, whilst the first tower burns. Soon after, both towers collapsed, killing some 2,750 people, including the passengers on the planes, and some of the firefighters and rescue workers who had entered the building to help.

▶ A fourth plane was headed for Washington DC, possibly aiming at the White House, but in an act of heroism the passengers on the plane realised what was happening and attacked the terrorists. As a result, the plane crashed in southern Pennsylvania, causing the deaths of 40 crew and passengers.

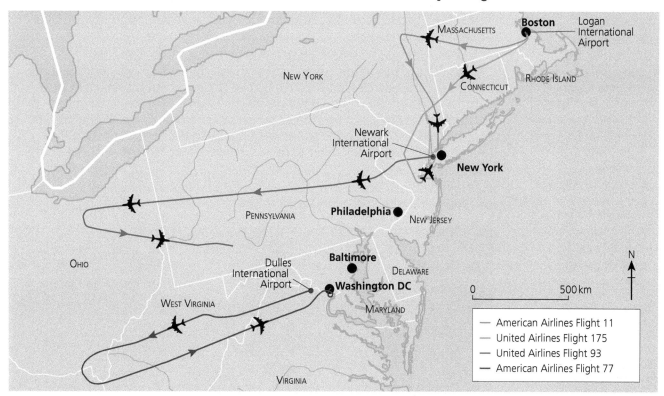

▲ The September 11 attacks.

SOURCE D President George W Bush, speaking to the nation at 8:30pm, 11 September 2001.

Today ... thousands of lives were suddenly ended by evil, despicable [dreadful] acts of terror... America was targeted for attack because we're the brightest beacon [light] for freedom and opportunity in the world. And no one will keep that light from shining....

SOURCE E President George W Bush, speaking to Congress on 20 September 2001.

Our 'war on terror' begins with Al-Qaeda, but it does not end there. It will not end until every terrorist group of global reach has been found, stopped, and defeated.

Activities

1 Create a timeline to show the key events leading up to the September 11 attacks, the events of the attacks and the immediate US response.

2 List all the things the 'war on terror' meant the US and other governments could now do.

3 Read Sources D and E. Was the US response of a 'war on terror' justified?

▶ President George W. Bush embraces a firefighter in New York at the scene of the attacks, 14 September 2001.

The response of the USA and its allies: the 'war on terror'

The 9/11 attacks, together with the huge damage and number of deaths which the attacks caused (see page 245), had a profound effect on the American people. The Western world suffered a huge shock – that terrorism could cause such carnage.

US President George W. Bush Jnr (son of President George H. W. Bush Senior) condemned the attack (Source D). He called for a 'War on Terror' which would:

▶ Find and kill terrorists such as bin Laden, who had taken credit for the 9/11 attacks, and destroy their organisations.

▶ Undertake 'regime change' – removing governments which supported terrorism and abolishing terrorist safe places.

▶ Strengthen weaker states such as Afghanistan to resist terrorism by building them into strong democracies.

▶ Improve security for US citizens and places at home and abroad.

On 14 September, Congress passed the Authorization for Use of Military Force Against Terrorists (AUMF) which gave the President the powers to do these things.

As a result:

▶ Afghanistan was attacked in October, and the Taliban regime there was removed by December 2001 (see page 247)

▶ In 2003, a coalition of forces invaded Iraq (see page 248)

▶ Almost 800 prisoners suspected of terrorist connections were imprisoned without trial at Guantanamo Bay.

Although the USA provided most of the forces and weapons, the invasion of Afghanistan was undertaken by a NATO International Security Assistance Force (ISAF), and the multi-national force which invaded Iraq involved 40 different countries.

Action abroad was mirrored by reaction at home. In the USA, the Department of Homeland Security was created to specifically fight against terrorism. The new Patriot Act (2001) gave the government the right to monitor phone calls and internet messages. Many US states introduced anti-terrorism laws, giving greater powers to the police to seek and detain suspects. In the UK, the USA's outspoken ally, the government tried (but failed) to give itself the power to detain suspects for 90 days without charge.

Gradually, the Al-Qaeda leaders were killed, some of them by the highly controversial method of drone strikes. In 2011, bin Laden himself was tracked down and killed by the US military.

The war in Afghanistan, 2001

Reasons for the invasion

There is good evidence that Afghanistan was a centre of Al-Qaeda terrorism. In 1996, Osama bin Laden had moved his Al-Qaeda organisation from the Sudan into Afghanistan, where it set up more than 120 training camps. One estimate suggests that as many as 20,000 jihadists were trained in these camps.

After 9/11, therefore, as one of their first steps in their 'war against terror', the US demanded that the Taliban government in Afghanistan hand over bin Laden and dismantle the Al-Qaeda organisation in Afghanistan. When the Taliban delayed, on 7 October 2001, America and Britain launched 'Operation Enduring Freedom' with waves of bomber and missile attacks on the Taliban army and the Al-Qaeda camps.

In December, an International Security Assistance Force (ISAF) – a military coalition of 18 countries – drove the Taliban out of government and chose Hamid Karzai to set up a new democratic government. In 2002, US Secretary of Defense Donald Rumsfeld claimed: 'The Taliban are gone. Al-Qaeda are gone.'

But the Taliban were far from gone. Mohammed Omar (see page 242) reorganised the Taliban into a guerrilla army, recruiting jihadists from Afghanistan and nearby Pakistan. Fighting in groups of about 50, sometimes helped by local warlords, they ambushed the ISAF forces with 'attack-and-scatter' raids, suicide missions and roadside bombs. They attacked or kidnapped Westerners, even aid workers. The coalition found itself in the same situation as the Soviets 30 years earlier, mounting large-scale operations to 'clear out' the Taliban, only to find that the enemy quickly reorganised and resumed operations.

There were still more than 8,000 US soldiers in Afghanistan in 2016. The war had become the longest in US history.

The impact on international relations

The war had a large impact on international relations:

▶ By 2016, more than 4,000 ISAF as well as some 15,000 Afghan soldiers and police had been killed in the war, along with nearly 20,000 civilians.

▶ On the surface, there was international support for the war. ISAF was authorised by the United Nations in December 2001, and 50 countries contributed to the force at some point in the war (see timeline).

▶ However, the war caused strains in the Middle East – only Bahrain, Jordan and the United Arab Emirates (UAE) actively contributed to the campaign. During the war, Pakistan complained about US military operations inside Pakistan (especially drone strikes on Taliban leaders). The Afghan government complained about civilian deaths.

▶ Most of all, there was increasing unease that growing anger amongst Muslims about the 'War on Terror' was actually increasing terrorist recruitment.

Operation Enduring Freedom, 2001: some of the troops deployed	
October 26	Britain will deploy 4,200 military personnel
November 1	Turkey, Australia and Canada agree to send forces
November 6	Germany offers up to 3,900 troops
November 7	Italy will provide 2,700 troops
November 9	The Netherlands will send up to 1,400 troops
November 16	France sends troops
November 22	Poland says it will send troops

Activities

1 What were the reasons for the NATO invasion of Afghanistan in 2001?
2 Can you link any of these reasons to the consequences of the Soviet war in Afghanistan, 1979–89 (see page 231)?
3 What were the consequences of the 2001 invasion?
4 Do you think Operation Enduring Freedom was successful?

The invasion of Iraq, 2003

As mentioned on page 243, Saddam Hussein was first a friend and then an enemy of the USA. Throughout the 1990s, relations remained tense between Iraq and the West, which suspected Saddam of trying to stock up on weapons of mass destruction (WMDs) – chemical, biological and nuclear weapons. The United Nations set up a special commission of inspectors (UNSCOM) to search for WMDs. Tension increased greatly when Iraq expelled the UN inspectors in November 1997.

These tensions led the USA to blame Saddam Hussein for the attack (Source F). A few days after 9/11, President Bush set up the Office of Special Plans (OSP) to prove the connection between Saddam and Al-Qaeda and that Iraq had WMDs. This approach suffered a setback when a UN inspection team in Iraq found no evidence of WMDs.

Bush and his ally, the British Prime Minister (1997–2007) Tony Blair, refused to accept the inspection results. In September 2002, the British Joint Intelligence Committee reported that Saddam had WMDs 'ready within 45 minutes of an order to use them'. In October, US senators were told that Iraq could attack the USA with chemical or biological weapons.

▼ Saddam Hussein (1937–2006).

Reasons for the invasion of Iraq

With many countries opposed to war, Bush and Blair decided to go to war without first getting the agreement of the United Nations. Instead, they secured the support of the US Congress and the British Parliament and attacked Iraq.

Bush and Blair gave as reasons for war:

▶ Saddam's support for Al-Qaeda.

▶ Iraq's possession of WMDs.

However, as it became increasingly clear that there was no firm evidence of either, a third reason was increasingly advanced:

▶ 'Regime change' – deposing a tyrant and giving the Iraqis a democratic government.

As time went on, it was suggested that the western powers wanted to secure Iraq's oil reserves for themselves, or that President Bush wanted to finish his father's war of 1991, or just that the United States wanted to dominate the rest of the world.

> **SOURCE F** In January 2002 American President George W. Bush told Congress:
>
> The terrorist attacks of September 11 on the USA are a major reason for attacking Iraq … We know that Iraq and Al-Qaeda have contacts that go back a long time. We have learned that Iraq has trained Al-Qaeda members in bomb-making and deadly gasses …

> **SOURCE G** British Prime Minister Tony Blair, speaking in America in July 2003:
>
> Even if there were no weapons of mass destruction, we removed the tyrant from Iraq.

◀ George W Bush and Tony Blair, 2003.

Activities

1 Using all the evidence you can find, make a list of all the different reasons for the Iraq war of 2003. Discuss in a group which you think was the most important reason for the USA and the UK.

2 What does Source G reveal about the reasons for the USA and the UK invading Iraq in 2003?

The downfall of Saddam Hussein

The Iraq war began on 20 March 2003 with an overwhelming 'Shock and Awe' aerial bombardment. The next day, 160,000 American, British and Australian troops invaded. While one advance secured the oil port of Basra in the south, 954 soldiers of the US 173rd Airborne Brigade parachuted into northern Iraq to join with Kurdish rebels.

The invasion broke the Iraqi military 200 miles south of Baghdad at the Battle of Nasiriyah (23 March – 2 April), and then advanced with little resistance. Overall, the Iraqis were defeated in three weeks.

The Iraqis surrendered, and the coalition forces entered Baghdad to cheers on 9 April. In a symbolic act, Iraqi crowds toppled and danced on a statue of Saddam Hussein. Saddam fled. (He was captured in December 2003 and tried and hanged in 2006.) The Iraqi government collapsed and the US army eventually captured most of its members.

The Coalition countries set about building a new democratic Iraqi state, but it soon became clear to the watching world that they were failing:

▶ The new Coalition-created government was largely made up of Shia Muslims and alienated the majority Sunni Muslim population – so sectarian violence flared between the two groups.

▶ The US insisted that much of the work of the new government (from security to rebuilding contracts) was given to US firms; this created economic and social hardship in Iraq.

▶ Iraqi loyalists and jihadist terrorists mounted guerrilla and suicide attacks on the coalition forces; before long all the westerners in the country were confined to a small, heavily-defended area in the centre of Baghdad called the 'Green Zone'.

▶ US troops were accused of abusing and bullying Iraqi prisoners in their care.

▲ Cartoon called 'Iraq OIL' published in the *Ventura County Star*, 2003. What is the message of this cartoon?

Source H A reflection on the causes of the war by Dr Shaid Athar, an American Muslim, in 2008.

Is it a war against Islam and Muslims by the Christian invaders and their reluctant [unwilling] allies, or is it a war of liberation of the Iraqi people? Is it a war of blood for oil by the only superpower … a war for the domination of the rest of the world?

Activities

1 Why was it important to the USA to remove Saddam Hussein from Iraq?
2 Do you think it was important to Iraqis that Saddam Hussein be removed?
3 How reliable is the cartoon to an historian studying the reasons for the Iraq War?

The impact of the Iraq War on international relations

Among the many consequences of the war:

▶ Saddam Hussein was overthrown, and the first free, democratic elections in 50 years were held in Iraq.

▶ There were, perhaps, 50,000 military deaths during the war (both coalition and Iraqi forces). A group called Iraq Body Count estimated civilian deaths from the war at 112,000, but some estimates are as high a one million.

▶ The war provoked terrorism in Iraq itself: there were 1,003 suicide bombings in the period 2003–2010.

▶ Several countries – including France, Germany, Canada and Russia – refused to support the invasion. Hundreds of thousands of people protested before and during the war because they saw it as illegal. Blair and Bush became hated figures throughout the world and some called for their impeachment.

▶ In 2003, the League of Arab States condemned the attack on Iraq and called for the immediate withdrawal of US and UK forces.

▶ Far from 'winning' the 'war on terror', terrorism (specifically anti-American, suicide attacks) has increased: since 2004, there have been over 2000 suicide attacks, compared to 343 during 1980–2003.

▶ The decision to invade Iraq without the UN Security Council's approval meant that the United Nations' reputation and authority suffered.

▶ There was anti-Muslim hostility in some western countries, especially when President Bush called the war on terrorism 'a crusade'.

Source I Excerpt from George W Bush's autobiography *Decision Points* (2011).

Almost a decade later, it is hard to describe how widespread an assumption it was that Saddam had WMD ... I believed that the intelligence on Iraq's WMD was solid ...

The nature of history is that we know the consequences only of the action we took. But inaction would have had consequences, too. Imagine what the world would look like today with Saddam Hussein still ruling Iraq. He would still be threatening his neighbours, sponsoring terror, and piling bodies into mass graves ... And the American people would be much less secure today.

Source J President Barack Obama, speaking at the National Defense University, 23 May 2013.

We must define our effort not as a boundless 'Global War on Terror', but rather as a series of ..., targeted efforts to [remove] networks of violent extremists... Our victory against terrorism won't be measured in a surrender ceremony at a battleship, or a statue being pulled to the ground. Victory will be measured in parents taking their kids to school; immigrants coming to our shores; fans taking in a ballgame; a veteran starting a business; a bustling city street.

Revision Tip ↻

When you answer the 'how did...' question in the exam, it is vital that – as well as describing and explaining each of the three 'guidelines' – you finish with an overview/conclusion which draws out and summarises the key principles

Practice questions ?

1 Describe two reasons for the September 11 attacks in 2001.
2 Describe two consequences of the Iraq War, 2003.
3 **a** How did the USA respond to the rise of the Taliban and Al-Qaeda in the 1990s and 2000s?
   Use the following guidelines in your answer. You must also use information of your own.
   - Events in the 1990s
   - The invasion of Afghanistan, 2001
   - The invasion of Iraq, 2003
  b How did international relations change in the years 1991–2003?
   Use the following guidelines in your answer. You must also use information of your own.
   - The consequences of the Soviet war in Afghanistan
   - The 'war on terror'
   - The impact of the Iraq War, 2003

Examination practice: International Relations, 1945–2003

This page provides guidance on how to answer question 6 in the exam. Choose **either** (a) or (b).

Question 6

(a) How did the USA respond to the rise of the Taliban and Al-Qaeda in the 1990s and 2000s?

Use the following guidelines in your answer. You **must** also use information of your own.

- Events in the 1990s
- The invasion of Afghanistan, 2001
- The invasion of Iraq, 2003 [22]

(b) How did international relations change in the years 1991–2003?

Use the following guidelines in your answer. You **must** also use information of your own.

- The consequences of the Soviet war in Afghanistan
- The 'war on terror'
- The impact of the Iraq War, 2003 [22]

Guidance

You should be looking to spend about 25 minutes on this question.

Your answer must address all three named 'guidelines'; you should analyse each in detail, making sure that you explain how each changed international relations.

Finish with a judgement which uses facts and arguments to reach a 'clear and full explanation' of the question.

The examples below are relevant to Question 6b, but give you a general idea of how to answer this question.

Step 1
Introduce the opinion in question

Example
International relations changed <to a certain extent / a great deal> after 1991.

Step 2a
Describe the first 'guideline', explaining in detail how it changed international relations

Example
Firstly, the Soviet war in Afghanistan affected international relations in the following ways …

Step 2b
Describe the second 'guideline', explaining in detail how it changed international relations

Example
Secondly, the war on terror affected on international relations as follows …

Step 2c
Describe the third 'guideline', explaining in detail how it changed international relations

Example
Thirdly, the invasion of Iraq in 2003 had a massive impact on international relations, namely…

Step 3
Write a 'clear and full' conclusion, drawing out some generalisations about the changes in international relations between 1991 and 2003. Do not just repeat things you have already said. Finish with a 'clincher' idea and fact which you have held back, and explain its significance.

Example
Thus we can see that the main changes to international relations in the years 1991 to 2003 were that … and that … The most significant difference was that …

Glossary

Abdication crisis The time in 1936 when Britain's King Edward VIII abdicated so that he could marry a divorced American woman, Wallis Simpson.

Absenteeism A pattern of absence from work or responsibilities.

Agent Orange A mix of chemicals used as a weapon during the Vietnam War.

Allies/Allied Powers The name given to Britain, France, the USA and the USSR (Russia) during World War I and World War II.

Amendment An official change to a law, mainly the US Constitution.

Anarchists Followers of the ideology that says there should not be a government and people should be allowed to rule themselves.

Anderson air raid shelter A particular model of air raid shelter designed to accommodate six people.

Antisemitism Anti-Jewish hatred.

Appeasement The policy of making concessions to an opponent in the hope that they will stop making demands.

Apprentice boys A loyalist club set up to remember the group of apprentices who closed the gates of Derry/Londonderry against the armies of King James II in 1689.

Ard Fheis Annual Party Conference (Irish).

Army Council The decision-making body of the Provisional Irish Republican Army.

ARP Air Raid Precautions. An organisation set up to protect civilians from the dangers of air raids.

Art Deco Art deco was a kind of design, popular in the 1920s and 1930s, characterised by geometric shapes, stylised forms and bright colours. It was used in everything from ornaments to architecture.

Asocial Someone who does not like social interaction and/or prefers to do things by themself.

Assimilate Absorb into another group.

Atheism Lack of belief in God or gods.

Atomic bomb A nuclear weapon.

Attorney General The politician in charge of justice in the USA.

Autarky A self-sufficient economy.

AWOL Absent Without Official Leave (a US army term to describe a soldier who has left their duties).

Backbencher An MP who is a member of the government party but who does not have a job in the government.

Battle of the Atlantic The naval campaign fought between the Allies and Germany 1939–45.

Black market When items are bought and sold illegally.

Boll-weevil A beetle that feeds on cotton buds and flowers.

Bolshevik Russian communist.

Bolshevism The communist form of government adopted in Russia after the 1917 Revolution.

Bootlegging Making or selling alcohol illegally.

Boycott To cut off connections with a person, group or organisation.

Brinkmanship Practice of almost, but not quite, going to war with the aim of gaining concessions off an opposing country.

British Commonwealth An association of countries that were formerly colonies of Great Britain.

Buffer zone A neutral area or area to be protected.

Bureau of Indian Affairs Initially set up by the federal US government to 'supervise' Native Americans.

Burqa An outer garment worn by some women in some Islamic cultures to cover themselves when in public.

Buying on the margin Buying stocks by putting some money down, then paying the rest of it later, when the stocks were sold.

By-election An election for an individual parliamentary seat held between general elections.

Campaign for Nuclear Disarmament (CND) A pressure group set up in Britain to oppose the possession and use of nuclear weapons.

Capitalist An economic system (or a person supporting it) which believes in private ownership and the making of profits.

Capitalist democracies A capitalist democracy is an ideology that combines capitalism and democracy (the people vote freely, by elections, for the people they want in power).

Censorship Prevention of the publication of unwanted viewpoints or information.

Central Intelligence Agency (CIA) A US government body set up in 1947 to collect information on international groups and governments.

Centre Party (ZP) Catholic political party in Germany.

Chaperone A person who looks after or supervises another person.

Civil disobedience Protesting peacefully against alleged injustice.

Civil rights The rights to political and social freedom and equality.

Civil service A government's administrative support.

Civil war A war between members of the same nation.

Coalition A government made up of different political parties.

Communism The ideas of Karl Marx who supported a system of rule where industries were run by the government for the good of the people.

Communists People who follow the ideas of Karl Marx.

Concentration camps Detention or death camps for political prisoners.

Concordat An agreement between the Catholic Church and government.

Congress The US Parliament.

Conscription/Conscripts Compulsory military service and those who serve.

Constitution A document setting out the rules by which a country is to be run.

Constitutional Relating to the law or approved by the law (in this case, the US Constitution).

Containment The policy of preventing expansion of a hostile influence or country.

Convoys Group of merchant ships sailing together with a military escort.

Coup A violent attempt to overthrow a government.

Corporation Town or city council.

Corset A tight-fitting garment, often reinforced with steel, to make women's waists thinner.

Criminalisation Turning something into a criminal offence by making it illegal.

Curly-top virus A common virus affecting crops.

DAF (German Labour Front) Organisation set up by the Nazis to control German workers.

D-Day The Allied invasion, on 6 June 1944, of Western Europe.

Decommissioning Removing weapons or equipment.

Deficit The amount by which a sum of money is too small.

Deposed Suddenly removed from an office or position.

De-Stalinisation A series of reforms by Nikita Khrushchev, to move away from Josef Stalin's policies in the Soviet Union, after Stalin's death in 1953.

Détente French word meaning 'a period of relaxation', in this case, the easing of Cold War tensions.

Dictatorial The behaviour of a ruler with total power.

Diktat A dictated peace (German).

Direct rule The system by which Northern Ireland was ruled directly from Westminster and not by its own local parliament.

Dividend A sum of money paid to shareholders in a company, usually out of the company's profits for that year.

Dominion A self-governing colony.

Domino effect Idea that political change in one country will lead to political change in other countries (like a row of dominos falling).

Downing Street Declaration A joint declaration issued on 15 December 1993, announcing Ireland's right to self-determination.

Draft cards Letters informing individuals they can be conscripted into the army.

Drone strikes A drone is a robotic vehicle, often aerial, that can be used as a weapon. Drone strikes take place when many drones fire missiles at one target.

Duties Taxes on imports.

Edelweiss flower Flower that grows on mountains.

Edelweiss Pirates A youth group set up in opposition to the Hitler Youth movement.

Einsatzgruppen Mobile units of SS responsible for rounding up and killing Jewish people in territories newly-occupied by the German Army.

Emirate A political territory ruled by an emir (a noble title of high office).

Espionage Spying by governments to gain intelligence.

Euthanasia Deliberately ending life to relieve suffering.

Family allowance Money paid to a family by the government to help cover expenses.

Fascist A person who follows or leads by authoritarian nationalism.

Fatwā A word typically used to mean 'death sentence', although the word is closer in meaning to 'ruling'.

Federal A political system with a central and local parliament each with their own areas of responsibility.

Fordney-McCumber Act The Fordney-McCumber Act (1922) used two principles to calculate what tariff an import should pay: (a) the 'Scientific tariff' (the lower the wages in the country of origin, the higher the tariff) and (b) the 'American selling price' (the higher the cost in America, the higher the tariff).

Foreclosed A property that has been shut down when payments on the mortgage have stopped.

Führer The German word for leader, strongly associated with the Nazi dictator, Adolf Hitler.

Fundamentalist A person who believes in a strict and often literal interpretation of scripture or texts in a religion.

General Army Convention The supreme authority of the IRA.

General election An election held for all the seats in a parliament.

Gerrymandering The practice of drawing electoral boundaries in a way that benefits one particular group at the expense of another.

Gestapo Official secret police of the Nazi regime.

Gleichschaltung Bringing people into an identical way of thinking and behaving.

Governor General Representative of the monarch in a dominion.

Great Depression Slump in the economy in the 1930s which led to high unemployment.

Guantanamo Bay US military prison located within Guantanamo Bay Naval Base in Cuba.

Guerrilla A conflict where one side tends to use hit-and-run tactics against a superior enemy.

Harlem Renaissance The period between the end of World War I and the mid-1930s when Harlem, USA, became a centre for all sorts of cultural innovations and artists, writers, poets and musicians.

Hitler Myth The view of Hitler as a saviour of Germany.

Hitler Youth (Hitlerjugend) Organisation set up for the young in Germany to convert them to Nazi ideas.

Home Guard A defence organisation of the British Army during World War II.

Home rule Self-government.

Impeachment A charge of treason against a country (being a traitor).

Imperialism The idea of a country having colonies.

Imports Goods brought in to one country from another.

International Security Assistance Force (ISAF) A NATO-led mission, began in 2001, meant to train the Afghan National Security Forces (ANSF) and help Afghanistan to rebuild after the war.

Inter-continental ballistic missiles (ICBMs) A missile built mainly for delivering nuclear weapons.

Internment Imprisonment without trial.

Irish Free State An independent state established in 1922 under the Anglo-Irish Treaty (1921), which comprised 26 of the 32 counties of Ireland. The remaining six states made up Northern Ireland, which opted out of the new state.

Irish Republican Army (IRA) Organisation dedicated to Irish republicanism and that political violence is necessary to achieve it.

Irrigation Controlled supply of water to plants at regular times.

Jihadism Often used as a way to describe the ideology followed by extremists who believe their religion requires them to go to war for Islam. The word 'jihad' is closer to 'spiritual struggle' rather than 'holy war'.

Jim Crow Name of the laws and system in the USA between 1877 and the mid-1960s that effectively segregated white and black Americans.

Judiciary The system of judges and courts.

Jurisdictions Official powers to make legal decisions and judgements.

KPD The German Communist Party, following the ideas of Karl Marx.

Kraft durch Freude (KdF) A youth club set up to promote Nazi ideology, as part of the DAF.

Kristallnacht The Night of Broken Glass, 9–10 November 1938: an attack on Jewish people in Nazi Germany, by the SA and German civilians.

Kurdish An ethnic group in the Middle East.

Laissez-faire A French phrase meaning 'leave-to-do'. In business it meant freeing businesses from things that would stop them making a profit.

Land annuities Money that the British government had loaned to Irish farmers before the Government of Ireland Act (1921).

League of Arab States A League of 22 Middle East states, formed in 1945.

Left-wing Reforming or socialist.

Leipzig Hounds Youth group in Nazi Germany, influenced by communists.

Liberal Having a more open approach to politics and society: the opposite of a conservative, who has more of a traditional approach.

Liquors Alcoholic drink, especially spirits such as gin, whisky and so on.

Lobbied To lobby someone is to try to influence a person, often someone who makes laws, on a particular issue.

Lone Wolf v. Hitchcock This case was brought by a Native American chief, Lone Wolf, who challenged the right of the government to give tribal lands away. The Supreme Court declared that Congress had the right to do as it wished, without contradiction by the courts.

Loyalists Supporters of the union between Britain and Northern Ireland.

Lundy An insulting term within unionism, meaning 'traitor'. Lieutenant Colonel Robert Lundy was the Governor of Derry/Londonderry during the siege of 1688–1689. Lundy recommended surrender rather than defence of Derry/Londonderry against King James II.

Lynching Death without trial, often by hanging.

Manifest destiny A concept in the USA during the nineteenth and twentieth centuries to justify white settler expansion across the Great Plains.

Marching season Usually the summer months of the year when different groups (mainly unionist) hold marches and parades.

Marxism The ideas of Karl Marx (see communism).

Mechanisation The process of changing production at work from people to machines.

Mein Kampf Adolf Hitler's autobiography, published in 1925.

Merchant shipping Ships carrying goods/produce.

Miscegenation Mixing between races by relationships or marriage. Typically used by white supremacists or people who disapproved of mixing. The word 'interracial' is more neutral.

Moderator The leader of a church (usually Presbyterian).

Mujahideen The term for a person engaged in jihad, commonly used to refer to the Afghan soldiers in the Soviet–Afghan War.

Napalm Flammable liquid used in warfare.

National Assistance (Act) Gave local authorities the responsibility to provide accommodation and services to people with disability or mental health problems.

National Security Council A group which advises the US President on foreign policy issues.

Nationalisation To bring industries under the ownership/control of the nation.

Nationalist A person who seeks to protect the interests of a particular nation.

Naval blockade Blocking of area by military ships.

Nazi Party (NSDAP) The Nationalsozialistische Deutsche Arbeiterpartei (National Socialist German Workers' Party), led by Hitler, that ruled Germany from the 1930s to 1945.

No-go areas Areas of Northern Ireland that were policed by Republican paramilitaries and which were not accessible to the RUC or British army.

Nomadic A wandering lifestyle rather than one that settles in one place.

Non-contributing pensions Pensions not involving contributions from workers. Instead the pension is fully funded by the employer.

North Atlantic Treaty Organisation (NATO) Established in 1949, a military alliance initially set up to oppose the spread of communism/Soviet aggression.

Occult Mystical or supernatural.

Official opposition The largest party in a parliament that is not the governing party.

Old guard Those people in an organisation or society who oppose change.

Ombudsman An official who deals with complaints from the public.

On licence Even though a prisoner has been released, the prisoner must be supervised and stick to certain conditions for the rest of their sentence.

Operation Motorman Large operation carried out by the British Army in Northern Ireland during the Troubles in 1972.

Operation Rolling Thunder A US aerial bombardment campaign against Vietnam from 1965 to 1968.

Pan-nationalist front A term used to define a nation but one not limited to borders.

Parity of esteem Where mental health is given equal priority to physical health.

Partial Test Ban Treaty A 1963 agreement between the USA and USSR which banned all test detonations of nuclear weapons except those taking place underground.

Partitioned The artificial division of a country.

Passive resistance To oppose a group without using violence.

Patriotic Devotion to one's country.

Peaceful co-existence The idea that communist countries could live together with capitalist countries.

Phonographs Device for recording and reproducing sound, also called a gramophone.

Planter An individual (or his/her descendant) who took part in the colonisation of Ireland in the 1600–1700s.

Plebiscite A type of referendum. A special vote where all the people of a country decide on a particular issue.

Plessy v. Ferguson This case was about the right of Homer Plessy, a mixed-race American, to sit in a whites-only train carriage. The Supreme Court declared that 'separate but equal' racial segregation was legal.

Points system A system for determining council house allocation. A certain number of points were needed to gain a house and points were awarded for a variety of reasons.

Privy Council Part of the British judicial system.

Proletarian A member of the working class, or 'proletariat'.

Promiscuous Having many sexual relationships.

Proportional representation A system of voting designed to create a result more in line with the way in which people voted.

Protection rackets When a group provides protection to another group via violence or illegal activities.

Proximity negotiations Discussions where opposing parties do not actually meet but are close to each other and talk through other individuals and/or groups.

Puppet government A government that is under the control or influence of another state.

Puppet ruler Person who is called a ruler but is actually being ruled by other people or forces.

Purge Remove.

Putsch A violent attempt to overthrow a government: a coup.

Radar System for detecting aircraft based on radio waves.

Radical Someone who believes in changing society through extreme measures or revolution.

Recession Economic decline.

Referendum A general vote on a particular issue.

Reichstag The German Parliament.

Reparations The fine placed on Germany at the end of the First World War. A general term for a fine imposed by one country on another.

Republic A form of government with no monarch.

Republic of Ireland Formerly the Irish Free State, until 1937, when the state was named Ireland and a new constitution was adopted. It was declared a republic in 1949.

Republican Believer in a republic.

Reservations The Reservations were the small areas of tribal lands promised to the Native Americans by the Treaty of Medicine Lodge, 1867.

Reserved occupations Job from which an individual will not be taken to serve in the armed forces.

Rollback Totally destroying an enemy's forces and occupying the country.

Rugged individualism The idea that each person should help themselves rather than have the government help them to succeed.

Russian Revolution When the Bolsheviks in Russia took control, in 1917, and which eventually led to the establishment of the Soviet Union.

Satellite States A country that is under the influence of another state.

Schizophrenia Severe, long-term mental health condition.

Schönheit der Arbeit (SdA) Nazi organisation, part of the DAF, that used propaganda to control German workers.

Schutzstaffel (SS) Hitler's personal bodyguard, established in 1925.

SDLP (Social Democratic and Labour Party) Established in August 1970 and led by Gerry Fitt. It sought political reforms within Northern Ireland and the eventual re-unification of Ireland. The SDLP immediately became the main opposition party in Stormont, replacing the old Nationalist Party (led by Eddie McAteer).

Search and Destroy A military strategy used by the USA in the Vietnam War to search out the enemy, destroy them and withdraw immediately.

Secretariat A group of civil servants supporting the work of the Anglo-Irish Agreement.

Secretary of State In the UK a politician who is in charge of a government department and who is usually a member of the Cabinet. In the US the term refers specifically to the Foreign Minister.

Sectarian Religious-based bias or hatred.

Segregation Separating someone or something apart from others. In the USA, this is commonly used to describe the separation of white Americans from black Americans.

Self-determination The process by which a country or person defines their own government or life.

Self-generating Generated by itself, rather than an external person or force.

Sharecropping A system of farming where parts of the crops are taken as rent.

Sharia law Islamic law.

Shia One denomination of Muslims, who follow teachings of Prophet Muhammad's successor, Ali.

Shock and Awe The military theory (also called 'rapid dominance') that a massive display of force will demoralise the enemy.

Sinn Féin Irish republican political party.

Solidarity A trade union in Poland in the early 1980s.

Sonderkommando Death camp prisoners, usually Jewish people, who were forced to aid with the killing of victims in the gas chambers.

Sovereignty The authority of a state to govern itself or another state.

SPD (Social Democratic Party) Main left-wing party in 1930s Germany, supported mainly by the working class.

Special category status The recognition that those convicted of crimes connected with 'the Troubles' had acted for political and not criminal reasons.

Speculators A person who trades on the stock market and takes large risks to make large profits.

Squatter/squatted An individual who occupies a house that he or she does not own or pay rent on/act of squatting.

State governments The governments of the individual states in Germany.

Statute of Westminster (1931) Stated that dominions were independent countries that could leave the Commonwealth without Britain's permission

Stock Exchange A market where stocks are bought and sold.

Stormont The name given to the Northern Ireland Parliament building opened in 1932.

Strategic hamlets A strategy used in the Vietnam War to isolate the rural population from the Viet Cong by forcing them to relocate.

Sturmabteilung (SA) The paramilitary 'storm troopers' of the Nazi Party.

Subsidies Sums of money granted by the state or a public organisation to help an industry or business.

Subsistence Making enough of something to support oneself.

Suffrage The right to vote.

Summit meetings A meeting between leaders of different countries.

Sunni A denomination of Muslims who follow only the teachings of Prophet Muhammad.

Super-corporations Large associations of companies.

Swing Youth A youth group set up in opposition to the Hitler Youth movement, centring on Swing and Jazz music and dance.

Taoiseach Irish Prime Minister (Irish for chief/leader).

Tariffs Customs charges, levied on imported goods, and designed to reduce imports by raising its price in the importing country.

Temperance Abstinence from alcohol.

Totalitarian A political system where all power is held by one person or by a small group of people.

Trade deficit When a country spends more money on importing goods than it makes from exporting goods.

Trade union Organisation set up to protect the rights of workers.

Tribunal A body set up to reach a decision on a particular issue.

Truman Doctrine The principle that the US should support people threatened by Soviet forces.

Tyrant A dictator: a cruel and oppressive ruler.

Ulster Volunteer Force (UVF) A paramilitary group originally set up in 1912 to oppose the introduction of Home Rule to Ireland.

Ulsterisation A strategy to disengage the non-Ulster regiments of the British Army from duties in Northern Ireland, and replace them with members of the local Royal Ulster Constabulary (RUC) and Ulster Defence Regiment (UDR).

Unionist A person who wishes the political union between Great Britain and Northern Ireland to continue.

United Nations (UN) An international organisation set up in 1945 to enable nations to co-operate in all areas and to achieve world peace.

UN Security Council The part of the UN which works to maintain international peace and security.

US Federal Reserve The central banking system of the United States – the American equivalent of the Bank of England.

US Supreme Court The highest federal court in the USA.

Vaudeville A type of entertainment involving comedy, song and dance.

Viceroy The representative of the monarch.

Victoria Cross The highest British military award for bravery.

Vigilantes People who take the law into their own hands rather than relying on the police.

Volksgemeinschaft The people's community. This was the Nazi idea of a community based upon the German race.

Wards of the state A ward is someone placed under protection, in this case, protection by the state.

Warlords A military leader in a particular region.

Weimar Constitution The laws that governed Germany during the Weimar Republic (1919–1933).

Welfare State A system where the government provides educational and health facilities for the people of a nation.

Western approaches An area of the Atlantic Ocean off the western coast of Britain. The majority of shipping to and from Britain made use of this route.

Westminster Borough in London, Britain, where the Houses of Parliament are.

Whip An official of a political party appointed to maintain parliamentary discipline among its members

Index